D1453486

Three chairs covered with 'Turkey Work' were in the parlour of Joseph Bonnington's farmhouse at Writtle (no. 156), and Henry Bright of Roxwell (no. 192) had eight of them in his hall. No doubt they closely resembled this example in the Victoria and Albert Museum, which is reproduced by courtesy of the Director.

FARM AND COTTAGE INVENTORIES OF MID-ESSEX 1635-1749

Edited by
FRANCIS W. STEER, M.A., F.S.A.

1897

PHILLIMORE

London and Chichester

First published in 1950 by
Essex County Council
as Essex Record Office Publication No. 8.
This corrected edition published
by
PHILLIMORE & CO. LTD.
Shopwyke Hall,
Chichester, Sussex, England
1969

SBN 900592 61 3

Printed in England by Stephen Austin
Hertford

PREFACE TO THE SECOND EDITION

It is gratifying to know that a book published for me in 1950 is still asked for in 1969. The only difference between this edition and the first is the incorporation of several corrections which have been collected over the years.

That the interest and importance of probate inventories has come to be recognized is manifest by the large number—either as collections or single documents—which have been published during the last twenty years. Increasing use of this class of record has been made by social, agrarian and economic historians who have seen how much valuable information can be gathered if inventories are interpreted with discernment. It is undoubtedly more rewarding to deal with the inventories of a small area or a town rather than with those relating to a whole county; the larger unit, however, can provide a subject for profitable research, especially into agricultural history, if great care is taken to allow for changes in soil regions and if the time of year when the inventory was compiled is taken into account.

I am indebted to the County Council of Essex for allowing this book to be reprinted and to Messrs. Phillimore & Co. Ltd. for the immense trouble they have taken in producing this new edition.

CHICHESTER, FRANCIS W. STEER
September 1969.

PREFACE

A PREFACE is often the last part of a book to be written; it is easier to express clearly the purpose of one's composition when the final pruning has been done and the work seen as a whole. It is after such a stage has been reached that I now consider my own effort, not so much to forestall the reviewer, as to determine whether the labour has achieved the desired result.

A writer is seldom satisfied with his production, but that is perhaps a good omen for it spurs one on to attain a higher standard in the future. I realise that the shortcomings of this book—as many as they are—would have been yet more numerous but for the good offices of friends and colleagues who have been always ready to give their advice and suggestions. But the book will, I hope, supplement a branch of English social history which does not enjoy a wide bibliography. Our ancient country mansions and their treasures, now, alas, rapidly passing from private to state or corporate ownership, have been described in great detail from many angles, but the homes and possessions of more ordinary people (which are, of course, in the majority) have been curiously neglected. The prime motive of this book is to draw attention to one kind of evidence which can remedy this deficiency.

As the years go by, many ancient houses of the smaller type are converted to meet growing demands for comfort and convenience, but their original lay-outs are lost in the process; these details can only be found by a study of surviving documents giving us a true picture of the past. The proud owner of a sixteenth-century house who proceeds to restore and refurnish it 'as it was' often falls far short of the truth through not knowing what a house of the period was actually like.

While persons living in old houses may gain something from these inventories, it is hoped there will be others into whose hands this book will come. Among such readers, it is the rising generation who has not known an England without gas, electricity and 'buses in most villages, who should benefit from this documentary picture of one facet of the Stuart and Georgian eras. This view is held by the Essex Education Committee who have, jointly with the Records Committee of the Essex County Council, sponsored the publication of this book. To the Chairmen and members of the two Committees, and to the Acting Chief Education Officer, I wish to acknowledge my indebtedness.

Among others who may find these documents of value are the philologist and the agriculturalist. Many of the inventories appear, at first sight, to be either a mass of printer's errors or a list of articles written in a foreign language. Those unacquainted with the Essex dialect may perhaps solve a difficult passage by reading it aloud in a slightly guttural tone. The -es ending to so many words is still used by some Essex folk, and is not, therefore, always a peculiarity of spelling.

Farmers may be amused with descriptions of implements and prices of crops and livestock until they recall how the value of money has fallen. These inventories supply, in homely and practical language, a picture of English agriculture during the seventeenth and eighteenth centuries which would not be readily obtained from other sources.

Only the briefest introduction is given to the evolution of homes, their furnishings, and rural life through the ages because the general background is to be found in many books dealing with these subjects.

The idea of publishing these inventories emanated from Mr. F. G. Emmison, F.S.A., County Archivist of Essex, whose work on a similar series of Bedfordshire documents is referred to later on. At all times in the preparation of this book, Mr. Emmison has been more than generous with his advice and encouragement. To others of my colleagues I am grateful for help and criticism in many directions, and particularly to Mrs. M. I. Thew who not only prepared a perfect typescript for the printer, but gave unstintingly of her knowledge of country life. I am likewise a debtor to all those who have permitted me to quote from their published works, answered my enquiries, or read through sections which they were qualified to judge.

I must also thank the Trustees of the British Museum for allowing me to use illustrations from Harleian MS. 2027, and for making casts of Daniel Leonard's token (Plate XIV); the Directors of the Victoria and Albert Museum, and the Science Museum, for permission to reproduce the Frontispiece and Plate IV respectively. Mr. H. M. Paterson, of Old Riffhams, Danbury, kindly let me use his sketch of Roxwell mill before its conversion. Mr. D. Gerken took the photographs from which Plates I and X were made, and Mr. G. W. Worrin lent the photograph of the table formerly at Little Dunmow (Plate XII). A special word of thanks is due to Mr. E. J. Rudsdale for lending me the excellent photographs used for Plates III and VIII; his work in reconstructing agricultural scenes deserves to be better known. Plate V from *Country Craftsmen* appears by kind permission of Miss Freda Derrick and her publishers, Messrs. Chapman and Hall, and Plate II by courtesy of Mr. A. Jobson and the Editor of *Country Life*.

The directors and staff of Messrs. Wiles & Son, Ltd., have spared no effort in the production of this book and I would like to thank them for the interest they have shown in it.

COUNTY HALL, FRANCIS W. STEER.

CHELMSFORD.

CONTENTS

LIST OF ILLUSTRATIONS

Figs. 2, 4-15, 17, 18 and 21 are reproduced from Harleian MS. 2027 in the British Museum. The blocks for Plate VI and the map have been kindly lent by the Records Committee of the Essex County Council.

NOTE

The compilation of this book was undertaken by Mr. Steer wholly outside his normal duties. The two Committees which have sponsored it wish to express their appreciation of the editor's offer to place the text at their disposal; they are gratified that the interest in the work, as shown by the number of pre-publication orders, has fully justified their acceptance of it.

A. LAVER CLARKE,

Chairman of the Records Committee.

INTRODUCTION

I

THE Stuart and early Hanoverian period is one so fraught with fundamental controversies that it can never be regarded as merely picturesque; and standing as it does, at the junction of the ways between Renaissance England and modern times, provides an unparalleled study in contrasts.

After the catastrophe of the Protectorate, economic revival under the Restoration regime brought about an improvement in standards of living and behaviour of all classes. The documents dealt with in this book help to create a picture of the homes of everyday men and women during this important phase in English history, and show that there was a story other than that of rich men broken by their adherence to the cause of Charles I, or of favourites scrambling for place at the Restoration. The picture drawn from the inventories shows the continuity of domestic life at a time when the careers of politicians and the fortunes of dynasties rose and fell. The problems arising from the Industrial Revolution such as the decline of the craftsman and the concentrations of population were still ahead when the last of these inventories was written. The countryman in his isolation regarded his social superiors with something akin to reverence; rural life has been well described by H. J. Massingham as a democracy within an aristocratic frame. The parish was the main unit of local government and controlled by its elected officers—the churchwardens, overseers, constable, and surveyors; movement from one's parish was restricted. They were days when sanitation was practically unknown, medical services were primitive, work was hard and unremitting, crime widespread, wages small, and life cheap.

From the meanness of domestic equipment many of the persons whose inventories are included in this book would rank as paupers if judged by modern standards, but they would not have been classed as such in their own day so long as they drew no parochial relief. The inventories of paupers in the technical sense are frequently found among the records of the parish overseer.[1]

Although the Civil War marks the end of one period and the Restoration the beginning of another, the change was gradual. As one writer[2] has put it :—

'Each historic age and social order gives place to new, but not at a single thunder-clap. Ebbs and flows go on through decades of adjustment, with spells of stress and crisis, separated by spells of comparative and illusory calm while the next birth-pang of the coming age gathers in the womb of time.'

[1] The low standard of living of the labouring classes in the seventeenth and eighteenth centuries has been attributed to their own improvidence rather than to the small wages which they received; the cost of living, the cost and sort of food, cost of clothes, and typical family budgets of the poor at the end of the eighteenth century are given by Eden in *The State of the Poor* (abridged and edited by A. G. L. Rogers, 1928, p. 100). Although Essex is poorly represented in this book, conditions were similar in most counties, provided that allowance is made for any local characteristics, such as industry; the inventories supplement Eden by showing what were the contents of the type of homes with which he was concerned.

[2] F. E. Kenchington, *The Commoners' New Forest* (1943), p. 49.

In these inventories we see the slow development of comfort, the introduction of new appliances and the discontinuance of some of the old, but what had been luxuries in the reign of Charles I became necessities in those of his sons.[1] We see, too, the survival of certain objects in spite of changing circumstances and fashions, and this is largely due to the fact that money was not plentiful and furniture was constructed to withstand hard wear and to descend from father to son.

II

In the following pages an attempt has been made to portray, by using documents prepared by their fellow-men, something of the domestic circumstances of poor and middle-class people living in two parishes in central Essex.[2] The varying degrees of personal well-being are perhaps shown more clearly in inventories than any other type of document, yet this source has been used but little. Sacks full of inventories lie at Somerset House and at other probate registries[3] waiting to be indexed and made available; thousands of others were, no doubt, destroyed at the abolition of local probate registries. The historical value of inventories cannot be too strongly emphasized, because these documents tell us precisely what goods a person had at the time of his death and what they were worth; they help, even more than manorial records, to determine the social positions of members of a community, and they supplement the evidence of past ages as shown in painting, literature, correspondence, and manuscripts.

Even in the days of restricted transport, household furnishings and utensils which were not of local manufacture were imported from those places which specialized in a particular production; there was a continual interchange of merchandise between counties, towns and villages, and small towns were under mutual obligations—they could never be entirely self-supporting communities owing to the lack of essential raw materials. Defoe gives an analysis[4] of the clothes and furniture of a man and woman living in Horsham, and it is noticeable that many of the centres now famous for a certain product were equally so in his time; there is ample evidence in early correspondence and elsewhere that members of a family travelling to distant parts of the country were asked to procure specialities not obtainable at home.

The invaluable work done by museum curators towards the preservation of examples of locally-made furniture, domestic and agricultural 'bygones', cannot be over-estimated, and Great Britain is not alone in this respect.

'Bygones'—a commonly-used expression—has, perhaps, a ring of insincerity about it; the word often implies the quaint or obsolete, and is used for want of something better to denote the destruction of the country life by the machine age. The individuality of the craftsman, whether he

[1] Sir Charles Petrie, *The Jacobite Movement* (1932), p. 37.

[2] Except 221 and 226 which relate to persons in Drury Lane, London, and Hadleigh, respectively.

[3] See B. G. Bouwens, *Wills and their whereabouts* (1939) for details of inventories known to exist.

[4] For details, see Thomas Burke, *The English Townsman* (1946), pp. 65-6.

worked on the land, in wood, metal, or stone, has almost gone, and mass-produced articles for the home, and mechanized farming, has taken its place. Few articles, other than necessities, were indigenous to the cottages of Stuart and Georgian England; the larger houses set the standard and the less wealthy either copied their superiors or accumulated such articles as were discarded with the changes in fashion.[1]

The majority of books dealing with furniture are designed for the connoisseur and therefore concentrate on those superb examples of craftsmanship emanating from Chippendale, Hepplewhite, and Sheraton, on the masterpieces in oak, walnut or mahogany, and on the products of France, Italy, and the East, which enrich our museums and galleries where the arts of the painter, the potter, and the silversmith are blended with those of the woodworker. This present book aims at recording the products of the humbler artisan whose work was sold to his neighbours at a modest price; carving and embellishment were the exception rather than the rule so far as the country joiner was concerned.

Of the work by other writers in this field of research special mention may be made of that of Mr. F. G. Emmison, F.S.A., whose book on Bedfordshire inventories of the Jacobean period[2] was the first to appear since the Surtees Society published five volumes between 1835 and 1929[3] of wills and inventories relating to the northern counties. Other smaller series, or single inventories, have been published from time to time[4], but Essex is poorly represented.[5] Mr. G. Eland, F.S.A., devotes a chapter, based on inventories,

[1] See R. L. Mason on Cottage and Farmhouse Furniture in *The Connoisseur*, July, 1913, pp. 27-32.

[2] Published by the Bedfordshire Historical Record Society, 1938.

[3] *Wills and inventories illustrative of the history, manners, language, statistics, &c., of the northern counties of England, from the eleventh century downwards*; *Wills and inventories from the Registry at Durham*; *Wills and inventories from the Registry of the Archdeaconry of Richmond.*

[4] The writer has seen the following in the course of collecting information for this book, but there are doubtless many more: *Norfolk Archæology*, vol. v, pp. 331-40; vol. xv, pp. 91-108; vol. xx, pp. 166-177; *Antiquary*, vol. xxxvi, pp. 50-2 (five inventories of wearing apparel and domestic linen, 1728, and one of fruit trees, 1727); two seventeenth-century inventories in *Yorkshire Archæological Journal*, vol. xxxiv, p. 170; *The Unton inventories relating to Wadley and Faringdon, co. Berks, in the years 1596 and 1620*, printed for the Berkshire Ashmolean Society, 1841; Chetham Society: *Lancashire and Cheshire Wills and Inventories*, O.S., vols., xxxiii, li, liv, N.S., 3, 28, 37; 'A Probate Inventory of goods and chattels of Sir John Eliot, late prisoner in the Tower, 1633', edited by Harold Hulme in *The Camden Miscellany*, vol. xvi (1936).

[5] An inventory of the goods of John Arnold of Great Warley is printed in the *Transactions* of the Essex Archæological Society, N.S., vol. x, pp. 58-9, and of Isaac Lemyng Rebow of Colchester in vol. xiv, pp. 16-25. For inventories of goods of Elizabeth Adly of Upminster, and Thomas Crush of Roxwell (no. 136), see *Essex Review*, vol. xv, pp. 67-9, 169-175. See also T. M. Hope, 'Two interiors. Toppingho Hall, Hatfield Peverel, in the 16th and 17th centuries', in *Essex Review*, vol. liii, pp. 121-4. Inventory of goods (taken either under distraint or possibly under an act of attainder) of an unknown person, *temp.* Henry VII, is in *The Red Paper Book of Colchester* (ed. Benham, 1902), pp. 66-7. *The Autobiography of Sir John Bramston, K.B., of Skreens* [in Roxwell], published by the Camden Society in 1845, is chiefly concerned with public affairs during the later years of the seventeenth century and does not give much light on local conditions.

to domestic comforts in *Shardeloes Papers of the 17th and 18th centuries* (1947), and Dr. E. P. Dickin, F.S.A., collected some useful information on houses and their furniture in his *History of Brightlingsea* (1939), pp. 201-29. Dr. W. G. Hoskins has used some of the inventories in the Leicester Registry in his *Short History of Galby and Frisby,*[1] and Miss L. J. Redstone has drawn on inventories and sale catalogues when describing home life from 1583 to 1915 in *Ipswich through the Ages* (1948), pp. 122-7.

In the Essex Record Office are numerous isolated inventories prepared for a variety of purposes; one of the more curious is, perhaps, the 'Lynnen delivered to Susan Gyllam for Winnifrid Barrington', 1589, and endorsed—by her mother or nurse—'my one Sweete hart'. The Barringtons of Hatfield Broad Oak were an important Essex family, and Winifred's inventory includes many items not found in the whole of the Writtle series. The inventories of some wealthy people such as William Pownset of Barking, *c.* 1555, and Thomas, earl of Sussex, *c.* 1588, and inventories concerning special classes of goods are noted in the *Guide to the Essex Record Office,* Part II (1948).

III

An inventory of the goods and chattels of the deceased, that is to say, his household stuff, money, debts, plate, clothes, jewels, cattle, poultry, corn, hay, and felled timber,[2] had to be produced at the time of the granting of probate of a will, or at the issuing of letters of administration if the person died intestate. Certain effects need not be listed, as, for example, fish, conies, deer or pigeons, found in pond, warren, park, or dovehouse, but the same animals and birds were liable for inclusion if tame.[3] Things affixed to the tenement and thereby made part of the freehold, were not put in an inventory, and neither were goods to which a husband was entitled in right of his wife.[4]

The obligation to produce an inventory was in the form of a bond, half in Latin and half in English; a typical example is given at the beginning of Appendix B. It seems to have been the usual practice for executors or administrators either to have entered into the bond at the time of exhibiting

[1] Reprinted, 1945, from the *Transactions* of the Leicestershire Archæological Society, vol. xxii, part III.

[2] Richard Burn, *Ecclesiastical Law* (1763), vol. ii, p. 645.

[3] *Ibid.*

[4] *Ibid,* pp. 647, 651. To illustrate this, it may be mentioned that when a person was in financial difficulties his goods were sometimes sold to discharge a debt. In such circumstances, an inventory was often taken, although the duty was not always a pleasant or easy one. For example, when Alice Thornton (a seventeenth-century Yorkshire widow and the daughter of an astute mother) found herself burdened with her late husband's debts, it was, to the great disgust of the appraisers, discovered that her mother had had her goods held in trust for her daughter and, therefore, could not be claimed for the discharge of another's debts (see Wallace Notestein, *English Folk,* 1938, p. 199). Similar circumstances where the wife maintained that certain goods were her property, may account for the absence of greater quantities of plate and other valuables than appear in the inventories of some of the wealthier yeomen.

the inventory, or else to date the inventory as being made on the same day as the bond. There is, however, evidence that inventories preserved in Diocesan and other Registries were fair copies of originals and certified retrospectively. The legal expenses[1] in obtaining a grant of probate or letters of administration were in the neighbourhood of thirty shillings; in the case of Henry Duke,[2] the sums paid were as follows: —

Dukes Administracion	0	18	2
Bond	0	1	0
Officer for ye pressing ye seale		1	0
Inventory Registring and Ingrossing	0	6	8
Exhibicion of itt	0	1	0
The Kings Duty	0	1	0
Oath	0	0	4
	1	9	2

[In the margin] Mortuary x^s^.

The inventory had to be made by, or in the presence of, some creditable persons who were qualified to assess the value of the deceased's goods. As Burn says,[3] 'it is not sufficient to make an inventory, unless the goods therein contained be particularly valued and appraised by some honest and skilful persons, to be the just value thereof in their judgments and consciences, that is to say, at such price as the same may be sold for at that time'.

Most of the inventories are written on paper which, although varying in size, was usually long and narrow; a few of the documents are on vellum or parchment. The earliest of the series to be on stamped material (under an Act of 1694) is that of Richard Maggett, 1700 (188).

Although appraisers were required to be 'honest and skilful persons', the majority of them were illiterate, and even allowing for the change in the purchasing power of money during the last two or three hundred years, some of their valuations were ridiculously low. There is a marked irregularity in prices, and the occasional omission of obvious articles (for example, although 102 is a very detailed inventory, there is no mention of beds) makes one doubt if the skill demanded was always present. A large number of totals are incorrect, and many of the documents are written in phonetic English (e.g. 113) with dialect words included; this has increased the difficulties of interpreting some of the terms. It is noticeable, too, that scholarship did not improve with the passing of time; nos. 86, 195, 196 and 211 are particularly illiterate, but none of the inventories in this series is quite so bad as that compiled by James Denny of Kirby-le-Soken:[4]

Novmbr : 22 : 1725

then Took an Envey Torey [inventory] of the Goodes and a destres for Rent dew to me James Denny to millmes [Michaelmas] Last ben the sum of won

[1] Two dilapidated sheets of expenses apparently prepared by the Commissary's clerk, together with indexes (211 names) of grants of probate or letters of administration made in the Writtle court, are in the Essex Record Office, D/APw P2.

[2] See Inventory 97.

[3] Richard Burn, *Ecclesiastical Law* (1763), vol. ii, p. 652.

[4] Essex Record Office, D/P 169/18.

Fig. 1. THE GREAT BARN AT LORDSHIP FARM, WRITTLE

Erected between 1490 and 1510, this fine building is thirty-seven yards long. It is one of the best examples of the carpenter's skill in Essex, and was carefully restored in 1939.

pond and sixten shillings and sixpens and heer follo what goods dis strayined as follow in the Hall houes 2 matkes [mattocks] and 2 Exes and a betell and to weges small and Greet and 4 oll[d] Chayires and won Tabell and won Gint stewell [joint stool] and a wor men [warming] pan and payir beloes a payir Tonges and firpan won Cabiren won Grid iren and Tramell and a Trensher Cas [trencher case] and other od things in the butrey won citell [settle or kettle] 2 skilets won frin [frying] pan won gren poot and won braspoot and 3 Tobes and won paybill and a hollf anker [anchor] and holl anker and won haff brell [? barrel] and won speet [spit] and a Long saw and som other small Emplements and in the Chamber won bee[d] and bolster and on oll[d] Ruge and a payir sheetes and mor small Linen of Litell valew thes goodes dis strayin[d] this day for Rent as a bof [above] sayd

by me James Denny and Willim formen ben Constebell ben in presens with me

Appraisers were in the habit of using such convenient collective terms as 'other implements' and 'other lumber' for goods which they did not want to list in detail; their use of punctuation may be said to be non-existent; capital letters were used indiscriminately, and the same word spelt in two ways in one line. Throughout the documents, one continually finds terms whose meanings are obscure; whenever possible, a definition (even if only a suggested one) has been given, but what is unintelligible to one reader is sometimes clear to another.

IV

The church of Writtle with the chapelry of Roxwell was a 'peculiar', that is to say, they were not subject to the same ecclesiastical jurisdiction (i.e. the ordinary of the diocese) as the majority of others, but under the control of the Commissary appointed by the Warden and Fellows of New College, Oxford, by whom they were acquired on the seizure of alien hospitals in 1391.[1] The College had, therefore, the privilege of acting, through the medium of its duly appointed Commissary, in the same capacity as the Bishop of the diocese, and its powers included the granting of probates and letters of administration.

There must have been a considerable quantity of documents in connection with the testamentary functions of the Commissary's court at Writtle, but the inventories now printed, a few bonds,[2] and some miscellaneous papers are all that remain. These documents were found in a chest in the church and were deposited in the Essex Record Office in 1939.[3] There are a number of similar inventories, described as 'ancient and irregular',[4] together with wills from 1637, in the Principal Probate Registry at Somerset House for this same peculiar.

[1] *Victoria County History*, Essex, vol. 2 (1907), p. 200. For an illustration of the seal of the Peculiar Jurisdiction of Writtle, see J. L. Fisher, 'The Petre Documents', in *Transactions* of the Essex Archæological Society, New Series, vol. xxiii, plate II, and p. 91.

[2] See Appendix B.

[3] Catalogue mark D/APw P4; see also *Guide to the Essex Record Office*, Part II (1948), pp. 94, 100, and *Essex Parish Records* (in the press). The E.R.O. has been approved by the Bishop of Chelmsford as the Diocesan Record Office.

[4] B. G. Bouwens, *Wills and their whereabouts* (1939), p. 53.

It is of interest to record that the headquarters of the Essex Institute of Agriculture are at Writtle, and the estate, including Lordship,[1] Daw's, Guy's and Sturgeon's Farms, covers much of the land once cultivated by the people whose inventories are given.

Detailed investigations into the history of the persons and properties mentioned in this book has not fallen within the scope of this study, but the extensive series of court-rolls, rentals, tax-rolls, and similar documents for Writtle and Roxwell, in the Essex Record Office, together with registers and other parish records, would provide a wealth of information in this respect. From such records it would be possible, not only to identify, but to trace the descent from generation to generation, of many of the houses to which the inventories relate. Appendix B, giving the names of those persons responsible for the production of certain inventories, has been added because of the relationships and occupations which are recorded; even this incomplete list shows that many inventories are missing.

HOMES AND THEIR FURNISHINGS

Types of Houses

An analysis of the houses[2] mentioned in the inventories gives a total of 1866 rooms or offices allocated as follows: —

			Rooms
Houses with	1 room	3 =	3
" "	2 rooms	1 =	2
" "	3 "	7 =	21
" "	4 "	18 =	72
" "	5 "	14 =	70
" "	6 "	32 =	192
" "	7 "	24 =	168
" "	8 "	28 =	224
" "	9 "	15 =	135
" "	10 "	13 =	130
" "	11 "	7 =	77
" "	12 "	18 =	216

			Rooms
Houses with	13 rooms	15 =	195
" "	14 "	5 =	70
" "	15 "	6 =	90
" "	16 "	4 =	64
" "	18 "	2 =	36
" "	19 "	2 =	38
" "	20 "	1 =	20
" "	21 "	1 =	21
" "	22 "	1 =	22
Total		217	1866

The rooms[3] may be further sub-divided into these classes: —

Hall	209
Chamber over hall	135
Parlour	183
Chamber over parlour	134
C' fwd	661

B' fwd	661
Great parlour	4
Old parlour	4
Little parlour	10
Chamber over little parlour	3
C' fwd	682

[1] See Fig. 1, p. 6.

[2] The majority of houses were six to eight roomed; Prof. Mildred Campbell arrives at a similar conclusion in *The English Yeoman under Elizabeth and the early Stuarts* (1942), p. 230, after extensive examination of inventories at Lincoln Probate Registry and elsewhere.

[3] Barns, stables and other outbuildings are not included. In a number of inventories the details are insufficient to be included in the analysis, and in others it is obvious that some rooms have been omitted; for example, in nos. 22 and 33, rooms *over* the buttery or *over* the parlour are given, but not the corresponding rooms below. The presence of rooms has not been assumed, and doubtful items have either been omitted or assigned to whichever category seems appropriate.

A Livery Cupboard in St. Albans Abbey.

Plate II

Interior of a Domestic Brewhouse at The Chantry Farm, Halesworth, Suffolk.

Room	Number
	B' fwd 682
Chamber or old chamber	30
Chamber next parlour	3
Bed chamber	1
Best chamber	19
Chamber over passage	1
Little chamber	11
Matted chamber	3
Middle chamber	2
New chamber	1
Pot chamber	1
Buttery	242[1]
Chamber over buttery	68
Little buttery	26
Cheese chamber or loft	48
Room next buttery	4
Kitchen	110
Chamber over kitchen	46
Little kitchen	1
New kitchen	1
Chamber over new kitchen	1
Old kitchen	1
Pantry or larder	15
Chamber over pantry	4
Dairy	75
Chamber over dairy	14
Milkhouse	51
Chamber over milkhouse	9
Brewhouse	65
Chamber over brewhouse	8
Malt chamber	14
Malt-house	22
Chamber over malt-house	1
Kiln-house	8
Quern-house or mill-chamber	9
Chamber over mill	3
Boulting-house	13
Chamber over boulting-house	1
Meal-house	7
	C' fwd 1621

Room	Number
	B' fwd 1621
Bakehouse or back-room	8
Room next boulting-house	1
Scullery	1
Sink-house	2
Chamber over sink-house	2
Shop	29
Chamber over shop	16
Workhouse	3
Iron Chamber	1
Corn chamber	22
Folks chamber	3
Lodging room	1
Servants chamber	32
Chamber over servants chamber	1
Entry	4
Chamber over entry	13
Staircase	3
Chamber at stair-head	3
Gallery	3
Closet	21
Garret	30
Cellar	11
Chamber over cellar	3
Old House	1
Slaughter-house	1
Wool-chamber	1
Wash-house	2
Chamber over wash-house	1
Passage	3
Music room	1
Best parlour	1
Falling-door chamber	1
Warehouse	1
Chamber over drinkhouse	1
Nursery	1
" Tufft-house "	1
Chamber over " tufft-house "	1
Interior rooms unspecified	15
	1866

The rooms listed in Zachariah Day's inventory, 1705 (189) correspond with those in Isaac Day's of 1715 (202), but the interchange of terms, i.e. parlour chamber for chamber over the parlour, is noticeable.

Although many books[2] have been written on the architecture and evolution of the English house, small houses of an early date were usually of two rooms or bays, known as the house (i.e. hall or living-room) and the parlour (or bedroom), divided by a partition and having a central chimney. To the hall was later added (often as a wing built at right-angles) the kitchen and buttery, thus separating the preparation of food from the sleeping quarters; the buttery was, perhaps, originally synonymous, or at least associated with, the ' bower ', which was essentially the women's part of the early house.

[1] Includes beer-butteries.

[2] See *The English Cottage,* by H. Batsford and C. Fry (1938), *The Evolution of the English House,* by Sidney Oldall Addy (revised and enlarged by John Summerson) (1933), and *The Englishman's Castle,* by John Gloag (1944), for further study on the smaller type of house.

Still later, rooms were added as an upper storey—the chambers over the hall, parlour, or other ground-floor rooms—while the kitchen wing was extended by such offices as dairies and brewhouses.[1] Barns or stables were often added to the domestic buildings, the resulting plan forming either an L-shape or three sides of a quadrangle. The wave of rebuilding was at its height between 1590 and 1640, and plans to include staircases (instead of newel-stairs in the thickness of the wall) and more than one chimney were evolved by about 1600.

The 'starr chamber' in John Holmes' inventory, 1685, shows the danger of coming to hasty conclusions about rooms; one might reasonably think that such a room was either a 'stair-chamber' (i.e. at the head of the staircase) or that its ceiling or walls were painted with stars. In a deed[2] of 1662, between Richard Wilton and William Garratt, both of Writtle, property is mentioned as lying between a tenement commonly called 'the Starre', in the occupation of John Holmes, cordwainer, and the orchard and tenement of Thomas Scott.

As with furnishings, the change from one type or plan was gradual, and we see in terms like 'the men's chamber' and 'the folk's chamber' a survival of the older order when farm workers lodged and boarded with their master, while the maids and mistress performed domestic duties in the kitchen, brewhouse, or dairy.

Further information on the size of seventeenth-century houses may be obtained from the Hearth Tax Rolls, which give the number of hearths in each house.[3]

It is doubtful if any of the houses mentioned in the inventories were without chimneys like the widow's cottage in Chaucer's 'Nonne Preestes Tale'. Much progress had already been made in housing improvements by the middle of the sixteenth century, when William Harrison (1534-1593), rector of Radwinter and author of the 'Description of England' prefixed to Holinshed's Chronicles, tells us of the changes which took place in his village during the lives of its oldest inhabitants,[4] including the erection of chimneys, the improvement in sleeping arrangements, and the replacement of wooden (treen) platters, dishes and spoons by pewter. Such changes become more apparent with the passing of the centuries and are more rapid today than ever before, and yet there are but few homes which do not retain something to remind us of a past fashion.

Houses in our period were built of local materials. In Essex, a stoneless county, we find weather-boarding and lath and plaster predominating; some

[1] An excellent example of this is Blamsters Manor, Halstead, where Arthur Golding, the Elizabethan scholar, spent his early years; the house is illustrated in the biography written by his descendant, Louis Thorn Golding (*An Elizabethan Puritan*, 1937).

[2] Essex Record Office, D/DB 456.

[3] A tax of two shillings for each hearth was levied under the Act of 13-14 Charles II, *c.* 10 (1662) and remained in force until 1688. See *Guide to the Essex Record Office*, Part I (1946), pp. 47-9.

[4] See Harold Smith, 'William Harrison and his Description of England' in *Essex Review*, vol. xxviii, pp. 100-5.

bricks were, of course, used, but a complete brick-built house was the exception rather than the rule. As many old houses have been remodelled to suit modern conditions, their original plans and appearance cannot now be determined with accuracy.

An interesting sidelight on the value of a house in 1654 is provided by a petition[1] presented to the county justices by George Furman, a husbandman, of Springfield: —

> 'A sudden sadd and lamentable fyer which consumed and burned downe ye sayd Dwelling howse and all ye weareinge apparrell of your sayd Peticioner his wiefe and Children except such as was upon theire backs and all theire howshold stuffe whatsoever theire Corne butter Cheese & poultry and other thinges to the valew of 103*li.* 6*s.* 11*d.* besydes the sayd Dwelling howse ye rebuildinge of which will cost neare 40*li.* to the utter undoeinge of your poore Peticioners and his famely'.

An inventory with the petition lists goods which were in the hall, parlour, dairy, buttery, chambers over parlour and hall, 'hovill' over the buttery, and the shed.

Although a few inventories relate to carpenters, bricklayers and wheelwrights,[2] there is not one dealing with the stock of a builder. Oddments of material for general repairs appear fairly frequently among the goods of yeomen and others who maintained their own premises, but such items are, in almost every case, confined to boards or planks, or simply listed as timber.

Some references, however, to boards and planks may refer to those used for table-tops (see pp. 12, 39) in kitchens or cheese-rooms, but prepared timber was seldom overlooked by appraisers. The mention of two boards and a tool box worth 3*s.* (26), a piece of old wainscot (49), two boards and old iron (58), a parcel of 'gysts [joists] and ploncke s' valued at £6 15*s.* (121), and the many references to axes, saws, wedges, timber-chains, and other gear used in tree-felling, all help to emphasize the importance of wood. Not only was is used for building purposes, but faggots and logs provided fuel, and bark was extensively used in tanning.

Bricks occur only twice. William Carnell had seven hundred bricks worth 14*s.*, and tiles to the value of £1 4*s.*; in John Chalk's malthouse (121) were seven hundred bricks and tiles valued, with four bundles of laths, five gate posts, a corn screen and two rakes, at £1 17*s.* Tiles are also listed in William Grudgfield's inventory (233) together with round wood, so termed here and in no. 218, to distinguish it from sawn timber.

A single reference to hair in a tanner's inventory of 1689 (152) reminds us of its use for mixing with plaster for walls and ceilings.

Tables

TABLES appear in practically every inventory, but it is not until relatively late in the series that we find anything described other than what must have been of good, plain, solid oak or elm. The earliest types were merely

[1] Among Quarter Sessions Records in Essex Record Office (Q/SBa 2/91).

[2] See also p. 43. The inventory of William Carnell, 1679 (104), has a good selection of timbers used in wheelwrighting, but a few items refer, no doubt, to general building requirements.

loose boards (or planks as they are sometimes called) on trestles or 'horses'. In an inventory of 1638 (14), the first entry is 'one planke Table wth the Dorments', i.e. the first form of a domestic permanent or 'dormant' table with its solid, but often decorative, ends joined by a single stretcher, as opposed to the more temporary type consisting of trestles and boards. This type of table was not, however, a new innovation; Chaucer, describing the Franklin in the Prologue to *The Canterbury Tales,* says:

'His table dormant in his halle alway
Stood redy covered al the longe day'.

From the table dormant was evolved the four-legged table; this variety, in turn, was improved by the addition of leaves which gave rise to the term 'drawing' tables, first noted in 1671 (70).[1]

Those described as 'falling' tables (166, 190) were of the 'gate-leg' type with hinged flaps supported by moveable gates.

The majority of tables in country homes of the seventeenth century were broadly classified into two main divisions: the long rectangular dining or kitchen tables, often described as 'joined' (i.e., with the frames morticed and tenoned, and the joints secured with wooden pegs), and the smaller ones which served occasional uses.

Oval tables are first recorded in 1672 (77), but square and round ones are listed from 1638 (19 and 7).

Although Spanish mahogany from the West Indies was used by Sir Walter Raleigh to repair his ships, this wood—eventually to become so popular for furniture-making—was not imported until about 1715 and then in very limited quantities.[2] The mention of a 'Spanish table' among the goods of Edward Sandford in 1687 (147) is of particular interest, and is an early reference to an article of furniture made of mahogany.

Livery boards or livery tables are occasionally noted, and seem to have been used either in place of, or as stands for, livery cupboards (see p. 15) in a few homes. They were possibly used also as benches, because in Thomas Osburne's inventory, 1672 (77), is an entry for a livery board with a Darnex cloth and two cushions upon it, which indicates a seat rather than a table. Sideboard or side tables (see p. 15) were accessory to the large table during the serving of meals, but the dresser or dresser-board was originally a simple, table-like article of kitchen furniture placed against the wall (and often with a series of shelves above it), where the food was 'dressed' preparatory to being cooked. The use of a dresser as a display stand for eating utensils was a much later innovation, and developed from a kitchen table into an important piece of furniture fitted with drawers and cupboards. In the hall of John Hillyard, 1727 (227), was 'one deal dresser board with doors and drawers'.

Table-chairs are listed seven times; these were armchairs or settles having hinged backs made of one piece of wood which could be swung over to form table-tops. A fine specimen, dated 1666, is in Stevenage church, Herts.

[1] A table of this type occurs in an inventory of 1558; see *A picture book of English tables,* in the Victoria and Albert Museum series of handbooks.

[2] *Old English Furniture* (M. Harris and Sons, 1938), p. 32.

A dressing table and glass is only mentioned once (1744, 238). A table in an inventory of 1725 (221), and described as ' broune ' (brown) provides us with a description spelt phonetically; the ' novill ' table which belonged to John Lord, 1696 (180), is merely another way of writing ' an oval ' table!

Seating

A HARD stool or bench was the poor man's seat until the early seventeenth century; chairs were only for important people and even they did not have much ease. The Woolsack of the Lord Chancellor was ' more a symbol of the foundation of the nation's wealth than an intentional contribution to his comfort.'[1]

Chairs, however, appear, in addition to benches and stools, in almost every inventory, but they were reserved for the owner of the house and his guests, and we are still reminded of this fact when a distinguished person is invited to become the ' chairman ' or ' to take the chair '. There can be little doubt that some of the earlier examples were either of the ' bobbin-frame ' type with triangular seats, or else like boxes fitted with a tall back and solid arms; both were remnants of the early sixteenth century, and as chairs, stools and benches are all recorded from the earliest times, it is a mistake to suppose that they are developments of the chest. The chairs of the second half of the same century, even if less cumbersome, were still heavy and obviously very uncomfortable.

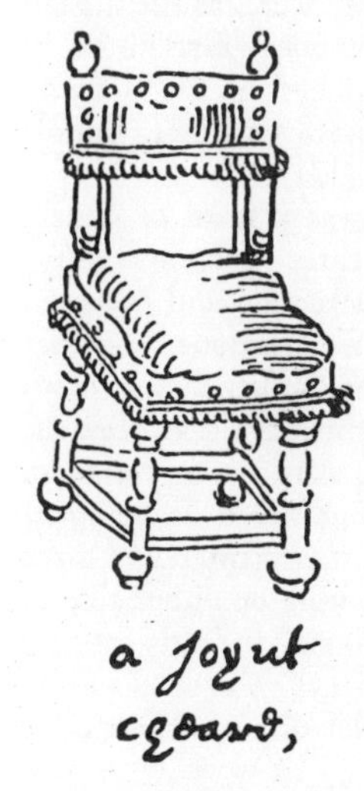

Fig. 2

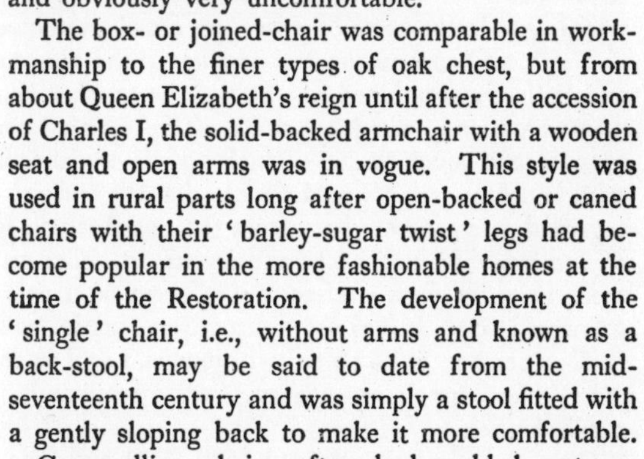

The box- or joined-chair was comparable in workmanship to the finer types of oak chest, but from about Queen Elizabeth's reign until after the accession of Charles I, the solid-backed armchair with a wooden seat and open arms was in vogue. This style was used in rural parts long after open-backed or caned chairs with their ' barley-sugar twist ' legs had become popular in the more fashionable homes at the time of the Restoration. The development of the ' single ' chair, i.e., without arms and known as a back-stool, may be said to date from the mid-seventeenth century and was simply a stool fitted with a gently sloping back to make it more comfortable.

Cromwellian chairs often had padded seats or backs (see 28, 1660) and, like the earlier ' farthingale ' chairs made in the reign of James I, were without arms. A lady attired in a farthingale could not sit in an armchair without damaging her dress or its supports, and as an additional precaution, the seats were often covered with 'Turkey work' (see Frontispiece), a woollen material worked on a loom in imitation of a Turkey carpet[2] (156, 192).

Caned chairs, although known in this country before the Commonwealth, do not figure in the Writtle inventories until 1690 (158), although a bass

[1] *The English Chair, its history and evolution* (M. Harris & Sons, 1937), p. 7.

[2] *Ibid.*, p. 20.

chair is recorded as early as 1665 (48), and wicker chairs from 1638 (5).[1]

The index to this volume shows the numerous types of chairs found in the homes of the period; many of the terms are obviously interchangeable, but the scarcity of chairs upholstered in cloth is remarkable. Those described as having arms, or as 'elbow' chairs, are few, and only one example is noted as inlaid (75).

Oak, ash, yew, or elm, and probably beech or walnut, were used in chair manufacture, and the Worshipful Company of Turners prescribed certain standards of workmanship. For example, in 1609, there was a complaint that chairs taken from Colchester to London had their seats made of poplar instead of ash, and the Court ordered that they should either be returned or remade in accordance with regulations.[2] In Jacobean times, chair-making was, however, becoming within the province of country joiners.

Rush-bottomed chairs, which are recorded shortly before 1700, were made either with or without arms and usually had 'ladder' backs; some were stained black as noted in nos. 198, 232, 245, while the red chairs in two of Richard Browne's rooms (198) were probably japanned.

Children's chairs are listed twice (61, 99), and high and low chairs once (26).

Stools appear in almost as many types as chairs; they were, as mentioned above, in more common use. Close-stools (i.e. commodes) first noted in 1682 (124) were, as the name implies, closed in, and distinct from the 'joined' stools which had four legs and stretcher rails. Stools were sometimes upholstered with leather or cloth; two are noted as quilted (171).

The most usual method of seating in the kitchen was a form or bench, and both are mentioned in one way or another in nearly every inventory; they were merely elongated stools of the simplest construction and designed to withstand rough usage. Bench boards are sometimes mentioned together with benches, and it would appear that the framing of the bench was often regarded as a separate item from the board which formed the seat. Settles, or benches with high backs and an arm at either end, were not so common, there being only two references to them, and only one noted as being of wainscot (153). It was not unusual for a settle, built to accommodate three or four persons, to be placed with one end against the wall, on either side of the kitchen fireplace; examples are occasionally found in old country public-houses.

Couches are not listed until 1689 (157) and then not often. Theophilus Lingard, 1744 (238) had a cane couch and squab.

Cupboards

CUPBOARDS[3] before the sixteenth century were not necessarily receptacles in

[1] In a series of extracts from advertisements in newspapers, 1662-1760, forming an appendix to Messrs. Harris's book on English chairs, the earliest wicker chairs are noted in 1674 (p. 167), and Russia leather chairs (mentioned as early as 1660 in the inventories) are not listed until 1708 (p. 168).

[2] *The English Chair, its history and evolution* (1937), pp. 14-15.

[3] See R. W. Symonds on 'Plate, Court and Livery Cupboards' in *Country Life*, vol. 102 (1947), pp. 1308-9; *Catalogue of Welsh Furniture from Tudor to Georgian times* (National Museum of Wales, 1936), p. 6.

which things were deposited, but rather side-tables on which they were placed; in other words, the original cupboard was simply a board supported by legs and covered with a cloth or carpet, on which household plate and vessels, especially drinking-cups, were put. Hence the word 'cup-board'. The term 'table-cupboard', showing the original intention of this piece of furniture, is used in 1638 (11) and on four other occasions up to 1689 (153).

But by the early sixteenth century, the difference between cupboards, aumbries and presses had become definitely established, the terms soon became interchangeable, and the medieval plate-cupboard was more generally quoted as, or superseded by, the court-cupboard. This was either of two open tiers rather like a sideboard, or else with the lower tier enclosed by doors and the upper fitted with small recessed cupboards leaving a shelf for cups or other articles. The earlier court-cupboards were not massive pieces of furniture: in 'Romeo and Juliet' (Act I, Sc. V) when the musicians are waiting to play for the dances, a servant says—'Away with the joint-stools, remove the court-cupboard, look to the plate . . .'.

At about the same time, livery cupboards became common, fulfilling the dual purpose of enclosed cupboard and shelf. They were generally small, and either on legs and surmounted by a canopy, or else made to hang on a wall; the front and sides were pierced with ventilation holes, or, more frequently, made of turned balusters set fairly close together. The name is derived from the liveries of wine or beer, and bread, which, with candles, each person took up to his bedroom on retiring for the night; the food was put in the cupboard, and the drink on the flat top. Livery cupboards in which bread for distribution to the poor was placed may still be seen in some churches; those in St. Alban's Abbey (see Plate I) are good examples and serve to illustrate the type which are noted at frequent intervals throughout the inventories; John Draper of Writtle, 1672 (75), had one made of juniper wood and covered with a striped cloth.

Press-cupboards (described on one occasion, 19, as a wainscot press) were wardrobes fitted with two doors and often decorated with simple mouldings or carving.

Numerous other cupboards designed to suit particular requirements are recorded, and mention may be made of keeps or safes in which to preserve meat during the summer. The inventory of Samuel Coaltburt, 1666 (51), describes such a keep as a 'hare' cupboard. This is not an early form of game larder, but a receptacle covered with a cloth woven of horsehair; in 1726 (225), the appraisers of John Battle's goods were more explicit when they described his meat-safe as 'a keep cupboard covered with haircloth'.

Beds and their Furnishings

So far as Northern Europe is concerned, beds were originally little better than those made by animals. Leaves, covered with skins were, perhaps, the first attempt at comfort, but a shallow box filled with dried vegetation was later found to be more convenient, and from this primitive form the mattress filled with wool, feathers, or hair, but still in a box-like structure, was developed in the early Middle Ages. The Crusades are credited with the innovation of a bed enclosed by a canopy or other draperies, and after the twelfth century beds are often shown in that style. From this stage, the evolution of the free-standing bed was rapid, and reached its peak in Elizabeth's reign.[1]

A man was sometimes judged by the costliness of his bed, it being regarded as one of the most important features in any seventeenth-century home. Shakespeare, like many others of his day, specially mentioned his beds in his will.

Only a few of the more wealthy people in Writtle and Roxwell had beds which may be described as elaborate; the majority had to be content with a solid framework, usually with a post at each corner (hence the term 'four-poster') which sometimes supported a tester or canopy from which hung curtains of local manufacture.

The framing of the bedstead was laced with stout cords or bed-lines on which rested the thin rush mat which was superseded by a mattress filled

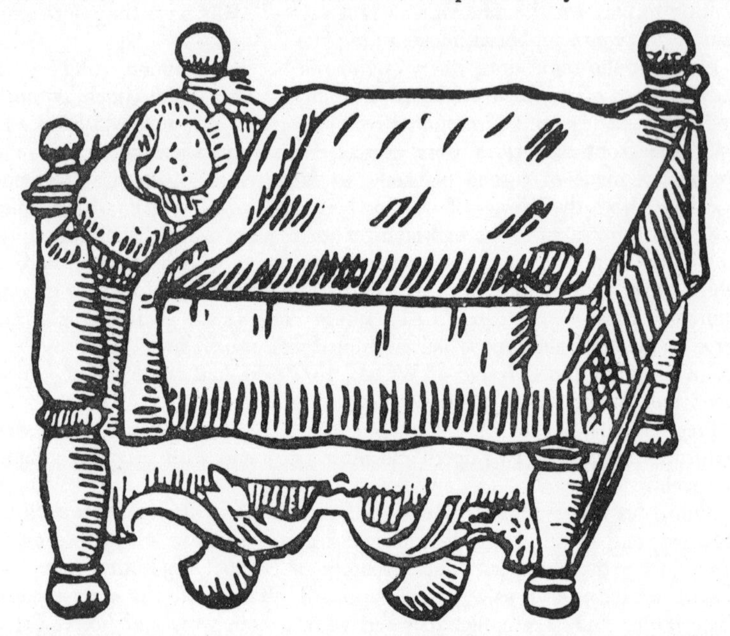

Fig. 3. From the brass in Boxford church, Suffolk, to David Bird, 1606.

with down, feathers, flock, or straw. Blankets and sheets were used as coverings, with rugs of a coarse material to provide extra warmth; these, like carpets, were seldom floor coverings. Pepys (13 July 1667) says 'Mighty hot weather, I lying this night, which I have not done, I believe, since a boy, with only a rugg and a sheet upon me'.

Although several types of bedsteads are noted in the inventories, there are

[1] A concise history of beds and their development is given in Aronson, *The Encyclopedia of Furniture* (New York, 1938), pp. 15-17.

167 documents in which this article of furniture is not given a definite description; of those which are described, fifty-seven are recorded as 'joined', and forty-seven as 'half-headed'. Joined bedsteads may be safely regarded as of the rigid four-poster variety with a canopy; the half-headed type had short corner-posts without canopies, but were, like most of the furniture of the period, soundly built.

Trundle or truckle beds were low frames fitted as beds, with castors enabling them to be rolled under the high or standing bedsteads during the day. Trundle beds, frequently used by children or personal servants, occur in no less than seventy-five of our documents.

Boarded or wainscot bedsteads had solid panels either at the head, or at both ends. Many of the bedsteads belonging to rich people had the head panel and posts richly carved, but the only example we have is that in Henry Turnidge's parlour (207).

Bedsteads are listed as 'sorry' on one or two occasions; this is an example of a dialect word meaning in poor condition, or of poor quality, and its use dates from the thirteenth century.[1]

The poorer classes did not have the luxury of sheets, and although blankets were much used, it did not follow that a family could afford many of them. Sheets and pillowcases (or pillowbeers as they were always called) were usually classified as coarse or towen, and flaxen or Holland; by our period, pillow and bolsters were in general use and no longer reserved for women in childbirth. Only once is a straw-filled bolster mentioned (26), and then it is additional to a feather one. Other than rugs, we find bed-coverings frequently listed in general terms with an occasional short description of the material; counterpanes[2] only occur three times, but quilts more often.

Widow Haward's feather beds were valued by weight (1729, no. 232); she had seventy-nine pounds of feathers priced at 7*d*. or 8*d*. per pound.

The tick, or case in which feathers or other bedding are placed, is twice listed (100, 224); the earlier entry is a good example of Essex dialect—'a node teck' is simply a local pronunciation of 'an old tick'. The six 'bed sticks' which belonged to Martha Meagle, 1690 (163), were, I think, also bed ticks.

One of the more important features of bedsteads were the hangings, nearly always listed as curtains and valances; on one occasion (222) the term 'bases'[3] is used instead of valances which were, however, generally recorded as 'valiants'. Reference to the index[4] will show the varieties of cloth used for bed and other curtains, but attention must be drawn to the obviously

[1] E. Gepp, *An Essex Dialect Dictionary* (1923), p. 104.

[2] This term is derived from the French *courtepointe* (a corruption of *contre-point*) and is the more modern equivalent of coverlet, also from the French *couvre-lit.*

[3] In the inventory of William Bird, 1691 (165), is an entry for a bedstead and bagis; the latter may be synonymous with bases, or, perhaps, it is a corruption of *bagasse* which is a probable variant of baggage, in the sense of being necessaries. (*N.E.D.*) Bird lived at Horsely Park, now Horsfrithpark Farm.

[4] *Art*: curtains.

elaborate hangings of William Bird's bed[1] in his parlour chamber; the outer curtains and valances were red 'cheyny' (?Chinee = Chinese) and the inner of a white material. Curtain rods were usually noted separately, and in 1671 (166) we have a collective term for curtains, valances and rods in the phrase 'one steale of yellow curtains & vallyans.'

In the later documents, bedding or bed-coverings are often described as a unit without any details.

Cradles, listed in fourteen documents, varied considerably in style; during the seventeenth century they were mostly low, box-like structures of panelled oak on rockers, and with wooden hoods which not only protected the children from draughts, but denied them of fresh air. The little bedsteads in Edmund Sterne's hall-chamber in 1683 (128), or the two low bedstedles[2] belonging to Samuel Woolfe, 1678 (111), were perhaps trundle beds. Although later in date, they may have been after the style of the bed shown on the brass (Fig. 3) in Boxford church, Suffolk, which has this appropriate epitaph:—

Dormitorium Davidis Birde filii Josephi Birde Rectoris istius ecclesia Obijt Vicess: Febru: 1606 Natus Septima: 22

Warming- or bed-pans—common articles in the home—were shallow containers of brass or copper attached to long handles and filled with hot embers. Beds were warmed by being ironed with this appliance, and the practice was one of the few comforts enjoyed by our forefathers.

a warmeing pan

Fig. 4

Chests, Hutches, Boxes and Trunks

ALL are closely akin to cupboards. The press cupboard was evolved because it was more convenient to suspend garments than to lay them in commodious chests. Many descriptive terms are employed, but mention may be made of three wainscot chests, two old sea chests, one little carved chest, and one made of juniper wood. The chest, derived from the coffer used mainly for storing money and valuables, is one of the oldest articles of furniture and was invariably constructed of wide oak or elm boards to reduce the joins to a minimum. There is only one specific reference to a boarded chest (6) meaning one made of narrow boards. A settle chest (55) had a back and narrow sides or arms to make the chest serve as a seat.[3]

[1] No. 165, see footnote on p. 17.

[2] Note the use of this term; 'steadle' is a variant of 'staddle', a foundation or stand.

[3] This should not be regarded as showing the evolution of the chair; see p. 13.

At least one chest is found in almost every home, and used for the storage of household linen; if carved or decorated, it would become a heirloom.

Hutches, used chiefly for clothes rather than linen, were generally smaller and less-strongly built than chests, but equally common. In poorer homes, the hutch was adequate to store the single change of clothing which the labourer and his wife possessed; in Robert Bloomfield's ballad of Richard and Kate we have the verse—

> 'She straight slipp'd off the Wall and Band,[1]
> And laid aside her Lucks and Twitches:[1]
> And to the Hutch she reach'd her hand,
> And gave him out his Sunday Breeches.'

An improvement to the chest, designed to give greater accessibility to its contents, was two drawers fitted at the bottom. This new piece of furniture, known as a mule chest,[2] was the forerunner of the chest of drawers which is first mentioned in 1673 (79), although a box of drawers—probably used for spices—occurs five years earlier (55). The olive-wood chest of drawers belonging to William Bird must have been a handsome piece.

Boxes are frequently mentioned, but their uses are seldom specified; except for George Bradford's little painted box (1671, 166), they do not call for comment. Owners of bibles no doubt kept them in oak boxes (known as bible-boxes), often carved and with sloping lids, but they are not mentioned in the inventories. Salt-boxes, usually kept near the fireplace or else in a specially constructed tunnel at the side of the chimney, are not listed so often as one would expect in view of the importance of salt.

There are many references to trunks, which were wooden boxes usually with domed lids, and covered with nail-studded leather. When not being used by travellers, they served as containers for bedding or linen.

Desks

DESKS, listed on ten occasions from 1670 (64), were originally portable boxes fitted with locks; later, they were put on legs, given sloping lids, and known as standing-desks.

Presses

SCREW-PRESSES for napkins and similar small linen appear early in the series, and there is one leaden hat-press (159).[3] The term 'hanging-press' was an alternative for a press-cupboard or wardrobe (see p. 15).

Mirrors

THERE is a surprising number of references to looking-glasses from 1663 (40). 'Seeing-glass' is often used for a mirror, but the latter term is,

[1] Terms used in spinning.

[2] No example is found in the inventories.

[3] Sir Ambrose Heal, in *The Sign-boards of Old London Shops* (1947), notes a hat-press as the sign of Bartholomew Flaggett, *c.* 1770, but the illustration accompanying this reference shows a large press being turned by a man using both hands on a cross-bar which controls the screw. The hat-press in the Writtle inventory must have been a small affair, probably for keeping flat the brim of a hat.

however, not employed. The frame of the looking-glass in William Bird's parlour chamber was, like his chest of drawers, of olive wood (165).

Clocks and Hourglasses

OUR first reference to a clock is in 1670 (64); the next is in 1679 (103) when John Putto's clock was valued at 30*s*. From that date, clocks become more frequent, but are never described in much detail.

The lantern clock[1] was, in the first half of the seventeenth century, the popular type for all who could afford such a luxury,[2] but after the Restoration, the production of weight-and spring-driven clocks rapidly increased in England. At the same time, the Dutch invention of the pendulum was developed, and long-case rather than wall clocks were made in this country. From about 1690 we have references to clocks and cases, which are listed simply as 'a clock and weights' (121, 159, 180), and are likely to have been wall clocks of the Dutch type.

Even with the growing popularity of clocks towards the end of the seventeenth century, hour-glasses did not go out of fashion, but it is strange that the hour-glass should not be noted until 1678 (102)—eight years later than the first reference to a clock.

Pictures and Maps

ALEXANDER REYNOLDSON, a grocer of Writtle, was evidently a man of taste; in addition to having the only musical instrument[3] mentioned in the series (see p. 48), his inventory (70) has the earliest reference to pictures. This form of decoration was infrequent as it is noted in only five other houses. Theophilus Lingard, 1744 (238), had two pictures in his best parlour, twenty prints in frames on the staircase, and two maps in the hall. In an unidentified inventory of *c.*1720 (245), four large pictures with gilt frames and a number of smaller ones are noted among the goods in the front chamber.

Soft Furnishings and Hangings

BED-CURTAINS and similar hangings are mentioned on pp. 17-18, but window-curtains—identifiable as such—do not appear until 1672 (74) and only then in a wealthy man's house; door-curtains (portières), however, although not mentioned in the inventories, are recorded at a much earlier date.

Hangings are still less frequent; in the inventories of William Bird, 1691 (165), and Richard Browne, 1713 (198), the hangings of their parlour-chambers (i.e. bedrooms) are noted. Bird also had a 'chimney peece in colours' which, although a painting or similar decorative panel, is more likely to have been, like wall-hangings, of tapestry or painted cloth.

[1] The writer recently saw a lantern clock by Stephen Levitt of Chelmsford for sale in the north of England.

[2] R. W. Symonds, *A Book of English Clocks* (1947), p. 31.

[3] A pair of virginals was the only musical instrument mentioned in the Bedfordshire Jacobean inventories (Beds. Hist. Record Soc., vol. xx, 1938); they belonged to a yeoman.

Reconstruction of a dairy exhibited at the Royal Show, Hereford, 1939. The central figure is using a plunger type of butter churn. Note the cheese-press, wooden butter scales, and cheese moulds.

AN EIGHTEENTH-CENTURY HAND-MILL.

This example of the millwright's craft came from Fyfield Hall, Ongar, Essex. The bevel gearing is of wood, but the difficulties in making it were solved by the general use of iron for mechanism at the end of the century.

Evidence of the latter art, known as early as 1419, is provided by the reference to the painted calico quilt on one of Bird's beds. Lingard's inventory, 1744 (238), gives us our sole example of paper hangings in a room.

Cushions, although listed from the beginning of the series, are described as embroidered in three instances (77, 132, 156).

To what extent carpets were used in the seventeenth century has not been satisfactorily determined, and there is frequently a doubt whether the entry refers to a covering for the floor or for a piece of furniture. The carpet on a livery cupboard or table, and the striped (86) and Darnex carpets (77, 93) were certainly not floor coverings. Carpets, in the modern sense of the word, did not become common even in the homes of fairly wealthy people until the first quarter of the eighteenth century.[1]

Artificial Light

It is not until 1725 (221) that we have any reference to lighting other than by candles, and even then tin lamps, lamp oil and matches among a shopkeeper's stock may not be regarded as typical of the average household.

The tinder-box, an essential feature of every kitchen before matches came into common use is, however, listed only once, 1744 (238). The probable explanation is that such an item, like candles (which occur only four times between 1671 and 1692) and rushlight-holders (which are not mentioned) were of very small value and not worth the trouble of listing.

Brass, iron, pewter, tin, or wire candlesticks are common throughout the series, and they would have been of the socket, rather than of the pricket, type. We find sconces, or wall brackets fitted with candle holders, in five houses between 1659 (26) and 1706 (190). Snuffers, an indispensable accessory with early candles, are noted on four occasions. They were a scissor-like arrangement fitted with a small box on one of the 'blades'; the charred wick, curling over the edge of the candle, was snipped off and retained in the box which closed when the handles of the snuffers were brought together.

Although the candle is of great antiquity—it is mentioned many times in the Old Testament—it did not give the relatively steady flame with which we are familiar. The best candles have always had a large percentage of beeswax in them, but the cottage homes of the seventeenth and eighteenth centuries could not boast such luxury. Even our modern cheap paraffin wax candles would have been the envy of the Writtle housewife of 1700; she probably had to be content with rushlights made from the pith of meadow rushes (with one rib of the outer skin left on to hold it together) which was dried and dipped in mutton fat. These primitive lights were laid in a piece of hollow bark to dry before being used in an iron holder; a rush about fourteen inches long would burn for about half an hour. Gilbert White, in a letter dated 1 November 1775 in *The Natural History of Selborne,* gives a detailed account of rushlight manufacture. The candles of the period were simply a larger edition of rushlights with a cotton wick dipped in tallow, or

[1] *Shardeloes Papers of the 17th and 18th centuries,* edited by G. Eland, F.S.A. (1947), p. 14.

in a mixture of tallow and wax, allowed to dry, then dipped again, and so on until the desired thickness was obtained; the finished articles were stored in a candlebox which was a development of the bark rushlight container. Eleven such boxes, which were normally fixed in a horizontal position on the wall, are listed.

Lanterns are noted between 1638 (8) and 1744 (238); in 1680 (115) we have one made of tin, but brass or sheet iron was the more general material. Light was emitted either through horn panels, 'bull's eye' glass windows, or through a series of punched holes; it is noticeable that this piece of equipment has hardly changed in shape from medieval times. Although the word is often written 'lanthorn', the name has nothing to do with the horn panels with which it was formerly fitted; the English form is from the Latin *lanterna*.

Miscellaneous Household Accessories

THERE are many articles in the inventories associated with one or other of the previous sections but not falling readily under a separate heading. Even today, we have various useful things in our homes so commonplace as to be scarcely noticed until, for some reason or another, we find that they are not to hand!

Fig. 5

Articles such as baskets of rush or wicker-work are often listed. There were coupled baskets to sling over a horse's back to take butter, poultry and other produce to market. An inventory of 1744 (238), refers to thirty 'mauns'; a maund, or hand-basket, was fitted with two lids, and used to convey butter and eggs. Flaskets,[1] or clothes baskets, are a fairly common item, but a basket known as a cob, carried by a sower as he broadcast seed in the fields, is only listed once (173).

Bins, barrels, tubs and other vessels for meal or corn were, with the 'powdering', 'aluming' or salting tubs or troughs, common in seventeenth- and eighteenth-century homes. Almost any kind of tub for household purposes was termed a kimnel, although the article is amplified occasionally

[1] This term is sometimes applied to a shallow washing-tub.

by being described as for milk, or (as in no. 6) a '3 legg chimnell'. The stalls and stands to support beer barrels, or to save the women-folk bending low over tubs used in the kitchens and butteries, are numerous. 'Tunnels' or funnels of wood or metal are also common, but 'stills' for distilling liquors (hence the term 'still-room') are not noted as often as would be expected during a period when the duties of a housewife included the preparation of medicines and cordials.[1]

Table forks are mentioned only three times from 1725 (222); beef-forks, pie-boards, saucepans, lids, saucers, dishes of pewter, wood, or earthenware are listed at frequent intervals. Tin-ware, however, was not common.

Fig. 6

The chafing dish, a small portable grate filled with burning charcoal to keep food warm, must have been a convenient form of hot-plate for the housewife dependent on wood fires. Coal[2] is only listed in nine inventories from 1672 (75) when two brass coal dishes are noted among the hearth appliances.

Brooms, brushes and mops are seldom mentioned, probably on account of their small value.

EATING AND DRINKING

Except for cheese (see pp. 37-9) very few items of food are mentioned; being of a perishable nature, it could not be regarded in the same light as furniture, fittings, or even livestock. Salt meat, which must have been such a monotonous winter diet and only relieved by an occasional pigeon or fowl, is noted twice (115, 236) as pork in 'powdering' tubs (see p. 27). There are fourteen references to bacon, but this is a small proportion of the total number of documents. Alum, used in curing bacon, is listed twice (169, 221).

Anchovies and red herrings occur but once and then in a London grocer's shop (221); this same man's stock also provides us with the solitary references to rice, tea, ginger, and capers. He also sold sugar and liquors, but the former is found in three forms, other than molasses, among the goods of a Roxwell grocer, 1692 (169), who also sold spice 'of all sorts'; this last-named commodity must have been in demand either to vary, or reduce, the strong flavour of salt meat.

There is only one reference to honey (87), and bees or bee-hives are recorded in 1638 (6), 1672 (75), 1678 (102) and 1719 (207), although it is hard to believe that apiculture was not more popular.

[1] Of the domestic recipe books in the Essex Record Office, that belonging to a certain Mrs. Slany, 1715 [D/DR Z1], is perhaps the most interesting; see illustration in *Guide to the Essex Record Office*, Part II (1948), p. 49.

[2] See also p. 27.

Porringers or porridge pots are frequently listed, but oatmeal is only referred to once (169).

Butter and milk have been dealt with in some detail under dairying, pp. 36-7; suet is noted in 1660 (30), and three pots of 'snett' (see p. 28) and grease in 1694 (174).

A human touch is provided when we come across a parcel of gingerbread among the stock of Widow George, 1687 (146), her total possessions were valued at 35*li.* 8*s.* 5*d.*, and she undoubtedly made and sold this speciality to augment her slender resources.

Tea and coffee do not make their appearance until 1725, and our evidence that the latter was consumed is not provided by the product, but by the references to coffee pots and a coffee mill.

Beer, the main beverage of a large proportion of the population until tea-drinking could be afforded by all classes towards the latter years of the eighteenth century, is not often specifically mentioned. The first occasion is in 1664 (41) and then not until 1685 (133); in both cases, the deceased persons were victuallers. Thomas Crow, 1687 (140), John Lord, 1696 (180), and John Portway, 1749 (240), are the only persons other than licensed retailers, who had beer (or ale) in their houses, or rather, who had a sufficient quantity to warrant its inclusion among their goods. The two remaining occasions when beer is noted are in 1724 (218) and 1729 (233), but the frequent mention of barrels, beer or drink stalls, brewing vessels and malting apparatus shows that a considerable amount of beer-brewing was carried on in ordinary homes (see pp. 32-6).

Brandy was worth 3*s.* 8*d.* a gallon in 1692 (169), and Theophilus Lingard of Writtle had home-made liquors (?wines) worth £10 in 1744 (238); no other similar drinks are recorded.

Preparing, Cooking and Eating of Food

As shown in earlier paragraphs, the variety of food was limited, and there must have been a marked distinction between the summer diet when fresh meat and vegetables were available, and the winter when salt meat invariably provided the main dish. Whatever the season, all boiling and roasting had to be done over, or in front of, an open fire, and the baking of bread or pastry in a brick oven. The first reference to a 'grate for seacoale' is in 1672 (77), and the term does not recur until 1725 (221), and only four times after that date.

Culinary equipment included many articles which have either gone out of use with improved conditions, or else have developed into utensils now known by other names. The more common items were brass or pewter basons and bowls; cleavers and various knives; pestles and mortars of bell-metal, fine-grained stone, or wood for grinding; colanders and sieves; metal—and later wooden or earthenware—dishes, pots, and pans; kneading troughs, and various other types of troughs and tubs.

Owing to the difficulties of cooking, the Stuart housewife—like her counterpart in earlier centuries—had to use utensils of a shape best suited to her conditions. Over every kitchen fire, a large iron or bronze cooking-pot or pottage (i.e. soup) pot was suspended from a hook and chain attached to a bar in the chimney; these wrought-iron pot-hooks, known also as trammells or hangers, were often adjustable and elaborate in design.

The posnets and skillets[1] of bronze—the fore-runners of saucepans—were fitted with short legs enabling them to stand in the embers of an open fire; their handles were long and occasionally decorated with a motto or the name of the owner or maker.

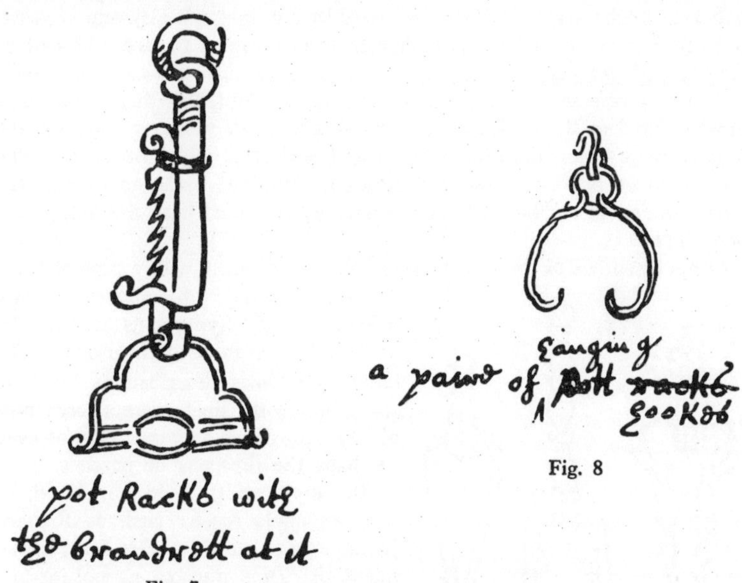

Fig. 7

Fig. 8

Roasting was accomplished by securing the joint to a slender iron bar (or to a series of bars forming a central cage but tapering to a single bar at the ends) known as a spit, which stood in front of the fire and was revolved either by hand or by a mechanical device. Spits were of various types according to the purposes for which they were required, and underneath the spit was a dripping pan to catch the meat juices with which the revolving joint or bird was continually basted to prevent its burning. Spits were supported by andirons (and-irons) which were large fire-dogs, although the latter term was usually applied to the small supports for the burning logs; we find them occasionally referred to as 'creepers' or 'dog-irons' (69, 93).[2] Cobirons, often employed instead of andirons, were long bars fitted with

[1] In some counties, particularly Suffolk, a thin perforated brass skimmer for removing cream is termed a skillet. Although the etymology of 'skilly' or skilligalee (a thin, and not very nourishing form of soup) is dubious, there seems to be some association with the pot called a skillet. See H. Bayley, *The Lost Language of London* (1935), p. 75.

[2] An amusing account of the various andirons in a gentleman's house was originally published in the *Gentleman's Magazine*, February 1789, and reprinted in the index to *The Unton Inventories relating to Wadley and Faringdon, co. Berks.* (1841).

hooks at frequent intervals; two cobirons leaned against the back of the fireplace at an angle of about forty-five degrees, and the ends of the spit were placed on which ever pair of hooks was most suitable. Sometimes each cobiron was fitted with another bar at the back to form a stand like a one-legged easel. When not in use, spits were placed in iron racks over the mantel-shelf.

Jacks, or spit-jacks, which made the spit revolve automatically, were an elaborate mechanical contrivance actuated by a weight and a system of gears, and are first noted in 1638 (19), having been invented towards the end of the sixteenth century.[1]

The only reference to a chimney-crane is in 1749 (240); this was an iron bracket fitted at the back of the fireplace and made to swing out over the hearth; some types had both vertical and horizontal adjustments to enable the pot to be put in any desired position. Iron fire-backs, to prevent the disintegration of the back of the fireplace by continual heat, are only noted once (61).

Other essentials to the hearth were bellows (of wood, with a pipe of brass or other metal),[2] fire-shovels, tongs, pokers, trivets, frying-pans and kettles of brass[3] or iron, and fire-irons. The latter, sometimes described as 'iron to stand before the fire', were a large type of trivet on which a simple form of oven (perhaps the fire-pans or pannets noted in the inventories) could be placed, or even an apple roaster such as Richard Josslin's (1668, no. 55). Fire-forks served much the same purpose as pokers and tongs. Gridirons were to be found in many homes; the seventeenth and eighteenth century varieties were either square or circular, and, like frying-pans, had long handles. Toasting-irons, used either for bread or bacon, occur four times. A fender is mentioned in 1681 (121); these additions to the hearth did not become necessary until fires were raised in either loose or fixed grates (see above).

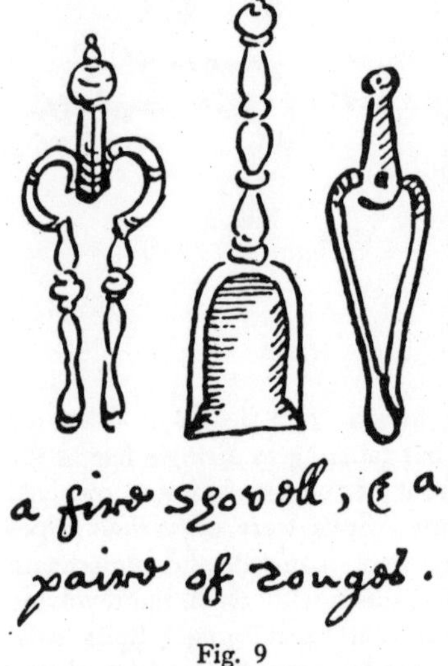

Fig. 9

Although not directly connected with cooking, mention may be made here of Theophilus Lingard's inventory, 1744 (238), where certain items relating

[1] A good account of kitchen and hearth appliances is in Seymour Lindsay's book, *Iron and Brass Implements of the English House* (1927).

[2] A pair of bellows, formerly belonging to the Mildmay family of Moulsham Hall, and now in Chelmsford Museum, is richly carved and inscribed 'Bellows like a qviat wife send ovt breath and make no strife 1673'; see illustrated description in *Essex Review*, vol. ix, p. 30.

[3] The word 'brass' is frequently used where 'bronze' is more likely to be intended.

to the hearth are not noted elsewhere. He had a pair of iron cheeks, and a fire-curtain and rod in his hall; the cheeks were the side-pieces of his coal-rack (or loose grate), and the fire-curtain may have been either the hangings from the mantel-shelf forming a fire-screen, or else a fire-guard. In this same room were three 'scquers' which is the oddest method of spelling 'skewers' that I have met. Lingard also provides us with the single example of a hearth brush and 'holders', but beyond the fact that it is a hearth appliance, the meaning of the latter term is obscure.

Fig. 10

Wood, as faggots or logs, was the fuel in general use, and coal is only noted on nine occasions, commencing in 1672; the bushel and chaldron were measures of coal, and in 1684 (129) a chalder[1] was valued at fifteen shillings, but in London in 1725 (221) a similar quantity was priced at double that figure. Sea-coal, so called because produced from mines near the coast, and transported by sea, occurs once (77); most of the inland coal-mines were opened at the time of the Industrial Revolution.

There are fewer references to baked food. Bread was invariably home-made in the larger houses, and the kneading trough and moulding board were, therefore, almost indispensable articles of kitchen equipment. The brick ovens were heated by faggots being burnt in them, the ashes afterwards raked out by a 'slice'—a long-handled iron implement like a spade—and the bread put in to be baked by the heat retained in the brickwork.[2] Another essential item was the peel (sometimes spelt as peeler or pelle), a long-handled iron or wooden implement with a broad, flat blade at one end used by bakers to insert or withdraw bread from the ovens. There is no definite evidence that brick ovens were used for anything except bread or pastry.

Moulding boards (i.e. benches where the loaves were shaped) are mentioned six times, flour is not listed at all, and meal (other than oatmeal) three times. There are two flour boxes (188, 237), and only four 'boulting' troughs, tubs or tuns where flour was 'bolted' or sifted to separate it from the bran.

There are many references to the salting or powdering troughs or tubs where pork and other meats were pickled for winter supplies. Salt and salt-boxes, although they must have been in everyday use are not often recorded; there is only one reference to spice (see p. 23), and only two to pepper[3] (169, 221), even though pepper boxes occur five times in other lists.

[1] A chaldron was 36 bushels or 25½ cwts. Note the Scotch form of chaldron used on this occasion.

[2] Seymour Lindsay, *Iron and Brass Implements of the English House* (1927), p. 61.

[3] Pepper had been used in England from at least 1180 when there was a gild of pepperers. The Worshipful Company of Grocers was evolved from the fourteenth century fraternity of pepperers.

Salt cellars (often described merely as 'salts'), while not common, are certainly less rare than pepper boxes, and were made of brass, pewter, or silver. Mustard querns are noted occasionally, and, as a farm crop, mustard was grown in several parts of Essex;[1] the seed was ground in the home for domestic requirements. 'The seede of Mustard ground with vinegar, is an excellent sauce good to be eaten, with any grosse meates, either fish or flesh, because it doth helpe digestion, warmeth the stomacke, and prouoketh appetite.'[2]

Dredgers, nutmeg graters, sieves, rolling-pins, funnels, ladles and skimmers, choppers, jars, jugs, filters, stills and other miscellaneous kitchen necessities are noted with varying frequency; these, together with the pots and pans of brass or other metals, and the dishes, pans and plates of pewter or earthenware,[3] were arranged on shelves round the walls and on the dresser-board.

Fig. 11 Fig. 12

Abraham Brecknock's inventory, 1694 (174), lists three pots of snett and grease; the former was deer fat, and our sole reference to this commodity.

In the humbler homes of Stuart England, the kitchen also served as the dining room. Food was eaten from wooden platters or trenchers[4] which eventually gave place to pewter and earthenware. Each person had an all-purpose knife, and as table-forks are only listed on three occasions (the first is in 1725, 222) we can only assume that food was transferred from the plate by means of pewter or wooden spoons aided by the fingers. From the frequent mention of table- or board-cloths, it would appear that meals were rarely served on an uncovered table; napkins were also used to a large

[1] [A. Young], *General view of the agriculture of the county of Essex* (1807), vol. ii, pp. 63-66. Mustard is not recorded as a crop in any of the inventories examined, but Young gives details of a crop at the neighbouring parish of Widford in 1800-1.

[2] *Thomas Tusser, his good points of husbandry,* collated and edited by Dorothy Hartley (1931), p. 151.

[3] Theophilus Lingard, 1744 (238), had 'fifty five pieces of Delph and earthen ware' in his pantry: this is the only reference to a specific variety of pottery.

[4] This word, as used in the inventories, signifies a wooden plate, but a trencher was originally a flat loaf made of coarse flour on which a person's meat was placed. Thus the loaf, serving as a plate, formed part of the meal. Platters were thin and round, while trenchers were square and had a hole in the rim for salt. Sometimes trenchers were hollowed on both sides, so that meat could be eaten off one side and a second course off the other.

AN ESSEX CART FITTED WITH LADDERS, AND A TILTED, OR COVERED, WAGGON.

PLATE VI (*overleaf*) INVENTORY OF ABRAHAM CHALKE OF WRITTLE, 1638 (no. 9).

An Inventorye of all and Singuler the goods that were Abraham Oakes late of Writtell in the County of Essex Husbandman, At the day of his deathe, Praysed the 10 day of November 1638 by Edward Bowyn of Roxfild & William Aylet of Writtle as ffolloweth Vizt.

Inprimis in the hale one table two formes wth a beilte borde and a cobberd and a payer of Cramells wth two cobyerns and two Spitts and other implemets — xx s

Ite in the Parlore one Boune bedstedell wth A fether bed and bolster, one cobberd and one Table and fower chests and a little table wth other implemets — v li

Ite in the chamber over the Parlor two bedstedles wth a bed and two chests wth other implemets — xl s

Ite in the Milkhouse one chees lacket two pootes one brasspoot another Iron poot and two kettels and two Tubbs and x peuter Disshes & other implemts — xl s

Ite in the buttery three barrels one kneding trofe two ~~tow~~ tubs and other implemets — x s

Ite two Carts wth one payer of wheles one Donncate and a payer of Harrowes one plow wth the yornes and other implemts — xxx s

Ite two Cowes and a wenall — vij li

Ite two Mares and the harnise in the Stable — vj li

Ite Nyne Sheepe and two lames — iiij li

Ite five gess —

Ite one Sowhogg — vij s

Ite six payer of sheetes and a Dusson of Napkines — iij li x s

Ite three Acres of wheate — viij li

Ite fower Acres of Bullimonger — v li

Ite three Acres of Otes corne — v li

Ite haye — xx s

Ite Sixtene ffowles — x s

Ite his wearing aparell And the mony in his purs — xxx s

Sume is 53 — 17 —

His
Edward E Bowyn
Marke

His
William W Aylet
Marke

extent—certainly by people other than the poorest—to wipe greasy fingers during the meal. Drink was served in flagons from which the pewter or horn mugs were replenished. There is a reference to three cruets in Lingard's inventory; it will be seen that he had many items not to be found in the homes of his neighbours.

This very incomplete picture of the kitchens of the period will serve to indicate their importance; housewives of that time held positions of great responsibility and they had to have a sound knowledge not only of all branches of the culinary and dairy arts, but also of brewing, medicine and weaving (see pp. 31, 33).

Fruit and Vegetables

THE average countryman has always been proud of his garden, but there are few references to garden produce, or to gardening tools; the latter were either included in implements of husbandry, or else covered by that all-embracing term, 'lumber'.

Although three people—Richard Bridgman, 1677 (98), George Bradford, 1671 (166), and John Bridgman, 1720 (211)—are definitely described as gardeners, we have to turn again to the goods of a substantial man like Lingard for references to bell-glasses, cucumber frames, young trees (including crab-stocks for budding or grafting), greens, turnips, parsnips and beans. Cucumber glasses are also noted among Bridgman's goods; the culture of this vegetable—one of the oldest—was popular in the seventeenth and eighteenth centuries.[1] Onions are noted in 1638 (19), and 'sallet' (i.e. salad) dishes in 1665 (46). A tin watering-pot and a rake, garden shears, spades, forks and hoes, are among gardening tools mentioned by name.

Apples occur five times from 1665 (49); plums and walnuts in 1729 (232). Unspecified fruit valued at £1 is in Robert Jackson's inventory, 1638 (8), and that of Charles Clark, 1659 (26), has the single reference to a fruit dish.

Raisins and plums are among grocers' stocks in 1692 (169) and 1725 (221) respectively; it was due to the enterprise of the East India Company that foreign produce such as dried fruits, sugar and spices were put within the reach of all but the very poor.[2]

Drinking Vessels and Bottles

DRINKING vessels of pewter or horn would have been common in most of the houses in Writtle and Roxwell, but there is no specific reference to horn drinking cups which were probably included under the general heading of vessels. Even pewter cups or tankards are not often listed separately as they would have been merged in the entry for so many pounds weight of that metal.

There are many references to glass cases or to glass shelves, which we may assume were not display cabinets, but wooden shelves or cupboards

[1] See F. W. Steer, 'The Account Book of an eighteenth-century Maldon tradesman', in *Essex Review,* vol. lvii, p. 48.

[2] John Hampson, *The English at Table* (1944), p. 28.

used to accommodate glasses; on the few occasions when the latter were listed, the numbers were invariably small, because glassware was an expensive item. It is not until 1744 (238) that we get the single instance of wine glasses and tumblers, a decanter and a punch ladle.

Pewter beakers are listed twice (75, 166), beer glasses once (163), and mugs six times between 1690 and 1749; in two cases (218, 233)—obviously those of ale-house keepers—mugs are described as double and single, or pints and half-pints, and would have been made of earthenware.

'One great Jack to drink in' was in the buttery of Thomas Osborn, a Writtle yeoman, 1672 (77); this was a large leather container, commonly known as a black jack, used until the end of the eighteenth century for small beer. Closely akin to jacks were leather bottles; from their frequency it would seem that they were more popular in this part of the country than the wooden variety, which are only listed twice and then not until late in the series (1690, 160; 1725, 222). Either type, usually known as harvest bottles because of the demand on them at that season, were filled, one for each man, with beer or cider, and laid out on kitchen tables of farmhouses for the men to collect on their way to work in the fields. Tusser commences his 'Points' for July husbandry with these words:—

Fig. 13

> 'Go muster thy servants, be captain thyself,
> providing them weapon, and other like pelf:
> Get bottles and wallets, keep field in the heat,
> the fear is as much, as the danger is great.'[1]

It is of interest to note that Hoare's Bank, Fleet Street, London, founded in the seventeenth century, still retains the Golden Leather Bottle as its sign. At Pleshey, Little Laver, Blackmore and Lexden there were inns or beershops having the sign of a leather bottle, and at the last-named place, it has given the name of 'Bottle End' to that part of the parish in which it stands.[2]

Unspecified bottles, either of leather, wood, pewter or stone, are listed from 1637 (3), but glass bottles, usually dark green in colour, with long necks and short, squat bodies, first occur in 1677 (96); they would have been used for wine, and it is not until 1725 (222) that quart and pint bottles are noted. A pewter bottle is recorded in 1637 (2).

To revert to drinking vessels: there are a number of silver cups and tankards which would be handed down from one generation to another and used only on special occasions; these items are either priced separately or included under the heading of plate. The word 'tankard' originally signified a wooden vessel holding two gallons or more, and is probably derived from the Latin *cantharus* which led to the Old French *tanquard*; its capacity has been, for at least two centuries in England, either a quart, pint or half pint.

[1] *Thomas Tusser, his good points of husbandry,* collated and edited by Dorothy Hartley (1931), p. 79.

[2] Miller Christy, *The Trade Signs of Essex* (1887), pp. 168-9.

William Bird, of 'Horsely Park,' Writtle, 1691 (165), had 'a lignum vite cup tip't with silver'; this cup, of very hard South American wood (*lignum vitæ*), must have been a treasured possession.

Tea cups do not make their appearance until 1729 (232) when Margaret Haward's inventory was made. She had two punch bowls, six 'slap' [i.e. slop] basins, a sugar pot, glasses, tea pots and cups worth together five shillings and sixpence which seems a low figure. Cups occur on three other occasions, but whether for tea or otherwise is not recorded. The saucers referred to in the inventories were not used as they are today; their function was to hold sauces and condiments.

HOUSEHOLD AND VILLAGE INDUSTRIES

Spinning and Weaving

THE seventeenth-century housewife, like her predecessors, was seldom idle. She had learned to spin in her girlhood, and one of her regular duties after marriage was to maintain the supplies of cloth and linen in the home. We find, therefore, many references to spinning wheels, or, as they are sometimes called, flax, linen, or woollen wheels, but as the Essex weaving industry was still an important one when the inventories were made, it is not surprising that home-weaving was less common in this county than others.

Thomas Raynebeard of Roxwell, 1638 (16), the only person described as a weaver, had three old looms with all the implements (unspecified) belonging to them in his shop; they were valued at £5 10*s*. We can imagine the women of the district taking the yarn which they had spun to be made up into cloth[1] by the local weaver.

Reels for winding yarn are sometimes noted, but not necessarily as accessories to spinning wheels. As so much depended on the diligence of the appraisers, we cannot determine whether the reels were spools or spindles, or were regarded as alternatives to the complete spinning machine. There are three references (26, 83, 84) to trap-reels which seem to be synonymous with wrap- or knacking-wheels used in conjunction with spinning wheels for measuring yarn into hanks or skeins. The wheel clicked after it had taken 120 revolutions; a hank is one hundred times round the wheel, but in the Highlands 120 times ensures good measure.[2]

Among the goods of Henry Turnidge, 1719 (207), was a carding stock and cards for combing out wool or flax; he also had a nobbing iron which was probably an instrument for rippling flax or hemp, i.e. removing the seed capsules.[3]

[1] For the varieties of cloth used for domestic purposes, see nos. 127, 169.

[2] This description is taken from a letter which appeared, with an illustration, in *Country Life*, 20 February 1948, p. 388.

[3] An illustration of this operation is in *Essex Review*, vol. viii, p. 253. Cf. *nob*, a flower-head, esp. of clover, and the Flemish *nobbeling*, the coarsest flax of which sacking is made.

Spinning wheels were not invented until the sixteenth century and they superseded the spindles (only once mentioned, 146), on which the yarn was wound by hand after the carded wool was pulled out from the distaff and twisted with finger and thumb. The introduction of the spinning wheel enabled the yarn to be wound on to the reel as it was turned by the wheel, and left the fingers free to feed out and twist the wool from the distaff attached to the machine.[1] The manufacture of spindles and wheels for spinning was formerly carried on at Great Bardfield.[2]

Yarn is listed on three occasions (16, 22, 79), but there are several references to wool in its raw state; Thomas Poultar, 1665 (49), had sixty pounds of wool worth thirty shillings.

Malting and Brewing

THERE is ample evidence to prove that the making of malt and the brewing of beer was carried on in many country homes. Barley was grown in considerable quantities, and part of the crop, at least on the larger farms, was reserved for malting. Before quoting any of the articles used in malt manufacture, it may be as well to briefly describe the process.

The barley was put into a large leaden cistern and steeped in water for about sixty hours to make it swell. After the water had been drawn off, the grain was 'couched' or placed in heaps for a day or two before being spread in wide rows about twelve inches thick on a floor where the temperature was moderate. The barley began to grow, but to ensure that the growth was uniform, the heaps were regularly raked over for a period of two to three weeks. The careful regulation of the growth of the shoots was, and still is, one of the secrets of a good maltster, and when the grain had germinated sufficiently, it was put on a kiln to dry. This part of the process occupied from one to four days according to the type of malt required; 'pale' malt was given slower treatment and less heat than that needed for mild beer.

Malt kilns were so constructed that the heat was well below a frame covered with a hair-cloth on which the sprouted grain was spread some three inches thick. Straw was considered the best fuel for malt kilns, but fern or wood were also used before the introduction of smokeless Welsh coal. The 'firing' burnt off the shoots and the composition of the grain was changed from a smooth, mellow corn to a white, chalky substance about one fifth less in weight; the husk of the grain did not undergo any noticeable change throughout the process.

The finished product was removed from the kiln and spread out to cool before being stored in bins for future use.[3] Good malt will float in water, but if the manufacture has been faulty in any one of its stages and the kernels retain any of their barley properties, beer made from such malt will be unsatisfactory.

[1] M. and C. H. B. Quennell, *A History of Everyday Things in England, 1066-1799* (1918), Part 1, pp. 163-4, Part 2, pp. 156-9. See also p. 46.

[2] *Victoria County History,* Essex, vol. 2 (1907), p. 401.

[3] Although these notes are written in the past tense, the essential features of malting are the same today; the introduction of modern plant ensures that the risk of spoiling a batch of malt is reduced to a minimum.

45 An Inventary of all the goods & Chattells of Thomas peach late of Roxwell in the County of Essex yeoman deceased taken valued & apprized by Josiah pepper and Alaxsandar Chalke this 25th day of September 1679

Imprimis. In the hall on table 5 stooles 6 Chaires firshovell tongs spits & other small things	02	00	00
In the parlor			
Two press Cubbards on table	01	10	00
In the Chamber over the parlor			
on doune bed with furniture belonging to it: 2 Cheastes on trunke 20 payer of sheetes 3 dozen of napkins 5 table cloaths & other small things	21	00	00
In the Chamber over the hall			
on fether bed with furniture belonging to it 4 Cheaste & other small things	06	15	00
In the Chamber over the entri			
on fether bed with furniture on table on silver boule 12 silver spoones	4	13	00
In the Chamber over the butteri			
on bed with furniture belonging to it	02	10	00
In the buttery			
six barrells bras & pouter & other things	07	18	00
In the kichin & Dary			
on leade bruing vessells & Darry vessells & shelves & other small things	07	18	06
The Corne & hay in the barns & hayhouse	30	06	08
fower horse & 2 coults			
Three Cous 2 heffers	08	00	00
Twelve shepe	09	00	00
fower hoggs	03	00	00
on waggon on long carte & tumbrill	03	04	00
plow & harrows	09	00	00
his waring apparill & monny in his purs	29	00	00
Sum totall	146	15	02

Josiah Pepper

Alaxsandar + Chalke his mark

Apud Writtle in Consistorio Episcopi 20mo die Mensis octobris Anno Domini 1679 Exhibitum fuit huiusmodi Inventarium per Hannam relictam et Administratricem pro vero et pleno protestando de addendo et quod si etc.

Jurat.

Inventory of Thomas Peach of Roxwell, 1679 (no. 109).

Plate VIII

This farmhouse kitchen, reconstructed for the Royal Show at Hereford in 1939, shows many items typical of those mentioned in the inventories. Nearly all these objects, like those on *Plate* III came from Essex houses.

Malt kilns are noted on the inventories of three yeomen (two in 1678, nos. 101, 102, and the other in 1687, no. 147), but we have hair-cloths (variously referred to as 'haire', 'hayre' or 'hayer' [cloths]) in ten other instances. The hair-cloth was of finely-woven horse-hair which permitted the heat to penetrate, but prevented the grain from falling on to the fire below. An interesting reference to the manufacture of hair-cloths occurs in the city records of York for 1487; a petition was presented to the mayor and corporation asking, among other things, that 'every roper and haster commyng to this Citie, and woll set up as a master within the same Citie in making ropes, kilne hares, teilds or eny othre thing, pertenyng or belonging to the said craft of ropers and haysters,[1] shal pay at his first setting up $xiij^{s}$ $iiij^{d}$.'[2]

By the beginning of the eighteenth century, the hair-cloth was being superseded by a very fine wire mesh, and one is listed in the inventory of Richard Browne, 1713 (198). As late as 1750 the hair-cloth was considered superior to the brass- and iron-wired frames, or to the tiled frames pierced with tiny holes.[3]

Malt shovels are specially noted three times, they were entirely of wood, but no doubt many more were included under the collective term, 'shovels'. Among other apparatus in malt-houses were various tubs and cisterns, large wooden rakes, scales and weights.

Before malt could be used for brewing, it had to be ground, and there are no less than twenty-seven definite references to malt querns or mills. There are also thirty-four references to stocks of malt; these facts indicate that there were many more people who bought malt than made it.

Malt was measured in quarters (336 lbs.) or seams (eight bushels); a quarter of malt was valued at eighteen shillings in 1665, and a seam at twenty-four shillings in 1681.[4]

Private brewing was done chiefly by the women of the house or, in larger establishments, by a maltster or brewer specially employed for the work. The method,[5] in smaller houses at least, was roughly as follows: into the great copper holding about thirty-six gallons of water was placed a peck of ground malt, and when the water boiled it was transferred to a mash vat and another four bushels of malt added. The mixture was stirred or 'mashed' until it was about the consistency of pudding, and then a further half-bushel or so of malt was added; the tub or vat was covered with sacks or cloths to keep in the steam or 'spirit' of the malt.

After two or three hours, bowls of hot water were allowed to percolate through the mass, and the impregnated liquid drawn off and put in a copper.

[1] Haysters; hairster; a worker in horsehair. *York Memorandum Book*, vol. ii, p. 171.

[2] *York Civic Records*, edited by Angelo Raine (1941), vol. ii, p. 16.

[3] *The London and Country Brewer*, by 'a Person formerly concerned in a Publick Brewhouse in London' (1750), p. 7.

[4] Other similar values can often be calculated from the inventories; these two are quoted as being typical.

[5] Only the broad principles are given here; methods varied considerably, and the reader interested in home and other brewing will find full particulars in *The London and Country Brewer* noted above.

Slow percolation of the water made a good ale, and a rapid process resulted in 'small' or weak beer. A canvas bag containing hops was added to the liquid (or 'wort') in the copper before boiling, and the quality of the beer was governed by the quantity of hops used. After the first brewing from the 'mash', a second often took place, and five bushels of malt were reckoned to be sufficient for a hogshead (fifty-four gallons) of ale, and the same quantity of small beer. When the boiling of the wort and hops was completed, the liquor was transferred to a 'working-tub' or vat, and yeast added to promote fermentation. This part of the process occupied two or four days according to the season, and then the yeast was removed from the top of the liquid which was then ready to be put into barrels.

In a large farmhouse it was necessary to brew considerable quantities of beer, and there are many references to the brewhouse as a separate apartment (see Plate II). The appraisers of Francis Allin's goods, 1718 (205), went so far as to describe the contents of his brewhouse as 'the office & utensills, 7*li.* 5*s.* 0*d.*'.

We find a large number of terms to denote the varied equipment used in this important domestic industry. For example, coppers (first noted in 1659, no. 25) are sometimes listed as being of brass, and it is not until 1687 that the word 'boiler' occurs. Brewing leads, pans, pails, bowls, and unspecified vessels are very frequent, but among vats, mention may be made of the 'guile vat' in no. 165; Halliwell[1] defines a guile of liquor as a quantity that is brewed at one operation. Tubs of all sorts are recorded, but the mash tub (often called the measin, mashing, or meatching tub) is not mentioned until 1672 (74). Wort tubs occur three times, and couls, coulles, cowls, cowlers, or coolers—noted frequently in one or other of these forms—describe any sort of large wooden tub found in brewhouses and kitchens. There are a few references to taps or cocks, and to tap-hoses, used to draw off the wort from the mash tub into another low, broad tub (known as an underback) before its transfer to the copper; underbacks are listed three times, and jets (large ladles with which to empty cisterns) twice (30, 218).

Among the more rare entries are tilders; these occur twice (180, 216) and were wedge-shaped machines interposed between a cask and the wall behind it, to tilt it up.[2]

A cover is listed with the goods in Thomas Crow's brewhouse (140), and a similar article of brass belonged to George Bradford (166); it is not unlikely that these articles were curfews (*couvrefeus*) used as a precaution against a conflagration when the work of brewing was abandoned for the day leaving the boiler fire still burning. The two pane-hangers in Richard Wolfe's brewhouse, 1678 (101) were probably pot-hooks (i.e., pan-hangers).

Beer was stored in butts (one hundred and eight gallons), hogsheads (fifty-four gallons), half-hogsheads, barrels (thirty-six gallons), casks, kilderkins (eighteen gallons), and runlits. Large quantities of beer were drunk in England before tea was within the reach of all except the very poor. There

[1] J. O. Halliwell, *A dictionary of archaic and provincial words* (1889).

[2] *Ibid.*

was no other liquid refreshment for the working classes, and it was also realized that water was not always wholesome; by boiling it in the process of brewing, a potential danger to health was partially, if not completely, overcome, and a nourishing beverage provided. William Harrison, in his valuable *Description of England,* gives the estimated cost of brewing two hundred gallons of beer as twenty shillings, and says that his wife and her servants brewed once a month.[1]

Four inventories record that hops were grown in Writtle and Roxwell. Thomas Crush of Dukes, 1686 (136),[2] was by far the most important grower; he had a crop valued at £150, and twelve thousand hop-poles worth £60. Richard Wolfe, also of Roxwell, 1678 (101), had poles valued at £45, and a stock of old and new hops at £77. A hop-ground of three acres was cultivated at Roxwell as late as 1883; the last hops grown in Essex were at Castle Hedingham in 1887.[3] Charles Vancouver, the agriculturist, writing in 1795 on hop-growing in the neighbourhood of Writtle and Chelmsford,[4] says that one acre of hops cost, on a seven-year average, £29 5*s.* 8*d.* to grow, and were saleable for £42 5*s.* 0*d.*, showing a profit of £12 19*s.* 4*d.* This confirms the view expressed in the *History of Essex,* by a Gentleman[5] [Peter Muilman], who, in his description of Moulsham, gives us this picture: 'Here are several plantations of hops by the roadside, which in summer-time have a pleasing appearance, and frequently turn out to the considerable advantage of the planters'. The same author mentions[6] the hop-grounds at Roxwell, and the over-shot corn-mill west of the church (see p. 40).

Hops were measured by the 'pocket' (1¼cwt.) or 'bag' (2½cwt.). Accessories used in hop-growing are not often noted, but 'pitches' or 'hop-pitches' occur in a few documents, and were iron crow-bars with a thick square point for making holes for hop-poles. Hop-sieves, listed six times, were for straining the hops from beer if the former had not been enclosed in a bag as mentioned on p. 34. Hops were dried by spreading them on a horsehair mat fixed above a charcoal brazier.

Tusser in his *Five Hundred Good Points of Husbandry,*[7] has a poem about hops, and a long digression on the hop-yard. The falsity of the couplet—[8]

> 'Turkeys, Heresy, Hops and Beer
> Came into England all in one year.'

[1] See Mildred Campbell, *The English Yeoman under Elizabeth and the early Stuarts* (1942), p. 251.

[2] This inventory is also printed, with notes, in *Essex Review,* vol. xv, pp. 169-175.

[3] *Victoria County History,* Essex (1907), vol. 2, p. 369. See also *A New and Complete History of Essex,* by a Gentleman (1772), vol. i, p. 299.

[4] Charles Vancouver, *General View of the Agriculture in the County of Essex; with Observations on the means of its improvement* (1795), p. 60.

[5] Vol. i (1769), p. 92.

[6] *Ibid.*, p. 299.

[7] Collated and edited by Dorothy Hartley (1931), pp. 89, 90.

[8] There are several versions dating from 1599; this one is probably the latest and was included by Rudyard Kipling in *Puck of Pook's Hill* (1906).

is established, because hops were in Norfolk in 1482.

Although cider-making was never carried on to any large extent in Essex, cider presses are noted in eight inventories from 1675. As troughs are sometimes mentioned as accessories, we may assume that the presses were of the screw type, and not cider-mills with great round stone troughs in which a millstone, mounted on an axle, revolved edgewise and crushed the apples as it was drawn round by a horse.

Dairying

THE dairy, or milk-house, was usually a stone- or brick-paved room with a slatted window on the coolest side (usually north-west) of the house; in it was to be found the churn, milk-pails, the keelers or coolers, and the cheese-making utensils (see p. 39). The shelves, stands and benches on which stood the milk bowls, trays or pans, the butter scales, butter pots, and other apparatus, lined the walls (see Plate III). A cool temperature was essential, and an eighteenth-century writer[1] recommends churning to be done in the morning before the sun appears, 'taking care to fix the churn where there is a free draft of Air'. A correspondent of this same writer remarks that 'he never knew any person whose hand was warm by nature make good Butter'.[2]

Most milk vessels were originally of wood and bound with iron hoops, but lead pans were also used for 'throwing-up' or 'rising' the cream from the milk; earthenware, first mentioned in 1673 (74), gradually came to be used in dairies and was certainly more hygienic. The obsolete word 'kimnel' occurs frequently among dairy goods and denoted almost any kind of tub. Ladles and skimmers were usually made of wood, but sometimes of metal.

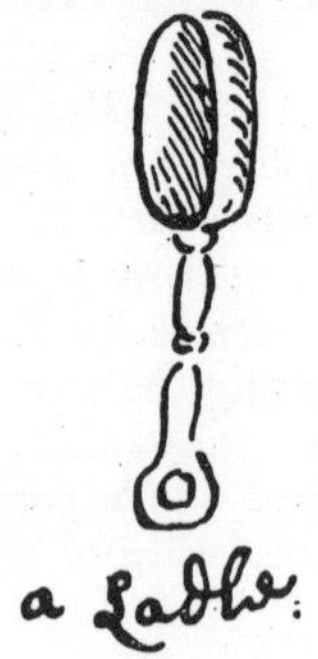

A churn, in the early days, was a conical shaped vessel fitted with a perforated plunger which was worked with an up-and-down motion.[3] Later, the revolving churn fitted on a frame by means of pivots came into use; it was barrel-shaped (see 216, 1723) and was less tiring to operate than the plunger and staff.

a Ladle:

Fig. 14

There are comparatively few entries for butter as it was undoubtedly considered by the appraisers to be a perishable commodity and, unless in quantity, not worth recording. Most of the butter made in farm-houses found its way to the local markets and fairs, and we have references to butter baskets which would have been used on those occasions. In the *Universal Magazine* for January, 1787, a contributor visiting the Epping

[1] J. Twamley, *Dairying Exemplified, or the Business of Cheese-making* (1787), p. 123.

[2] *Ibid.*, p. 124.

[3] A drink made of rancid butter, salt, and boiling tea is made in Tibet by mixing these ingredients, by means of a plunger, in a cylindrical wooden churn similar to the old butter churns; an excellent illustration of a Tibetan using such a churn appeared in *The Listener* of 12 February 1948.

district noted that butter was made up for market in long rolls each weighing one pound.

Butter firkins occur in 1673 (79) and 1744 (238) from which we may infer that it was the practice of some farmers to send considerable quantities of butter a long distance; a firkin of butter weighs half a hundredweight.

Cream pots are occasionally noted, but their use, whether for keeping the cream preparatory to butter-making or for dispatch to market, is not apparent.

Fig. 15

Cheese

ESSEX cheeses, after having been famous for many centuries, no longer have a place with those of Stilton, Cheddar, Wensleydale and other localities, but if the county ever failed to head the list for quality, it must surely have done so for weight of cheese. In the accounts of the officers of St. Osyth's priory for the year 1512,[1] we have 20 'Weighz' of cheese at ten shillings the 'weigh' of 336 pounds; eight barrels of butter at ten shillings the barrel, four and a half gallons of cream at three pence a gallon, and two gallons of poor milk at one penny a gallon.

John Skelton, a former rector of Diss, Norfolk, and a poet-laureate of Henry the eighth's reign, who 'is said to have fallen into some irregularities, too natural to poets, and by no means suitable to the clerical character',[2] provides us with an interesting note on Essex cheese. In his ballad of Elynour Rummin, the famous ale-wife of Leatherhead, we have a picture of one Margery, an habituée of the inn; he describes her as:—

'Crooked-neck'd like an owle,
And yet she brought her fees,
A cantle of Essex cheese,
Was well a foot thicke,
Full of magots quicke;
It was huge and great,
And mighty strong meat,
For the Deuill to eat,
It was tart and punicate'.[3]

Another sixteenth-century writer, John Norden, whose *Speculi Britanniæ Pars: an historical and chorographical description of the county of Essex*

[1] See *Essex Review*, vol. xxx, pp. 1-13, 121-127, 205-221, for a full translation of these accounts; the originals are among the records of the Duchy of Cornwall.

[2] J. Granger, *A Biographical History of England* (1824), vol. i, p. 131.

[3] *The Harleian Miscellany*, edited by Henry Savage (1924), p. 81.

(1594)[1] contains such a delightful description of the country, speaks in glowing terms of Essex cheese when he writes: [2]

> 'The hundreds of Rocheforde, Denge, Dansye, or Dansing, which lye on the sowth-easte parte of the shire, yelde milke, butter, and cheese in admirable aboundance: and in those partes are the great and huge cheeses made, wondred at for their masiuenes and thicknes. They are made also in Tendring hundred, wher are manie wickes or dayries'.

Norden was, however, like Camden in his *Britannia,* referring to the marshlands of Essex where great quantities of 'those huge thicks Cheeses are made that are vented and sould not onely into all parts of England, but into forraigne nations also, for the rusticall people, labourers, and handicraftes men to fill their bellies, and feed upon.' [3]

Except for the marshlands, there is no evidence that cheeses were made elsewhere in Essex from anything but cows' milk; the industry has died out, and the last cheeses (other than 'cream' cheeses) were made at Steeple Bumpstead about 1900.

We have throughout the inventories, not only numerous references to stocks of cheese, but to the various utensils employed in its manufacture. Good cheese not only demanded the skill and knowledge of the housewife or her dairy-maid, but also the experience of the farmer; an over-rich pasture could be as harmful as an inferior one, because the flavour and quality of the cheese would be affected by the food of the cows. Thomas Tusser, whose *Good Points of Husbandry* may be regarded as specially applicable to Essex, makes these remarks about the wife who entrusts her cheese-making to a maid:

> 'Ill huswife unskilful, to make her own cheese
> through trusting of others, hath this for her fees:
> Her milkpan and cream pot so slabber'd and sost:
> that butter is wanting and cheese is half lost'.[4]

Briefly, the process of cheese-making was to slightly warm the milk and curdle it by adding rennet,[5] and when the curd had firmly settled at the bottom of the tub, the whey was drawn off. Within a short time, the curd was broken into small pieces, thoroughly squeezed to make it close and firm, and then transferred to the cheese mould with its muslin lining. The moulds were sometimes put into a press to express any superfluous moisture and to consolidate the curd; otherwise, the moisture gradually drained away or evaporated. The old presses, weighted with stones, were superseded by wooden screw presses.

Great care was taken with the final stage of 'ripening' cheese. We read in *Dairying Exemplified, or the business of cheese-making,* by J. Twamley (1787), that 'when Cheese goes from the Press, let it be kept in as warm a

[1] Published, with a map, by the Camden Society, 1840.

[2] Page 8.

[3] William Camden, *Britain, or a chorographicall description of the most flourishing Kingdomes, England, Scotland, and Ireland* (1637), p. 443.

[4] *Thomas Tusser, his good points of husbandry,* collated and edited by Dorothy Hartley (1931), p. 64.

[5] Originally a preparation extracted from the fourth stomach of a suckling calf; vegetable matters are also used.

state as you can, till it has had a sweat, or is got pretty regularly dry, and stiffish: It is warmth that makes Cheese ripe, improves the colour, and causes Cheese to cut flakey, the surest sign of excellent quality.' As it was considered detrimental to hardened cheese to keep it in the same room as the new, moist cheese, we often find a cheese loft or storage room in addition to the dairy or buttery. A cheese room or dairy was exempt from window-tax imposed by statute, 7 Wm. III, c. 18, if a notice was affixed in a conspicuous position stating that the room was used for that purpose; such a notice is preserved in the Holly Trees Museum at Colchester.

Cheese-making utensils occur many times in the inventories, and there are often two or three alternative names for one article; perhaps the greatest number of variants is for the moulds which are termed motes, moots, moles, mooles, moults, or cessmouts. The uses of planks, shelves, racks, bearers, stands, tables, boards, and so forth are fairly obvious, but such items as a cheese-coller (probably a cooler, or perhaps a mould), lathes or laves, lar, and breads, are likely to be local terms for articles generally called by other names.

In most museums may be seen specimens of cheese-making apparatus, and some are shown in Plate III.

A 'lead', or fifty-six pounds of cheese, is a measure used occasionally, and in the inventory of John Sapsford, 1660 (28), was valued at ten shillings. Among Richard Wolfe's goods, 1678 (101), six score of cheeses at two shillings each were in the cheese chamber; these would have been a small variety about nine inches high, six or seven inches in diameter, and weighing about eleven pounds.

Daniel Bridges, a grocer of Drury Lane, 1725 (221), had 'a chease taster and a nife' valued at ninepence; we can imagine him sampling the cheeses brought to his shop from Essex, and the carrier taking back to the farm some item of luxury not to be found on the shelves of the country grocer.

Milling[1]

FROM the time when man ceased to depend on herbs and uncooked food for his sustenance, he has ground corn; of all industries, that of flour-milling must surely be the oldest. The Fayum people who inhabited the shores of the former lake of that name in Egypt had saddle-querns as early as 6000-5000 B.C., and from this primitive method of crushing grain by rubbing it with a stone roller on a flat stone with a hollowed bed, developed the various types of revolving mill. The earliest of these, driven by animals or slaves, appeared in the Mediterranean area about 500 B.C., but as a large mill was not a practical proposition for all families, a smaller type, rotated by hand, was evolved. Among the goods of Samuel Sumers, a victualler of Roxwell, 1685 (133), a 'horcmill' [horse-mill] is listed; this is the only direct reference in the inventories to a mill rotated by an animal.

It is beyond the scope of this book to trace the evolution of hand-mills,

[1] See Wilson Marriage and C. Fell Smith on 'The history of corn milling in Essex', in *Essex Review*, vol. xvi, pp. 184-195, and F. W. Steer on 'Two Essex Mills' in *Notes & Queries*, vol. 193, pp. 425-7.

but archæologists assert that rotary querns were introduced into England about 100 B.C.[1] The stone used for querns varied according to localities, but micaceous schist, Old Red Sandstone, or a pebbly conglomerate known as ' pudding-stone ', are the most common. Although their form varied with the passing of centuries, the principle was constant, until finally, large stationary mills driven by water or wind were developed and became a common and pleasing feature of the countryside. But this progression did

Fig. 16. ROXWELL MILL BEFORE ITS CONVERSION INTO A HOUSE.

not mean that hand-mills were entirely discarded, and even in the seventeenth and eighteenth centuries we find abundant documentary evidence of the survival of querns for a variety of uses. By this time, hand-mills mounted on stands (see Plate IV) were used chiefly for grinding malt, mustard, and other grain unsuited to the more powerful types of mill. At the time when this series of inventories comes to an end, malt mills, of which a good example

[1] E. C. Curwen, *Plough and Pasture* (1946), p. 109.

may be seen in Colchester Castle museum, were being made of iron and were much easier to work than the old stone variety.

The inventories of John Putto, 1679 (103), Henry May, 1693 (171), and John Overill, 1720 (208), are of particular value for the details they give of milling accessories. In the oldest of these three documents, the value of a pair of windmill stones, the bras(s)es (or renewable parts of a bearing taking the friction), the 'gabellrop cloath',[1] and a hammer were appraised at £9 14*s*. 0*d*. Putto also had a watermill with one pair of stones, weighing apparatus, measures and sundries worth £13 5*s*. 0*d*.

Henry May worked the mill belonging to Lord Petre, and the items so carefully listed and qualified by the phrase 'if nott my lords' were valued in all at £16 14*s*. 6*d*. The terms are of interest: the 'payer of cullen stones' were black mill-stones quarried at Andernach and shipped from Cologne—hence the name. These stones ground finer flour than the English ones as Ralph Sheldon of Beoley writes in a letter dated 22 January, 1588-9:—

> 'The blacke Myllstones you wryte of I provyded for a very Lytle Mill I made at Beoley, only for the provision of my house, the w'ch I alwaies use when I kepe my howsholde there, in myne absence comon stones of o'r contrey are in place of them used because for suche p'sons the fynesse of the bredd is not Respected.'[2]

The 'Peek' mill was so called because it contained one 'Peak' or Derbyshire stone, and a French or 'burr' stone. An 'axtree' was undoubtedly the windshaft on which the sails were mounted, while the 'bredg wheell tree' was the local description of the bridge-tree on which the stone spindle rests. Brays were a system of levers used to raise or depress the bridge-tree and with it the stone spindle and runner (or upper) stone so that the fineness of grinding could be maintained whatever the speed of the mill.

'Bills', a special type of chisel for re-cutting the grooves in the grinding faces of the stones, and spileing chisels are listed among the gear in the mills of May and Overill. This latter term is likely to denote a type of mill-bill, but Mr. Wailes suggests that if it was a wood-worker's chisel then it may be the name for a tool which looks like a cross between a taper reamer and a gouge. It was used to bore the taper air vent in the top of a barrel into which the spile peg was inserted. Alternatively, it could have been used in connection with boring holes or preparing large timbers used as piles or foundations.[3]

Miller May also indulged in fishing for we have a flew and a fishing bray worth, with a riddle (or sieve), five shillings. A flew was a small fishing net, but the meaning of a fishing bray is not clear; was it a form of trap-net to spread across a stream, or another form of lever for raising or lowering stones as mentioned above? The meaning of an appliance called a 'ruffle

[1] Mr. Rex. Wailes, M.I.Mech.E., to whom I am indebted for technical help in this section, suggests that the gabelrope was the main cord down the edge of a sailcloth and that the counterline was one of the pointing lines attached to it.

[2] E. A. B. Barnard, *The Sheldons* (1936), pp. 38-9.

[3] Cf. *Spile*: a pile, i.e. a heavy beam of timber usually sharpened at one end; a number of such timbers are driven into the bed of a river or marshy ground for the support of a bridge or other building.

heaven ' has not been found, but two pairs of trundles were carriages on low wheels. A ' sheluch ' (sluice) hammer is a typical example of phonetic spelling.

The contents of John Overill's mill-house were valued at £4 13*s.* 8*d.* Other millers were Henry Groves, 1674 (82), John Godfrey, 1728 (229), and Joseph Goodman, 1730 (235), but no details of equipment are given. It would appear that there was a separate inventory for John Godfrey's water-mill, but the document is missing from the series.

There was a windmill in Writtle as early as 1274,[1] but none of the three windmills and one watermill clearly shown on Chapman and André's map of Essex, 1777, survive in working order today; the place-name of Cooksmill Green is a survival of the time when Richard Cook's windmill stood there.[2]

In no. 69 is a reference to a bolting mill which was a machine for ' dressing ' or sifting flour (see p. 27).

Fig. 17.

Some Village Tradesmen

ALTHOUGH there are several shop-keepers, there is only one mention of a sign (221), and six to counters, or shop-boards, as they are twice called. No doubt a certain amount of trade was carried on in the homes of the people where counters were not deemed necessary; this was probably the case with Widow George, 1687 (146) whose modest stock was valued at five shillings and one penny, whereas her scales and weights, measures, and ' sum small implements ' were worth ten shillings and sixpence.

In Edmund Butler's inventory, 1713 (200), there is a single item of £114 2*s.* 3*d.* for stock in his shop and warehouse, which indicates a considerable business, but there is no clue to its type. Zachariah Day, a blacksmith of Roxwell, 1705 (189), had unspecified stock valued at thirty pounds; here, as so frequently, the appraisers did not list the individual items from which we might have learned a lot about village trades, but

[1] Donald Smith, *English Windmills* (1932), vol. ii, p. 4.

[2] P. H. Reaney, *The place-names of Essex* (1935), p. 280, n. 11.

the omission of details for a complete smithy is partly rectified by examination of William Poole's inventory, 1684 (129). This man's stock is interesting, and includes 'gloomes *alias* anvills'; it is fortunate that the alternative term is given by the appraisers because it does not appear in any of the dialect dictionaries consulted.[1] Another noteworthy entry in this inventory is the 'slick-trough' or water-trough invariably found at the end of a blacksmith's hearth and near the anvil. The interest is in the word 'slick', used here in the sense of a dash or stroke;[2] i.e., the iron is dashed into the water-trough for rapid cooling after being hammered into shape.

The stocks of Joseph Clarke, grocer and draper, 1692 (169), and Daniel Bridges, tobacconist and grocer, 1725 (221), are, like that of William Craig, draper, 1683 (127), of particular interest for the assortment of goods and the many obsolete terms describing them. It would, no doubt, be impossible to find indigo in a village store today, but three pounds of it appear among Clarke's goods at one shilling and two pence per pound.

A glover's stock is recorded in no. 49 (1665) where the values of dressed and raw hides are in much greater detail than in Nathan Wade's inventory, 1680 (116). John Waylett,[3] a tanner, *c.* 1689 (152), had a stock of hides worth £471 14*s.* 0*d.*; tanning was carried on in several parts of the county, and large quantities of bark were supplied for this industry from nearby woods.[4] An aluming trough is among Wade's goods; this article was used in the process of 'tawing', or whitening skins with alum, salt, and other substances.[5] The shoemaker, Francis Quy of Roxwell, 1681 (117), had a small stock of leather which, with the other equipment in his shop, was valued at £3 6*s.* 6*d.*

Henry May's inventory, 1693 (171), and that of John Overill, 1720 (208), are informative on the contents and value of mills, of which further details are on pp. 41-2.

A wheelwright was an important person in the days of horse-drawn vehicles, and the extent of William Carnell's stock, 1679 (104), shows the varied accessories for implements and carts. In his inventory we have mention of 'Pollenger' timber which was wood from pollard trees; spokes reckoned by the 'trann'[6] which measure was also used for 'felleyes'

[1] In a deed of Thaxted, 1653, in the Essex Archæological Society's collection at Colchester, is a reference to a common field called 'Glome worke'. Thaxted was formerly noted for a small cutlery industry, and the 'Glome worke' field indicates a connection between iron or steel working and the use of the term for an anvil as in Poole's inventory. Cf. French, *enclume,* anvil. There is a Glumangate in Chesterfield.

[2] *N.E.D.*

[3] For details of his will, see *Transactions* of the Essex Archæological Society, New Series, vol. xix, p. 46.

[4] See F. W. Steer, 'The Account Book of an Eighteenth-century Maldon Tradesman' in *Essex Review,* vol. lvii, pp. 45-52.

[5] See *Victoria County History,* Essex (1907), vol. 2, pp. 458-60, for particulars of the leather industry (especially the manufacture of chamois or 'wash' leather) at Writtle.

[6] A tran is twenty-five spokes or thirteen fellies. A. E. Baker, *Glossary of Northamptonshire words and phrases* (1854).

(fellies), or the curved pieces in the circumference of a wheel. The 'knaves'[1] mentioned at the beginning of this inventory were the hubs of wheels through which the axles passed, while rave pins were for fixing the raves, or framework of rails or boards, added to the sides of a cart to enable a greater load to be carried. Elm was used for the naves of wheels, oak or ash for the spokes, and the last-named timber for fellies and shafts.

Throughout the inventories are references to tradesmen's tools, but seldom in detail; often the entry is simply 'his working tools'. Mention may be made here of the tools belonging to Edmund Turnidge, 1678 (102); they included a hand-saw, three [spoke]-shaves, a gouge and a pacer, all of which he kept with articles of a more domestic nature in the hall of his Roxwell farm. The pacer was almost certainly a perambulator or measuring-wheel used by surveyors and others;[2] it is not listed in any other inventory.

Scales and weights used in many trades occur at frequent intervals, and are dealt with under weights and measures, pp. 65-7.

WEARING APPAREL

THE inventory of Jane Barnard, 1638 (15), is the only early one where there is anything approaching a detailed list of garments; a number of the items are described as being old. We learn that the ruff was still worn, and, as Dr. Willett Cunnington said in his lecture on 'The Scientific Approach to Period Costume',[3] this article 'corresponded to the Victorian top hat and bonnet, symbols that may have been inconvenient to wear but how convenient to demonstrate your social rank!' Mrs. Barnard also had six coifs valued at sixpence each; these were white lawn or silk head-coverings.

Charles Clark of Writtle, 1659 (26), had two waistcoats, five petticoats and one pair of 'bodies' (i.e. bodices) worth two pounds; three aprons and three handkirchers (i.e. handkerchiefs) are included in his household linen.

Widow Poole, 1672 (76), had a black scarf, a green apron, four petticoats, a waistcoat and a hat worth, in all, twenty-eight shillings.

From the 'accompt of the countrie debt of the deceast William Craig drawn out of his book', we gather that this Roxwell inhabitant who died in 1683[4] was a travelling draper with an extensive connection. His large stock of cloth included some of local manufacture.

Fabrics such as 'bays', serges, broad-cloth, Linsey-Wolsey, Kersey, fustian, buckram, linen, calico, cotton, silk and crape, with the prices per yard or ell,[5] are among the stock of Joseph Clarke, 1692 (169); he also had haberdashery such as tapes, filletings, bindings, laces, ribbons, 'ferritts',[6]

[1] Now spelt 'naves'. Another definition of 'knave' is given in the *N.E.D.* (and listed as a rare obsolete word) as a contrivance in which a spool or spindle revolves; the connection is, therefore, apparent. See also the chapter on 'The Wheel-wright and Wagon-Builder' by Thomas Hennell in *The Countryman at Work* (1947).

[2] See *Catalogue of Maps in the Essex Record Office*, 1566-1855 (1947), p. viii.

[3] Printed in the *Museums Journal*, Oct. 1947, pp. 125-130.

[4] No. 127.

[5] 1¼ yards.

[6] Ferret: ribbon woven from spun silk.

buttons, pins, needles and thread. Among his ready-made garments were hose at prices between sevenpence and two shillings a pair; coats (probably children's waistcoats) at sixpence each, and two petticoats of broad stripe worth eight shillings.

Shirts, neckcloths, caps and a handkerchief are with the goods of Joseph Taverner, 1695 (178). An incomplete, unidentified inventory of *c.* 1720 (245), is apparently that of a person on a higher social scale than the majority, for it records 'suites' of red and blue silk, Holland shirts, linen shifts, 'turnovers',[1] breeches and woollen capes[2]; in this inventory (which is not priced) three wigs and a pair of silver buttons are noted.

Boots, cloaks, frocks, face kerchers, muffs and smocks are each noted but once, while gloves and gowns are specially mentioned on only two occasions. It was the general rule to value the deceased's apparel and enter it, with his ready money, as a single item at the end of the inventory.

We must not imagine that the people whose goods we are considering were dressed in the rich clothes such as are shown in paintings of Stuart courtiers. The seventeenth century may be divided into two distinct periods so far as the dress of the upper classes is concerned. The year 1667 is the important date which marks a change in costume which passed from lace-edged collars and cuffs or fur-trimmed gowns for men, and silk, satin or velvet dresses, caught back to reveal embroidered petticoats, for ladies, through the more sober days of the Commonwealth, to the revival of colours and frills in the year following the Great Fire of London. This picture applies only to the wealthy; the poorer classes were invariably dressed in hard-wearing, dull clothes made either of home-spun or locally-produced material, with a slightly better, but still plain, frock and petticoat for Sunday or holiday wear for the women, and a smock rather more elaborate than usual for the men. The nearest approaches to personal adornment (other than a very few articles of jewellery, p. 48) are found in the inventories of John Freeman, a barber-surgeon of Writtle, 1721 (213), who had, in addition to fifteen shirts, a pair of silver spurs worth one pound, and the unknown person who possessed the silver buttons mentioned above.

The seventeenth century was, in costume as in most other things, an age of comparisons, and the similarity between the clothes of one section of the community and another did not exist as it does today.

WASHING OF CLOTHES

WHETHER in the mansion or the cottage, the washing of linen and wearing apparel was an irksome task for the seventeenth century housewife or laundry-maid. In a large establishment there would have been a room set apart as a laundry, but as no mention is made in these inventories of such

[1] A turnover was a woman's shawl.

[2] This entry may refer to caps. By an Act of Parliament of 1571, an attempt was made to enforce all persons of common degree to wear English woollen caps on Sunday; they were fined 3*s.* 4*d.* if they broke the law and were discovered, but it is not suggested that this entry has any connection with an Act of Parliament of one hundred and fifty years earlier.

an office, we must assume that the work was done either in the kitchen, or, during fair weather, in the yard. Perhaps it was a fine washing-day when William Garrat's inventory (159) was taken, as two pairs of sheets, valued at two shillings, are described as 'upon the hedge'.

Water was heated in great boilers and used in circular wooden tubs placed on low benches; the clothes were well soaked before being beaten with flat wooden bats.[1] There are numerous references to tubs with no indication of their use, and only seven wash(ing) tubs are specifically noted. Flaskets are occasionally listed, and this term may be applied either to a shallow washing tub, or to a clothes basket.

In three out of the four inventories where soap is mentioned (the first in 1687), it is part of a shop-keeper's stock, and in the fourth, half a firkin is noted among a yeoman's goods, 1694 (177). A solution made from the ashes of burnt wood or other vegetable matter was in general use instead of soap. The process of manufacture, given at length in the *Victoria County History,* Essex (1907), vol. 2, pp. 372-5,[2] was to put the ashes in a tub having a perforated bottom, and to wash out all the soluble potash salts. The resultant liquid, known as lye, ran into a second tub placed below the first and called a lye-letch;[3] the latter, together with lye troughs or tubs, occur several times in the inventories. Wheat, oat, or barley straw was steeped in the lye, then dried and slowly burnt, and the ash from it gave a still richer potash which made a concentrated solution, and helped the housewife to soften her hard water on washing days. As an industry, it was of considerable importance in Essex, but ceased about a century ago; only field, wood, and farm names remind us of it.

Starch is only listed in the inventories of two grocers, and mangles are not mentioned.

There are three main varieties of irons. Box and lock irons,[4] heavy to use and supported on three-legged stands, were heated by means of a piece of hot iron inserted at one end. These 'heaters' are mentioned several times from 1689 (153), and a stove 'for to heat lock iron heaters' occurs in 1725 (222). Smoothing irons, similar in shape to the modern flat-iron, are often noted, but cloth irons and flat irons only once.

LINEN AND OTHER CLOTH

THROUGHOUT the centuries it has been customary for a prospective bride to accumulate a supply of household linen and, until about 150 years ago, to maintain it after marriage by spinning yarn from prepared fibres of the flax plant (*Linum usitatissimum*), and, in some cases, weaving it into cloth. All classes of women were employed in spinning yarn, for which task a spindle and distaff (or a spinning wheel) were the fundamental implements; the operator was known as a spinster.

[1] See illustration in G. Jekyll & S. R. Jones, *Old English Household Life* (1945), p. 27, of a sixteenth-century washing day.

[2] See also P. Benton, *History of the Rochford Hundred* (1867-85), p. 902.

[3] C.f. *leach*—to wash or drain away by percolation of water.

[4] This term is not common; it occurs as 'lackirn' in a Great Bentley, Essex, document, 1706, in the E.R.O. [D/P 171/8/2].

The linen mentioned in the inventories may be broadly classed as table-linen and bed-linen, and further sub-divided into two main qualities, viz.: coarse, or towen, and Holland, or fine. The finer linens were made from the inner fibres of the flax stalks, while the coarse or towen linens—less white than the other and sometimes called canvas[1]—were manufactured from the fibres nearer the rind and called *stupæ* or tow. Holland linen was so called because the fertile lands of the Low Countries, resting upon moist subsoils, were particularly suited to the growth of flax from which linen of a high quality was produced.

In the inventories, bed-linen is confined chiefly to sheets, and pillow-cases or pillowbeers. This latter term is an ancient one; Chaucer, in the 'Prologue to the Canterbury Tales', says of the pardoner—

> 'Ne was ther swich another pardoner.
> For in his male [bag or wallet] he hadde a pilwe-beer,
> Which that, he seyde, was our lady veyl: '

There are few references to damask or that linen in which a pattern—sometimes even a scriptural story—was woven in imitation of the silks originally made at Damascus. Diaper (*qu.* so called because the special weave originated, many centuries ago, from Ypres in Belgium—hence d'Ypres), a form of twilled, unbleached linen, was frequently patterned with slightly defined figures and made into table-cloths and napkins. Darnex, a coarse variety of damask used for carpets, curtains, etc., was originally manufactured at Tournay, called in Flemish, *Dornick.*[2] Towels, sometimes described as of linen, are often mentioned, and are our only evidence that men and women of the seventeenth and eighteenth centuries were concerned with personal cleanliness; there is a marked absence of references to washing facilities even in the inventories of the wealthy classes.[3]

For the more common varieties of cloth, other than linen, there are not many references. Silk occurs but once (245); calico is listed occasionally from the third quarter of the seventeenth century and was sometimes painted (see p. 21); woollen cloths such as 'bays' and serges were in demand for bed-curtains and coverings.

Hair-cloth, woven from horsehair, was used in malting (see p. 32) and for the doors of 'keeps' or meat-safes. Barn-cloths, of a coarse material, were spread on barn floors during threshing, the grain, beaten from the ears with flails, being gathered up in the cloth to be taken out and winnowed.

Wearing linen is referred to in the section on apparel (see p. 44).

The inventories of William Craig, 1683 (127), and of Joseph Clarke, 1692 (169), are important for the many varieties of cloth listed; some are obviously of local manufacture, while others are from more distant places.

[1] Canvas is usually made from hemp fibres, but appears to be synonymous with coarse or towen linen in the inventories.

[2] J. O. Halliwell, *A dictionary of archaic and provincial words* (1889).

[3] See also *Shardeloes Papers of the 17th and 18th centuries,* edited by G. Eland (1947), pp. 16-18.

JEWELLERY

JEWELLERY, or similar items of personal adornment, is but rarely mentioned, and this may be due to the absence of inventories of many wealthy people. Except in the case of Thomas Crush, of Dukes, 1686 (136), where five gold rings are listed as worth £4, we have only three gold (122, 166), one silver (76), two plain and two cipher rings (245). The latter were undoubtedly engraved with initials in the form of a monogram.

MUSIC

THE only reference to musical instruments is to an old pair of virginals among the goods of Alexander Reynoldson, a grocer, 1671 (70).[1] A virginal, like an early organ, was often referred to as a pair when it had two keyboards, and the instrument is reputed to have been so called because of its popularity with ladies in general, or with Queen Elizabeth—the 'virgin queen'—in particular.

BOOKS AND PAPER

BOOKS are occasionally noted from 1638 (12)—'It'm baks with other Implements, 13*s.* 4*d.*'—but, except for the Bible and one reference to the Book of Martyrs, no titles are given. The Bible is first listed in 1639 (20), and there are isolated cases of it being described as a large, great, or folio volume; only once do the appraisers attempt any detail and note the Bible belonging to William Garrat (159) as a folio, 'Cambridge print'. 'One Booke of martirs' belonging to John George, of Writtle, 1638 (19), would have been that by John Foxe (1516-1587), whose work, together with the Bible, was considered essential to the library of any seventeenth-century gentleman.

Book-shelves and a little bookcase are each specifically noted on one occasion, but the numerous other references to shelves may include those used for books. In the inventory of Edmund Sterne, of Skiggs Farm,[2] Writtle, 1683 (128), is '1 little table & a library' which we may take to mean a bookcase or similar piece of furniture, and its contents.

Writing-paper in the stock of Daniel Bridges (221) was sixpence a quire in 1725; this commodity is, like waste paper in the same inventory, only listed once in the series.

TOBACCO AND SNUFF

KING JAMES I described smoking as 'a custom loathsome to the eye, hateful to the nose, harmful to the brain, dangerous to the lungs, and in the black, stinking fume thereof nearest resembling the horrible Stygian smoke of the pit that is bottomless'. Although tobacco had been introduced into England in the latter years of the sixteenth century, it is not until 1689 that we find a reference to it in the inventories; among the goods of Henry Bullen, a yeoman (157), was a tobacco box, presumably of silver.

In the detailed grocery stock of Joseph Clarke of Roxwell, 1692 (169), we have tobacco powder (snuff) and probably tobacco pipes, but the latter are mixed up with such diverse goods as alum, bedlines, and brooms.

[1] See p. 20.

[2] Now Skeggs Farm.

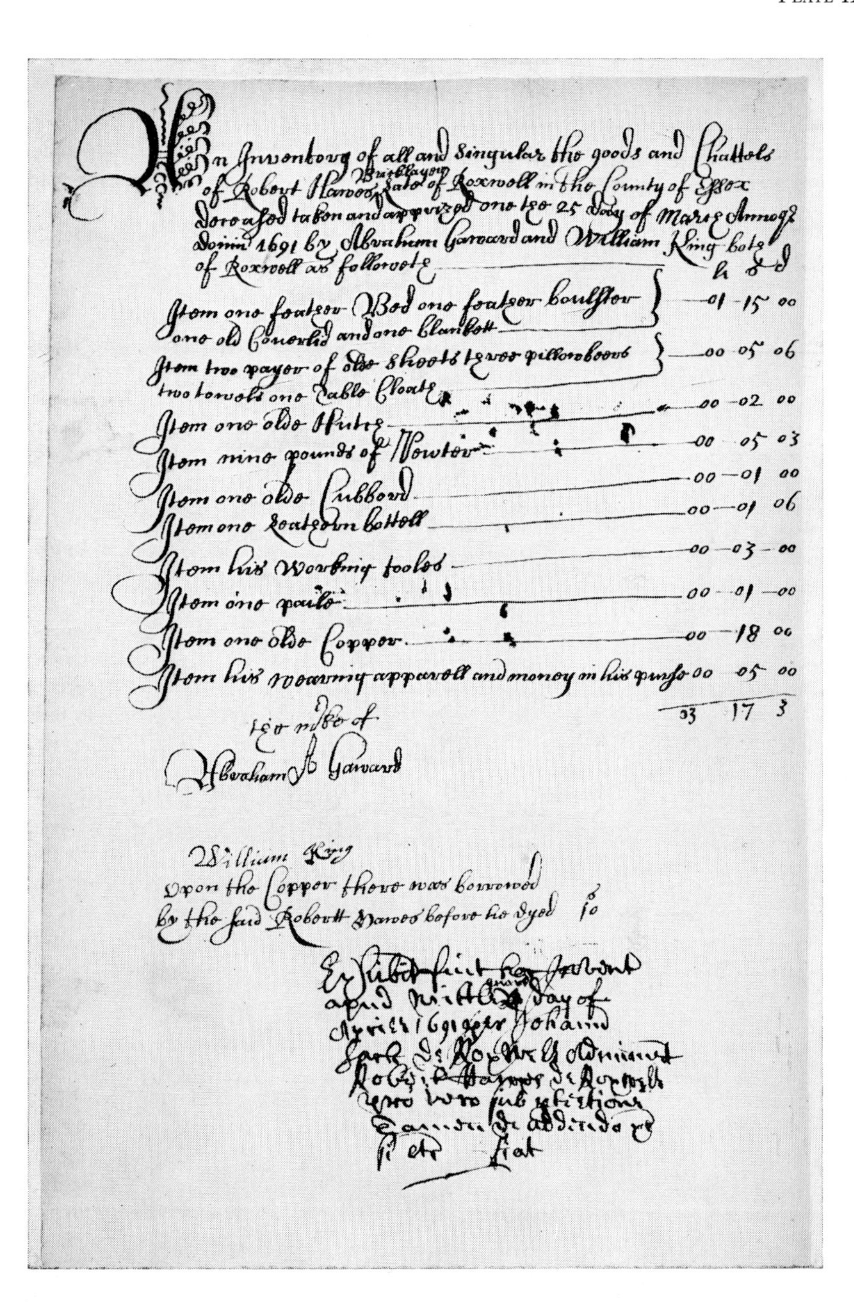

An Inventory of all and singular the goods and Chattels of Robert Hawes Bricklayer late of Roxwell in the County of Essex deceased taken and apprized the 25 day of March Anno Domini 1691 by Abraham Garrard and William King both of Roxwell as followeth

	li	s	d
Item one feather Bed one feather boulster one old Coverlid and one blankett	01	15	00
Item two payer of olde Sheets three pillowbeers two towels one Table Cloath	00	05	06
Item one olde Hutch	00	02	00
Item nine pounds of Pewter	00	05	03
Item one olde Cubbord	00	01	00
Item one leathern bottell	00	01	06
Item his Working tooles	00	03	00
Item one paile	00	01	00
Item one olde Copper	00	18	00
Item his wearing apparell and money in his purse	00	05	00
	03	17	3

the marke of
Abraham A Gaward

William King

Upon the Copper there was borrowed by the said Robert Hawes before he dyed 10s

Exhibitum fuit hoc Inventarium apud Writtle [illegible] day of April 1691 per Johannem Clark de Roxwell Administratorem Roberti Hawes de Roxwell [illegible] sub protestatione [illegible] de addendo [illegible] Fiat

INVENTORY OF ROBERT HAWES, BRICKLAYER, 1691 (no. 164).

A FARMER'S 'COAT-OF-ARMS.'

This tombstone in Redbourne churchyard, Herts., is in memory of Jonathan Rose who died in 1813. The first 'quarter' of the shield is occupied by a wheat-sheaf; the second by a harrow; the third by a hand-mill and sieve; the fourth by a sickle and rake. A pick, shovel, flail, scythe, and hoes are arranged on either side, while a plough forms the 'crest.'

Another grocer—Daniel Bridges of Drury Lane, 1725 (221)—whose connection with Writtle is obscure, has several references to tobacco which varied in price between eightpence and one shilling a pound; Bridges also sold snuff which he stored in pots, and tobacco pipes which would have been of clay and of the long, 'churchwarden' type. Mention is made in the same document of the 'two black boys' valued at three shillings; the Black Boy was the recognized trade sign for a tobacconist and is referred to in Ben Johnson's Bartholomew Fair": —

> 'I thought he would have run mad o' the Black Boy in Bucklersbury, that takes the scurvy roguy tobacco there.' Act i, Scene 1.

The definition of what appears to be 'old siferies tobaccoe block' remains unsolved.

A silver snuff box is listed in an inventory of *c.* 1720 (245) and a pipe-ring in one—presumably of an ale-house keeper—of 1729 (233). A pipe-ring may be described as a sort of iron cage fitted with rings to contain long clay pipes when they became foul; the whole thing was placed in an oven when the fire was lighted in it (see p. 27) and there thoroughly burned to sweeten the pipes.

FIREARMS AND OTHER WEAPONS

WEAPONS may be divided into two classes, viz. of warfare, and for sporting purposes. Those noted in the inventories are varied even if not numerous, and some were probably relics of the trained bands of Elizabeth's reign, or Civil War souvenirs.

The cross-bow and the English long-bow had both fallen into desuetude many years earlier than 1665 and 1674 at which dates we find them mentioned (49, 83).[1] There are two pikes (121, 242), but again, they are late survivals; the pike, sixteen to eighteen feet long and tipped with iron, was formerly considered to be the only weapon with which foot-soldiers were able to resist mounted men-at-arms. Halberds, noticed three times between 1663 and 1696, were shorter and easier to handle than pikes, but about the middle of the seventeenth century both weapons were superseded by the bayonet. Among edged weapons, swords occur fifteen times between 1663 and 1726, but the cutlass—a comparatively short weapon midway between a sword and a dagger—is only referred to once (1690, no. 159). The one example of defensive armour is a head-piece, or helmet, among the goods of William Boosey, 1675 (85).

Cannon, invented in the fourteenth century, were soon followed by similar, but smaller, weapons which could be carried by men in their arms. This led to the invention in Spain, in the first half of the sixteenth century, of the arquebuse, and from this, the musket, a heavier weapon, was rapidly developed; it occurs in the inventories from 1638 (19) until 1720 (210).

[1] 'As late as 1621 a keeper was accidentally killed in the Park at Bramshill by an arrow from the Archbishop of Canterbury'. (J. Simpson, *History of South Warnborough in Hampshire* (1946), p. 37, note 22.) It is not unlikely that the cross-bow, being a noiseless weapon, was occasionally used by poachers at a late period.

Before being discharged, it was placed upon a forked rest of which one is noted in Widow Perry's inventory, 1662 (33); she also had a carbine—a short, light type of musket, accurate in fire, but not often used because of its poor range and difficulty in loading. The actions in musket drill given in Hexham, *The First Part of the Principles of the Art Military* (1637), show a soldier wearing a head-piece such as mentioned above, and a bandolier or leathern belt for carrying ammunition. Bandoliers are listed five times in the inventories between 1662 and 1681.

The wheel-lock carbine in which a flint instead of the inconvenient 'match' supplied a spark was invented in the early sixteenth century, and from it developed the pistol of which we have references in 1678 (111) and 1681 (121).

Gunpowder or shot is listed only among grocers' stocks in 1692 (169) and 1725 (221).

From weapons of war we pass to sporting guns, commonly termed birding- or fowling-pieces; they were long-barreled light firearms for small shot. Excellent illustrations of them can be seen in the paintings of pheasant and partridge shooting by George Morland and other artists of the seventeenth and eighteenth centuries. In the Curtis Museum at Alton, Hants., is a fine specimen of a birding-piece which has been dated to *circa* 1620, but the earliest reference found in these inventories is 1638 (19).

SPORTS AND PASTIMES

SUCH firearms as would have been used in the killing of game or vermin, either as sport or from necessity, are included in the preceding section. There is little else to consider under the heading of sport, as the solitary reference to foxtraps in 1685 (134) is hardly comparable to the paraphernalia attached to the destruction of foxes today. From at least the sixteenth century until the early years of the nineteenth, it is not unusual to find payments for vermin destruction recorded in churchwardens' accounts.[1] Every opportunity of exterminating foxes, badgers and, to quote an Act of 1566, 'Noyfull Fowles and Vermyn', was taken, and the rigid preservation of foxes for the pleasure of the Hunts is a comparatively modern practice.

'One shrapnett' occurs in Francis Taverner's inventory, 1673 (79). A shrap was a snare in the form of a place baited with corn or chaff, and over it a net suspended in such a manner that when the birds had settled, the trapper, concealed behind bushes or a tree, contrived by means of strings, to drop the net on his victims.

Lastly, we have mouse traps listed among the grocery stock of Joseph Clarke, 1692 (169). Traps were of various sorts; that known as the 'deadfall', where a heavy block of wood dropped on to the mouse when he entered a box, was in common use, together with the 'cage' type of trap which survived until recent times.

In the Quarter Sessions records of some counties will be found numerous presentments of alehouse keepers 'mayntayning of an unlawful game . . .

[1] A book by J. Steele Elliott dealing with this subject was published by Luton Museum Committee in 1936, under the title of *Bedfordshire Vermin Payments*.

callyd Shovyll a borde and Slyde grote contrary to the Statute'.[1] This game, now familiar as 'Shove-ha'penny' since the groat has ceased to be legal currency, finds a place in the inventories; a shuffle board table and a set of shuffle board pieces were among the goods of Margaret Allen of Roxwell, 1724 (218), who may be described, almost certainly, as an inn-keeper.

LAND UTILIZATION

RELIABLE information on land utilization cannot be obtained from such a mixed series of inventories, but an analysis of one hundred[2] of these documents shows the following results: —

FARINACEOUS CROPS		
Wheat	890½ acres	
Barley	410½ acres	
Oats	122¼ acres	
Rye	27 acres	
	——	1450¼
LEGUMINOUS CROPS		
Peas	154½ acres	
Peas and beans	13 acres	
	——	167½
BULLIMONG		
Bullimong	89 acres	
Peas and bullimong	33 acres	
Barley, peas and oats	14 acres	
Peas and tares	23½ acres	
Oats and peas	74 acres	
	——	233½
MESLIN		
Wheat and rye	34 acres	
Wheat and barley	157¾ acres	
	——	191¾
MISCELLANEOUS		
Etch corn	50 acres	
Hops	¾ acre	
Clover seed	10 acres	
	——	60¾
UNCROPPED ARABLE LAND		
Barley Land	249½ acres	
Fallow	938 acres	
	——	1187½
CROPS NOT STATED		77½
GRASS		192
		3560¾ acres

It will be seen that the acreage of wheat was more than twice that of any other crop. The table given on p. 53 shows the varying acreage, with the

[1] See *Guide to the Essex Record Office*, Part I (1946), p. 99.

[2] This is not a selected number, but nos. 46, 58, 90, 95, 97, 107, 125, 128, 140, 160, 161, 195, 197, 199, 200, 209, 222, 236, 238, 240 and 242 have been omitted because no useful information would be gained by their inclusion.

highest and lowest corn prices[1] at short intervals, and that sixty per cent. of the holdings were thirty acres or less in extent; none were over one hundred and fifty acres.

In the folding table given opposite, the value of growing crops or available land may be compared with the total value of the deceased's goods (no allowance has been made for the time of year at which the valuation was made); the figures in the last two columns are the corrected ones (to the nearest £) for the total value of each inventory.

Difficulties also arise with regard to the rent of land and cost of cultivation; these particulars are specially noted in some inventories, e.g. nos. 140, 162, 197, but there is no guarantee that appraisers always took such items into consideration. The term 'tilth', or its archaic form 'tilt', is frequently used to denote the number of times the land has been ploughed, i.e. what degree of fineness of soil has been reached; the costs are often recorded.

The categories to which certain mixed crops belong are in the summary on p. 51. Bullimong is a word which has been in literary use since the fourteenth century, while meslin (now regarded as an almost archaic term) was used in country districts up to the middle of last century.[2] Household bread for servants was usually made of rye, while meslin-bread, made with equal quantities of wheat and rye, was for the master's table and considered very good and wholesome.[3]

Although etch is the late pasture or 'aftermath' in stubble following an early harvest, Vancouver refers to bean *etche* or stubble being 'well cleaned in the autumn and sown again with wheat: a small portion of these etches are occasionally sown with tares'.[4]

Barley land is that prepared several weeks in advance of sowing; the object is to allow the seeds of weeds to germinate and they are then destroyed when the barley is sown. Winter barley is sown during September-October, and the Spring variety in March-April.

Fields were manured by the cattle feeding on the stubbles, and except for one reference in 1663 (38), we do not find stocks of manure until 1729 (232) and then only on four subsequent occasions. The three-course system of crop-rotation (wheat, barley or another corn crop for two seasons, and then a fallow period) was customary, and the figure of 938 fallow acres represents rather more than one third of the total area under cultivation throughout the period. During the time that land was fallow it regained heart; farmers were continually fighting a hard battle to restore fertility to land which had the benefit of so little manure. As Lord Ernle says in *English Farming, Past and Present,* 'on land which was inadequately manured, and on which neither field-turnips nor clovers were known . . .

[1] 'A Collection of Papers relative to the Price, Exportation, and Importation of Corn . . . ' from *Three tracts on the corn-trade and corn-laws,* 1795. The figures given are for the average price of wheat in Windsor market.

[2] E. Gepp, *An Essex dialect dictionary* (1923), p. 25.

[3] R. Forby, *The vocabulary of East Anglia* (1830), p. 213.

[4] C. Vancouver, *General view of agriculture in the county of Essex* (1795) quoted by J. Britten, *Old country and farming words* (1880), p. 120.

PERIOD	5	10	15	20	25	30	35	40	45	50	75	100	125	150	TOTAL NO. OF HOLDINGS	ACRES OF WHEAT	HIGHEST CORN PRICE PER QTR.		LOWEST CORN PRICE PER QTR.	
	NO. OF HOLDINGS OF 15 … ACRES IN EXTENT																	£ s. d.		£ s. d.
1638–40	5	4	—	—	—	—	—	—	—	—	1	—	—	—	10	34¾	1638	2 17 4	1640	2 4 8
1658–70	4	2	—	—	—	3	—	—	2	—	2	1	1	—	15	77½	1662	3 14 0	1666	1 16 0
1672–80	4	2	—	1	—	—	—	—	1	2	2	2	2	—	16	126	1674	3 8 8	1676	1 18 0
1681–90	3	3	—	3	1	2	1	1	3	—	1	—	1	3	22	288½	1681	2 6 8	1687	1 5 2
1691–1700	—	4	1	3	—	1	—	2	2	—	2	—	—	—	15	130¼	1696	3 11 0	1691	1 14 0
1705–15	2	2	—	1	—	1	1	—	—	—	—	—	—	2	9	70	1709	3 18 6	1706	1 6 0
1716–27	—	1	—	1	—	3	—	—	1	—	1	1	1	—	9	153	1725	2 8 6	1723	1 14 8
1729–44	2	1	—	—	—	—	—	1	—	—	—	—	—	—	4	10½	1740	2 10 8	1743	1 4 10
	20	19	1	9	1	10	2	4	9	2	9	4	5	5	100	890½				

CLASS OF ANIMAL	TOTAL NO. OF REFERENCES	TOTAL NO. OF ANIMALS	PERCENTAGE OF PERSONS OWNING 1–3 ANIMALS	4–6	7–9	10–12	13–15	16–18	19–21	22 or more
Cows	266	1163	60·15	20·68	9·4	5·26	1·13	1·5	—	1·88
Horses	228	528	78·5	17·55	3·95	—	—	—	—	—
Pigs	209	952	50·24	24·4	14·36	8·13	1·91	—	—	0·96
Sheep	207	4889	10·15	14·49	14·01	9·18	8·21	6·28	8·21	29·47
Total No. of references examined	910									
Total No. of animals . .		7532								

there could be no middle course between the exhaustion of continuous cropping and the rest-cure of barrenness. The fallow was *un véritable Dimanche accordé à la terre'*. After the introduction of turnips, there developed the four-course rotation which has been handed down to the present day; this consists of wheat, roots, barley undersown with seeds, and finally hay, but peas or beans sometimes take the place of roots.

Turnips had become scarcely more than a culinary crop by the time that this series of inventories comes to an end; there are references to rye and turnips worth £10 (236, Jan. 1731/2), and to seven roods of the latter among the roots on Theophilus Lingard's land in 1743/4 (238). Potatoes are not recorded anywhere in the inventories as it was not until the second half of the eighteenth century that this vegetable 'started on a slow rise to popular favour'.[1]

Rye, clover, and hops are insignificant so far as the analysis of crops is concerned, but hop-culture is referred to in more detail on p. 35.

Throughout the inventories there are numerous references to stocks of grain, and, to a lesser extent, of peas, beans and tares both threshed, and 'in the straw' or unthreshed. Sometimes, as in no. 225, there are stocks of grain in the barns, but no mention of land under cultivation.

Hay was obviously an important commodity, although the comparative absence of straw is noticeable. Owing to the ever-present shortage of manure, all the straw not required for thatching purposes would have been used in stock-yards or put in places frequented by cattle so that every available load of humus could be made and returned to the soil. Chaff is not often noted; it was likely to have been cut as required.

We have a reference (6) to grass 'about the dooles' which were balks or strips acting as boundaries across a ploughed unenclosed field, or along its borders.

FARM STOCK

ALTHOUGH cattle were often described in vague terms, we are able to get a reasonably good idea of the types, local names, and numbers of animals kept by various householders. Over nine hundred references have been tabulated (see opposite) to show the varieties of animals, the first and last dates when they appear, the number of inventories in which they figure, and the total number listed in the series. It will be seen that there is a complete absence of donkeys, mules and goats, but the inclusion of 'cauts' on an inventory of 1698 (181) presents a difficulty as no definition of this word has been found.

As many of the terms applied to livestock are synonymous, or their exact meaning is not always clear, a shortened table showing the percentage of persons owning from one to twenty-one, or over, in any of the four main divisions of animals is given on p. 53.

It has not been possible to sub-divide these four main classes into (a) stock kept for breeding purposes and (b) for fattening and slaughter, because of the variation in the descriptions given in the documents. Hogs, stores,

[1] J. Hampson, *The English at table* (1944), p. 25.

sheats, shots, and pigs, for example, were probably all destined to be slaughtered while the sows were kept for breeding; the small number of the latter specially noted, supports this theory. The same conclusion, though not to such a marked degree, may be drawn from the comparative figures for bullocks and bulls.

The table on p. 53 shows that while sheep greatly out-numbered all other types of animals, the percentage of farmers who kept them in quantity is considerably higher than for farmers who had small numbers. On the other hand, it was the smaller farmers who kept the largest numbers of cows, horses, and pigs.

In a series of one hundred and sixty-six Bedfordshire inventories, 1617-1620, edited by Mr. F. G. Emmison, the total number of animals listed[1] is 2,630, made up as follows: —

Cows	....	689
Horses	....	145
Pigs	....	414
Sheep	....	1,382
		2,630

This figure shows that the localised area in Essex now under consideration fed far more livestock than did Bedfordshire. If the Bedfordshire figures were applied to the same number of inventories as in this present series, the result for that county would be approximately 3,900 animals, whereas the Writtle and Roxwell numbers exceed 7,500.

Norfolk sheep are listed as early as 1678 which was more than a century before the experiments to determine the respective merits of Norfolk and Southdown sheep were carried out at Finchingfield. Charles Vancouver, the agriculturist, refers to these tests,[2] and he records that after taking everything into consideration, the Norfolk breed of sheep were worth five shillings and eight pence each more than the Southdown variety although producing less wool. The ideal animal was a cross between a Southdown ram and a Norfolk ewe, because it fattened well and was much approved by the butcher.[3] Norfolk sheep were thought to waste pasture by their impatient ramblings which excited a continual appetite; this characteristic of the Norfolk Black Face sheep is attributed to its argalian forebears who have roamed, in a wild state since the earliest days, over an area extending north-eastwards across central Asia.[4]

Sheep were kept in substantial numbers for food, they benefited the land, cost little to maintain, and provided the greatly needed wool; cheese could also be made from their milk. Even so, Essex could never be

[1] 'Jacobean Household Inventories' in vol. xx of the Bedfordshire Historical Record Society Publications, p. 38.

[2] C. Vancouver, *General view of the agriculture in the county of Essex; with observations on the means of its improvement* (1795), pp. 20-1.

[3] *Ibid.*, p. 27.

[4] E. C. Curwen, *Plough and pasture* (1946), pp. 30, 32.

classed as one of the great wool-producing counties; Norden, writing in 1594,[1] says 'Ther are noe great flockes of sheep in this shire. Yet are ther sundrie places, that yealde verie fine woull; but not in the depe countries: the moste barren and heathye groundes yelde best woull . . .'

Cows, next in order of popularity, provided milk, butter, cheese and meat, but were, generally speaking, animals of poor quality; it was not until the second half of the eighteenth century that men like Robert Bakewell of Leicestershire, and Coke of Norfolk, devoted their energies to the improvement of the standard of cattle by cross-breeding. It is likely too, that during the period covered by the inventories, the major portion of the cattle were of a reddish colour, being descendants of those brought over to eastern England by Saxon invaders many centuries before.[2] The very small number of Welsh cattle specifically mentioned shows, however, the introduction of some of the original 'black' breeds from the west of England to the east. The transfer of cattle from one part of the country to another is occasionally noted in records,[3] but the greater number of cattle owners in the inventories are unlikely to have been much concerned with movement of stock; an exception may have been John Duke whose inventory of 1681 (123) includes a small number of cattle on Stow[4] marshes where there would be good pasture for fattening.

The Complete Grazier: or Gentleman and Farmer's Directory (1767) written 'by a Country Gentleman, and originally designed for private Use', has a chapter on the stocking of one hundred acres of pasture with cattle to fat for the markets 'according to the Manner in Essex; with the Expence and Profit'. The author recommends the purchase, in April, of one beast to each acre and a half, and allowed four months for the fattening of these cattle which were sold in August. The stock was replenished in October with small beasts 'such as are brought from Scotland or Wales'; each animal was allowed three acres and a little hay for winter feed and was sold off in February. It would seem impossible for the eighteenth-century farmer to lose money if he followed the directions in this book which, although a mine of information on cattle farming, includes chapters on the rearing of turkeys, pigeons, rabbits, pheasants, and bustards.

Pigs were not so common as one would expect, but this may be attributed to the fact that a great area of the woods had been cleared with an attendant loss of natural food supplies. It was customary to kill pigs, other than those reserved for breeding, after the acorns and beech-mast had been consumed and before the hard winter days set in. This fact would also account for the relatively small number of pigs noted in the inventories, and as salt pork is only listed twice (it was regarded as a perishable commodity), we cannot estimate how much of this meat was preserved for winter use in an average house.

[1] J. Norden, *Speculi Britanniæ Pars: an historical and chorographical description of the county of Essex,* ed. by Sir Henry Ellis (1840), p. 9.

[2] G. Uden, *Farm History* (1946), p. 52. The common grazing arrangements did not help to improve the strain of cattle as there was much inbreeding.

[3] See Tyrrell account book, 1539-40, in Essex Record Office, D/DP A2.

[4] Presumably Stow Maries on the river Crouch.

Essex ss }
Roxwell } June the 14th 1694

An Inventory of the goods and Chattels of John Crush late of Roxwell aforesaid deceased xx taken and aprized on the day above said by xxx Edward Boggas and William Browne both of x Roxwell aforesaid as followeth xxxxxxxx

	£	s	d
In the Parlor Chamber			
one bedsted mat and cord one trundle bedsted 5 stript curtains and valions and curtaine Rods one feather bed two boulsters two pillows two blankets one Ruge one old feather pillow 5 chests and one box three cushions one chayer two [illegible]	05	00	00
In the maids Chamber			
one feather boulster two pillows two trussells	00	08	00
In the Hall Chamber			
one bedsted a payer of greene curtains with Rods one trundle bedsted one hutch four payer of sheets two table cloaths six napkins one silver spoone one looking glasse two shirts five pillowbers four hankers five neckcloaths	02	07	00
In the Parlor			
one bedsted mat cord and curtin Rods five stript curtings and valions two feather beds one boulster two blankets one coverlid two tables two stools x two carpets one cubbord cloath one press cubbord one court cubbord and cloath one payer of curtin Rods one fire shovell a payer of tongs one chaier one dumbstalo	05	00	00
In the mens Chamber			
one flock bed and boulster one pillow four blankets	00	14	00
In the Hall			
two tables four forms two joyne stools one cubbord two chayers two cushions a payer of cobirons one forke one fire pan one paier of tongs one jack one wayt two spitts one warming pan two trammils one hower glass and frame and one skreen	03	05	00
In the Drink buttry			
two half hogsheads one hanging shelf one bowstall	00	08	
In the small beere Buttry			
two kettels one skillit one porridg pot one dripping pan a rosting iron pewter dishes four small pewter candle stiks one frying pan	02	09	00
Item ten bookes	00	05	00
Item his wearing apparell and money in his pursse	01	16	00
Sum totall	21	12	00

By us William Browne, Edw: Boggas } Appraisers

INVENTORY OF JOHN CRUSH OF ROXWELL, 1694 (no. 176).

'IN THE HALL—ONE JOYNED TABLE . . .'

This table, formerly in the Priory House at Little Dunmow, Essex, is typical of those sturdy pieces of furniture used in the larger farmhouses during the seventeenth and eighteenth centuries.

Horses were essential to all people who had to till land, take produce to market, or travel from place to place, and yet it is surprising to find (even allowing for the comparatively low value of money in the seventeenth century) a horse valued at four shillings, but similar low sums are noted on several occasions;[1] there is the possibility that many good horses were sold as soon as they were broken in. Young, writing on the agriculture of Essex, gives[2] information on the number of horses required to work a specified acreage in various parts of the county, and his figures are unlikely to vary much from those prevailing at the time the inventories were written.

Owing to the divergence in values, it would be unreliable to assess the wealth of substantial yeomen according to the sum entered for their livestock, but the student of agricultural history may obtain information on the relationship between acreage and quantity of stock on a series of farms by analysing the figures on inventories.[3] It is necessary, however, to pay attention to the season of the year when the inventory was made.

Cow and sheep racks, presumably to accommodate fodder, are each specifically noted on one occasion; cribs, used either as mangers, or more probably as cattle folds, are listed four times. Cow tyings, or fastenings used to keep a restive animal under control when being milked, are recorded in the inventories of Richard Clary (173) and Joseph Westwood (177). Alternatively, the term 'cow tying' may be a local word for the ox-stock, or trevis, which was a heavy wooden contraption for securing the animal while being shod;[4] this theory is further supported by the reference to a shoeing iron among Clary's goods. The reference to cow soles (102) is a reminder of the days when cattle were driven for long distances and needed protection for their feet.

Livestock were branded with their owner's mark before being put out to graze on common pasture. An elaborate system of cattle marks was used by the reeves of the Forest of Essex where cattle belonging to the 'commoners' of eighteen parishes were put on the waste lands; each commoner had to mark his own animals in a distinctive way in addition to seeing that they bore the parish brand.[5] Evidence that a similar procedure existed at Writtle and Roxwell is provided by the references to an iron brand among the goods of John Herridge, yeoman (216), and an iron seare belonging to Henry May, miller (171). Pitch pans used in the branding operation are listed in

[1] See nos. 70 and 74 (1671), a blind horse, 10*s.*, (1672), four horses, 16*s.*

[2] [A. Young], *General view of the agriculture of the county of Essex* (1807), vol. ii, pp. 352-4.

[3] See the table op. p. 52 showing comparison between value of growing crops and total wealth of the deceased.

[4] See note in *New York History,* Oct., 1946, p. 500, and its accompanying illustration. A similar apparatus, used when shoeing horses, is still at Gressenhall, Norfolk, and was the subject of an article by Dr. E. I. Puddy in the *East Anglian Magazine,* Feb., 1947.

[5] For illustrations of some parish cattle marks, details of the procedure for branding, and particulars of the pasture and pannage rights of the commoners, see W. R. Fisher, *The Forest of Essex* (1887), pp. 265-311.

Herridge's inventory and in those of William Garrat (159) and Richard Maggett (188) although the latter did not possess any livestock at the time of his death. Pitch is listed in nos. 98 and 111, but we cannot assume that it was necessarily for use in branding cattle.

POULTRY

POULTRY plays a small part in the farming stock, and this is due either to the fact that the number of birds kept by the poorer classes did not warrant their being noted, or, where the numbers were larger, the appraisers could not be bothered to round them up for counting.

Hens, poultry, or fowls occur under one or other of these names in fourteen inventories, of which those of Robert Jackson, 1638 (8), who had fowls worth three pounds, and Abraham Chalke, 1638 (9), whose five geese were valued at seven shillings and thirteen fowls at five shillings, are worth quoting as examples of prices. Two pullets belonging to John Burrows, 1638 (10), were listed at one shilling and four pence. Thomas Crow, 1687 (140), had poultry worth five pounds. A gander and four geese were priced at two shillings each in Joseph Taverner's inventory, March, 1695 (178), which compares favourably with the twenty-nine geese listed among Abraham Boosey's stock, July, 1723 (217), for £1 14*s.* 0*d.* Sixteen geese belonging to John Battle (225), were worth thirty shillings, but that was in September, when the birds would have been in prime condition.

Geese were profitable as they could fend for themselves on the commons, but they are only mentioned on seven occasions; ducks are only noted once.

There are sixteen references to capon, hen, or chicken coops, and four other similar articles are simply described as coops. These wicker cages in which fowls were confined for fattening or transport are usually found among the kitchen or buttery equipment.

AGRICULTURAL IMPLEMENTS AND ACCESSORIES

FARMING implements have been divided, for present purposes, into two categories, viz. heavy and light.

The first class includes ploughs, harrows, rollers, and vehicles; the second, and wider class, is devoted chiefly to hand tools. It would be outside the scope of this introduction to consider the evolution of farm implements in much detail, but Essex, like other counties, had types best suited to its soil. In some cases, difficulty has been experienced in identifying certain tools, as they are recorded by their local names whose definitions have not survived.

Swing-ploughs, designed for use on the heavy Essex clay, had the land-handle in a straight line with the beam, and the furrow-handle, passing beneath the mould board, was socketed into the 'slade' or ground-wrest; this form clearly demonstrates a development from the primitive one-handled plough.[1]

[1] T. Hennell, *Change in the Farm* (1936), pp. 75-6.

Harrows, although more crude in design than the modern implement, had altered but little from those depicted in the Luttrell Psalter of *circa* 1340.

In a stoneless county like Essex, it is probable that field rollers were of wood, and although they performed their function as clod-crushers, they were never entirely satisfactory because the soil was rubbed in turning at the headlands. This defect was not remedied until the invention of rollers made up of a number of small sections.

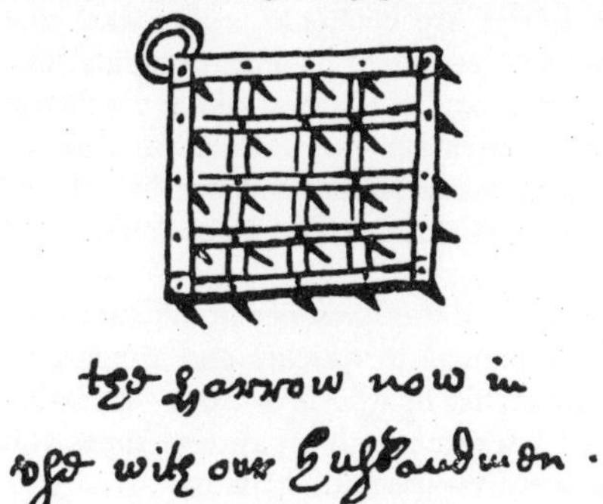

Fig. 18

A common implement was the dew-rake. This is an alternative name for a horse-rake, but was originally a large rake dragged by hand and lifted up for unloading only when full; it was also called a hobby-rake. Dew-rakings are those left after sheaves or swathes are cleared, and said to be easier to handle when damp in the morning.[1] Only once is a drag-rake recorded (1687, 140); this was a large hay or corn rake and probably synonymous with a dew-rake.

The absence of a seed-drill shows that Jethro Tull's revolutionary invention[2] had not penetrated into this area, any more than in others, until some years after his death in 1741. Seed would have been broadcast or dibbled into the soil, and we have one reference to a 'payre of setters' (63) which consisted of two irons each having a handle at one end and a bulbous piece, tapering to a point, at the other. The operator held an iron in each hand and, stepping backwards along the line to be planted, made holes about an inch deep and four inches apart into which two grains were dropped by a woman, boy, or girl, who accompanied the dibbler. It has been estimated that a dibbler and three 'droppers' could set an acre in two days by this method; the seed was covered at the end of each day by a horse drawing over it a gate bushed with thorns.[3]

Waggons and carts, like ploughs, are often peculiar to certain counties. There are many references to 'load-carts', apparently so named from the Middle English 'loode', and as a generic term for any cart used on a farm with the exception, perhaps, of dung-carting, for which special vehicles are frequently listed. Load-carts seem to have had detachable bodies fitted to a pair of wheels and drawn by a single horse. Long-carts occur occasionally, and the name is probably an alternative for waggons; the East Anglian

[1] See C. Partridge, 'A Suffolk Yeoman's Farming Stock and Crops, 1794', in *Notes & Queries,* vol. cxciv, p. 117, n. 1.

[2] Tull (1674-1741) is also claimed to have introduced horse-hoes.

[3] For an account of this method of sowing, see *Country Life,* vol. 101 (1947), p. 41. Accounts vary the number of seeds dropped into each hole.

word 'buck', meaning the body of a waggon, is noted four times, which fact confirms that the terms 'waggons' and 'carts' were interchangeable. Tumbril carts are noted on eight documents from 1663, but it does not follow that this type of vehicle was uncommon, because, as is shown above, a cart was frequently listed without a detailed description. There are three references to sledges.[1] Carting accessories are common: coops and tilts (i.e. covers), wheels in variety, cart ladders (see Plate V) and ropes, and one reference in 1729 (232) to 'copses',[2] or that part of a wagon which overhangs the thiller—or shaft-horse, all occur. Mention may be made here of 'thillbells' which occur several times in many forms, and are the chain-tugs fixed from a horse's collar to the shafts; a 'thill' is an alternative name for a cart shaft.

Other parts of waggons or carts are noted in the inventory of William Carnell, 1679 (104), a wheelwright. The references to winches and winch-pins are not to hoisting apparatus, but to the cranks of wheels or axles—probably the latter as is shown in an entry for '1 waggon with a payer of ropes and winch pins' in Abraham Boosey's inventory—used for hauling.

Carriages are listed three times, that belonging to Richard Clary, yeoman, 1694 (173), being valued at one pound. The single reference to a coach-box among the goods of William Eree, 1677 (96), undoubtedly refers to a travelling trunk and not to part of a conveyance.

Harness, designated as applicable either to ploughs or carts, is often listed, but when given the collective title of horse-furniture or tackle would include plough chains and the like; in three inventories (140, 198, 238), the term 'gears' is used for harness or similar equipment. Of the less common items barlines (i.e., traces or reins), fetters, stirrups, spurs, a wanty,[3] and pannels or pads used as rough saddles,[4] may be mentioned. Bridles, collars, halters and saddles—the latter including side-saddles for ladies—all occur at frequent intervals, as does the pillion (a form of cushion or small mattress upholstered in leather) used by a lady passenger who held on to the rider's belt. A crupper, listed once (232), is the roll of leather fitting under a horse's tail and helping to keep the harness in position.

Whipple-trees to which the traces or barlines were fixed, were the swinging bars of a plough or other horse-drawn implement.

Axes, bill-hooks, dung- and pitch-forks, spades, rakes and wheel-barrows and other hand tools were common. The mattock was also a widely-used tool, and an interesting reference to it is in a letter of 1753 sent by a Cheshire woman to her landlord; she writes 'and when my Father enter'd upon your Estate the Ground was most cover'd with Gors or Fuzz, but

[1] Mention may be made here of G. Berg, *Sledges and Wheeled Vehicles* (1935), issued by the Northern Museum, Stockholm. The book is in English and copiously illustrated.

[2] The singular is 'cop': see J. O. Halliwell, *A dictionary of archaic and provincial words* (1889). See also G. Sturt, *The Wheelwright's Shop* (1942), p. 155.

[3] This is a fourteenth-century word for a horse's belly-band; see E. Gepp, *An Essex Dialect Dictionary* (1923), p. 121.

[4] Pannels date from the thirteenth century. *Ibid.*, p. 84.

He being lusty and willing strove daily to subdue it; and so constantly employ'd his Mattock that it was a common Saying (where a strict Union was), "as true as Thomas Leech to his Mattock".'[1]

Hooks for cutting bushes, peas, weeds, and grass are noted, and the use of the word 'brome' for specifying grass-hooks is of interest; brome-grass is a variety bearing a strong resemblance to oats. Sickles, as distinct from the broad, smooth-edged 'fagging' hooks, are not mentioned as frequently as scythes. Snaths or scythe-handles (of willow, with hand-grips, or nibs, preferably of apple wood), and cradles used during the cutting of corn or barley, are sometimes noted; the cradle was a light wooden frame curved parallel with the scythe blade, and it collected the corn during the process of mowing so that it fell into a compact and even row.[2] In Abraham Brecknock's inventory, 1694 (174), we find, in the malt house, 'three sythes with their kilter', which gives us a reference[3] to the use of an Essex word meaning the component parts of anything; in this case, the scythes with their handles, and possibly cradles.

Fig. 19. WINNOWING-FAN FROM THE BRASS TO SIR ROBERT DE SEPTVANS (died 1306) IN CHARTHAM CHURCH, KENT.

This family, who held the manor of Little Wigborough, Essex, under the Earls of Gloucester during the 13th and 14th centuries, bore for arms, *Azure, three winnowing-baskets or.*

Threshing apparatus such as barn-cloths, riddles, sieves and screens, and casting-shovels were essential to the farmer; flails are, however, only recorded

[1] *Shardeloes Papers of the 17th and 18th centuries,* edited by G. Eland (1947), p. 113.

[2] J. Britten, *Old Country and Farming Words* (1880), pp. 13-14.

[3] See also p. 67.

four times.[1] Grain was threshed out with flails on a raised wooden floor in a barn and winnowed by shaking it through a fan or sieve on a windy day; the kernels fell on to a cloth and were then screened, riddled, or put through a caving-sieve to get rid of the larger pieces of chaff which had not blown away. The dialect word 'cavings', meaning such residue as broken ears of corn after the grain and chaff have been removed, gives us the word 'cave' which, according to Gepp,[2] is of eighteenth-century origin, but the inventories show that the caving-sieve was in use as early as 1659 (26). The man or boy who carted away the chaff was called the 'cavey'. Casting shovels were also necessary during threshing time, and the uses to which some of the above implements were put are adequately summarized by Tusser[3] under 'November's Husbandry':

> 'Some useth to winnow, some useth to fan,
> some useth to cast it, as clean as they can.
> For seed go and cast it; for malting not so,
> but get out the cockle,[4] and then let it go.'

Such implements as the flail, seed dibbler and cob, the sickle, and many others went out of use almost suddenly after being familiar objects for many centuries—almost from the earliest days of civilization. But some husbandry tools, like the chaff-box or cutter, thatching and ditching tools, are conspicuously absent from the inventories even though they must have existed.

Sacks were a valuable asset, and care was often taken to quote the exact number. Archdeacon Thomas Plume, D.D., who died in 1704, left to his native town of Maldon, '£1000 or more to establish a Trade of weaving Sackcloth, to the end that the Poor might be maintained comfortably for ever by their Labour'.[5]

Crowbars, pickaxes, and hoes were not often listed, but ladders—used for converting a two-wheeled cart into a form of hay waggon (see p. 60)—were common. There is also a number of references to screws or screw-presses; they were either cider-presses (see p. 36) or corn-presses, but the function of the latter is not apparent. In Abraham Brecknock's inventory, 1694 (174), the term 'corne skrew' is used.

Wood being the chief fuel and building material in this part of the country (see pp. 11, 27), we have references to beetles (or large mallets) and wedges with which to split logs.

Among John Ruskin's goods, 1686 (138), there was 'an old hovell' valued at two shillings and six pence; this has several definitions of which one is an out-house or sty (not necessarily in a state of squalor as implied by its modern usage), or part of a dwelling-house. As Ruskin also had a

[1] For information on flails see H. W. Lewer, 'The Flail' in *Essex Review*, vol. xvii, pp. 177-185; also Dag Trotzig, *Slagen och andra tröskredskap* [The flail and other threshing implements] (1943, Northern Museum, Stockholm), in Swedish, and extensively illustrated.

[2] *An Essex Dialect Dictionary* (1923), p. 28. Gepp says that the verb 'cave' is only used in Essex in the term 'caving-sieve' or 'cave'.

[3] *Thomas Tusser: his good points of husbandry*, collated and edited by Dorothy Hartley (1931), p. 105.

[4] A pretty purple-flowered weed, *Agrostemma Githago*, which is often found growing in cornfields.

[5] T. Cox, *Magna Britannia* (1700), p. 691.

hog's 'coate' worth ten shillings, the hovel may, in his case, have been a timber framework under which sheaves, hay, or turves, were laid to protect them from the weather. Tusser[1] says:

> 'With whins or with furzes, thy hovell renew,
> for turf and for sedge, for to bake and to brew.'

Hammers, pulleys, and grindstones are noted from time to time, and there are three references to wimbles. The latter may be either augers, or else an instrument consisting of two wooden bars joined together and parallel to one another, with an iron pin passed through them, upon which the framework can revolve. The pin secures the instrument to a post or wall, and a handful of straw is hooked over the end of one of the bars; by spinning the wimble with one hand and adding more straw with the other, a skilled man can make a straw rope or bond very quickly. The process is difficult to describe, and still harder to perform, by anyone who has not had considerable practice in the art of drawing out hay or straw bonds.[2]

Mention may be made here of the monument in Writtle church to Sir Edward Pinchon (died 1627) and Dorothy Weston his wife, which is reputed to be the work of Nicholas Stone and identical with a monument on a larger scale in Southwark cathedral. The pilasters, flanking a rock on which stands an angel holding a sickle, are carved with harrows, rakes, spades, scythes and other husbandry tools; the inscription is on a tablet within a winnowing fan, and the family arms on the blade of a spade.[3]

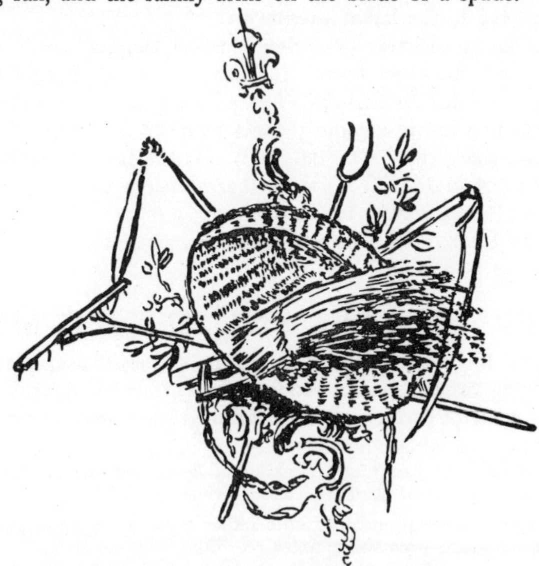

Fig. 20. DECORATION FROM A MAP OF MISTLEY BY BERNARD SCALÉ, 1778.

[1] *Thomas Tusser: his good points of husbandry,* collated and edited by Dorothy Hartley (1931), p. 76.

[2] A good description of this craft will be found in Hennell, *Change in the Farm* (1936), p. 153. The implement is sometimes spelt 'windle'.

[3] J. H. Upton, *A history of Writtle church* (1930), pp. 72-8, and *Essex Review,* vol. xiii, pp. 115-6.

FINANCE AND TAXES

BANKING, as understood today, was not established in Essex until between 1760 and 1770,[1] and transactions earlier than this period were chiefly on a cash basis. Bills[2] and drafts, perhaps negotiated for country people by an agent with a London connection, occur in the inventories from 1638 (18). Bonds, or promissory-notes, are listed from 1637 (2) and are about twice as numerous as bills. There is only one mortgage (93). Debts, usually noted at the end of an inventory and often described either as 'desperate' (i.e., doubtful of recovery) or good, are fairly numerous, and were naturally accounted as part of the deceased's estate. Less frequent, is a record of the monies owing by the testator, but where these are given, the names of his creditors often appear. In almost every inventory is a note of the cash in the purse or pocket of the deceased.

The entry of four shillings for chimney-money in Hezekiah Godsafe's inventory, 1687 (145), is the charge for hearth tax imposed under the Act of 13-14 Charles II, *c.* 10 (1662) on every householder except those exempted from parochial rates, on the basis of two shillings for each hearth. The duty was abolished by the Act of 1 Wm. & Mary, sess. 1, *c.* 10 (1688).[3]

In the inventory of Caleb Carter, of Writtle, 1682 (125), is the only entry described as taxes, but there are no details. In this document and in no. 145 are single entries for servants' wages; ten shillings tithe payable to Mr. Butler[4] is quoted in the latter inventory.

Expenses during sickness (including nursing charges) occur once (125), and burial costs but seven times. In 1638, the burial charges for Francis Banks (13) amounted to 3*s.* 10*d.*, but as his goods were only valued at £3 10*s.* 10*d.*, this bill is obviously for a pauper's interment. In 1678, we find a funeral charge of £3 1*s.* 0*d.* (100), and the few entries between this date and the last in 1689 (154) show that a charge varying between three and five pounds was normal for this service.

Some of the few references to rent for lands include the cost of preparation for sowing (see p. 52).

PEWTER, SILVER, AND OTHER METALS

PEWTER[5] was the most common metal in domestic use; plates, basins, dishes, drinking vessels, spoons, candlesticks, chamber-pots, and many other articles now made of earthenware or enamelled ware, were formerly made of

[1] For the history of banks and banking in Essex, see Miller Christy in *The Journal of the Institute of Bankers*, October 1906, pp. 319-330.

[2] Probably used for a promissory note rather than in the strict sense of a Bill of Exchange, although promissory notes are often listed as such.

[3] *Guide to the Essex Record Office*, Part I, p. 47. Hezekiah Godsafe does not appear in the Hearth Tax Roll, 1662, in the Essex Record Office [Q/RTh], but the membrane for Roxwell is partially mutilated.

[4] Rev. Robert Butler, of Roxwell, died 8 August 1703.

[5] The Pewterers' Company of London was incorporated by Royal Charter in 1414, but may have been in existence long before that as the records of the Pewterers' Guild of York dates from 1272.

January: 4: 1724-5 A true and purfect Inventory of the goods
and Chattles of Joseph Wollward of Writtle Deceased Aprysed
by Saml Shettleworth and John Sawell

		£ s d
Item in the Hall	one table 2 Joyned stooles two puter dishes 3 Chayers one lanthorn one Cubard	0-12-6
Item in the Buttery	one porrigpot 2 Cettles bras one Churn one Chaynes	1-3-0
	one beer vessell one tub	0-6-0
Item in the parlor Chamber	Two Beds 2 sorry Bedsteds 2 Indeferant Bolsters 2 Indeferant Blankets one pair of Shets three pillobers	2-0-0
Item in the Barn	3 Rakes 2 forks one wier sive one Ridle one half Bushell	8-0
In the stable	A parcell of old horstakel	0-8-0
	Item one Cart one pair of Harros one plow which wheels Belong to it one doorrake	2-0-0
Item	one Hors 2 Cows	8-0-0
		14:17:6

Wittnes our hands
Saml Shettleworth
John Savell

JOSEPH WOLLWARD'S GOODS, 1724/5 (no. 220)

Note the 'sorry' bedsteds and 'indeferant' bolsters and blankets.

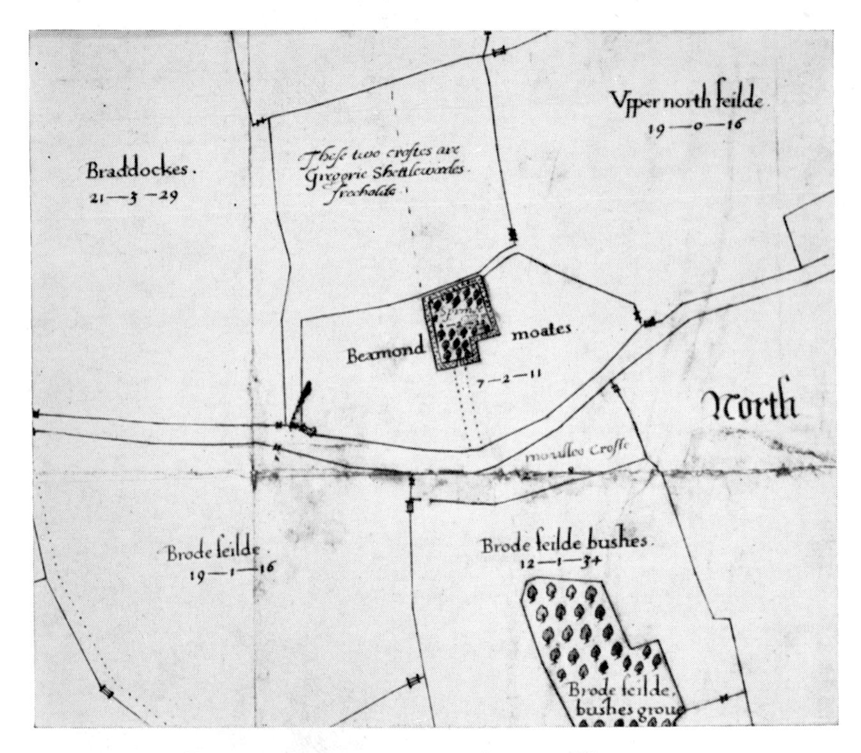

BEAMOND OATES, THE HOME OF JEREMIAH WESTWOOD.

Westwood's inventory (no. 119) was made in 1681, while the map from which this illustration is taken was drawn in 1599, by John Walker, the Essex cartographer. The crofts marked as 'Gregorie Shettlewoodes freeholde' belonged, no doubt, to an ancestor of Gregory and John Shettleworth, whose inventories are nos. 23 and 54 respectively.

HALF-PENNY TOKEN ISSUED BY DANIEL LEONARD OF WRITTLE, 1668.

[Twice full-size].

Leonard's inventory is no. 69.

pewter. In the larger houses, the appraisers often weighed it in bulk and assessed the value at so much a pound; in 1658 (24), 53 lbs. of pewter were priced at a shilling a pound; this is the highest figure recorded as two other lots (29, 37) were at ten pence, three lots (156, 203, 232) at eightpence, one lot (140) at sevenpence, and another (146) at sixpence. Henry Isaacson, 1714 (201), had a hundredweight of pewter, valued at £2 10*s.* 0*d.* Collectively, pewter articles are known as a 'garnish', and the sparkling metal must have looked very fine when set out on the oak furniture darkened with age and polished with wear.

Brass was also in great demand for pots and pans, but only once is it priced—at a shilling a pound (232)—in bulk.

Bell-metal was sometimes used for mortars, and lead was the usual metal for cisterns of which the finer examples often had decorative panels enclosing dates, initials, or coats-of-arms, although it is unlikely that any of the persons whose goods we are considering had such elaborations on their tanks.

Fig. 21

Tin-ware becomes more common in the later inventories, but never entirely supersedes the earlier metals.

The possession of silver bowls, cups, porringers,[1] spoons, salts, and other articles fashioned in precious metals was a source of pride in all classes of society, and such items were often specific bequests in wills. Eleven inventories contain references to silver bowls, and that of William Boosey, 1675 (85), to an 'Old Silver Guilt [gilt] Boule' worth £2. Silver spoons[2] are listed on thirty-two occasions, and silver tea-spoons once; salts (i.e. salt cellars) and porringers each occur three times. Other silver articles are noted under wearing apparel (p. 45) and drinking vessels (p. 30).

Sometimes the plate, either silver or pewter (or both), is listed as a single item; that belonging to Edmund Butler (200) is described as 'All the silver pleat, 8*li.*', and Thomas Crow's (140) as 'Parcell linen & plate, 6*li.* 10*s.*'.

Gold and other rings are dealt with under jewellery on p. 48.

WEIGHTS AND MEASURES

APPRAISERS employed a variety of terms for what we may assume to be reasonably accurate estimates of cereals and liquids.

The bushel and half-bushel were used for cereals measured by bulk, and eight bushels made a quarter. The quarter, however, varied in weight according to the grain; for example, a quarter of wheat was 504 lbs., while similar measures of peas and beans weighed 532 lbs., of barley 448 lbs., and oats and malt 336 lbs. Pecks, and half-pecks—a quarter and an eighth

[1] These were not saucepans, but small dishes for porridge.

[2] Silver spoons were sometimes used for applying poultices or ointments to sores or wounds, as they would have been cleaner than those of other metals. See G. Home, *Evolution of an English town* (1915), pp. 217-8.

part respectively of a bushel—do not occur so frequently, but are sometimes used as seed measures. The seam[1] was a popular term for a quarter of any of the above cereals. The quarterns listed in no. 192 as a measure for oats and barley are obviously a mistake for quarters. Cants[2] of barley in nos. 95 and 102 denote small crops grown in odd corners of a field.

A cock of hay was an alternative name for a stack; in Hertfordshire, hay was raked into wind-rows and then put into grass-cocks. The next day it was shaken into square leets and made into bastard-cocks which were twice as big as grass-cocks. On the third day 'we cock it up into heaps . . . [The fourth day] we put it into staddles, load it, and carry it away into a barn, cock or stack'.[3] A 'little Jag' of straw (67) is an Essex dialect word for a cart-load.

Butter is listed twice (79, 238) in firkins which weighed 56 lbs.; but where firkins are noted elsewhere, it is presumably the liquid measure of nine gallons.

Hogsheads[4] are invariably used as measures of beer (54 gallons), but a wine hogshead belonging to Abraham Brecknocke (174) and apparently empty, varied from 46 gallons if of claret, to 52½ imperial gallons or 63 old wine gallons. Pipes are listed three times and were wine barrels having a capacity of 162 gallons. The kilderkin, a barrel holding 18 gallons, occurs in sixteen inventories, but the small wine measures of a quart, a quartern and half-quartern (the two latter being a gill and half-gill respectively) are only noted in no. 218. In this same inventory is a Winchester quart and a pint, which remind us that the 'Winchester measure' was the standard from the days of Edgar in 972 until an Act of Parliament in 1824 established an uniformity throughout the United Kingdom as from 1 January 1826.

The larger measures were of wood with metal or wooden bands; some, however, such as the standard bushel ordered to be provided by lords of manors under an Act of 1670[5] were of bronze. The smaller liquid measures were invariably of pewter.

There are numerous references to scales of all sizes; some with wooden pans for butter, others of iron or wood and described as weighing beams (or merely beams) for heavier goods. Steelyards (or stillyards) were presumably the same as weighing beams; in this form of scale, also known as the Roman balance, a counterpoise was moved along a graduated beam. Weights, of lead or iron, are not usually specified.

Among the more rare descriptions of quantity, we find 'streaks' of old iron included in the stock of William Poole, blacksmith, 1684 (129). These

[1] An early reference to this measure is quoted by L. T. Golding in *An Elizabethan Puritan* (1937) from *The Chronicles of Battel* [Battle Abbey, Sussex] written *c.* 1176; part of the customary service from each tenant was the making of a seam of malt.

[2] J. O. Halliwell, *A dictionary of archaic and provincial words* (1889).

[3] W. Ellis, *Modern Husbandman* (1750) quoted by J. Britten, *Old country and farming words* (1880), p. 23.

[4] See also p. 34.

[5] That provided for Hingham, Norfolk, is still preserved in the church, and is claimed to be the only one surviving in such a place.

were probably strakes or strakers as the iron sectional rims of wheels were sometimes called,[1] but there is the possibility that the term is an obsolete one for a given quantity of iron.

SOME DOUBTFUL WORDS

THE definitions of certain terms used by the appraisers have not been satisfactorily determined, and although it is undesirable to introduce more doubts than necessary in a book, the attempted explanation of some obscure words may save the reader from going over ground which has been explored previously. It must be remembered that many of the inventories were written wholly or partially in the Essex dialect, and one person's interpretation of a phrase may be quite different from that of another. The meaning of some of the words given below may be readily apparent to the reader, while obscure to the present writer.[2]

BARKINGS (67). May be a variant of barlines (see p. 60) or barkhams; the latter is a horse's collar and is sometimes called a barholm.

WINDING BLADES (85). Perhaps a variety of windlass or hoisting apparatus. Alternatively, connected with the spinning of straw bands or yarn.

ROWELL BOARD (171). Circular timbers or trees waiting to be sawn into joists or planks.

A BOSHE FOR AND SACKS (139). Indistinctly written; more likely to be a bushel, fan, and sacks.

BRACPOT (100). A brass pot. The 'c' is pronounced as 's'.

CAULS (181). *Qu.* Calves as the item appears immediately after cows. The Kentish word *cawl,* a coop, does not seem to apply.

ONE OULD CLACK (219). The value and position of this article indicates that an old clock is intended, and not part of mill fitting more commonly known as a 'damsel'.

CILTER (188). A kilter: usually a scythe, sometimes a plough, but is applied to a tool or implement of any kind (see p. 61).

COABS (101). Almost certainly seed cobs (see pp. 22, 62) or baskets for carrying chaff.

COBARS (149). May be a form of grate, i.e. coal bars. Or perhaps intended for crowbars.

COBLARD (87). *Qu.* mis-spelling for cupboard.

CROPS (63). The only suggestions are, (i) a variant of crupper (see p. 60); (ii) intended for *cropiers,* saddle-cloths.

CUERLINS (OR CVERLINS) (94). From its context, this term is intended for (bed) coverings.

CULLERD (94). May be another mis-spelling for cupboard, a word which seems to have presented some difficulty to appraisers; note, however, the spelling *cuberd* in the parlour furnishings in this inventory.

[1] J. O. Halliwell, *A dictionary of archaic and provincial words* (1889), *art.* strake (5), and T. Hennell, *The Countryman at Work* (1947), pp. 48, 62.

[2] Further information on any of the terms will be welcomed for adding to Gepp, *An Essex Dialect Dictionary,* and other Essex word-lists of which annotated copies are in the library of the Essex Record Office.

DIXNARY (86). Probably dictionary.

HOOPE (140). A variety of cheese-vat, and a measure varying from a quart to four pecks, both have this name. The second form is derived from three hoops on a quart pot, and if three men were drinking, each would take his *hoop,* or third portion.

KEVE (191). A keeve, or vat in which beer is put to ferment before being barreled, seems the most likely explanation.

LANNDLES (198). Obviously a dairy utensil and may be intended for *kimnel,* which word is spelt ' kimdle ' later on in the same document. Unlikely to be *laniers,* which were whip lashes.

LEKERS (21). May be some connection with taps or stills in the sense of the dialect word *leck,* to leak. The word is not very clear in the inventory and could be ' bekers ', i.e. beakers.

CROSE LOATHES (15). *Qu.* Cross-clothes. A cross(e) cloth was a knitted kerchief or head-cloth.

PANYARDS (94). Probably intended for *panniers* which are light baskets thrown across a horse's back for carrying produce to market.

PEYBOARD (94). Pie-board.

PIDGS (103). *Qu.* Piggins. These were small wooden vessels or pails, with one stave longer than the rest to serve as a handle.

RIDEL (118). Either (i) a riddle, or sieve; or (ii) the ring to which the neck-rope of an animal is fastened in a stable.

SHAINE (105). Chain is probably intended, although ' plowchaines ' are the preceding item.

CORNE SITCH (155). A corn scythe may be meant here; Halliwell quotes *site* for scythe from *Nominale sub compendio compilatum de fixis et mobilibus.*

SKEULERS (8). Although *skewers* appears to be the obvious explanation, it is not unlikely that *coolers* are the articles referred to. Coolers or cowls were large open tubs, or sometimes pails. Evidence that there was a difference between a cooler and a cowl is provided in nos. 136 and 150 where the terms follow each other. Gepp, in his *Essex Dialect Dictionary* (1923) defines a cowl as a tub with two ears on the upper edge, and used in brewing; the word dates from the thirteenth century. A cooler, in the sense of a butter cooler, was probably a much smaller vessel. The two articles are indexed under one heading, which includes the forms *coulle, coule, cowler, cowl,* and *cooler.*

THATBANDS (105). Probably back-band, a strap or iron chain passing over the cart-saddle in a groove, and supporting the shafts.

TRAPP RULE (49). *Qu.* Trap-cowl, being identical with a trap-dish in the Norfolk dialect. Such an utensil was a perforated dish through which milk or other liquid was strained to relieve it of hairs or similar foreign bodies. See also trap-reel, p. 31.

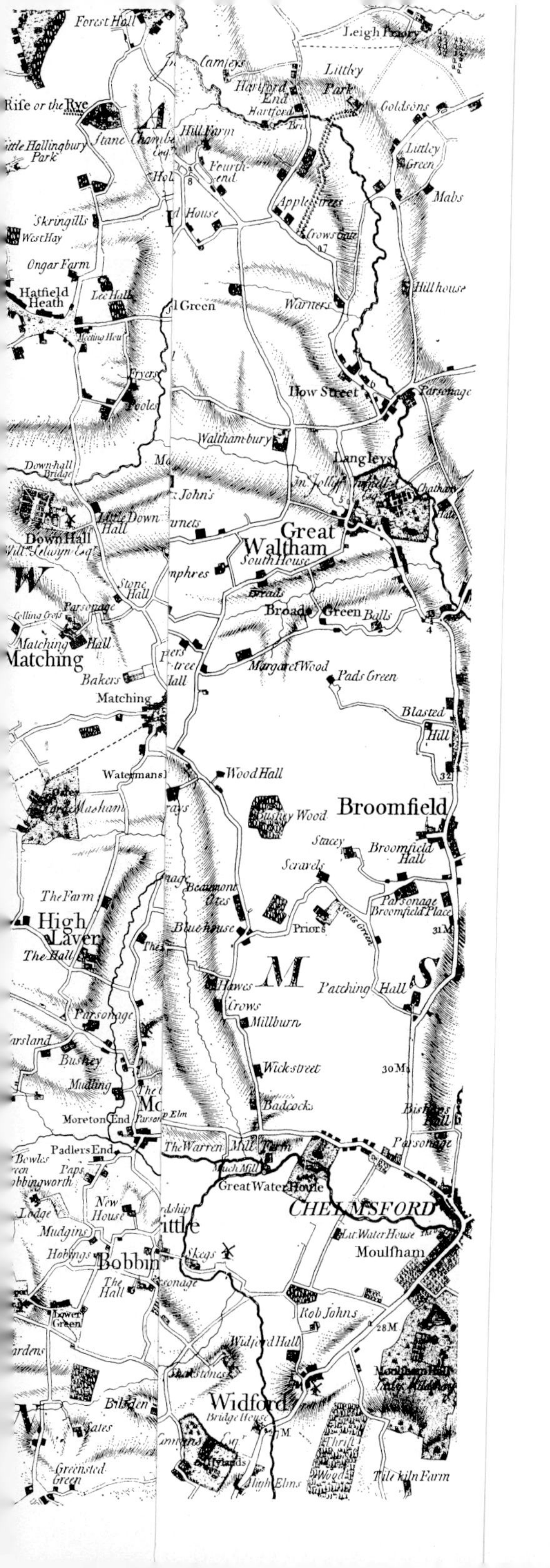
Forest Hall
Leigh Priory
Camleys
Littley Park
Hartford End
Goldsons
Rife or the Rye
Hill Farm
Littley Green
Fourth end
Mabs
Apple trees
Crows Gate
Skringills
West Hay
Ongar Farm
Hill house
Hatfield Heath
Lee Hall
Warners
Meeting House
Fryers
How Street
Parsonage
Walthambury
Langleys
Down-hall Bridge
Great Waltham
South House
Down Hall
Stone Hall
Broads Green
Balls
Parsonage
Matching Hall
Matching
Margaret Wood
Pads Green
Bakers
Matching
Blasted Hill
Watermans
Wood Hall
Broomfield
Bushey Wood
Stacey
Broomfield Hall
Scravels
The Farm
Beaumont Otes
Parsonage
Broomfield Place
High Laver
Blue house
Priors
The Hall
M
Patching Hall
S
Hawes
Crows
Millburn
Parsonage
Bushey
Wick street
Mudling
Badcocks
Moreton End
Padlers End
The Warren
Mill Farm
Parsonage
Paps
Great Water House
New House
CHELMSFORD
Mudgins
Lit. Water House
Moulsham
Hobings
Skeys
Bobbin
The Hall
Lower Green
Rob Johns
Widford Hall
Widford
Bridge House
Thrift
Wood
Tile kiln Farm
Greensted Green

EDITORIAL METHOD

THE original inventories were prepared, more or less, to a standard form. The indiscriminate use of capital letters, lack of punctuation, use of abbreviations, archaic and illiterate forms of spelling according to the whim of the appraisers or their scribe, have made a certain amount of editing necessary, but as much as possible of the original form has been preserved. It is realised that no printed text can fully represent, and certainly not supersede, the actual document; there is no general agreement on how documents should be transcribed, and the responsibility of making the printed version as easy, or easier, to read than the original, rests solely with the transcriber.[1]

Although every care has been taken in the preparation of the text, the expert palæographer may come across a few minor inconsistencies or even errors which seem to creep in however rigorously one tries to suppress them. The risk of such mistakes is greater where a long series of documents in many handwritings (most of them illiterate) is involved, and the work done—as in the present case—intermittently. But as Christopher Morley writes in *John Mistletoe,* 'The rule of clearness is not to write so that the reader can understand, but so that he cannot possibly misunderstand', and it is with that aim that the transcripts, with the following notes, have been prepared.

The transcripts which follow differ from the original documents in so far that after inventory no. 20, the headings have been condensed and the names of the appraisers given at the end of each document; if, as in a few isolated cases, there are notes of interest in the heading, these have been printed. Capital letters have always been used for names of persons and places, and at the beginning of lines, but their use at random in the documents has been observed only in the first ninety transcripts. Obvious errors, except those of spelling, have been corrected; the original spelling has been retained throughout. Surnames are printed as spelt in the originals, but the index gives modern forms with the variants, where necessary, in brackets. Punctuation marks have been inserted, and the description of goods put in paragraph form for each room. The words 'Imprimis', 'Item', or 'to the value of' have been omitted where they occur frequently.[2] Sums of money have been printed, with *li.* or *£,* as they are written; where there has been any doubt or omissions, the prevailing usage of the period has been adopted.

The use of the letters i and j, and u and v, as they appear in the originals has been retained, but where there has been doubt about u and v, the modern usage has been followed. Generally accepted abbreviations have been extended, but those which are doubtful are indicated by an apostrophe. Numerals and the ampersand have been reproduced as

[1] V. H. Galbraith, *An Introduction to the Use of the Public Records* (1934), pp. 77-8.

[2] Inventory no. 3 is, however, an exception.

written. The old dating has been given in the text, editorial notes give double dates; the use of the development of 'thorn' (as in 'ye') has been retained, and the initial 'ff' has been reproduced as a capital letter.

The documents are presented in the order in which they are filed in the Essex Record Office, which is not quite strictly chronological, e.g. 166 is among those for 1691 instead of for 1671, and 243 is a copy of 18. Where a misleading title is given (as in 242, headed 'Widow Watts' instead of 'James Watts' who was the deceased person), a correction is given.

If the *index of subjects* is found to be occasionally tautological, the inclusion of items in their many forms must be the excuse for this. As a rule, articles described as 'old' or 'broken', or where any doubt has existed as to their state, are included in those designated as 'unspecified'; articles simply listed as 'furniture' or 'lumber' have not been indexed; certain objects, e.g. barrels, have not been separated into classes, and where the same article appears more than once in the same inventory, it is only listed once in the index. When using the subject index readers are advised to look through the sub-headings under the main article, because the various descriptions may necessitate the inclusion of the same type of article under two or more headings; for example, spinning wheels are listed under 'Wheels—flax, linen, spinning, unspecified but probably spinning, and woollen spinning'. Where there are a large number of references to a common article, only the inventory in which it first appears is given, but the total number of references is in brackets after the words *et passim.* A full list of these references is kept at the Essex Record Office; readers unable to attend in person may apply in writing to the County Archivist for brief details.[1]

The *index of places* does not include Writtle when that place is only mentioned in the Commissary's certificate; the Court always sat at Writtle.

The certificates of exhibition have also been omitted, but the date of exhibition and the persons concerned, with their relationship to the deceased, where known, have been added in square brackets.

[1] See *Guide to the Essex Record Office,* Part II (1948), p. 113, for information about postal inquiries.

TRANSCRIPT OF THE INVENTORIES

1.—An Inventary of all and singuler the goods Chattells and debts of William Coleman of Writtle in the County of Essex Mason Deceased made taken valued and appraised the twentith Day of Aprill Anno Domini 1635 by William Aylet and John Georges as followeth vizt.

In the Hall—One oulde presse Cupbord, viij*s.*; one ould powderinge tubb, ij*s.*; one brasse Kettell, ix*s.*; two payles, xij*d.*; Three Chayres, ij*s.*; one payre of Trammells, one payre of potthookes, one grydiron and other Implements, iij*s.*

In the Buttery—One ould Iron pott, ij*s.* vj*d.*; eight pewter dishes, one saltseller, five pewter Spoones, v*s.*; one greate woodden Dishe with other smale wooden Dishes and other Implements, xij*d.*

In the Chamber over the hall—One Joyned Table and sixe Joyned stooles, xiij*s.* iiij*d.*; one halfeheaded bedstedle with one small featherbed and feather boulster, one blanket, one ould Coverlid, xx*s.*; one Chayre, one Cushion, x*d.*; one payre of scales and waightes with other Lumber, ij*s.*

In the Chamber over the Shopp—One halfe headed bedsted, one Featherbed, one feather boulster, one blankett, one Coverlid, xviij*s.*; one Little flockbedd, v*s.*; fowre ould huches and two little boxes, vj*s.*; fower payre of Towen sheetes, xvj*s.*; one Table Cloth, ij*s.*

His workinge tooles, v*s.*
His wearinge apparell and money in his purse, x*s.*
Summa totalis—vi*li.* xj*s.* viij*d.*
One Desperate debt due from John Luckyn of Little Waltham, xix*li.*
[Exhibited 16 April 1635 by Helen Coleman, relict and administratrix.]
Endorsement: the fees of this Inventorie come to ix*s.*

2.—An Inventory of the goods & Chattells of William Carding Late of Roxwell deceased taken & praised by William Thurgood, Kenelm Browne & Phillip Cragg November y[e] 27th 1637.

In the Halle—One Joyned table with a frame & a ioyned forme, 12*s.*; a ioyned press, 18*s.*; a Chaire, 2*s.*; a little table, 2 little chaires, 2 stooles, 2 bench boards, 3*s.* 4*d.*; a pair of bellowes, 1*s.* 2*d.*; a tramell, cobirons, a spitt, a dripping pan, a grediron, a chopping knipe, a pair of sheeres, 4*s.*; working tooles for husbandry, 7*s.* 6*d.*; 4 peeces of pewter, 5*s.*; a great kettle, 7*s.*; a warming pann, 2*s.* 6*d.*; one midling kettle, 7*s.*; one little kettle, 2*s.* 6*d.*; a posnett, 1*s.* 6*d.*; a frying pan, 1*s.* 6*d.*; an Iron pott & pothoocks, 4*s.* 6*d.*; Som is 3*li.* 19*s.* 6*d.*

In ye Parlor—One sheete, 6 napnins, 2 towells, 1 lay, 8*s.*; a Joynd press, 2 boxes, a chest, 14*s.*; a Wollen & a limen wheele, 3*s.*; a pewter dish, a platter, 2 poringers, 2 saucers, a spone, & a pewter bottle, a skillett, a wire candlestick, a cushing, 5*s*. 6*d*.; a little table, 6*s*. 8*d*.; a little beere vessell, 2*s*.; a payle, 1*s*.; [total] 2*li*. 0*s*. 2*d*.

IN THE BUTTERY—Two Beere vessells, a kimnell, a tub, woodde boules & dishes, a meale seive, a paile, 7*s*.

IN YE CHAMBER—7 bushells of wheate, at 5*s*. ye bushell, 1*li*. 15*s*.; a featherbed, 2 pillowes, a blankett & an old bedsteede, 1*li*. 3*s*. 4*d*.; a flock bed & bolster, a blanckett & bedsteede, 6*s*. 8*d*.; 2 chaires, 1*s*. 4*d*.; 5 new sheetes, 1 pair old sheetes, a tablecloth & other linnen all, 1*li*. 4*s*.; 2 Cests, 3*s*.

3 store piggs, 12*s*.
Wearing apparrell, 1*li*.
2 bonds, one for 7*li*, ye other for 4*li*., 11*li*.
Som totall is—23*li*. 12*s*.
[Exhibited 5 January 1637/8.]

3.—An Inventorie of all the goods moveables & Chattells of John Burrag thelder of Roxwell husbandman late Deceased Taken & prised the third Day of March Anno Domini 1637. by these whose names are hereunder written prised as Followeth: viz.

Inprimis for one bed, one boulster and one pillow, xxvj*s*. viij*d*.
Item for ij ould coverings, one old blanket and an old boulster, iij*s*. iiij*d*.
Item for A morter and a pestle, j*s*. viij*d*.
Item for pewter, iiij*s*. vj*d*.
Item for his wearing apparell, xj*s*.
Item for two pillow beers, iiij*s*.
Item for one chist and one box, vj*s*.
Item for one brasse kettle, xiij*s*. viij*d*.
Item for old brasse, vj*s*. viij*d*.
Item for one old yron pott and one old payle, ij*s*.
Item for two old siths, viij*d*.
Item for three broken chairs and one old kushin, j*s*.
Item for working Tooles, vj*s*. viij*d*.
Item for one old barrell and one old kneading trough, ij*s*.
Item for two old bottles, one bruch and old old sickle, j*s*.
Item for one bedstedle and two old Tubbs, vj*s*. viij*d*.
Item received since of Jeremy Danish of White Nottley being parcell of ye goods of the said Testator, v*li*.
Summa Totalis—ix*li*. xvij*s*. vj*d*.
Appraisers—Henry Cornish, Christopher John Clarke
An Inventory of the goods of John Burredg deceased remayning in his howse in Blacknotley praised by Jeremy Davenish and Edward Capron ye sixteenth day of September 1637 amount to ye value of thirty and two shillings. Hereunto wee have set to our hands.
Received in money being in a Cupboard at his said house, 19*s*. 9*d*.
Summa totalis—2*li*. 11*s*. 9*d*.

4.—An inventorye taken of the goodes of Bennett Gue of Writtle Deceased prized and valued by Thomas Casbolte, Richard Bridgeman and John George the 21th of Aprill 1638.

IN THE CHAMBER—One Fether bed & boulster, iij*li.* xv*s.*
Twoe payer of sheetes, xviij*s.*
One Brasse pott, vij*s.*
Twoe possnets, v*s.*
One Cheste, vj*s.* viij*d.*
One salte Boxe with other smale things, xij*d.*
In maulte, 28 quarters [blank] bushells, lx*li.* iiij*s.*
Sixe sackes, xvj*s.*
His wearinge Apparrell—xl*s.*
In monye in his purse, xiij*li.* vj*s.* viij*d.*
In bondes & other good debtes, xxvj*li.* viij*d.*
In desperat Deptes, vj*li.*
Debtes due by him to others x*s.* x*d.* ; vj*s.* viij*d.*
Summa—112*li.* 18*s.* [Should be 114*li.* less 17*s.* 6*d.* = 113*li.* 2*s.* 6*d.*]
[Exhibited 15 January 1638/9.]

5.—The goodes and chattles of John Osburne late of Writtle in y[e] Counte of Essex [?yeoman] praysed the 25th of Aprill 1638.

IN THE HALL—One great ioyned table, eigght stooles and one forme, 1*li.* 10*s.* ; one litle ioyned table, 2 stooles and one great ioyned chayer, 8*s.* ; one cubbard & one settle with 3 boxes in it, 1*li.*

IN THE NEW KITCHIN—One table & a forme and 3 bench boordes, 13*s.* ; one drippinge pann & one spitt, 8*s.*

IN THE BUTTERY—Six shelves & one plancke & a charne, 7*s.* 6*d.* ; six other shelves & 2 old cubbordes, 10*s.*

IN THE CHAMBER OVER THE HALL—One great ioyned chest, one glasse case and one table hutch, 1*li.* 2*s.*

IN THE CHAMBER OVER THE NEW KITCHEN—2 dosen of pewter & other smale sawcers and one salt seller, 2*li.* 12*s.* ; one beddsteddle, one feather bedd, one flocke bedd, 2 bolsters, one payer of curtoynes, one pillow, three blanketts & one coverlitt, 5*li.*; 3 old chests, 10*s.*; 8 payer of sheetes, 6 pillow beeres, 10 napkins & one table cloath, 3*li.* 5*s.*

IN THE CHAMBER OVER THE BUTTERY—One beddsteddle, one feather bedd, one trundle bedd, 3 blanketts, one coverlett, one feather bolster, one flocke bolster, 2 pillowes, one chest & one wicker chayer, 4*li.* 2*s.* 6*d.*

IN THE GALLERY—One trundle bedd, one boarded bedsteddle, one old table, 2 old formes, 12*s.*

IN THE CHEESE CHAMBER—3 brasse potts, one kettle, one brasse pann, one warmeinge pann, 3 brasen candlestickes, one morter and pessell, one chaffen dish of brasse, one skillet, 2*li.* 10*s.*

IN THE OLD KITCHIN—The capons coope, the beere stalle, one mouldinge boorde & a ploncke, 5*s.* 8*d.*

IN THE MILKE HOUSE—One powdringe troffe with a cover & other implements, 12*s.*

IN THE QUARNE HOUSE—one quarne, 13*s.*

His apparell and mony in his purse, 62*li.*
One flocke bedd att Thomas Osburnes, 2 blanketts & one flocke bolster, 12*s.*
One horse att Thomas Osburnes, 2*li.*
[Total—90*li.* 12*s.* 8*d.*] [Appraisers—John Woolmer, James Wattes.]
[Exhibited 15 January 1638/9.]

6.—An Inventory of the goodes of Joane Harris widdow deceased the firste of June 1638.

IN THE HALL—One table, one forme & one stoole, 9*s.* ; 3 chayres, 1*s.* 6*d.* ; one cubbord, 9*s.* ; one cobiron, 2 spitts, one trammell, one fier shovell, one payer of tongs, 3*s.* 4*d.* ; 2 bench boordes & other implements, 1*s.*

IN THE PARLOR—One ioyned beddsteddle, one feather bedd, one feather bolster, one pillow, one coverlett, 2 blanketts, one payer of cutaines, 5*li.* ; one cubbord, one chest, 17*s.* ; one ioyned chest, one wicher chaire, 9*s.* ; one greene rugg, 1*li.* 5*s.* ; 5 chusheons, 8*s.* 4*d.*

IN THE MILKE HOUSE—One cheese presse, one musterd quarne, one 3 legg chimnell, one charne, 7 cheeses, 2 milke bowles & other implements, 15*s.*

IN THE BUTTERY—3 kettles, 2 posnetts, one fryinge pann, one tubb, one dripping pann, one kimnell, 2 barrells, 2 wheles, one kneding troffe & other implements, 1*li.* 13*s.* 4*d.*

IN THE CHAMBER OVER THE PARLOR—One feather bedd, one flocke bedd, 2 feather bolsters, 3 pillowes, 4 blanketts, 4*li.* 10*s.* ; one ioyned chest 2 boorded chestes, one box, 1*li.*; 5 payer of sheetes, one casting sheete, 2*li.* 10*s.*; 2 long towells, 2 table cloathes, napkins and other linnen, 1*li.* 10*s.* ; the pewter, 13*s.* 4*d.*

IN THE CHAMBER OVER THE BUTTERY—3 bushells of wheat, 3 peckes of malt, one half bushell wooll, a warming pann & other implements, 1*li.* 10*s.*

2 acres of oates and pease and the grass about the dooles, 3*li.*
2 cowes & one calfe, one mare and colt, 5 sheep & 2 lambs & one pigg, 12*li.* 16*s.*
The wodd in the yard, 13*s.* 4*d.*
One acre of fallow, 6*s.* 8*d.*
The henns, duckes & geese, 14*s.*
2 heves of bees, 6*s.* 8*d.*
Her wareing apparrell & mony in her purse, 25*li.*
[Total—66*li.* 1*s.* 6*d.*] [Appraisers—John Wallis, John Woolmer.]
[Exhibited 15 January 1638/9.]

7.—A true and perfect Inventory of all the goods Cattle Chattell monye utensells mooveables & houshould stuffe of Henry Sharpe late of Writtle yeoman deceased Taken and Indifferently valewed & prised this 24th day of September Anno Domini 1638 by John Woollmer and William Chalke as followeth

IN THE HALL—One Table with Tressell & one forme & 3 bench bordes, 12*s.*; One Cubbord, one rounde Table with other goods amounting to the vallew of 1*li.*

IN THE PARLOR—One ioyned Table with 3 stooles, 13*s.* 4*d.*; One Bedsted with featherbed and Boulster & Trundlebed With furniture belonging to y[e] same, 5*li.*; One Cubbord with other goods amounting to the vallew of 1*li.* 10*s.*; Pewter, 1*li.* 10*s.*

IN THE GREAT BUTTRY—Twoe brasse Potts, 2 kettles, one Possnet, twoe dripping pan, 2 Spitts, one pillion & saddle with other goods amounting to the vallew of 3*li.*

IN THE LITTLE BUTTRY—Three Hoggsheads, one Binn with other Implements, 13*s.*

IN THE KITCHING—One Leade, one moulding borde with other goods, 1*li.* 5*s.*

IN THE OLD MILKE HOUSE—One Cheese presse, one Charne with other Implements, 1*li.*

IN THE MILKE HOUSE—One powdring Troffe with other Implements 1*li.*

IN THE CHEESE LOFT—Cheese, 10*li.*

IN THE SERVANTS CHAMBER—One borded Bed with furniture belonging to the same, 1*li.*; One old Chest with other Implements, 10*s.*; one paire of Scales & waights, 10*s.*

IN THE CHAMBER OVER THE PARLOR—One ioyned Bedsted with other furniture & Chest, 2*li.* 10*s.*

IN THE CHAMBER OVER THE PARLOR [*sic*]—One borded Bed with furniture & one Cradle, 1*li.* 6*s.* 8*d.*

IN THE CHAMBER OVER THE HALL—One Chaire, twoe blankets, 6*s.*; Ten paire of Sheets with other lynning, 5*li.*

IN THE BARNE—Wheate & Barley, 30*li.*; Otes & Pease, 12*li.*

IN THE HAY BARNE—Hay 40 loade, 40*li.*

IN THE STABLE—Cart Harnesse, plowe Harness with other furniture belonging to the same, 1*li.*

IN THE YARDE—Five Hoggs, 7*li.*; Twoe dung Carts Coops, one Loade Carte with a paire of drug wheeles, Two paire of harrowes, one plowe with furniture, 3*li.*
[Total—131*li.* 6*s.*] [Exhibited 15 January 1638/9.]

8.—An Inventory of the goods and Chattles of Robert Jackson late of Writtle desesed taken the first day of Novembre Anno domini 1638 by John Woollmer and Samuell Perey as Followeth

IN THE HALL—One table, 2 formes, one Joyned stole, 1*li.* 6*s.* 8*d.*; 2 little tables, 2 chayres, 8*s.*; 1 bench bord, 4 cushens, 1 payer of coberns, 1 tramel, one fiershovell, one payer of tonges, one clever, one payer of bellows, one gredgen, 13*s.*

IN THE PORLER—One Joyned bedsted with all that belongeth to it, 5*li.*; 2 chayers, 1 little table and one Joyned stole, 1 Cuberd, one warming pan, 1*li.* 15*s.*

IN THE CHAMBER OVER THE PARLER—One bedstedle with the furnytuer, 1*li.*; 3 Chest, one box, 2 Chayers, 1*li.*

IN THE CHICHIN—One leade, 2 tubes, 1 tramell, 1 pell, one forme with other Implementes, 2*li.*

IN THE BOWLTING HOUS—One bowlting tub, 2 sives, one Lanturne, one linenwhell, 4*s.*

IN THE MILKE HOUSLE—One bras pott, 3 cettles, 1 keller, 3 little cellers, 2 charnes, 2 posnettes, one musterd quarne, 2 skeulers [?coolers] with other Implementes, 3*li.* 6*s.*

IN THE QUARNE HOUSE—One quarne, one Cheaspres with Cheasmoles and Chesbreades, 10*s.*

IN THE BUTTRE—3 barells, one great tub, 2 spetts, 1 dripinge pan, 2 shelfes, one forme, 1*li.* 10*s.*

IN THE CHESESCHAMBER—7 leade of Chese, 5*li.*; for butter, 1*li.*; 3 shelvs and 3 bushells oates, 6*s.* 8*d.*; 8 peueter dishes, 2 sawtes, one dusone of peuter spownes, 1 Candlesticks, 4 sasers, 1*li.*

2 bord clothes, 6 payer of sheates, 5 napkins, one payer pillowbears, 3*li.*
2 acers of wheate, 4*li.*; one acer and a halfe of oates, 1*li.* 10*s.*
For hay, 15*li.*
4 Cowes, 16*li.*; 2 stears, 10*li.*; one Cowbollocke, 2*li.*; 2 hors, 7*li.*; 12 sheate, 6*li.*
2 acers of wheate sone, 4*li.*
One loade cart and one dungcart, 2*li.* 10*s.* one plow, 10*s.*; Cartharnes and plow harnes, 1*li.* 10*s.*
Fowles, 3*li.*
Frute, 1*li.*
One farm [fann], lodders, pichforks with all other Implementes, 10*s.*
His waringe Aparell and money in his purs with other desperit detts, 100*li.*
Summe is—203*li* 8*s.* 4*d.* [should be 203*li* 9*s.* 4*d.*] [Exhibited 13 March 1638/9.]

9.—An Invatorye of all and Singuler the goods that were Abraham Chalkes late of Writtell in the County of Essex Husbandman, At the day of his death, Praysed the v of Nouember 1638 by Edward Bowyn of Roxfilde [Roxwell] & William Aylet of Writtle as Followeth Viz[t].

IN THE HALE—One table, tow formes with a bentch borde and a kobberd and a payer of Tramels with tow kobyerns and tow spites and other implemetes, xx*s.*

IN THE PARLORE—One Goyne bedstedell with A fether bed and bolster, one kobberd and one Table and fower chests and a little table with other implemetes, v*li.*

In the chamber ouer the Parlor—Tow bedstedles with a bed and tow chestes with other implemetes, xl*s*.

In the Milkhouse—One chees laethe, tow pootes, one braspoot, another Iron poot and tow kettels and tow Tubbs and x peuter Deisses & other implemtes, xl*s*.

In the buttery—Three barrels, one kneding trofe, tow tubbs and other implemetes, x*s*.

Tow Carts with one payer of wheles, one Dewreake and a payer of Harrowes, one plow with the yornes and other implemtes, xxx*s*.
Tow Cowes and a wenall, vij*li.*; Tow Mares and the Harnise in the Stable, vj*li.*; Nyne Sheepe and tow lames, iiij*li.*; five gess, vij*s.*; one Sowhodg, x*s*.
Six payer of shetes and a Dusson of Napkines, iij*li.* v*s*.
Three Acers of Wheate, viij*li.*; fower Acers of Bullimonge, v*li.*; three Acers of Etch corne, v*li.*
Haye, xx*s*.
Thirtene Fowles, v*s*.
His waring aparell And the mony in his Purs, xxx*s*.
Sume is—53*li.* 17*s.* 0*d.* [Exhibited 15 January 1638/9.] See Plate VI.

10.—Nouember the sixte 1638. An Inuitary taken of such goodes as ware lefte by John Bur'owes Late of Writtell.

In the Chamber—Two bedsted and a flockbed and a blanket and anowld Ciuerin, on flock boulster and pillow, xiij*s.* iiij*d.*; on pare of sheetes, on pare of pillowbeares and two napkines, x*s.*; two litle Chistes, iij*s.* iiij*d.*; thre litell pewter dishes and on salt, iij*s.*; for other owld Lumber in the Chamber, ij*s*.

For his waring parell and the mony in his purs, xj*s*.

In the butery—Two kettelles, v*s.*; on brasspoot and on posnet, j*s.*; thre tubes and two kimneles, ij*s*.

In the hall—On owld table, two owld Chares, on Joyne stowle and apar of tramelles and a Wheele, iij*s.* iiij*d*.

In the Yeard—On Pige, xij*s.*; two pulletes, j*s.* iiij*d.*; two Ladderes, vj*d*.
The som is—3*li.* 7*s.* 10*d.*
[Appraisers—Thomas Borne; John Rowning.] [Exhibited 6 November 1638.]

11.—An Inventary of the goods and Chattels of Henry Carr late of Writtle decesed taken the Six and twenty day of November Anno domini 1638 by Symon Brecknot and John Woolmer as Followeth.

In the hall—One table, one forme, one benc bord, 16*s.*; one table Cuberd, 8*s.*; 5 Chayers, 4*s.*; one payer of Cobirens, fier shovell and tongs and tramells, 5*s.*; 4 stowles with other Implements, 10*s*.

IN THE PARLER—One Joyned bedstedle with the furnetuer, 4*li.* 4*s.*; one tabe [table], 5 stoles, 10*s.*; one Chest, 6*s.*; one Cuberd, 18*s.*; 15 payer of sheates, 5*li.*; one wicker Chayer, 2*s.* 6*d.*; one trundlebed, 3*s.* 4*d.*; 20 pouter dishes, 1*li.* 10*s.*; 4 Candlesticks, 2 Poringers, 2 saltes, 4*s.*; boles, 10*s.*

IN THE CHAMBER OVER THE PARLER—One Joyned bedsted with the furnetuer, 4*li.*; one other Joyned bedsted with the furnetuer, 3*li.* 10*s.*; one bedstedle with the furnetuer, 1*li.*; 4 Chest, 1*li.*

IN THE CHAMBER OVER THE HALL—One trundlebed with the furnetuer, 2*li.*; 10 pownd of woll, 8*s.*

IN THE BUTTRE—6 Cettles, one bras Pott, 3*li.* 10*s.*; 4 Posnetts, 6*s.*; 5 shelfs, one Charne, one Chese Coller with other Implements, 3 firkens, 1*li.*

Cartes, Plow and harnes, 2*li.*

IN THE BOULTINGE HOUS—One Cheslene, one quarne, 2 Caponcopes, one hogshed, 4 tubs, 3*li.*; one Kneding trof, 3 whels with other Implements, 10*s.*; one bord, one forme, 2 baskets with other Implements, 3*s.* 4*d.*

IN THE BARNE—Wheate, 8*li.*; barley 1*li.*; pese and oates, 2*li.* 10*s.*
Hay, 5*li.*

4 Cows, 12*li.*; 2 mars and 2 Cowlts, 5*li.*; 5 shepe, 1*li.* 10*s.*; 6 hogs, 4*li.*
Fowls, 1*li.* 10*s.*
Wheate sowne and 2 acers of barleland, 6*li.*
His waring Aparell and money in his purs—12*li.*
Summe is—96*li.* 8*s.* 2*d.* [Exhibited 13 February 1638/9.]

12.—An Inuentory of the goods and Chattles of Peter Woolmer Late of Writtle desesed taken the Six and twenty day of November Anno Domini 1638 by Siman Breckenot and John Woolmer as followeth.

IN THE HALL—One Joyned table, one forme, 1*li.*; one other table with a stole and a forme with 2 bench boards, 13*s.* 4*d.*; 3 Chayres, 2*s.*; one Whele, 2*s.*; one other Whell, 1*s.* 6*d.*; one payer of Cobeirons, tangs and fiershovell and tramells, 2 spetts, 8*s.*; Six Cushins, 4*s.*; baks [books] with other Implements, 13*s.* 4*d.*

IN THE C[H]AMBER OVER THE HALL—One Joyned bedstedle with the furnetuer, 5*li.*; 2 little tables, 15*s.*; one forme, one Chest, 5*s.*

IN THE CHAMBER OUER THE CHICHEN—One borded bed with the furnetuer, 3*li.*; one trundlebed with that belongs to it, 3*li.*; 2 Chest with the linen in them, 6*li.*

IN THE CHICHIN—One lead with 5 Cettles, 3*li.*; one Chespres, one Kneding trof, 13*s.*; 5 tubs with other Implements, 1*li.* 6*s.*

IN THE CHESCAMBER—Chese, 1*li.* 10*s.*; oats, 1*li.* 5*s.*; woll, 2*li.*

IN THE MILK HOUS—2 Charns, one Ches tub, 13*s.* 4*d.*; one forme, one plonke, one Pott of butter with other things, 16*s.*

IN THE BUTTRE—2 hogsheds, one musterquarn, 8*s.*; one bras pott and peuter, 2*li.* 16*s.*

One owld Cart and a dunge Cart Cope, 1*li.*
Plow and harowse, 10*s.*; Cart harnes and plow harnes, 10*s.*

IN THE BARNE—Barley, 15*li.*; hay, 5*li.*

14 shepe, 9*li.*; 3 Cows, 12*li.*; 2 hoges, 2*li.* 10*s.*
One serve [sieve], one boshell, one fann with other things, 10*s.*
2 acers of wheate sone 3*li.*; 4 acers of barle lond, 4*li.*
Fowls, 1*li.*
His waringe a parell and money in his purse, 5*li.*
Summe is—94*li.* 5*s.* 6*d.* [should be 93*li.* 11*s.* 6*d.*] [Exhibited 13 February 1638/9.]

13.—An Inventory of the goods of Francis Bancks the elder Late of [Roxwell] Taken & praised By Robert Sharp and William Crush the 5th of January 1638.

A table, a forme & a bench board, 5*s.* A kettle & a pott, 10*s.* A Cupboard, 8*s.* Two old bedsteads & sheetes & bedding belonging to them, 1*li.* 10*s.* Two Cobirons, a paire of tramells, a greediron, a fire shovle & a paire of bellowes, a how & a shovell, 4*s.* A tubb & a bottle, 4*s.* A barrell, a little tubb & a chaire, 2*s.* A Spitt, a posnett & his weareing apparrell 6*s.* 8*d.* Lastly a Cradle, 1*s.* 2*d.*
Som Totall is—3*li* 10*s.* 10*d.*
The charg of the buriall iij*s.* x*d.*
[Exhibited 15 January 1638/9.] [Also a copy on parchment.]

14.—An Inventorie of all the goods Chattells and moveables of Henry Bright thelder late of Roxwell in the County of Essex yeoman late Deceased Taken & prised the 5th Day of January Anno Domini 1638 by Thomas Saye yeoman and John Collin yeoman as followeth viz:

IN THE HALL—One planke Table with the Dorments, iij*s.* iiij*d.*; 5 joyne stooles, iiij*s.*; one glasse case iij*s.* iiij*s.*; 4 Chayers ij*s.*; one wicker Chayer, j*s.* vj*d.*; one other little Table, 2*s.*; 4 Cushions, 2*s.*; one payer of Trammells, 4 Cobirons, 2 payer of tongs, one fire shouell, one slice, a payer of bellowes with other ymplements in the Hall, vj*s.* vj*d.*

IN A BACKE ROOME—4 little tubbs, 4*s.*; one Mattocke, one grubbing axe, one bill, one axe with other small implements, 4*s.*

IN ANOTHER ROOME—7 boards & a Capens Coope with other implements, iij*s.*

IN THE LITTLE BUTTERY—3 Dozen of pewter Dishes, iij*li.*; one Duzen and 8 of saucers, v*s.*; one Flaggon, 2 salts, one Bason, 2 little pewter Candlesticks, 4 Chamber Potts with other implements, vj*s.*

BRASSE—2 brasse Potts, xx*s.*; 8 Kettles, 3 skilletts, one frying pan, one scummer, 1*s.*; 3 brasse Candlesticks, one Morter & pestle, vj*s.*; one baking Pan, iij*s.* iiij*d.*; 6 little shelves, a forme, & a stoole, a little Chest with other small implements, iij*s.* iiij*d.*

IN THE OTHER BUTTERY—4 little Barrells 4*s.* ; 3 Duzen of trenchers, 9*d.* ; 2 old Dripping pans, 3 spitts, 2 basting ladles, halfe a Duzen of woodden Dishes with other Implements, v*s.*

IN THE CHAMBER OVER THE HALL—Linnen, 13 payer of sheets, vij*li.* ; 6 Table Clothes, xx*s.* ; 10 Towells 8*s.* ; 6 pillow beeres, 10*s.* ; 4 Duz' of Napkins, 1*li.* 6*s.* 8*d.* ; his apparrell 30*s.* ; 5 silver spoones, 30*s.* ; one feather bed, one boulster, 2 pillowes, 1 Couerlett, 2 blanketts, one Joyne bed & y[e] Curtaines, vj*li* ; one halfe headded bedsted with 2 feather beds, 2 boulsters, 4 pillowes, 2 blanketts, one Coverlett & a rugg, vj*li.* ; one Trunke with 5 blanketts & 2 peeces of striped stuffe and small peeces of Darnax, xxx*s.* ; in the same Trunke, 2 Couerletts & one Carpett, 1*s.* ; 4 Curtaines, vj*s.* viij*d.*; 2 Chests & 3 trunkes, a Chayer & a stoole with other implements, x*s.*

IT IN THE CHAMBER OUER YE BUTTERY—One old joyn bed with a feather bed, 1 bolster, 2 pillowes, 2 blanketts with a trundle bedsted, iiij*li.* ; a nother old bedsted, 4 Chests, one boxe with other implements, xvj*s.*

An acre or neere of wheate on y[e] ground, xl*s.*
Summa totalis—xlvj*li.* xvj*s.* v*d.* [Exhibited 12 September 1639.]

15.—Januarye the 14th 1638 A True Inuentorye off the goods off Janne Barnard widow off Writtell the wyffe off John Barnard.

A bed Steadell & a Settell, 6*s.* 8*d.* A Flock bed, a boullster and Strawbed and a boullster, 12*s.* A Fether bed and a boullster and three pilious, 2*li.* 10*s.* Two darnikell Couer Lyds, two blankelts and a peese of a blankelt, 1*li.* 5*s.* Hallff off the Curtyans, 7*s.* A tablle, three Stoolles and a Forme, 10*s.* 4 pairs off Sheetts, 1*li.* 8*s.* 5 aprones, 10*s.* 3 pillowbeeres, 3*s.* 4*d.* 10 napkins, 3 towells, 6*s.* 8*d.* 3 Smoakes, 4*s.* 6 Coyffes at 6*d*, 3*s.* 5 Crose Loathes, 3*s.* 12 doubll Clouts, 3*s.* A Littell Small Linene, 2*s.* 2 Chestes and a box, 8*s.* 3 Cheyres, 4 kusens, 8*s.* 6*d.* One presse, 16*s.* One beareing kull and Face kercher, 12*s.* One old dish Cuboard and one old boull, 3*s.* 3 old peest kettells, 12*s.* 2 ould posnetts, 2*s.* 6*d.* One old goune, one ould Red pettecoat and 2 ould Wast Coats, 18*s.* 4*d* 2 ould Ruffes, 5*s.* One ould hatt, 6*d.* In money, 9*li.* 6*s.* 11*d.* *ob.* *qz.*
Total—22*li.* 6*s.* 5*d.* *ob.* *qz.*

An Inventory off the goods bequeathed In her Will as heareaffter Followeth

One black searge gowne, 2*li.* One Red pettecoat, 6*s.* One hatt, 6*s.* 8*d.* Her best Ruffe, 7*s.* One ould Cloak, 2*s.* One searg pettecoat, 10*s.* One gren aprone, 1*s.* 6*d.*
[Total]—3*li.* 13*s.* 2*d*
[Appraisers—Allexander Reynolld, Thomas Reeve, John Rowning.]
I Richeard Bridgman In the presenc off us whose names are heare written have destrayned all these goods heare mentioned For Rent and dyett which the said Janne Barnard widow have Received and houlden the tyme off Seawen yeares and upward
[signed] Richard Bridgman
[Exhibited 13 February 1638/9.]

16.—An Inventary of all the goodes moveables and Chattels of Thomas Raynebeard late of Roxwell in the County of Essex Weaver late Deceased taken & prysed the xxviij[th] Day of January Anno Domini 1638 by Reignald Sumpner Frances Purkas & Henry Pavett as followeth:

IN THE HALL—One Table & a frame, 2 Formes, two little ioyne stooles, the bench & bench board, one little playne table, one fyre shovil, a payer of tongs, two Cobyrons, 2 potthookes, one payer of Bellowes, the painted Clothes with other ymplements prised at 1*li.* 13*s.* 4*d.*

IN THE PARLOUR—One halfe headded bed stead, one old Feather bed with stript feathers, one boulster, one pillow, 2 blanketts, one Coverlett at 2*li.*; one presse Cupboard, 13*s.* 4*d.*; 20*li* weight of pewter, 6*s.* 8*d.*; 3 earthen Dishes & 3 glasses at 1*s.*; one ioyne Chest & 2 plaine chests, one Chayer with other ymplements in y[e] Parlour, 13*s.* 4*d.*

IN THE CHAMBER OUER YE HALL—One plaine bedstead, one Flockbed, one boulster, one pillow, 2 blanketts, with other ymplements at 1*li.*

IN THE BUTTEREY—Two little barrells, one Kneading troffe, two little Tubs, one little troffe, the shelves with other ymplements at 1*li.*

THE BRASSE—Three Kettles, one little brasse pot, one little postnett, one frying pan, one gridiorn at 1*li.* 10*s.*

IN THE SHOP—Three old Loomes with all other ymplements belonging to them at 5*li.* 10*s.*

One old Cowe & one bullock at 5*li.*
One Pigg & the Hay, 1*li.*

LINNEN—3 payer of sheets, 4 pillowbeeres, 4 table napkins, one table Cloth, 2 small towells, 1*li.*
His wearing apparrell, 1*li.* 6*s.* 8*d.*
Sum' is—22*li.* 14*s.* 4*d.*
[Exhibited 13 February 1638/9.]

17.—An Inventary of all and singular the goods of John Taverner of Writtle in the Countie of Essex husbandman deceased Taken & prized the 13th day of February Anno Domini 1638 by John Woollmer & Thomas Casboult as followeth

Two ould Chests, one boulster, one spade, one Cubord, his wearing Apparell with other Implements, x*s.*
In monye, xj*li.* xiiij*s.*
Summa totalis—xij*li.* iiij*s.*
[Exhibited 13 February 1638/9.]
[Also a copy on parchment on which a shovell is listed in addition to the items given above.]

18.—An Inventary of all and singular the goods & Chatell of Christopher Bellsted late of Writtle in the Countie of Essex Husbandman deceased taken and prized the [blank] of [blank] Anno Domini 1638 by Thomas Robbinson and James Watts as follweth vidz.

In the Hall—One Table, one forme, twoe Chaires & other Implements, xiij*s*. iiij*d*.

In the Parlor—One old featherbed and Bedsted, one Presse, twoe Chests, one Table with other Implements, iij*li*.

In a chamber—Three Chests, one Coverled and other Implements, xiiij*s*.; one Chest, twoe paire of Sheets, one Table cloth, one paire of pillowbeers & one dozen of Napkins, j*li*. x*s*.

In a Roome—Twoe ould flockbeds, two Bedsteds and other things amounting to xiiij*s*.

In the Buttry—Twoe brasse kettles, twoe brasse Potts and other implements, ij*li*.

In the milkhouse—One Querne, one Cheese Lar, Eleaven pewter dishes and other implements, j*li*. x*s*.

In the Barne—Wheat and Hay, in the Hay house, x*li*.

In the yarde—One Horse, one Mayre, one Coulte, iiij*li*. x*s*. ;Twoe Cowes, iij*li*. ; One Dung Carte, one paire of Wheeles, ij*li*.

His Apparrell and monye in his Purse, ij*li*.
By Bondes & Bill despearete, 79*li*. 8*s*. 6*d*.
Summa totalis—110*li*. 19*s*. 10*d*.
[See also No. 243.]

19.—A true and perfect Inventory of all the goods Chattle Cattle monye napery utensells & houshold stuffe of John George yeoman late of Writtle deceased Taken valewed & Indifferently prysed this [blank] day of [blank] Anno Domini 1638 by [blank].

In the Hall—One ioyned Table with a frame, one ioynd forme & 7 ioynd Stooles, 1*li*. 10*s*. ; one square Table, 2 foote stooles, one ioynd st[oo]le, 5*s*. ; 3 bench bords, 2*s*. 6*d*. ; one wenscot Presse, 1*li*. 4*s*. ; eight Cheires & one forme, 6*s*. 8*d*. ; twoe payre of Andrions, 5*s*. ; twoe paire of Tongs, one fire forke, one fire shovell, one fire yren, 3*s*. 6*d*. ; twoe paire of Tramells, 5*s*. ; a Jack, 10*s*. ; one musket, one birding peece with furniture, 1*li*. 6*s*. 8*d*. ; one pounde of yarne with other Implements, 2*s*. ; 5 Cushings, one paynted Cloth with other Implements, 8*s*.; one Booke of martirs, 2*li*.; other Books, 4*s*.

In the Parlor—One faire ioynd Bedsted & Trundlebed, 2*li*. 6*s*. 8*d*. ; one Featherbed, 2 boulsters, 2 pillowes, 3*li*. 10*s*. ; one grene Rug, 2 blanckets, 1*li*. 6*s*. 8*d*. ; one paire of vallance Curtaines, 1*li*. ; one wenscot Presse, one Cubbord cloth, 16*s*. ; one square Table & 3 stooles & one Box, 14*s*. ; one glasse case with glasses, 5*s*. ; twoe Chaires, 6*s*. 8*d*. ; 14 pounde of yarne, 1*li*. 1*s*. ; 71 pounde of Pewter, 3*li*. 5*s*. ; 2 brasse Candlesticks, 6*s*.

IN THE BUTTRY IN THE HALL—3 shelves, one little forme, one little Barrell, 2 Juggs, one strayner with other Implements, 6*s.* 8*d.*

IN THE GREAT BUTTRY—One Cubbord, one livery Table, 4*s.*; Three Hoggsheads, 10*s.*; one shelfe, one dishe case with other Implements, 9*s.*

IN THE KITCHIN—Twoe brasse Potts & one brasse possnet & one yron Pott, 2*li.*; five brasse kettles & one brasse pan, 1*li.* 10*s.*; 4 brasse skillets, 4*s.* 6*d.*; one yron dripping pan, 5 Spitts, 2 gridyrons, 17*s.*; one brass skimmer, one clever, one ladle, one morter, one chopping knife, one basting Ladle, 5*s.* 10*d.*; one frying pan, one Querne, one payre of Andyrons, 5*s.*; one dishe Case, twoe plancks with other Implements, 14*s.* 4*d.*

IN THE BREW HOUSE—One brewing led, 1*li.*; 4 brewing vessells & one Cooler, one under fatt, 2*li.* 10*s.*; one Querne, one cheese presse, one kneading Troffe, one meale Troffe, one Cheese Tubb with 7 cheese metts & 2 breads, 2*li.* 5*s.* 6*d.*; one old kettle, one Coope with other implements, 11*s.*

IN THE MILKE HOUSE—One salting Troffe, 8*s.*; one Table & Twoe Charnes, 10*s.*; Twoe powdring Tubbs, 6*s.* 8*d.*; Seaven kimnells, 11*s.*; one chopping block, one planck, 2 formes, 2 shelves, 4*s.*; 5 old Tubbs, one butter basket with other implements, 3*s.* 6*d.*

IN THE SERVANTS CHAMBER—One Trundle bed, one borded bed, 8*s.* Twoe flock beds, twoe boulsters, 1*li.* 10*s.*; Twoe [illegible, but ? coverlets], twoe blanckets, 16*s.*; Twoe leather Bottles, one broone hoock, one paire of winch pinnes with other implements, 6*s.* 8*d.*

IN THE CHAMBER OVER THE SERVANS CHAMBER—One Table with Tressells, 7*s.*; one Corne Binn, one bushell, one peck, one halfe pecke, 14*s.* 8*d.*; 4 Tubbs, 3 Riddles, one Sive, 5*s.* 6*d.*; [?Eight] Pitchforks, one dew Rake, 4 meade Rakes with weeding hoocks, 9*s.* 4*d.*; one Twoe hand Sawe with other yron worke, 15*s.* 4*d.*; one old Troffe, 3 Barrells, 4*s.* 6*d.*; Twoe paire of Scales & waights, 8*s.*

IN THE CHEESE LOFT—Cheese, 3*li.* 6*s.*; one Cheese planck with Tressells, 4*s.* 6*d.*; onnions, 3*s.*; shelves, 2*s.* 6*d.*

IN THE CHAMBER OVER THE PARLOR—One Standing Bed, 13*s.* 4*d.*; one feather bed & twoe feather boulsters, one flock boulster, 2 pillowes, 4*li.* 15*s.*; Curtaines & fringe, 10*s.*; one Kiverled, one blancket, 1*li.* 6*s.* 8*d.*; one Presse, 1*li.* 10*s.*; Six paire of Sheets, 2*li.* 8*s.*; Sixe pillowbeers, 10*s.*; one dozen of napkins, 6*s.*; halfe a dozen of napkins, 3*s.*; 5 table clothes, 8*s.* 8*d.*; Towells, 3*s.*; 3 wallets, 2*s.* 4*d.*; 3 baggs, 1*s.* 6*d.*; one Chest, Twoe Truncks, 16*s.*; 2 hampers, one basket, 4*s.* 6*d.*

IN THE CHAMBER OVER THE BUTTRY—One Standing Bedsted, 13*s.*; one featherbed & boulster, 3*li.* 10*s.*; one flock bed & boulster, 13*s.* 4*d.*; one Kiverled & blancket, 1*li.* 6*s.* 8*d.*; Curtaines & fringe, 13*s.* 4*d.*; one warming pan, 5*s.*; one Chaire, one Trunck, 8*s.*

IN THE CHAMBER OVER THE KITCHING—2 halfe headed bedds, 18*s.*; 2 feather bedds, 2 boulsters & 2 flock boulsters, 5*li.*; Twoe kiverleds, 2 blanckets, 1*li.* 6*s.* 8*d.*; Twoe sheets, 2 chaires, one old Trunck, 11*s.*; one one borded Cradle, 1*s.* 8*d.*; one standing Still, 12*s.*

IN THE CHAMBER OVER THE BREW HOUSE—Twoe flax wheeles, one Coope with other implements, 5*s*.

IN THE YARDES—One Waggon, 4*li*. ; one loade Cart, 5*li*. ; one loade Cart bodoye, 8*s*. ; twoe Dung Carts, 2*li*. 6*s*. 8*d*. ; twoe Cart Ropes, 6*s*. 8*d*. ; Six Gates, 2 Cribs, 5*s*. ; Wood 3 loade, 1*li*. 10*s*. ; one paire of winch pinnes, 2*s*. ; 2 Ropes, one Axe, 5*s*. 10*d*. ; 2 Sithe snaths & Cradles, 1*s*. 6*d*. ; one horse block, 2*s*.

IN THE BARNE—One [ba]rne cloth, one shovell, one sive, 10*s*. ; 6 Sacks, 2 fanes, 14*s*. ; five Cowes, & Twoe Bullocks, 26*li*. ; 24 Sheepe, 12*li*. ; eight Lambs, 2*li*. 13*s*. 4*d*.

IN THE STABLE—Three Cart Collors, with their Harnesse & foure paire of Harnesse with their furniture 1*li*. ; One Cart Sadle, one Collor with 2 paire of fill bells, 5*s*.; foure plow Collors with harness, one paire of new harnesse, 9*s*.; [illegible] bitt halters, 8*s*.; three Coller halters with yron Raines, 2*s*. 6*d*.; one paire of fetters, one paire of Cuplings, 2 barlings, 2*s*. 6*d*. ; one Saddle, one bridle, one pannell, 12*s*. ; one Corne hutch & j chaffe binn, 6*s*. 8*d*. ; one plowe, one paire of Harnesse & one Coulter, 2 plowe sha[torn away] with Chaines, 14*s*.

His wearing Apparell & monye in his Purse, 6*li*. 13*s*. 4*d*.

IN THE HAY BARNE—Thirty loads of hay, 25*li*.

Foure Cart horses & one Coult, 30*li*. ; twoe Hoggs, 2*li*. 10*s*.
Fifteene Acres of wheate, 47*li*. 10*s*.; eight Acres of otes & pease, 16*li*.; fourteene Acres Barley pease & otes, 18*li*. 13*s*. 4*d*. ; five Acres of fallow in Broadefeild, 16*s*. 8*d*.; fourteen Acres & a halfe fallow Preistsfeild, 2*li*. 8*s*. 6*d*.

Oweing the Testator By Bonde, 100*li*.
Summa totalis—389*li*. 4*s*. 6*d*.
[Appraisers—Thomas Eve, John Woolmer, Thomas Purcas, Richard Bridgman. Exhibited 6 November 1638.]

20.—An Invetrie of all the goods and chattels of Jeffre Bradley Late of Writle Decessed taken the 29th of Aprell Anno Domini 1639 by John Crush John Woolmer & Isacke Bowsey as Followeth

IN THE HALLE—One table, one forme, one Chayer table, two chayers, one bench, one bench borde, 15*s*.; one payer of cobiernes, one payer of tramells, one fiershovell, one payer of tongs, two spettes, one short forme with other Implements, 5*s*.

IN THE PARLER—One Joyned bedsted, one trundle bed with the furnetuer theorto belonginge, 3*li*. 10*s*.; two Cuberds, 15*s*.; one Chest, two chayers, two stowles, 9*s*. 0*d*.; thre cushens, one bible, 6*s*. 8*d*.; eight pewter dishes, one peauter pott, one pewter candsticke, 15*s*.; five payer of towin sheats, six napkins, one bordcloath with other linen, 1*li*. 10*s*.

IN THE BUTTRE—Two barells, one chearne, two shelfes with other Implements, 6*s*.

INE THE CHAMBER OVER THE PARLER—Tenn bushells Wheate, one coverlet, two ould Chests with other Implements, 3*li.* 6*s.* 8*d.*; two bedstedles and two flockbeds with other things belonginge, 1*li.* 6*s.* 8*d.*; two Chests, two seves with other things, 13*s.* 4*d.*

IN THE MILKHOWSE—One Cheselave, thre barells, fower owld tubs, one braspott, fower cettles, two posnetts with other Implements, 3*li.*
Eyght Cupples and seven sheape which are dry sheape, 5*li.*

Two Acers thre Roads of Wheate, 5*li.*; one Acer thre Roads of peson, 1*li.* 10*s.*
His wearinge Aparell and munneye in his purse, 1*li.* 10*s.*
Sum is—29*li.* 18*s.* 4*d.* [Exhibited 12 September 1639.]

21.—Thomas Larkin of Writtle, husbandman. 17 October 1639.

IN THE HALL—One Table, six stooles, one Joynd Cubbord, 4 Chayers, 2 little Joyne stooles, one little table & 2 formes & one bench ij*li.*; thirteene pewter dishes, fower pewter saltes, twe pewter Candlestickes, two lekers [?beakers], two porrengers, one bowle, one flagon & six sawcers and two plates, j*li.* 10*s.*; 3 spitts, 3 Cobkarnes with a payer of tonges, a fier pannet, 2 tramells & an Iron bar & a drippinge pan with other Implements, j*li.*

IN THE PARLOR—One halfe heded bedsteede with a fetherbed & 2 fether boulsters with all things belonginge to it, iij*li.*; one Joynd Cubbord, 3 Chestes, one Chayer & a box, xiiij*s.*; a warming pan, 2*s.*

IN THE CHAMBER OVER THE PARLOR—One Joynd bedsteed, one flockbed with all things belonginge it, j*li.*; one longe Joynd table & 2 formes, 2 stooles, & 2 Chests, x*s.*

IN THE CHAMBER OVER THE BUTTERY—One Troundle bedsteed with a flockbed & the things belonginge to it with other lomber, j*li.*; in Linen, 2 payer of flaxen sheets & 2 payer of towen sheets with six diaper napkins and two flaxen Table Clothes with other linen, j*li.*

IN THE MILKHOUSE—4 brasse kettles, 4 possnetts, one brasse pott & a skimmer with a morter & a bastinge ladle, j*li.* vj*s.* 8*d.*; a Cheesepresse, one Tub with a knedinge Trowf & other potts & things x*s.*; one greate planke, one powldring Tub, a planke upon Trestles, 4 shelves, one Chirme, 2 keelers, with milke pannes & other things, xiij*s.* 4*d.*

IN THE STABLE—One malte Querne, one Tub, one pannell with Carte harnes & plow harnes & other things, xiij*s.* 4*d.*

A lode Carte, a dung Carte, a payer of Harrowes, a plow & an Iron Chayne, j*li.* 13*s.* 4*d.*
Eight sheepe & 3 lambes, 4*li*; 2 mares & one mare Cowlte, ix*li.*; three Cowes, xij*li.*
2 acres of wheate, 2 acres of barly & an acre & halfe of pease & tares, x*li.*
His wearinge Apparell & Redy money j*li.* 13*s.* 4*d.*
Summe—53*li.* 6*s.*
[Appraisers—Matthew Marston, gent., John Wolmer.]
[Exhibited 17 October 1639.]

22.—William Bearman of Writtle. 21 April 1640.

iij acres of Wheat, 7*li.* 10*s.*
viij sheep, 5*li.*
One plow and Chaynes, 10*s.*
iiij Cowes and iiij bullocks, 23*li.*
Cart and Cart harnesse, 2*li.* 10*s.*
5 piggs, 2*li.* 5*s.*; iij Mares and one Colt, 5*li.*; iij sheep 15*s.*

IN THE CHAMBER OVER THE BUTTERY—Woolline yearne, 6*s.* 8*d.*; The lynen in the Chamber over the butterye, 1*li.* 14*s.*; vj bushells of Wheat, 1*li.* 2*s.*; one Chest, 4*s.*

IN THE KITCHIN—2 Capon coopes, iij basketts and other implements, 17*s.* 6*d.*; j tub, 5*s.*

IN THE CHAMBER OVER THE KITCHEN—2 quarters of Mault, 2*li.*

IN THE MILKHOWSE—2 hoggesheads, 2 barrells, one Flaggon pott, a Chamber pott, 2 brasse possnetts, one Cherne, and other implements, 1*li.* 4*s.*

IN THE CORNE CHAMBER—14 bushells of horscorne, 18*s.*

In wood, shovells, Spades and other implements, 10*s.*
Apparrell and money in his purse, 3*li.*
The powltry, 15*s.*
Summe—lix*li.* vj*s.* ij*d.*
[Appraisers—Peter Whetcombe, John Woolmer, John Weall, Thomas Robinson.]
[Exhibited 7 May 1640 by Elizabeth Bearman, widow and administratrix.]

23.—Gregory Shettleworth of Writtle, yeoman. 14 May 1658.

IN THE HALL—A table, thre forms and one Cubert and a paire of Coberns, tongs and fire pan and Certaine other things, 2*li.* 6*s.* 8*d.*

IN THE PARLER—A table and Carpet and a liveree Cubert and Carpet, five Jointe stools and Eight bucket stools and two Chaires and twelve Cushins, 4*li.*

IN THE CHAMBER OVER THE PARLER—A Joined bedstidle, Curtains and Valliants and two feather beds, one bolster and three blankets and two great Chists and three huches and two Chairs, 12*li.*

7 peuter Dishes, a flagon and other small peuter, 2*li.*
His wearing aparell and redie moniy—3*li.*

IN THE CHAMBER OVER THE HALL—One bedstid, Curtains and Vallants, one feather bed and bolster, one Civer lid and blankett, a trundle bed, one feather bed and bolster, one blanket, one trunke, two huches and one box and two Chaires and a paire of Coberns, tongs, and fire pan and other small things, 10*li.*

A silver bowle and thre silver spoons, 3*li.* 10*s.*
All the linin, 2*li.*

IN THE CHAMBER OVER THE ENTREE—Foure Brase potts, a brase pan and foure brase kettles and other small things, 3*li.* 10*s.*

The Chamber over the buttree—A plaine bedstidle, one floke bed, an bolster, an small things, 1*li.*

The buttre—An old Cubert and one barrell, six spitts and a Driping pan and a kneading trough and boulls and Dishes and other things, 1*li.* 10*s.*

In the kitchin—A lead and a peell and a Dresser bord and a quarn and a Coulle with other small things, 1*li.* 10*s.*
The some in all—46*li.* 6*s.* 8*d.*
[Appraisers—Humphry Glascock, William Boosey. Exhibited 9 February 1664/5.]

24.—William South of Writtle, husbandman. 3 July 1658.

In the Hall—One Cubard, two forms, one table, three chairs, one pair of Andireons, fire shovell, tongs & a pair of Bellowes, 1*li.* 6*s.* 8*d.*; one Ketle, thre brass skillits, one Chafeing dish and one warming pan, 10*s.*; twenty fower peeces of Peauter, of Severall Sorts waighing fifty thre pound at 12*d.*, 2*li.* 13*s.*; one Salt box, one pair of Tramills, three Joynt stools & a benchboard, 5*s.*

In the Butrey—Fower brewing vessells, three runlits, one halfe hogshead, one beerestal, one funnell, two bouls & some other implements, 1*li.* 12*s.*

In the Chamber over the Hall—One flock bed, feather boulster, one Bedstead, three pillows, one Covering, two blanckits & a matt, 2*li.* 15*s.*; two Chists, one box, fower pair of Sheets, two doz Napkins, 6 towells, five table clothes, 2*li.*

In the Chamber over the Butrey—One Meale tub, one sive, & some smal implements, belonging to husbandry, 5*s.*

In the Parlor—One feather bed, boulster, two pillowes, one blancket, one Covering, one Bedstead, & a trundlebed, 4*li.* 10*s.*

In the yeard, & ground—One Mare, five sheepe and two lambs, 5*li.*; two Acres of Barly, 4*li.* 16*s.*
In Wearing Clothes and redy Money, 11*li.*
[Total]—36*li.* 12*s.* 8*d.*
[Appraisers—Richard Crow, Robart Thorwgood.]

25.—Thomas Reeve of Roxwell, husbandman. 28 July 1659.

In the Hall—A Table, 6 ioynt stooles, five Quishons & a bench board, 1*li.* 4*s.*; 5 chaires & a little Table, 4*s.*; A payre of cobirons, trammell, peele, tongues, bellows & other implements, 5*s.*

In the Buttry—Fower beere vessells, 16*s.*; Nine Tubbs, 1*li.* 2*s.*

In the little Roome next to the Buttry—A Copper, 4 Kettles, 2 skilletts & a scummer, 3*li.*; Seaven cheese moots, a cheese bread & a bowle, 4*s.* 6*d.*; Shelves & a Tub, cooler, Kneading trough & other Implements, 14*s.*

In the milke house—A churne, 5 milke vessells, a powdring tub & 2 bowles, 14*s.*; fower shelves, 3*s.* 6*d.*; Frying pan, Gridgiron, dripping pann, 2*s.*; Earthen potts & other Implements, 2*s.*; Two payre of scales and weights & box Iron, 10*s.*

IN THE PARLOUR—A Feather bed & straw bedd, 2 boulsters, 3 pillows, a Coverlid, blankett, curtains & vallns & bedstedd & matt, 7*li*; A featherbed & flockbed, flock boulster, 2 feather pillows, a Coverlid, blanket, matt & halfe bedsted, 2*li*. 5*s*.; Nine payre of sheets & an odd one, 3 pillowbeers, 5*li*. 10*s*.; Table cloats & napkins, 1*li*.; A Cupboard Table, 2 chests & a chaire & box, 16*s*.; Two silver spoones, 10*s*.; Nine peuter dishes, 2 porringers, 2 sawcers, 6 spoones, 1*li*.; 2 dozen trenchers, 8*d*.

IN THE CHAMBER NEXT THE PARLOUR—A Feather bed, a flockbedd, 2 Feather pillows, flock boulster, bedsted & curtains, Coverlid and a blankett, 4*li*.; Two chests, 8*s*.

IN THE ROOME OVER THE PARLOUR—Wheat & barley, 2*li*.; Wool, 10*s*.

Wheeles & tubbs & old Lumber, 10*s*.; Two Carts & plough Irons, 3*li*.; Harness & pannells, 10*s*.
A horse & maire, 7*li*.
A paire of Harrows, 7*s*.
3 cows, a wennell & a calfe, 10*li*.; Two sowes & 2 piggs, 2*li*.; Nine sheepe, 3*li*. 10*s*.
3 Acres of wheat, 10*li*.; 2 Acres of barley, 6*li*.; 5 roods of pease, 2*li*. 10*s*.
A bushell, Fann, casting shovell, spade, mattock, shovell, Axe, bill, pitchforke & flayle, 13*s*.
Weareing Cloaths & money in his purse, 3*li*.
The summe is—83*li*. 0*s*. 8*d*.
[Appraisers—John Collyn, Richard Thurrowgood.]

26—Charles Cleark of Writtle. 20 December 1659.

IN THE HALL—One Large Cubbard, 1*li*. 10*s*.; one lesser Cubard, 1*li*.; one Table, forme, & one Joynt Stool, 10*s*.; Three Woollen Spining Wheels, 8*s*.; one Trapp Reele, 2*s*. 6*d*.; two high Chairs, two low chairs & one low Wicker chair, 5*s*.; Six Cushions, 5*s*.; one Glass-case & a Brass Sconce, 2*s*. 6*d*.; Two pair Andireons, two Spitts, one pair Tramells, & a pair Tongs, 8*s*.; one Warming pann, 3*s*.; Two old Cubard-cloths, 1*s*. 6*d*.; one Lead, 1*li*. 10*s*.; one Brass Candlestick, one Wyer Candlestick & a Baskitt, 2*s*.

IN THE PARLOUR—One Larg Cubard & Cubard cloth, 1*li*. 10*s*.; one Table and forme, 10*s*.; one letle Cubard, 5*s*.; one Chair, 2*s*.; one great Wicker Chair, 4*s*.; 2 Waistcoats, five petticoats & one pair Bodies, 2*li*.; one feather bed, two Bolsters, three pillowes, one Covering, two Blanckets, one Strawbed, Bedstead, Curtans & Vallance, Curtan-rodds, 7*li*.

IN THE BUTTREY—One great Ireon pott, 8*s*.; one Hogshead, one halfe Hogshead, two Brewing Vessells, one Keeler, one Cheesestand, & a Beerstall, 1*li*. 10*s*.; one letle Ireon dreaping pann, 2*s*.; one Kneading trough, 1*s*. 6*d*.; one Bushel & a halfe peck, 4*s*.; one Mustard quarne, 2 old Sives, 2*s*. 6*d*.; one pair Baskits, & their Cuppleings, 3*s*.; one old Brass Ketle, 5*s*.

IN THE CHAMBER OVER YE PARLOR—One flockbed, three Blanckits, one Bedstead, Matt, chord, one feather Bolster, one Straw Bolster and two feather pillows, 2*li*; one feather bed & Bolster, one flock bolster, Bedstead, Covering, one pair old Blanckets & two Matts, 3*li*. 10*s*.; one Chist with Cross

Barrs, 6*s*. 8*d*.; one letle Chist Carved, 3*s*. 4*d*.; one Chist with a lock above, 4*s*. 6*d*.; one other Chist, 2*s*. 6*d*.; two old Chairs, 2*s*.; one dozon of Table Napkins, five pair of Sheets, two Table-cloths, three pillow beers, three Aprons, thre Handkirchers and a Board-cloth, 4*li*.; Tenn putar dishes, two trencher plats, one pie-plate, one flaggon, fower Sausers, fower Spoones, one poringer, one Salt, and a letle frute dish, 3*li*.

In the Chamber over ye Hall—One old flock Bed, 5*s*.; one Table, 1*s*. 6*d*.; one old Chair, 6*d*.; two old Chists & a Trunck, 5*s*.; one Bedstead, and some part of another unsett upp, 15*s*.; two Boards and a Toole Box, 3*s*.; one Caveing-Sive & a fann, 4*s*.; one Childs Cradle, 1*s*. 6*d*.

In the Butrey—One Swill-tubbe & 2 washing tubs, 5*s*.; one Salting trough for Bacon, 4*s*.; one Capon-Coope, 1*s*. 6*d*.; two letle Stools & a Chair, 8*d*.; one old frying pan, & two gridireons, 4*s*.

In the Milk-house—One Cheese-press, 6*s*. 8*d*.; one Chirne, 5*s*.; one Butter baskitt, 1*s*.; five panns and potts, 2*s*.; fower Cheese-moats, 3*s*.; one Brass pott, & an old Ketle, 10*s*.; one Keeler, 2*s*.; two Skillits, 2*s*. 6*d*.; Two Pails, 2*s*. 6*d*.

In the yeard & upon ye ground—One Lye trough, & Leash, 1*s*.; Two Cowes, 8*li*; Eleaven Sheepe, 3*li*. 10*s*.; fower Henns & a Cock, 3*s*. 4*d*.; Two Acres of Wheat the rent deducted, vallued, 3*li*.

In debts & Redy Money, 18*li*.
Somme—71*li*. 3*s*. 2*d*.
[Appraisers—William Garrat, James Tavernere. Exhibited 9 May 1661 by Mary Hinson (*recte* Emson), daughter and administratrix.]

27.—Robert Harris of Writtle. 20 June 1660.

In the hall—Two tables, one forme, five chayres, one flax wheele, a payre of andirons, fier shovell & tongs, bellowes, one iack, three spitts with other implements, j*li*. 10*s*.

In the parlor—One table, one cubbord, one feather bedd, one feather bolster, one pillow, one ioyned bedsteddle, one flock bedd & bolster, one blankett & coverlet & other implements, 4*li*.

In the kitchen—One lead, 4 tubbs, a kneading trough, 3 sives & other implements, 3*li*.

In the milke house—One cheese presse, 5 cheese mooles, one stand, 5 milke vessells, & other implements, 13*s*. 4*d*.

In the chamber over the hall—One half headed bedsteddle, one flock bedd, bolster, one coverlett, 2 blanketts, 2 chests & other implements, 1*li*.

The linnen—7 payre of sheetes & other linnen, 3*li*.

The pewter—15*s*.

In the chamber over the parlor—One ioyned bedd, one feather bedd & bolster, one blankett & coverlett, one pillow, one ioyned table & forme, one presse cubbord, one chest, 4*li*.

The wheate, 10*li.*; the barley, 6*li.*
6 cowes, 18*li.*; 2 mares, 6*li.*; 3 hoggs, 3*li.*; 5 sheepe, 1*li.* 5*s.*
The cart, plow, harrowes & other implements, 10*li.*
The timber & his workeing tooles, 5*li.*
Pease & bullimong, 5*li.*
His wareing apparell, money in his purse, bonds, bills and desperate debts, 3*li.*
Summa totalis—87*li.* 3*s.* 4*d.* [should be 85*li.* 3*s.* 4*d.*].
[Appraisers—John Wallis, John Stonard. Exhibited 9 May 1661 by Mathew Harris, son and executor.]

28.—John Sapsfoard, senior, of Writtle. 28 January 1660.

IN YE HALL—One long Table with a Joynt frame, one forme & a Bench, 1*li.* 0*s.* 6*d.*; Three Chairs, Six old Cushins, one Glasscase with some implements, 6*s.* 6*d.*; one Court Cubard, 6*s.*

IN THE PARLOR—Fower Russia lather Chairs & one green Chair, 18*s.*; one Table & frame, and one forme, 6*s.*; one pair of Andireons with Brass Knobbs, and one pair of Small ons Suteable [torn away], 16*s.* [torn away]; one Covering for a Bedd, two feather pillows & a Bolster, 18*s.*

IN THE CHAMBER OVER YE PARLOR—One Joynt Bedstead, darnix Curtans & vallance, one featherbed, three pillows, one Bolster, two Blanckets & a Covering, 5*li.*; one Trundle Bedstead, feather-bed & Bolster, one Blanckett & a Covering, 1*li.* 15*s.*; one Wainscott Chist, 8*s.*; Twenty pair of Sheets, 10*li.*; one diaper Table-cloth & twelve Napkins, 1*li.* 2*s.*; five pair of pillowbers, 10*s.* Two Table clothes and twenty Table Napkins, three Towills & a Cubard-cloth, 1*li.* 5*s.* 6*d.*

IN YE CHAMBER OVER THE BUTREY—One Bedstead with green Curtans & Vallance, one feather Bedd, two Pillows, one Bolster, two Blanckits, & one Covering, 4*li.* 3*s.* 4*d.*; three old Chists, & one Box, 11*s.*; Sevarall Peeses of Peauter waighing 60*li.*, 3*li.*

IN YE CHAMBER OVER YE KITCHIN—One Bedstead with a Flox Bedd, one feather Bolster & a pillow, one Blancket & a Covering, 2*li.* 10*s.*; one Boarded Bedstead, one flox Bed & Bolster & Covering, 1*li.* 10*s.*; one old Chist with some implements, 2*s.*

IN YE BUTREY—Seaven Beere-Cask, and two Beere-stalls, 1*li.* 11*s.*; one Wooden Beame & Scales, 52*li.* Iron & 54*li.* Lead waights, Several Shelves, one pair of Hand Scales & other implements, 16*s.* 4*d.*

IN THE BREWHOUSE—Two Leads, 3*li.* 5*s.*; Two Malt-tubbs, 1*li.* 6*s.* 8*d.*; fower Brewing-tubbs, one Kneading Trough, with other implements, 1*li.* 2*s.*

IN YE DARY—One Cheese press, one Cherne, fower Cheese-moats, one powdering tubb, one Stand, three Keelers, fower Trayes, fower pales, fower Cream potts, fower Shelves, one powdering-trough & some implements, 2*li.* 1*s.*

IN THE KITCHIN—One great, & one letle Brass ketle, two Skillits, two brass Potts, one litle Brass Ketle, one old warming pan, one pestle and Morter, one Chafeing dish, Two Lather Botles, *2li.* 18*s.;* Three Spitts, two pair of Tramills, two dreaping pans, one pair Andireons, one pair of Tongs, one fire shovel & two pair of pothooks, 1*li.* 2*s.* 6*d.*; one press Cubard, 10*s.*; two Tables & frames, fower Joynt Stooles, fower Chairs, one Benchboard, with other implements, 16*s.*

Two Silver Spoones, redy Money & weareing Clothes, 8*li.* 5*s.* 8*d.*

IN YE BARNE & UPON YE GROUND—Seaven Cowes & a Bull, 30*li.* 10*s.*
Wheat Unthrash't, 40*li.*; Barley unthrash't, 16*li.*[torn away]; Twenty Quarters of Barly, 20*li.;* fifteene Quarters Bullimung, 10*li.*; Six Bushels of Tairs, 12*s.*
Tenn Store piggs, 5*li.*
One Wagan, one Load Cart & one dung-cart, 12*li.*
Three Horses, 16*li.*
20 load of Hay by Estimacon, 20*li.*
Ploughes, Harrows, & Hors-Harness with other implements, 3*li.* 10*s.*; Tenn Corne-Sacks, 1*li.*; two fanns, one Bushil & a Scrine, 14*s.*
two and twenty dry Sheepe, 12*li.*; Twenty yeare old Lambs, 5*li.*
Twenty five Acres Wheat & Rie, 50*li.*; twelve Acres of Barley Land, 15*li.*; five Acres of Pease, 2*li.* 10*s.*
Ten Lead (or 5Cwt) Cheese, 5*li.*
Somme Totall—324*li.* 18*s.*
[Appraisers—Richard Crow, James Taverner, William Garrat. Exhibited 9 May 1661 by John Sapsford, executor.]

29.—George Ramsaye *alias* Laurance. 2 February 1660.

IN THE HALL—One ould Cuboard, one tablle and forme, fyve Cheyres, two Littell formes, one Joynd Stoolle, one pair of Littell Cob Irones, fyre pan and tounges, a pair of ould bellowes, one warming pane with other Implements at twentye Shillings, 1*li.*

IN THE PARLOUR—One ould bedstsed, one fettherbed and two flocke boulsters, one Coverlyd, two blanketts, three Chests, two Cheyres at two pound fyve Shillinges, 2*li.* 5*s.*

IN THE CHAMBER OVER THE HALL—One bedsteed, an ould flocke bed, one flocke boulster, two ould blanketts, two Chests, one Littell tablle, two Joynd Stoolles, two wheells, one Reell at fourtenth Shillings, 14*s.*

IN THE CHAMBER OVER THE SHOPE—One bedsteed, one flocke bed, two blanketts, one Chest with other Implements at tenn Shillings, 10*s.*

IN THE BUTERYE—Two firkins, Sex Tubbs, one kneading Trough, three kettells, peuter—twellve pound at 10*d.* a pound, two pottes, one palle, two posnetts, one frying pann at two pound two Shillinges foure pence, 2*li.* 2*s.* 4*d.*

IN THE CHAMBER OVER THE HALL—Fyve Sheetts, one tablle Cloath, Sex napkins, one Littell tablle Cloathe at 15*s.*

For his Wearinge parrell and money In his purse fyve Shillinges, 5*s.*
The Tottall Soome is—7*li.* 11*s.* 4*d.*
[Appraisers—Allexander Reynoldson, Richard Bridgman, John Cooke.]
[Exhibited 9 May 1661 by Alice Laurence *alias* Ramsey, widow and executrix.]

30.—Humfrey Smith of Roxwell, yeoman. 23 February 1660.

IN THE HALL—A long Table, 2 Joynt formes, 3 chaires, a presse cupboard, a great cobiron, one spitt, fier shovell & tongs, 2 paire of trammells, 4 cushions, 2*li.* 6*s.* 8*d.*

IN THE ROOME OVER THE HALL—Two Bedsteds, one great chest & a little one, one Table & a forme, eight peuter dishes, a peuter bason, a peuter Candlestick, 2 salts, one chaffeing dish, & wooll, 2*li.* 12*s.*

IN THE PARLOUR—One Feather bed & bedsted, 2 boulsters, 2 blanketts, one pillow, one Coverlid, one chaire, one little Table, one ioynt stoole & a warming pan, 3*li.* 15*s.*

IN THE MILKEHOUSE—Two kettles, a brass pan, a brasse pott, 2 skilletts, a dripping pan, a frying pan, a Churne, a powdring tub, 2 milke bowles, a chesse presse, 4 cheese moots, a cheese bread, 12 Trenchers, a mustard querne, a payre of scales & weights, 4 wooden dishes & other Implements, 2*li.* 12*s.*

IN THE BUTTRY—Two Beere Vessells, a Tunnell, 2 Tubbs, a Kneadind trough, 2 axes, 2 wedges, a bill, 1*li.* 10*s.*

IN THE CHAMBER OVER THE MILKEHOUSE—One flock bed & bedsted & other Implements, 15*s.*

IN THE KELL HOUSE—A Copper, 3 Tubbs, a querne & a pale, 1*li.* 6*s.* 8*d.*

IN THE MALT HOUSE—Three Seame & sixe bushells of malt & Barley, 4*li.* 2*s.*; Two Tubbs, a Jett, a trough, a hairecloath, 2*li.* 8*s.*

A Cart, cart ladder & Harrowes, 2*li.* 10*s.*; Harnes, Collers, pannell, cart-saddle, rope, 12*s.*
Hay in the Hay house, 15*s.*
Mare & colt, 1*li.* 13*s.* 4*d.*
Wood in the yards, 2*li.*
Two Cowes, 6*li.* 15*s.*; 4 sheepe, 1*li.* 6*s.* 8*d.*; Two piggs, 1*li.* 6*s.* 8*d.*
Two Hoggs of Bacon & sixe pound of suet, 3*li.* 5*s.*
Old Dung Cart, plough & dew Rake, 10*s.*
14 Bushells of wheat, 3*li.* 14*s.* 8*d.*
Tenn Seame of malt in the Chamber over the parlour, 11*li.* 10*s.*
Weareing apparrell & money in the house, 2*li.*
The summe is—58*li.* 15*s.* 8*d.* [should be 59*li.* 5*s.* 8*d.*].
[Appraisers—John Colin and Philip Richmond, of Roxwell.]
[Exhibited 9 May 1661 by Joan Smyth, widow and executrix.]

31.—An inventorie of the goods & Chattells of Suzan Aylett late of Writle in the Countie of Essex widdow deceased take & apprized the eight daie of October in the yere of the lord one Thowsand six hundred, threescore & two by us Thomas Poole & Abraham Brecknock both of Writle aforesaid yeomen as followeth. now in the howse of Robte White of Writle aforesaid

One Joyned bedstedle with Curtens, one Featherbedd with boulster & blanketts to the same, one chest, two paire of sheete with some other lynnen, one presse, Cubbard with some other smale thinges in the Parlor, alsoe certen pewter and her monie in her purse with her waringe apparell. And alsoe the brasse with other smale ymplements, 7*li.* 2*s.* 4*d.*
Item from William Aylett for oates, 5*li.* 10*s.*
Item from John Aylett, 2*li.* 13*s.*
[Exhibited 11 June 1663.]

32.—Thomas Sharpe of Writtle. 23 March 1662.

IN THE HALL—One long table, one forme, six chayres, 1 chayre table, two litle stooles, two payre of trammells, one Jacke, five spitts, one dripping pann, eleven chusheons, one payre of bellowes, fier shovell, tongs & other implements, 3*li.* 10*s.*

IN THE PARLOR—One ioyned bedd steddle, two feather bedds, three feather pillowes, three feather bolsters, five blanketts, one coverlett, one rugg, one ioyned presse, one long ioyned table, eight ioyned stooles, two ioyned formes, one glasse case, foure chayres, one livery cubbord, one payre of curtaines, 12*li.*

IN THE CHAMBER OVER THE HALL—One Joyned bedd steddle, one feather bedd, two feather bolsters, one feather pillow, one ioyned table, one forme, fower chests, one wicker chayre, one presse cubbord, two blanketts, one coverlett with other implements, 5*li.*

IN THE ROOME OVER THE PARLOR—One trundle bedd steddle, one litle table, two chests, one box, one livery cubbord, 1*li.* 5*s.*

IN THE CHAMBER OVER THE LITLE BUTTERY—One bedd steddle, one chest & other implements, 13*s.* 4*d.*

IN THE TWO CHAMBERS OVER THE BUTTERY—One boorded bed steddle, two flockebedds, two flocke bolsters, two coverletts & old lumber, 2*li.*

IN THE TWO BUTTERIES—Five vessells, two drinke stalles & other implements, 3*li.*

IN THE LITLE MILKE HOUSE—One charne & other implements, 1*li.*

IN THE DAYRY—One ploncke table, one cheese presse, one forme, the milke vessells & other implements, 3*li.* 10*s.*

IN THE KITCHEN—Two leades, with brewing vessells & other lumber, 3*li.*

IN THE QUARNEHOUSE—One quarne & other implements, 10*s.*

IN THE CHEESE CHAMBER—The cheese & butter, 15*li.*

The pewter, 2*li.* 10*s.*; the brasse, 3*li.*; the linnen, 4*li.*

The Corne in the house & barne, 5*li.*

IN THE STABLE—Two horses & two mares, 26*li.*; one load cart, two dung carts, two ploughs, two payre of harrowes, the Collars & harnes & other old lumber, 13*li.*

IN THE STALL—Three fatt oxen, 36*li.*; Tenn hoggs, 8*li.*; sixteene Cowes & one bull, 66*li.*; Twenty three sheepe & Twenty seven lambs, 12*li.*; the hay, 5*li.*; five Colts, 13*li.*; twelve dry sheepe, 5*li.* 10*s.*

Tenn acres of wheate, 22*li.* 10*s.*; Twelve acres of pease & bullimong, 10*li.* 16*s.*; three acres & three roodes of fallow for barly, 5*li.*
His wareing apparrell, mony in his purse, bonds, bills & desperate debts, 200*li.*
[Total]—487*li.* 14*s.* 4*d.*
[Appraisers—Gabriell Collin, John Wallis, Anthony Browne. Exhibited 11 June 1663.]

33.—Widow Pery, late wife of John Pery of Roxwell. 1662.

IN THE HALL—One Joynd tabell with 2 formes and a sid bench, 2 litl tabells and one Joynd stoll, 4 chayers, one Joynd cubert, a litl glascase, 2 tramells, 2 cobyrons, a fier shovell and tonges, a curbine, a musket, a rest and banddoleres, one warming pane, 2 smothing yrons, 3 cushins, one cubert cloth, 3*li.* 14*s.* 10*d.*

IN THE CHAMBER OVER THE PARLOUR—One Joynd bedstedl, one fether bed, 2 blankets, one coverlet, 2 bolsters, curtaines and valianc, 5*li.* 6*s.* 8*d.*

IN THE CHAMBER OVER THE DAYRE—One bedstedl, one fetherbed, one blanket, one coverlet, one bolster, 2 pillowes, 2 chests, 6 payer of shets, half a dossen of napkins, 2 tablecloth, 2 pillow beres, 4*li.*

IN THE OLD CHAMBER—A bedstedl, one flockbed, one bolster and 2 blankets, 10*s.*

IN THE CHAMBER OVER THE HALL—One tabl and tressells, 6*s.* 8*d.*

IN THE BUTRY—2 spits, 2 posnets, 2 brase ketls, 3 hogs heads, a brase pot, 6 pewter dishes, one salt, 2 poringers, 6 pewter spones, one candellstick, 2*li.* 17*s.* 4*d.*

Wearing cloathes and monny in her purse, 5*li.*
Summe—21*li.* 15*s.* 6*d.*
[Appraisers—George Bayly, Abell Baker.]

34—Mary May of Writtle, widow. 8 April 1663.

IN YE HALL—One Cubard, one Table, Tressells, and forme, one Setle & an old chair, 15*s.*

IN YE PARLOR—One old Bedstead, one featherbed, two Boulstars, two pillowes, thre Blanckets, & one flock bed, 3*li.* 10*s.*

IN YE CHAMBER—Two Chaires, one old bedstead, Curtans, one Covering & a blanckit, 10*s.* 6*d.*; two Cobireons, one pair of tongs, one fire shovell, one Spitt, & one broken Warming pan, 8*s.* 6*d.*; one Wainsscott Chair, two Stooles, tow Wheeles, thre old pillowes, one table, a flaskitt, two Chists, & Severall other Small implements, 1*li.* 6*s.* 8*d.*
Wearing a parell & redy Money, 1*li.* 9*s.* 6*d.*
Some Totall—8*li.* 0*s.* 2*d.*
[Appraisers—William Garrat, Thomas Poole.]

35.—Jane Poole of Roxwell, widow. 15 April 1663.

IN THE HALL—One press Cubbord, one Cubbord, twoe Tables, one Forme, Twoe Joyned stooles, Three Chayers, 10*s.*

IN THE PARLOR—Twoe Bedstedles, one Bedd, one Press, Three Chestes with Linen and other lumber, one Table, Twoe Joyned Stooles, 1*li.* 3*s.* 4*d.*

IN THE PARLOR CHAMBER—One Table, Two bedstedles and bedds with Blanketts and Kiverlids, 11*s.*

IN THE BUTRY—Twoe Potts, Fower Kitles, Fower skilletes, one Cheese press, 16*s.*; Twoe hogsheads, Twoe barrells and a kneadinge Trough, 5*s.*

IN THE KITCHEN—[?Six] Pewter Dishes and six Sawcers, Fower Tubbs and one Querne, [?7*s.*].

IN THE CORNE CHAMBER—Twoe seame of Maulte & thre sackes, 2*li.* 10*s.*

IN THE BARNE—A parcell of unthrast wheate, and one skreene, one shovell, one Fann, 3*li.*

IN THE YARD—One Load Cart & one Tumbrill, 15*s.*; One Plough and Plough harness, 5*s.*; One Cowe and Twoe Bullockes, 4*li.*; One Horse, 2*li.*

IN THE [illegible]—[illegible] Sheepe and [?]Three piggs, [?]1*li.* 3*s.* 6*d.*
Ready money in the howse, 10*s.*
[Total]—17*li.* 5*s.* 10*d.* [should be 17*li.* 15*s.* 10*d.* if the figures inserted are correct; this deed is partially illegible.]
[Appraisers—J. Pulley, Matthew Nightingale. Exhibited 11 June 1663.]

36.—Robert Thurgood, senior. 2 June 1663.

IN THE HALL—2*li.*

IN THE PARLER—The linin, 3*li.*; on fetherbed, to coverlets, on boulster, to blanckes, and curtens, 4*li.* 10*s.*; on chest, pe[w]tter, 5 chushens and a buckstins, 2*li.*

THE CHAMBER—To fetherbeds, thre boulsters, on flockbed, thre flockboulsters, on Rugg, on paier blanckets and a chest, 5*li.* 13*s.*

CHAMBER OVER THE BUTTRI—Certain goods, 1*li.* 15*s.*

THE BUTRI—Bras and other things, 1*li.* 10*s.*

IN THE OWLD HOUS—to lables [*recte* tables], thre ould bedsteeds and other lumber, 3*li.*

THE BARN—On scru [one screw], 10*s*.
The Som is—23*li*. 18*s*. 4*d*. [should be 23*li*. 18*s*.]
[Appraisers—Richard Bridgman, sen., William Allet, sen. Exhibited 11 June 1663.]

37.—Richard Porter of Writtle, baker. 9 June 1663.

One stack of Faggot wood and some other wood In the yeard—4*li*.
One ligh-trough, 2 laders, 2 Baskits, 2 panils & some other things, 10*s*.
One White horss, 3*li*. 10*s*.

IN THE KITCHEN—18 Severall peeces of Puter, waighing 24*li*. at 10*d*. a pound, 1*li*.; one Ireon pott, and 9 Severall peeces of Brass vallued at 1*li*. 6*s*. 8*d*.; one Jack, two pair of Cobireons, fire shovel, Bellowes, tongs & a Spitt, 1*li*.; 4 Ireon Wedges, one Saw, one ax, a Hatchit and some other Smal things, 10*s*.; one dresser, one letle Table, a Cubard, 5 Chairs & a lanthorn, 13*s*. 4*d*.

IN THE BAKE-HOUSE—One Quarter of Wheat meale, 1*li*. 12*s*.; one Seame of Wheat, 1*li*. 12*s*.; two Kneading troughs, one Moulding boord, two tubbs, a Baskit, a Bush: Sacke, one Empty hogshead and two plancks, 1*li*.; one pair Scales, three Stone Weights, one beame and some other implements, 10*s*.

IN THE HALL—One Table & frame, two Chairs, one Court Cubord, one pair of Andireons, fire shovell & firefork, 1*li*. 10*s*.

IN THE PARLOR—One Cradle, three old Baskits, one forme, one frame for a Table, one planck, 1*li*.

IN THE CHAMBER OVER THE PARLOR—One Feather Bed and Bedstead, Curtans, Vallance, one Covering, one Rugg, two Blanckits, 6*li*.; one Chair, and a Letle table, 5*s*.

IN THE BUTREY—Two Barrills, one Hogshead, one powdering tub, one Side Sadle & a pillion, 1*li*. 5*s*.

IN THE CHAMBER OVER THE KITCHIN—One Bed, Bedstead, Curtans & Vallance, Blanckit, Covering, 4*li*.; one Trundle bedstead, one flock bed, two pillowes & a Bolster, 1*li*.; two Chists, thre truncks, one Box, one pair of Bellows, one Sword & a halbert, 1*li*.

4 dozen of Napkins, 5 Table Clothes, 6 pair of Sheets, 4 pair of Pillow beeres, & 6 Towills, 6*li*. 10*s*.
In redy Money and wearing Cloths—5*li*.
[Total]—44*li*. 14*s*.
[Appraisers—William Garrat, John Cooke. Exhibited 11 June 1663.]

38.—John Woolmer of Writtle, yeoman. 20 August 1663.

IN THE HALL—Two tables, & eight joind stooles, A forme, a presse Cubboard, a livery Cubbard, a Jack, 4 Spits, An Iron dripping pan, 6 chair's, two pair of Cobirons, tongues, & fier shovell, with other implements belonging to the hall, 5*li*.

IN THE PARLOR—A joind bedstead, a fetherbed, a bowlster, two pillows, a pair of blankets, a trundle bedstead, A greate Chest, a table, 6 joind stools, 5 chairs, 6 cushions, with other implements, 10*li*. 10*s*.

In the little buttery—3 barrells, a glasse case with other implements, 1*li.*

In the buttery—An iron pott, a brasse pot, 3 posnets, a brasse candlestick, an hogshead with other implements, 1*li.*

In the Milkhouse—A powdering tub, a stand, Churne, two keelers with other implements, 1*li.* 4*s.*

In the brewing house—Two leads, a great trough, a wash bowle, 5 tubs with other implements, 4*li.* 5*s.*

In the bowlting house—A cheese presse, a kneading trough, a meale tub with other implements, 1*li.*

In the chamber over the parlor—Two bedsteads, two fether beds, 3 bowlsters, two Coverlets, 3 blankets, two pair of Curtains, & valians, a Rug, two presses, two chests, a chair, two pair of Cobirons, with other implements, 12*li.*

In the Corn Chamber—Three chests, a skreene, malt, & Oat's, with other implements, & woole, 4*li.* 6*s.*

In the cheese chamber—Cheese, 2 pair of baskets with other lumber in the next Roome, 3*li.*

In the buttery chamber—A fetherbed, bowlster, pillow, a blanket, a coverlet, cutains, two stooles, 2 livery Cubbards, 2 Wicker chairs, 4*li.* 10*s.*

In the Quern house—A Quarn with other lumber, 1*li.*

In an old chamber—A bedstead, 3 blankets, a coverlet, one tub, some pease with other implements, 1*li.* 10*s.*

A paire o scales, weights, wedges, forks, & other necessarys belonging to husbandry, 1*li.* 4*s.*

Pewter & warming pan, 2*li.*; Linon, 4*li.*; Bookes, 1*li.* 2*s.*

Four cowes, two heifers, 19*li.*; A horse, & Colt, 5*li.*; Sheepe—thirty one 9*li.*
The Corne abroad, 10*li.*; The Hey in the barn, 18*li.* 10*s.*
The wood, Cribe, timber & other things, 8*li.*
Horse harnish, 1*li.* 10*s.*
Sow, & piggs, 3*li.*
Carts, ploughs, and harrow's, 8*li.* 5*s.*

In the malt house—A malt tub, 2 ladders, & other things, 3*li.*

The Dung, & fallows, 6*li.* 18*s.* 6*d.*

Mony in his purse, & his wearing cloaths, 19*li.* 6*s.* 8*d.*
Summe—90*li.* [should be 170*li.* 1*s.* 2*d.*; the total shown on the inventory is in a different hand, and appears to have been altered from 80*li.*]
[Appraiser—William Boosey. Exhibited 17 December 1663.]

39.—Henry May, senior. 2 December 1663.

In ye Chamber over the Butrey—One Bedstead & feather bed, one pair of Blanckits, one Rug, Curtans & Vallance & a Trundle bedstead, 4*li.*; two Chists, five Chaires, fower stooles, fower Cushins & some other small implements, 13*s.* 4*d.*; one Cubard, and one livery Cubard, one round table, one glasscase & a letle Box, 1*li.* 6*s.* 8*d.*; two pair sheets & one doz of Napkins, one pare pillowbers, one Table cloth 18*s.*; Nine Severall peices of pewter waighing by Estimacion 25*li.*, 1*li.*

IN THE CHAMBER OVER THE LITLE BUTREY—Two Bedsteads, one old featherbed & a flock bed, one course rugg, one pair Curtans & vallancs of Linsey Wolsey to one of the beds, & one Covering, 2*li.*; one old Chist, one broken Cubard, & a frame for a stoole, 5*s.*; one brass pott, three Small panns or Ketles, one skillitt & some other small things, 1*li.*

IN THE BUTREY—One Table & frame, one Beere-stall, two old Tubbs & some old lomber, 6*s.*

IN THE PARLOR OR GREAT BUTREY—One Cubard, one Kneading trough, two boards, two Small Ketles, one Ireon pott & one pair of Cobireons, 15*s.*
[Total]—12*li.* 4*s.*
[Appraisers—William Garrat, Richard May.]

40.—Gamaliell Rathbane of Writtle, gentleman. 2 March 1663.

IN THE BEST CHAMBER—One featherbedd, one Flocke bedd, one feather Bolster, one Pillowe, one Bedsted with Matt and Corde, Two Coverletts, Three Blanketts, Three Curtaine Rodds, Three Blanketts, Three old stayned Curtaines, 4*li.*

MORE IN THE BEST CHAMBER—Three Chests, two Trunkes, two little Tables, sixe Jointstooles, one Joynd chaire, Three Cushions, one Glasse Case, two lookinge Glasses, a Birdinge peece, one paire of Cobirons, a fire shovell and Tonges, a paire of Bellowes, a Saltboxe, a paire of Trammells, fower old Candlesticks, a smoothinge Iron, Two paire of flaxen sheets, three Pillowbeeres, a Dozen of Napkins, Three Towells, two shirts, two Table Cloathes, 4*li.* 8*s.*

IN THE OLD CHAMBER—One Cupboard with Drawers, two Chests, one Trunke, fower boxes, a Napkin Presse with two swords & other Lumber, 2*li.* 10*s.*

MORE IN THE OLD CHAMBER—A parcell of Bookes, Twenty Pewter Dishes, Twelve Sawcers, sixe Porrengers, one Pewter Bason, one Quart pott, one Pewter Chamber pott, three Brasse Potts, one Chaffer, one Pestle and Morter, Three Skilletts, Two small kettles, one fryinge Panne, one Drippinge Pann, Three Spitts, an Iron Spade, 6*li.* 10*s.*

IN THE SHOPP—Turninge Tooles, 13*s.* 4*d.*

IN WEARINGE APPARELL AND MONEY IN HIS PURSE—9*li.* 19*s.* 4*d.*

Due to the deceased in debts upon bond & otherwise about—70*li.*
The whole summe of this Inventary . . . doth amount unto—98*li.* 0*s.* 8*d.*
[Appraisers—Anthony Sturgeon of Chelmsford, woollen-draper; Michael Grove, junior, of Moulsham, yeoman.]
[Exhibited 11 June 1663.]

41.—Thomas Lines of Roxwell, victualler. 28 March 1664.

For the goods in the halle—1*li.* 10*s.*
For the goods in the parller—4*li.*
For the goods in the buttery—hogsheads, bere, pewter and tine [tin], 4*li.* 1*s.*
For the goods in the Chichin—Copper, brase, bruing vessels and other inplements, 4*li.* 10*s.*
For the goods in the best Chamber—4*li.* 10*s.*
For the goods in the Littelle Chamber—3*li.* 1*s.*
For the goods, pewtter and lining—2*li.* 15*s.*
For the haye in the barne—1*li.* 15*s.*
For the wood in the yarde—3*li.* 1*s.*
For olde hoppols [hop-poles]—1*li.*
For a soue and 4 pigs—1*li.* 10*s.*; for 2 shipe and fower lambs—1*li.* 2*s.*
For bills, bonds and desperret deptts—4*li.*
For wearing apearrelle and mony in his purse—2*li.* 10*s.*
Some—39*li.* 5*s.*
[Appraisers—Thomas Crush, senior, Thomas Coxe.]
[Exhibited 2 June 1664.]

42.—William Stringer of Writtle. 26 April 1664.

In Bonds—60*li.*
In Bonds—75*li.*
In Ready money—50*li.*
5 Parye of Sheetes, 2*li.* 10*s.*; 5 Table Cloathes, 1*li.* 5*s.*; other Smale Linnen 10*s.*
5 Smale Silver spoomes, 1*li.*; 2 Chests 10*s.*; a pillow & a little Chest 1*s.*; a large Bible 10*s.*; other Smale Bookes 2*s.*
His weareing Apparrell 3*li.*
In his pocketts 1*s.* 6*d.*
Summa Totalis—204*li.* 9*s.* 6*d.* [should be 194*li.* 9*s.* 6*d.*]
[Appraisers—John Holmes, senior, Richard May.]
[Exhibited 2 June 1664.]

43.—An inventory of the goods & Chattels of Thomas Hakins late of Rittle in the Countie of Essex yeman deceased take & aprised the eight Day of June in yere of oure Lord 1664: by Abraham Breknok & Thomas Turnige both Wittness aforesaid yeoman as foloweth now in the house of Robert White as writtiten aforesaid.

In the hall—One bible, one table and a form and one little tablle, one Chaire, 2 spits, one driping pan with a few other inplements, 13*s.* 4*d.*

In the parler—One Joined tablle with 6 stooles & one press Cubbard, one Chest with some other small inplements, 1*li.* 13*s.* 4*d.*

In the Chamber over the hall—One Joined bedsted & Curtains, with a featherbed & one feather bolster & one feather pillow, one Covering & 2 blankets: one little table & 2 stooles, 2*li.* 13*s.* 4*d.*; 2 huches and one old trunck, 2 paire of sheets & a Dosen & a halfe of napkins, a dosen small dishes of peuter, 1*li.* 6*s.* 8*d.*

IN THE CHAMBER OVER THE MILKHOUSE—One halfe headed bedsted with one feather bed, with one bolster & a pillow & one Covering & ablankett with other small inplements, 13*s.* 4*d.*

IN THE MILKHOUSE—2 brasse kettels, 1 scillet & one Cheesepresse & one Churne & other small milk vessels, 15*s.* 6*d.*

IN THE BOULTING HOUSE—One kneading trough & one planke, 3*s.* 4*d.*

IN THE BUTTERY—2 barells & some other smal innplements, 3*s.* 6*d.*

IN THE KICHING—one lead & 3 tubs and some other small inplements, 1*li.* 3*s.* 4*d.*

2 old Cows, 4*li.*, & an old mare & her fole, 1*li.* 15*s.*
One old Cart, one paire of harows with some other innplements, 13*s.* 4*d.*
One acre of Wheat and five roods of barly, 2*li.* 6*s.* 8*d.*
His wearing aparell & mony in his purse—1*li.* 3*s.* 4*d.*
[Total]—18*li.* 14*s.* [should be 19*li.* 4*s.*]
Written by Sam Kent this eight day of June. [Exhibited 2 June 1664.]

44.—Mary Mitchell of Roxwell.

IN YE PARLOR—[torn away] fether beed, on fether boulster, [torn away] fether pillows, 2 blanckets, [torn away] Coverlid, 3*li.*
[Torn away] flock beed, 2 flocke boulsters, [torn away] blanckets, 1*li.*; [torn away] Cupboard, 12*s.*; one short tabill with adrawer in it, 12*s.*; one Chest and one small box, 5*s.*; on plonck, on Chayer, 2 litelt stoolles, on short forme, on salt box, one oatmeale box, 8*s.* 6*d.*; 2 payer of Canvit sheets, one short tabill Cloath, 2 napkins, 2 pillow beers, 1*li.* 4*s.*; one warming pan, on litill kitill, 2 litill ould postnets, on bird spit, 7*s.* 6*d.*
The pewter, and on ould morter and pesltill, 12*s.*
On paye of quarnes stoones, 3*s.* 6*d.*
On old bibill, 2*s.* 6*s.*
[Total 8*li.* 7*s.*]
[Appraisers—Thomas Bogas, Thomas Warner, William Coallman.]
[Exhibited 21 July 1664.]

45.—Henry Dorington of Writtle.

IN THE HALL—One table, 4 chaires, one stoolle, one forme, fire pan an tonges, and other small things, 16*s.*

IN THE PARLER—One bedstedle, one flock bed, one bolster, 3 Chest, one Cubert, 3 boxes, 2 Chaires and other small things, 1*li.* 10*s.*

THE CHAMBER OVER THE PARLER—A trundle bed and beding, 2 Chest with all other od things, 1*li.* 11*s.* 6*d.*

IN THE BUTTREY—4 tubs, 2 barrells and a kneading trough, and one paill with other small things, 1*li.* 9*s.*

3 kettles, 2 pots, 3 skellets of Brase, 3*li.* 6*s.* 8*d.*
3 peuter Dishes, six spoons, 6*s.* 8*d.*
3 paire of sheets and all other linin, 1*li.* 2*s.* 6*d.*

4 sheep, 1*li.* 6*s.* 8*d.*; 2 pigs, 13*s.* 4*d.*
A spade, a shovell, a mathock, other tools, 5*s.*
A malt quarne, 6*s.* 8*d.*
Fire wood, 4*s.*
Wearing parell and ready money, 12*li.*
[Total]—24*li.* 18*s.*
[Appraisers—William Boosey of Writtle, Lawrence Poole of Broomfield.]
[Exhibited 9 February 1664/5.]

46.—Edward Halden of Writtle. 12 September 1665.

IN THE HALL—One great table, one litle table, two formes, two benches & one bench borde, two litle stooles, one cubborde, three chayers, two payre trammells, two andirons, fire shovell & tongs, one payre of bellowes, one bible & other implements, 1*li.* 15*s.*

IN THE PARLOR—One ioyned beddsteddle, one feather bedd, two feather bolsters, one feather pillow, 2 blanketts, 2 coverletts & one strawbedd, 5*li.*; one borded beddsteddle, one flock bedd, one feather bolster, 2 blanketts, one coverlett, 13*s.* 4*d.*; one great ioyned chest, 10*s.*; one ioyned table, six ioyned stooles, 2 leather chayres, 1*li.* 6*s.* 8*d.*; one presse cubbord, & one litle table, 1*li.*

IN THE KITCHEN—2 brasse potts, 3 brasse kettles, 3 skilletts, one lead, one warming pann, 2*li.* 10*s.*; one boulting tunn & other implements, 6*s.* 8*d.*

IN THE BUTTERY—2 hoggsheades & 3 litle barrells, 4 old tubbs with other implements, 1*li.* 16*s.*

IN THE MILKE HOUSE—One cheese presse, one powdring trough, one stand, one cheese tubb, one powdring tubb, 2 trayes, 5 bowles, 4 cheese mooles, one charne, 5 shelves & one forme, one frying pann, one spitt, one dripping pann, one clever & other inplements, 3*li.*

IN THE CHAMBER OVER THE HALL—One ioyned beddsteddle, one feather bedd, two feather bolsters, 5 feather pillowes, one mattrice, 2 blankett, one rugg, one payre of curtaines, 5*li.* 5*s.*; 5 chests & one box, one wicker chayer & other implements, 1*li.* 5*s.*

IN THE CHAMBER OVER THE PARLOR—The wheate, 6*li.* 8*s.*; the cheese, old & new, 6*li.*; 3 shelves & other inplements, 10*s.*

THE LINNEN—8 payer of towing sheetes, 2 payer of flexen, 1 dosen of napkins, 4 towells, 5 tables cloathes, one cubbord cloathe, 4*li.* 10*s.*

THE PEWTER—One salt seller, 16 peeces of pewter, 2 sallett dishes, one dosen & halfe of spoones, 2*li.* 13*s.* 4*d.*

IN THE CHAMBER OVER THE KITCHEN—One borded bedsteddle, one flock bedd, one flock bolster, one old blankett, one coverlett with other implements, 13*s.* 4*d.*

IN THE CHAMBER OVER THE BUTTERY—2 dew Rakes, one screw, one bushell, 5 pitch forkes, 3 siths, one spade, one shovell, one mattock, one saw, 9 old sacks, one fann, one caving sive & othe implements, 3*li.*

The woole, 1*li.* 10*s.*
Barley & oates in the chamber, 2*li.* 9*s.*
5 horses, 27*li.*; 6 cowes, 19*li.*; 2 wennell calves 1*li.* 12*s.*; 4 hoggs, 3*li.*; 10 sheates, 3*li.* 10*s.*
The wheate in the barne, 24*li.*; the barley in the barne, 20*li.*; the pease & oates, 6*li.* 10*s.*; the hay, 3*li.* 6*s.* 8*d.*
The fallow, 17*li.*
2 load carts, 4*li.* 10*s.*; 3 dung carts, 2*li.* 10*s.*; one plough & chaines & shares & coulter, 8*s.*; one payre of harrowes, 6*s.*; two payre cart & 4 payre plough harneis, 7 collars, 2 pannells, 2 cart sadles, 4 bitt halters & other implements, 1*li.* 15*s.*
16 sheep & 7 lambs, 7*li.* 6*s.* 8*d.*

IN THE OUTHOUSE—The quarne & other implements, 8*s.*

His wareing apparell, money in his purse, bonds, bills & desperate debts, 4*li.*
Summe—198*li.* 4*s.* [should be 198*li.* 3*s.* 8*d.*]
[Appraisers—Abraham Brecknocke, Edmund Turnidg.]
[Exhibited 20 September 1665.]

47.—Henry Battle, junior, of Cocksmill Green in Roxwell. 2 September 1665.

On [one] acre & halfe of wheate, 4*li.*; two acres & halfe of barly, 4*li.*; on acre & halfe of bulemong, 3*li.*
Two Cows, 6*li.*; on sow & eight pigges, 3*li.*; six pigges, 12*s.*
On long Cart & harnes, 3*li.*

GOODS IN THE PARLOR—On Joynd bedstedell & trondell bedstedell, on fetherbed & boulsters & pillows, rug, blankets, curtens & valients, 4*li.*; on table & forme, on levery table & pres, fouer Chayers, on glascase & a trunke, 2*li.*; seven peuter dishes, a flagin & Candelstic, and a Chamberpot & other small things, 1*li.* 15*s.*

GOODS IN THE HALL—On table & sevn stooles, 1*li.* 10*s.*; six Chayres, five cushens & a bench, 4*s.*; two dripin pans & a spite & tramells, coboyrns, fire shovell & tongs, belles [bellows], grigoyrne [gridiron] & locoyrn [lock-iron], on wollin whele & linin whele & a handrele, 3*s.*

GOODS IN THE HALL CHAMBER—On fetherbed & flocbed & fower blankets, on halfheded bedstedell, two Cradles & a Cheste, 3*li.* 10*s.*; five payer of shets, two tabelcloaths, on dozen of napcins, two towells, 2*li.*

His waring Cloaths & mony in his purs—1*li.* 10*s.*

GOODS IN THE MILKHOUS—On Chorne & stane & two payles & shelfes, a tray & two boules, scoalles, wayts & a frying pan, thre Chesemots & other small things, 1*li.*

GOODS IN THE BUTTERY—On kneading trough & chespres & two tubs, thre barells, two drenkstalls & a tunell, 1*li.*; two Cettles [kettles], on bras pot, on scellet [skillet], on scumer, a bras pan, on Candelstick, on morter, wooden platers, dishes & trenchers, 1*li.* 10*s.*

GOODS IN THE CHAMBER OVER THE MILKHOUS—on fan, shovell, spade, bill, axe, mathock, sithes & other old things, 10*s.*

Sume Totall—44*li.* 14*s.*
Dets that he ought when he dyed—19*li.*
[Appraiser—Richard Thurrowgood. Exhibited 20 May 1666.]

48.—Andrew Hall of Writtle, tanner. 7 December 1665.

IN THE CHAMBER OVER THE HALL—One Bedstead, one Chest, Curtans and Vallance, with Chord, 18*s.*

IN THE CHAMBER OVER THE PARLER—One old Chist, 3*s.*

IN THE PARLOR—One Court Cubard, 6*s.* 8*d.*; one Feather bed & Bolstar & one Rugg, 2*li.*; one Press & one Cushin, 16*s.*; one flaggon & five other peces of peauter, 10*s.*

IN THE HALL—One Hanging Cubard, 8*s.*; one glass-case, one Jugg, one brass flower pot, & a brass salt with some other inplements, 5*s.*; one Table, Six Joynt Stooles, one Chair & a Cushin, 18*s.*; one pair of Andireons with brass knobbs, fire shovel & tongs, one Spit, one Warmingpan, one Candlestick & a Sconce, 10*s.*; one Bass Chair, 1*s.*

Redy Money and Wearing apparill, 1*li.* 13*s.* 4*d.*

At Chelmsford at M[r] Jeglins—29 quarters of Malt at 18*s.* the quarter is 26*li.* 2*s.*
One debt owing by Mistris Harvey of Chelmsford—11*li.*
[Total]—45*li.* 11*s.*
Owing Unto Severall men—19*li.* 16*s.* 10*d.*
Remanes—25*li.* 14*s.* 2*d.*
Debts owing by the sade John Hall viz[t].
To the wid Barnard, 8*li.*; to James Terill of Springfield, 2*li.*; To Sarah Cleark, 3*li.*; To Andrew Hall, 5*li.*; To William Lucas, 1*li.*; To John George, 16*s.* 10*d.*; Total—19*li.* 16*s.* 10*d.*
[Appraiser—William Garrat. Exhibited 28 May 1666.]

49.—Thomas Poultar of Writtle, glover. 8 March 1665.

IN THE HALL—One table & frame, 3 old Joynt Stools, one Bench board, one wicker Chair & 2 other old Chairs, 11*s.*; one pair of Bellows, one pair of Andirions, Fire shovill & Tongs, 2 Candlesticks, one Lanthorne, one old Jack, one peece of old wainscott, with some other implements, 10*s.*

IN YE PARLOR—One Bedstead, Featherbed, Boulstar, 2 Pillows, one Covering, one rugg & a Blanckit, 2*li.*; Two old Truncks, two Chists & two Boxes, one Baskit, with other Small implements, 10*s.*; 3 pair of Sheets, one Table cloth, 4 Napkins, 2 Towills, & some other old Linen, 1*li.*

IN YE BUTREY—One Hogshead, one Barrell, two letle Runlits, three Tubbs & one Kneading trough, 12*s.*; Two letle brass Ketles, 3 Skillits, one Ireon pott with Severall Earthen potts & other implyments, 1*li.*; two letle peauter dishes, 2*s.*

In ye Chamber over the Parlor—One Parcell of Wooll by Estimacion 60*li.* at 6*d.*, 1*li.* 10*s.*; two old Boxes, one broken Cross-bowe, two Bushills of aples, two sives, & some old twools, 4*s.*

In ye Chamber over the Hall—One Boarded Bedstead, one flock Bed, one Wollen, & one linen Whele, one flaskitt, two Baskits, 3*li.* of Cource Wooll, one old Sadle, 26*li.* of lead waights, one Beame & Scailes, & one heape of Shreds, with other implements, 1*li.*

In redy money & wearing aparell, 2*li.*

In ye Shop—One shopp-board, one stake a with, one pairing knife, Severall Plancks & boards, one Beame knife with some other implements, 10*s.*; one Bullock hyde drest, 5*s.*; one dozon of Sheepe skins, & one dozen of lambe skins, 8*s.* Tenn Calve-skins drest, 7*s.* 6*d.*; twelve pair of Gloves, 6*s.*; fower broken Hydes, 16*s.*; Seaven Broken Calve skins, 4*s.*

In ye yeard—Three raw Hors-hyds, 7*s.* 6*d.*; Eaighteene Raw Pelts, 2*s.*; forty Skins in the drench-tubb,5*s.*; one Drench-tubb, three brewing tubs, one Allam trough, one ligh-trough & leach, one powdering tubb & one Trapp rule, 12*s.*; halfe a load of Wood, & a grindston, 5*s.*

In ye Barne—Two hundred waight of Hay, one Tubb, a lather, & other Lumber, 4*s.*; one Mare, one Horss & two Coults, 5*li.*
Some Totall comes to—20*li.* 11*s.*
[Appraisers—John Wallis, William Garrat. Exhibited 3 April 1666.]

50.—John Playle of Roxwell, yeoman. 27 May 1666.

Twenty five acres of wheat at Three pounds & Tenn shillings per acre, 87*li.* [should be 87*li.* 10*s.*]; Thirty foure Acres of Barley, 85*li.*; for the follow [fallow], 36*li.* 8*s.*; five Acres of pease, 6*li.*
Twenty sheepe, 14*li.*; Three Bullockes, 4*li.*; Three Calves, 1*li.* 10*s.*; Twelve Cowes & a Bull, 44*li.*; six horse and a Colt, 48*li.*
Seaven Acres of grasse, 9*li.* 6*s.*
A waggon, 8*li.*; Three Dungcarts, 8*li.*; Collers & harnesse, 4*li.*; ploughes and harrows, 1*li.* 10*s.*
Hoggs and piggs, 5*li.* 10*s.*
Sacks, a skreene and spades, 2*li.*
Brewing vessells, 1*li.*; A Quarne, 1*li.*
A lead and other things in the dary, 4*li.* 10*s.*
Hoggs heads & other things in the Buttrey, 2*li.*
Wayts and skoyles, 1*li.*
Goods in the parlour, 7*li.* 10*s.*
Three Seame Wheate, 3*li.* 10*s.*
Goods of Twoe roomes over the great parlour, 8*li.*
Goods in the great Chamber over the hall, 8*li.*
Goods in other Three Chambers, 10*li.* 10*s.*
Lynnen, 11 *li.*; pewter, 3*li.*; Brasse and other thinges in the kitchen, 9*li.*
Goods in the hall, 1*li.* 5*s.*
Cheese, 3*li.*
In money, 20*li.*

Totall—461*li.* 19*s.* [should be 458*li.* 19*s.*].
[Appraisers—William Sandford, Matthew Nightingare.]
[Exhibited 28 May 1666.]

51.—Samuel Coaltburt. 20 August 1666.

IN THE HALLE—One Table, one form with an ould Cuboard, three Cheyres, one birding peese, one wheell, Sex Cushanes, one pair of Andrianes, one tramell, a pair Tounges and a fyre-pann, a pair of bellowes, 2*li.* 2*s.*

IN THE PARLLOURE—One Tablle, fowre Stoolles, one forme, Sex Cheyrres, one pres Cuboard, one sydboard Cuboard, one pair of Cob Irones and Tounges, one glas Case and a Littell one with some bookes and Trenchers, one bedsteed, one fetther bed, One boullsters, two blanketts, and one Coverlyd with Curtians and Valliants, 8*li.* 10*s.*

IN THE CHAMBER OVER THE PARLOURE—One bedsteed, Curtians and Vallianes, one fetther bed, two boullsters, one Rugge, Two blanketts, two Chests, 5*li.* 10*s.*

IN YE CHAMBER OVER THE HALL—One ould bed stead, Curtians and two Coverlyds, one blankett, one fetther bed, one boullster and two pillowes, one Trundell bed, one flocke bed and boullster, two Blankett, one pres, two Chests, 6*li.*

THE CHAMBER OVER THE KITCHING—One flocke bed, one headed bed, one forme, 1*li.* 10*s.*

IN THE CHAMBERS AND THE ROOMES ABOUT THE HOUS—Nynethenth pair of Sheets, Ten pair of pilliow beeres flexen and holland; the Tablle Linene—thirre dosen of napkenes, four Tablle board Cloathes; the Cuboard Cloathes —thrree, and sydeboard Cloathes, 13*li.* 10*s.*

Thrre Sillver spoonnes with other Implements, 1*li.* 14*s.*

IN THE BUTERY—Two barrells, In the next Roome Two barrells more, one kneading Trough, one musterd Corne [quern], one hare [hair] Cuboard, one boullting Trough witth other Implements, with a kneading Trough, 2*li.*

IN THE KITCHINGE—One Chespres, 8*s.*; Sex Tubes, 30*s.*, one Lead 2*s.*, Thrre bras kettells, 15*s.*, one Copper, 20*s.*, thrre Littell posnetts, 3*s.*, one Iron pott with other Implements; the Soome is 4*li.*

IN THE DARYE—One kettell, one Stand, two Chernes, three Trayes, one poudering Tub, thrree bowlles with other Implements, 2*li.*

IN THE CHESE CHAMBER—Cheese, 2*li.*; one pair Scolles, Two Basketts, 6*s.* 8*d.*

The peuter with other Implements, 2*li.*
The Corne In the barne, the wheat and the barelley, 60*li.*
The Corne on the Stacke and the Littell barne, 22*li.*
The haye In the Littell barne, 5*li.*
The fallow—twenty Sex akerres, 24*li.*
Four horse and a Coult, 17*li.*
The harnes, ploughes and Carttes, the harroues, 10*li.*

Fyve Cowes and one bull, 20*li.*
One fann, one Screw, matockes and spads, [?Ten] Rackes, 2*li.* 3*s.*
Thrre Weanells, 3*li.*; four hogges, one Sowe and Sex pigges, 6*li.*
For his wearinge parrell and money In his purs, 10*li.*
[230*li.* 5*s.* 8*d.*; original not totalled.]
[Appraisers—James Taverner, Allexander Reynoldsone.]
[Exhibited 11 October 1666.]

52.—Samuel Hanbery of Writtle. 24 July 1667.

37 acers of followed land which was sowen with wheate and barly at two and thirty shillings an acer, 59*li.* 4*s.*; 13 acers of eatch corne at five and twenty shilling an acer, 16*li.* 5*s.*; 43 acers of followed ground, 40*li.*
Five and thirty seame of wheate, 35*li.*; three skore and ten seame of malte at 18 shillings a quater, 63*li.*; A percell of barly not threshed, 5*li.*; A cocke of pease, 5*li.* 5*s.*
Six horse at 8 pound a horse, 48*li.*; Five cowes and a yearein bulloke, 16*li.*; 26 sheepe and 22 lambs, 14*li.*; 6 hoggs and 8 piggs, 7*li.*
One waggon, one loade carte, and one dunge carte, and all implements of husbandry, 17*li.* 10*s.*

One table, one coberd, 4 spits, a paire of cobirons and other things all standing in the hall, 1*li.* 15*s.*

One bedstead, one trundle bed, two feather beds, and two boulsters, two pillows, two coverlids, three blankits, two matts and cords, with red curtins and valence belonging to the bed, 5*li.*; one table, 4 Joynd stooles, one livery coberd, one cheast, two chaires and a cushing stoole, all standing in the paler, and a paire of Cobirons, 2*li.* 1*s.*

In the chamber over the hall—One bedsteed, one feather bed and boulster, one coverled, one blanket, one matt and cord, with greene curtaines and vallance belonging to the bed, 4*li.*; two tables, two cheasts, eight chaires, a paire of cobirons and a hanging presse, 2*li.* 8*s.*

In the chamber over the entry—One bedsted, one feather bed and boulster, three pillows, one coverled and three blankets, 3 cheasts, 4*li.* 15*s.*

Two bedsteds, one feather [and] one flock bed, three blanketts, two coverleds, three boulsters and one pillow all standing in the chamber over the buttery, 4*li.*

In the garett—Wooll, cheeses, two tables, one halfe hundred waight, a pocket of hops and a paire of skoles, 9*li.* 1*s.*

Five vessells, one tin coberd, two powdering tubs and kneeding trofe and other things standing in the stronge bere buttery, 2*li.* 2*s.*

Five hoggsheads in the smale buttery, two driping pans and an Iron pottage pott, 2*li.* 5*s.*

One powdering troafe, one churne, milke vessells and other things all standing in the milkhouse, 1*li.* 15*s.*

One brase copper and bruing vessells, 6*li.* 5*s.*

Foure brase kittells, one brase pott, three brase skillitts, two warmeing pans and an ould brase copper, *5li.* 10*s.*
Forty nine pound of pewter, *3li.*
Sheets, table cloathes, napkins, pillow beares and other linin, 12*li.*
One bedsted, two flocke beds, two boulsters and 4 blankets standing over the milkhouse, 1*li.* 5*s.*
The silver boule and ready money, 20*li.*
His wareing apparell—5*li.*
Totall is—418*li.* 14*s.* 4*d.*
[Appraisers—William Boosey, Jeremy Westwood, yeomen.]
[Exhibited 5 August 1667.]

53.—A noat of all the goodes in John Atwood house. 12 March 1667.

The goodes in the paller ar valued at 3*li.*
The Chamber over the paller at 1*li.* 1*s.*
The goodes in the hall at 1*li.* 5*s.* 6*d.*
The goodes in the buttere at 2*li.* 10*s.*
All the meterialls bee longing to his tread at 2*li.* 15*s.*
For 7: Sheepe at five shillinges apeese, 1*li.* 15*s.*
For two piges at 10*s.*
The wood in the yarde at 6*s.* 6*d.*
Total—13*li.* 3*s.*
[Appraisers—Francis Taverner, John Sapsforde.]
[Exhibited 16 April 1668.]

54.—John Shettlworth of Writtle, yeoman. 14 April 1668.

Two Bullocks, 3*li.*; One Coue, 3*li.* 10*s.*; One Colt, 3*li.*; Six & thirty Sheepe, Fourteen Lambs, 14*li.*
Three Bedds, 10*li.*; Two Beadsteadles, 1*li.*
Brasse & pewter, 2*li.*; Brueing Vessells & Tubs, 2*li.*; Tables & one presse & Chaires, 2*li.*; Other Implements & Lumber, 1*li.* 10*s.*
One Cart, one plow & 1 Slead, 1*li.* 5*s.*
One Sem of Wheate, 1*li.*
Linning, 5*li.*; One Trunke, two Chests, 10*s.*
A payre Andirons, fire Shovell & Tongues, 10*s.*; One Warmeing pan, gridion, bellows, 6*s.*
Timber & loggs, 1*li.*
One Cheesepresse & Capon Cups [coops], 5*s.*
In ready Mony, 10*li.*; One Severall Bonds, 80*li.*
His Weareing Apparell, 7*li.*
Summe is—148*li.* 16*s.*
[Appraisers—John South, junior, Francis Taverner.]
[Exhibited 16 April 1668.]

55.—Richard Josslin of Roxwell. 27 May 1668.

In the Hall—One longe table and another short one, one longe foorme and another short, Eight Joyne Stooles, Leaden Wayts waying 107 pounds, one Jacke and three Spitts, two Beames y[e] one Iron y[e] other Wood, 2 payre of Scales, one short Settle, Chest, one Little box of Drawers, a glasse Case and two Chayres, *3li. 13s. 2d.*

IN THE PARLOUR—One Beddsteadle and feather Bedd, two Blancketts, two Coverings, two feather pillowes, one Boulster and one payre of Curtaines and Valens, one presse Cubbard, one longe table, Six Joyne Stooles, three Chayres and Seaven Cushens, *5li. 13s. 4d.*

IN THE KITCHIN—One Short table, two Formes, one bench, fowre Shelves, one Smal Cubbard, two payre of tramells, one payre of Cobb Irons, one fire Shovell and tongues, one Iron Slice, on tinn Collingdor, two little brasse potts, fowre Kittles, three skillits, two Drippinge pans the one Iron the other tinn, one Mortter and pestle, fourteene dishes great and Small, twelve Spoones, five Sausers, one Candle Sticke, one Chamber pott, one tinn Apple Roster, three dozen of trenchers, *5li. 8s.*

IN THE BREWHOUSE—One Brewinge Leede and a Cheese Leed, one Cheese presse, one flock bedd, three Blancketts, one Beadstedle, fowre brewinge tubbs, one little old table, two payre of tramells, one Cleaver, one Shreedinge Knife, two Smooth Irons, fowre Cheese Mootes, one Cheese bread, *3li. 3s. 4d.*

IN THE BUTTERY—Fowre hoggsheads, one barrill, one needinge troph, a Little meall barrill, one tunnell, two Leather Bottles, one Shilfe, three Suives and other Lumbar, *1li. 2s. 6d.*

IN THE MILKE HOUSE—Three Iron potts, Six shelves, one Cheese table, one foorme, one powdring tubb, one powdring troph, three Kimnells, three treys, two Churnes, one Mortter of wood, one Stand, one frying pan, two payre of potthooks, three payles, *1li. 15s.*; One Iron punch, one Saw, two Matthooks, two Axes, Six Wedges, two Shovells, one Spade, three bills, *1li.*

IN THE CHAMBER OVER THE KITCHIN—One feather Bedd, one bolster, two blancketts, one Coverlead, one Joynt Beddstedle, two Chests, one old trunke, one Warming pan, two Cobb Irons, one old Chayre, *2li. 6s. 8d.*

IN THE CHAMBER OVER THE MILKEHOUSE—Two bedds, two bolsters, two pillowes, two blancketts, two old bedsteedles the one a standinge bedsteedle the other a trundle bedsteedle, two Hutches, one old trunke, two old Coverleads, *3li. 6s. 8d.*

IN LINNEN—Three payre and one flaxing Sheets, three payre of holland pillowbys, two table Clothes, two dowzen of Napkins, Six payre of Corse Sheets, one flaxen towell, two Corse towells, one Costinge Sheete, *5li. 10s.*

IN THE CHEESE CHAMBER—One Cheese table, two Joyne Stooles, Six boards, two Castinge Shovells, one old trundle beddstedle and other Lumber, *2li. 10s.*

His wearing Clothes and Moneys in his pockett, *2li.*

IN THE BARNE—One Boshell, three Corne Seives, one Skreene, two Casting Shovells, one Ridle, three boards, one Scope, fowre forks, eight boshells of Corne, Seaven sacks, *2li.*

In the Stable—Cart Harness, Plow Harnesse, Collours, Cartsadles, thill belts, an old Sadle and Ropes, 1*li.*; two Horsses, one Mare and a Colt, 8*li.*

One Waggon, one Load Cart, two old Dung Carts, one Plow, two old payre of Harrowes and three old Ladders, 9*li.*
Seaven Cowes, 24*li.* 10*s.*; three Hoggs, one Sow and Piggs 3*li.* 5*s.*; Nine Sheepe and five Lambes, 3*li.* 5*s.*
Fifteene Acres of Wheat, 22*li.* 10*s.*; Six Acres of barley, 9*li.*; Six Acres of Pease and teares, 7*li.* 4*s.*; one Acre and halfe of Bollymon, 1*li.*
Summa Totalis—128*li.* 2*s.* 8*d.*
[Appraisers—Henry Bright, Richard Thorowgood.]
[Exhibited 24 January 1668/9.]

56.—Rubin Mason of Roxwell, yeoman. 5 August 1668.

In the hall—One Cubard, 5*s.*; one Table, three Stooles, fower Chaires & two Cushins, 9*s.*; two pair of Tramills, two Cobireons, two Spitts, one fireshovel & tongs, one gridireon, one Smoothing-Ireon, one pair of Bellowes and a Basting ladle, 10*s.* 3*d.*

In ye Parlor—One Bedstead, one Bed & bolstar, three blanckets & a Covering, 2*li.* 6*s.* 8*d.*; one Trundle bedstead with a flock bed & boulstar, two pillowes & two Blanckets, 10*s.* 6*d.*; three Chists, two Boxes, one Cubard, two Chaires, one Stoole, one forme & a Warming pan, 18*s.*; Seaven peauter dishes, two Saucers, one poringer, fower Spoones & two Candlesticks, 19*s.* 6*d.*; three pair of Flaxen Sheets, Eaight pair of Towen Sheets, Six pillowbears, ten Napkins, fower Table clothes & a Cubard cloth, 5*li.* 15*s.* 9*d.*

In ye Butrey—Fower Ketles, three Skillits & one Brass pott, 2*li.* 2*s.* 8*d.*; one Ireon pott, two pair of tramells, two Cleavers, one fryingpan, the Beame Scailes & Waights, 18*s.* 2*d.*; fower tubbs, fower Barrills, one Tunnill, one Beerestall, one Kneading trough, three Shelves, 4 old formes, two Boules, two pailes, one Ax, one Bill & a Spade, one Mattock, one Shovill, two pitch forks with inplements, 1*li.* 12*s.* 8*d.*

In the Chamber over ye Parlor—One Bedstead, one feather bed, three feather pillowes, one Coverlett, three blanckits & a flock boulstor, 2*li.* 6*s.* 8*d.*; two chists, two Boxes, one Side Cubard, 6*s.* 4*d.*

Ten Bushills of Wheat & three old Sacks, 1*li.* 16*s.* 4*d.*

In ye Chamber over ye Hall—One fann, one rope, two wheeles, two Baskits, with other old Lumber, 13*s.* 4*d.*

Bonds, Bills & other desperate debts—52*li.* 6*s.* 9*d.*
Wearing apparrell & redy Money, 5*li.*
[Total]—78*li.* 17*s.* 7*d.*
[Appraisers—Nathan Wade, Francis Taverner.]
[Exhibited 16 January 1668/9.]

57.—Thomas Motte of Writtle, yeoman. 13 January 1668.

In the Hall—One long table, one forme & one bench, 12*s.*; one little table, two chaires, a paire of andirons & trammells, 10*s.*; one dripping-pan, two spits & other implements, 5*s.*

IN THE PARLOR—One cubbord, foure peuter dishes & other implements, 1*li.*

IN THE BEST CHAMBER—One bedstead, bed and coverings, 3*li.*; one chaire, one chest & other implements, 10*s.*

IN THE CORNE-CHAMBER—In wheat, 2*li.* 10*s.*

IN THE QUERNE-HOUSE—One querne, one wheele-barrow, two tubs & other implements, 1*li.*

IN THE DAIRY-HOUSE—One brasse-pot, 3 kettles, one candle-stick & a skimmer, 2*li.*; in cheese and butter, 3*li.*; two barrells, foure cheese-motes and other implements, 10*s.*

IN THE BARNE—In hay, 3*li.* 10*s.*; in barlie, 1*li.*

WITHOUT DOORES—Two cowes, 4*li.*

His wearing apparrell and money in his purse, 4*li.*
In money due upon bonds, 100*li.*
[Total]—127*li.* 7*s.*
[Appraisers—John Collin of Roxwell, yeoman; John day of Norton Mandeville, carpenter. Exhibited 16 January 1668/9.]

58.—Richard Bright of Roxwell, 18 March 1668.

IN THE HALL—One long Table, one short Table, One Forme, One Chaire, One Benchboard, One Old Kettle, Two three Legg Stools, one paire of Trammels, one paire of Cobirons, one warminge pann, one Ax, one Bill, 16*s.*

IN THE PALER—One Joyne Bedsteed, one Feather bedd, one Boulster, one Coverlett, Two Blanketts, one Table, one Forme, one old Cuboord, two old Chessts, one wicker Chaire, two Pewter Dishes, one Skillett, one paire of Flaxen sheets, One Pillow Beare, 4*li.* 0*s.* 6*d.*

IN THE BUTTREY AND MILKHOUSE—One pouderinge Trowth, one Stand, one Boule, one Kettle, one Iron pott, one Charne, one old Table and Forme and Cheesepress, two Boords, and other Imployments thereunto belonginge, 18*s.*

IN THE BUTTREY—Two kettles, a Small Tub, one Peell, one old Spade, two Barrells, one Forme, one kneadinge Trowth, one Kemnell, one Iron Dripping Pann, one Seed pecke, one Capons Coope, one Panell, one Boord, 2*li.* 9*s.* 10*d.*

IN BUTTREY CHAMBER—One Feather Bedd, one Boulster, two Feather pillows, two old Bedsteeds, two old Chests, two Coverletts, one Blanckett, 3*li.* 2*s.* 2*d.*

IN THE HALL CHAMBER—One tub, one Sadle, one paire of Skalles, one Chest, two Boords and old Iron, one old Fann, three paire of Towinge Sheetts, 1*li.* 14*s.* 4*d.*

IN THE PARLOR CHAMBER—A little old wheat, a paire of Carte Harness, a old Cart Sadle, and one Boord, 1*li.* 3*s.* 4*d.*

Two ould Carts, one Quarne, 12*s.*
The Corne upon the Ground, 3*li.*
A Cowe & Calfe, one Hogg, 3*li.* 8*s.*; nine Sheepe, Five lambs, 3*li.* 4*s.*

The hay in the Barne, 13*s.* 4*d.*
His wearing Apparel and his mony, 1*li.* 13*s.* 4*d.*
Summa Totalis—26*li.* 14*s.* 10*d.*
[Appraisers—Henry Bright, Thomas Crush.]
[Exhibited 24 September 1669.]

59.—Robert Meade of Writtle. 8 July 1669.

IN YE HALL—One presse Cubburte, two tables, two formes, thre Chaiers, one spite, one paers of Cobiorns, one grigins, paies of tongs, one payer of bellowes, two paier of tramells, one fier yorn [iron], one paile, one mortar, one smothing yorn, one salte box, 1*li.* 6*s.*

IN YE CHAMBER OVER YE SHOP—One fether beed, two floke bolsters, two fether pillows, one Coverline, one Joyn beedstadle, thre Cheastes, thre paier of towen sheets, two pillow beers, one brush, one bill, 2*li.* 10*s.* 5*d.*

IN YE CHAMBER OVER YE HALL—One floke baed, one floke bolster, one blancate, one Coverline, one half heded bedstadle, one Chaier, two Cheasts, one pillow, one pautar Chambar pote, 1*li.*

IN YE CHAMBER OVER YE BUTTREY—One bill, one axe, one sawe, one sickle, one sith, 2*s.* 11*d.*

IN YE BUTTRY—Thre [k]ittels, one scillute, [skillet], one pauter dish, one yorn potte, one friing pane, two barrills, one neding trofe, one drinkstall, one warmeing pane, two lether bottells with other small Implments, 1*li.* 5*s.*

IN YE SHOPE—Two wheels, one Relle, two bibels, 5*s.*

IN YE YARDE—One pege, one henn: one hoges tube, 11*s.*

The sume is—7*li.* 0*s.* 4*d.*
[Appraisers—Thomas Gray, John Cooke. Exhibited 8 July 1669.]

60.—Widow Argo. 4 February 1669.

IN THE HALLE—One long tabell, six Joyne Stolles, 1*li.* 3*s.* 4*d.*; in the same rome—a littell tabbel, one cubberd, 2 chaires, 2 boockes, 1 spit, 1 trammell, gridgin, and tongs, 1 mortter, 1 C[?lever], 11*s.* 6*d.*

IN THE PALLAR—One Joyne bedstede, 1 fether bed, 2 bossters, 3 pillows, a paire of blanckets, Curttains and valliants, 3*li.* 15*s.*; in the same rome—1 Joyne Colbord, 1 Joyne Chest, 2 huches, 1 boxe, 2 Cushins, 1*li.* 3*s.* 2*d.*; in the same rome—4 shetts, 4 pillowberes, 5 napkins, 2 aporns [aprons], 1 hatt, 2*li.* 2*s.*

IN THE PALAR CHAMBER—One Coatt, hallf a seame of Wheatt, a boshsshel and a halfe of barly, 1*li.* 1*s.* 6*d.*

IN THE BUTTERY—4 putter dishes, 12*s.* 4*d.*; in the same rome—2 brase Cittels [kettles], 1 pott, 2 tubs, a barrell and otther small things, 1*li.* 17*s.* 6*d.*

For eidght fowlles, 5*s.* 4*d.*
Hir Wearing aparrell, 1*li.*
[Total]—13*li.* 8*s.* 4*d.* [should be 13*li.* 11*s.* 8*d.*].
[Appraisers—Jonathan Sapford, Thomas Crosse.]
[Exhibited 1 August 1670.]

61.—Richard May of Writtle. 7 February 1669.

In the Hall—One Cubard, one table, fower Joynt Stooles, 6 Chairs, *2li.*; a pair of fire shovill & tongs, a pece waniscot, & implements, 10*s*.

In the Parlor—One Bedstead, feather bed, Bolstr, Curtans & Vallance, *5li.*; one Trundle Bedstead, 5*s*.; one Cubord, 3 Chaires, 2 formes, one Table & frame, 1 Chist, a Glass-case, 2 Boxes, & mplements, 3*li*.

In ye Chambr over the Parlor—2 Beds & Bedsteads, 2 feather beds, 2 Coverings, Curtans & Vallancs, 3 Chists, 2 truncks, 8 pair sheets, 4 dozen Napkins, 8 pillowbers, 4 Tableclothes, & one press, 15*li*.

Chamber over the hall—One old forme, a Setle, a Childs Chair, a Chist, one box with severall implements, 10*s*.

In the Butrey—26 peces Peauter, 3li.; five Beere vessells, one Beerestall, 3 spits, 3 shelves, 2 Ketles, one Pot, & implements, 4*li*. 10*s*.

Kitchin—2 Coppers, 2 Ketles, a Stoole, one Ireon Back, & implements, 4*li*.

In ye letle Butrey—One Kneading trough, 6 Tables, 2 berestalls, a Skillit, Scales & waights, & implements, 3*li*. 10*s*.

In ye Barne—2½ load of Hay, 2 Mills, 2 lathers, & implements, 9*li*.

Barly Chamber—6 Seame of Barly, 6*li*.

Malt Chamber—6 Seame Malt, one fan, one Screne, a Bushell, 6 sacks, 7*li*.

Malt house—9 Seame Malt, a Cestarn, a hare, & implements, 14*li*. 10*s*.

In redy Money & wearing apparill, 4*li*.
Somme—81*li*. 15*s*.
[Appraisers—Thomas Woolfe, William Garrat.]
[Exhibited 13 February 1669/70.]

62.—John Sells of Roxwell, yeoman. 4 June 1670.

In the Halle—One Long Table, One Forme, Three Joyned Stooles, one Small Table, Three Chaires, Fower Cushins, and other Implements, 1*li*. 4*s*.

In the Parlor—One Table, One Cuppboard, One Forme, Fowre Chaires, Two Stooles, one Boxe, One Feather bedd and Boulster, Two Blanketts, one Coverlet, one Beddstedle, Curtaines and Valliens, 4*li*. 15*s*.

In the Kitchin—One Table, one Cuppboard, Two Chaires, one Side Board, one Little Cuppboard, Two Cobirons, a Fire Shovel, a paire of Tongs, Two paire of Tramells, one Gridgiron, a Spitt, a Cleiver, Three Dripingpans, and other Implements, 1*li*. 10*s*.; In Brase and Pewter, and One Iron Pott, 3*li*. 8*s*.

In the Bruhouse—Two Leads, Five Bruing Tubbs, one Trofe, Two pailes, a paire of Scooles, a Flaskett, Spades, Axes, Mathookes, Bills, Wedges,

Sawes, Pitchforks and Wimbles, and other Implements of Husbandry, *6li.* *18s.*

In the Milkhouse—One Table, one Cheise Presse, Fowre Shelves, one Forme, Two Whay Tubbs, One Churne, Five Milke Vesells, one Frying panne, Two Cheeise Moots, one Cheese Bread, Five Earthen poots, and a Butter Baskett, *1li.* *12s.* *4d.*

In Two Butteryes—Three Hogsheads, Fowre Barrills, one Pouldring Tubb, a peece of Wainscott, a Peeile, Three shelves, one Forme, and Two Drink stalls, *1li.* *12s.* *4d.*

In the Boulting House—One Boulting Trough, Two sives, and other Lumber, *4s.*

In the Halle Chamber—One Trundle Beedstedle, an Old Wheele, and other Lumber, *5s.*

In the Parlor Chamber—One Beddstedle, Two Chests, one Boxe, One Feather Bedd, One Flock Bedd, Two Coverlitts, Fowre Blankets, Two Boulsters, Three Pillowes, One Warmeing panne, and Two Cobirons, *4li.* *0s.* *6d.*

In Linin—Two payre of Flaxen sheets, Five payre of Towin ones, Three Table Clothes, One Douzen of Napkins, Three payre of Pillowbeires, *2li.* *12s.*

In the Chamber over the Bruhouse—Two Boarded Beddstedles, Two Flock Bedds, Two Boulsters, Two blanketts, and Two Coverletts, *1li.* *1s.* *8d.*

In the Kitchin Chamber—One Screene, Tenn Bushells of Wheate, Seven Old Sackes, a Fanne, a bushell, a shovell, One Riddle, and other Lumber, *3li.* *8s.* *6d.*

In the Carthouse—Two Old Wagons, one Dungcart, a payre of Harrowes, Two Ladders, plows, and plowirons, *10li.* *9s.*

In the Quearnehouse—One Maulte Quearne, *10s.*

In the Stable—Five Horses and there Harnesse, *13li.*

In the yards—Five Cowes, Eleven Sheepe, Five Lambs, Fower Hoggs, a Grinstone and a Hogg Troufe, *19li.* *13s.*

For Twenty Fowre Acres of Wheat and Barly and for Thirteene Acres of pease (That is to say) for the seed, Sowing, Plowing, Harrowing, and the Reente then payd upon the same at the Tyme of the Intestates Death, *55li.* *3s.* *9d.*
For the Halfe yeares Reent paid at Lady daye Last paste for Thirty seven Acres of Meaddow and pasture and Fallowes for the Farme Called Westhouse, *6li.*
For weareing Apparrell and Money in the purse of the Intestate, *2li.*
Summa Totall'—*139li.* *7s.* *1d.*
[Appraisers—Robert Birchwood, Richard Thorowgood, Thomas Cheveley.]
[Exhibited 8 October 1670.]

63.—William Irons, senior. 25 June 1670.

In the hall—The bookes, one bible, & other small bookes, 5*s*.; one ioyned table, one forme, one bench board, one presse cubbord, 6 chayres, one payre of bellowes, fier shovell & tongs, one payre of cobirons, & other implements, 2*li*.; one hogg of bacon, 1*li*. 10*s*.

In the parlor—One bedsteddle, one trundle bedd, two feather bedds, two feather bolsters, one feather pillow, one flock bolster, one coverlett, 3 blanketts, & other implements, 9*li*.; one chest & two hutches, 1*li*.

In the litle parlor—Two bedsteddles, two flock bedds, three flock bolsters, foure blanketts, & other implements, 3*li*.

In the chamber over the hall—The cheese with other implements, 2*li*.

In the chamber over the butteries—One beddsteddle, one feather bedd, one feather pillow, two blanketts, two flock bolsters, 2*li*. 10*s*.

In the chamber over the milke house—One ioyned bedsteddle, curtaines & vallance & curtaine rodds, one feather bedd, one feather bolster, one flock bolster, two blanketts, one coverlett, 6*li* 10*s*.; one litle table, two hutches, two chayres, two crops, one rugg, & other implements, 1*li*.

The linnen—8 payre of sheetes, two boord cloathes, three payre of pillow beeres, three smale board cloathes, & other smale linnen, 4*li*.

In the buttreyes—The pewter, 1*li*. 15*s*.; the brasse, two iron potts, 2*li*.; one hoggs head, three barrells, two drink-stalls, one old table, & other implements, 1*li*. 6*s*.

In the kitchin—Two payres of trammells, one lead, one frying pann, one dripping pan, one spitt, one kneading trough, one moulding board, one quarne, 6 old tubbs, & other implements, 4*li*.

In the milk house—One cheese presse, one charne, two tubbs, one stand with other milke vessells, & other implements, 2*li*.

In the barne—One Screw, one caving sive, one bushell, two fanns, foure ladders, one casting shovell, 1*li*.

In the stable—Foure payre cart harneis, foure payre of plow harneis & halters, one pannell, one saddle, one mattoch, one shovell, two spades, two axes, two bills, one payre of setters, with other implements, [illegible] ropes, 2*li*. 12*s*. 6*d*.

One waggon, one load cart body, two dungarts, two payre of harrowes, one plow chaines & plow irons, one dew rake, one carryage, & one payre of wheeles, 16*li*.
The corne in the chamber & other implements, 2*li*. 13*s*.
The wood in the yard, 1*li*.
Foure hoggs, 3*li*. 10*s*.; one horse & three mares, 8*li*.; five cowes, 14*li*.; foure sheepe, 16*s*.
The grasse & old hay, 10*li*.; 6 acres wheate, 12*li*.; 10 acres barley, 15*li*.; 12 acres pease & tares, 15*li*.; 13 acres fallow, 2*li*. 12*s*.
Three seame of oates, & other implements, & sacks, a payre of horse baskes, 2*li*. 14*s*.

His wareing apparell, bonds, bills, & desperate debts, & money in his purse, 12*li.*
[Total]—150*li.* 13*s.* 6*d.* [should be 162*li.* 13*s.* 6*d.*]
[Appraisers—Abraham Brecknoeck, John Wallis, John Aster.]
[Exhibited 1 August 1670.]

64.—John Collyn, yeoman. 27 [?June] 1670.

In the hall—The Bible, & other smale bookes, 10*s.*; one table, one forme, one round table, one carpett, 6 chussheons, foure chayres, two payre of trammells, one payre of Andirons with other implements, 4*li.*

In the parlor—Two ioyned tables, one forme, seven ioyned stooles, two chayres, one livery cubbord, one clock, one glasse casse, one carpett, 7*li.* 10*s.*

In the litle parlor—One ioyned bedsteddle, one feather bedd, one feather bolster, two feather pillowes, one litle table, curtaines & vallances, two hutches, one blankett & coverlett, one leather stoole, 3*li.* 10*s.*

In the chamber over the hall—One ioyned bedsteddle, curtaine & vallance, six hutches, one deske, one payre of Andirons, one payre of bellowes, two chayres, one litle stoole, 3*li.* 10*s.*

In the chamber over the entry—Three hutches, one old bedsteddle, one blankett, with othe implements, 12*s.*

In the chamber over the parlor—Two ioyned bedsteddles, two feather bedds, two feather bolsters, two feather pillowes, two coverletts, foure blanketts, curtaines & vallance & curtaine rodds, one round table, one presse cubbord, three chayres, one payre of brass andirons, one fier shovell & tongs brasse, one chest, two litle stoole, one glasse case, with other implements, 20*li.*

In the chamber over the litle parlor—One ioyned bedsteddle, one trundle bedd, two feather bedds, foure feather bolsters, foure blanketts, one coverlett, one rugg, curtaines & vallance & curtaine rodds, two chests, one trunck, and other implements, 7*li.*

The linnen—20 payre of flexen sheetes, three dosen napkins, two diaper table cloathes, 3 flexen table cloathes, with other smale linnen, 24*li.* 10*s.*

The plate—12 spoones, two smale bowles, 7*li.* 10*s.*

8 payre of sheetes goeing about the house & 6 payres of pillow beeres, 6*li.*

The pewter—3 dosen smaale & greate, one flaggon, two pewter candlesticks, 6 porringers, one dosen saucers, one dosen spoones, 6*li.*

In the kitchen—The brasse, two leades, 4*li.* 10*s.*; three kettles, foure skilletts, two brasse potts, two iron potts, one warmeing pann, two chaffer dishes, one morter & pessell, three brasse candlesticks, one skimmer, one brasse pott lidd, 3*li.* 13*s.*; the iron, one payre of trammells, one payre cob-irons, foure spitts, two dripping panns, one iake, fierpann, one payre of tongs & other implements, 1*li.* 16*s.*; two litle tables, three ioyned stooles, three chayres, & other implements, 1*li.*

IN THE MILKE HOUSE—The cheese presse, one leaden sisterne, one stand, foure kinnells, two charnes, five payles, three trayes, six cheese mootes, the shelves & other implements, 5*li.*

IN THE BUTTERIES—Six hoggs heades, one pipe, three drink stalles, the shelves, three leather bottles, & implements, 3*li.*

IN THE CHAMBER OVER THE BUTTERY—One bedd with other lumber, 1*li.*

IN THE MAULTING HOUSE—One tubb maulting, eight tubbs, one kneading trough, one payre of markett basketts, one payre of iron racks, one iron beame with scales & weights, & other implements, 4*li.*

The woole, 2*li.*

IN THE MALT CHAMBER—The corne, 3*li.*

IN THE CHEESE CHAMBER—The cheese, 7*li.*

3 payre of cart harneis & collars, two cart saddles, 5 payre plow harneis & collers, three pannells, one saddle, one payre of thilbells & halters & tropers, three horses & mares, 35*li.* 10*s.*; one waggon, one cart, 2 dungcarts, 2 payre of harrowes, two plows & irons, & one payre of wheeles, 22*li.*

The wheat in the barne, 7*li.* 10*s.*
One screw, one bushell, one casting shovell, one fam [fann], one caveing sive, 15*s.*; 5 wedges, 3 spades, two shovells, two dew rakes, 12 pitch forkes, two mattocks, one pick axe, two axes, three bills with other implements of husbandry, 1*li.* 10*s.*
3 swordes, one musknet, one birding peece, 1*li.* 5*s.*
The ladders, & wood in the yard, 15*s.*
14 Cowes, 42*li.*; 27 sheepe, 9*li.* 9*s.*; 4 hoggs, 4 piggs, 4*li.*; 8 dry heifers, 16*li.*; 14 lambs, 2*li.* 12*s.*
The fallow, 20 acres, 4*li.* 12*s.*; the wheate, 11 acres, 27*li.* 10*s.*; the barly, 13 acres, 24*li.*; the pease, 4 acres, 5*li.*; the grasse, 18 acres, 20*li.*
His apparell, bonds, bills, & desperate debts, & money in his purse, 77*li.* 1*s.* 1*d.*
Summa totalis—478*li.* [should be 428*li.* 0*s.* 1*d.*]
[Appraisers—Abraham Brecknoeck, John Pond, John Wallis.]
[Exhibited 1 August 1670.]

65.—Henry Burlinge of Writtle. 30 July 1670.

IN THE HALL—4 smale chayres, one payre of tramnels, one payre of cob-irons, fier shovell & tongs & bellowes, one woollen wheele with other implements, 6*s.* 8*d.*

IN THE PARLOR—One litle table, two old bedsteddles, one feather bedd, one chest, two boxes with other implements, 2*li.*

IN THE CHAMBER OVER THE PARLOR—One old bedsteddle & bed, one old hutch, 10*s.*; the linnen, two payre of sheetes, 5*s.*

IN THE BUTTERY—One barrell, two tubbs, one brasse kettle, one cheese presse with other implements, 1*li.*; two pewter porringers, 6*d.*

Two Cowes, 4*li.*; 13 sheepe & lambs, 2*li.*; one mare & colt, 1*li.* 10*s.*

3 acres wheate, *6li.*; one acre barley, *1li.*; the hay, *10s.*
Two hoggs smale, *1li.*
[Total]—*20li. 2s. 2d.*
[Appraisers—John Wallis, John Barrowes. Exhibited 6 May 1671.]

66.—A true and perfect Inventary of all and Singuler the Goods Chattells Debts and Howeshold stufe of John Perry Late of Roxwell in the County of Essex Yeoman Deceased as they are now standinge being and Remaineing in the House of One Christopher Perry of Roxwell aforesaid Taken Vallued and Appraized the Tennth Daye of November in the Two and Twenteith yeare of the Raigne of our Soveraigne Lord Charles the Second now King of England &c., in the yeare of our Lord 1670; by Tho: Chevely and John Bowtle as Followeth viz;

IN THE PARLOR—One Long Table, Five stooles, One Forme, One Chayre, One Cuppboard, One Little Table, and Two Dousen of Trenchers, *2li. 11s.*

IN THE NEW CHAMBER—One Feather Bedd, Five Feather Pillowes, Three Flock Boulsters, Two Blanketts, one Coverlitt, One Joyned Beddstedle, Curtaines and Curtaine roods, One Chest, one Chayre, one Forme, Five Cushins, *4li. 16s. 10d.*

IN THE KITCHIN—One Potte, One Pott posnett, One Spitt, One Dripping pann, and One Brase Candlestick, *2li. 4s. 6d.*

IN THE CHAMBER OVER THE KITCHIN—One Flock Bedd, One Feather Boulster, One Feather Pillow, one Blankett, One Coverlitt, Three Chestes, *1li. 18s.*

IN THE CHEEISE CHAMBER—One Trunke, One Chest, One Trundle Beddstedle, one Flock Bedd and Boulster, and one Blankett, *18s.*

In Pewter—Tenn Pewter Dishes, One Pewter Chamber Pott, One porringer, one Sault, Two sawcers, Eight spoones, One Bason, One Pewter Candlestik, and one Little Cupp, *1li. 1s. 6d.*
In Linnin—Five Flaxen Sheeites, Eight Payre of Towin sheeites, Two Dozen and Three Napkins, Five Pillowbeires, Fowre Table Clothes, and Sixe Towells, *4li. 18s. 6d.*
In Five quarters of Maulte in the Mault Chamber, *5li.*
In Two Eue Sheepe, *10s.*
In Wearing Apparrell and Money in his Purse, *4li. 4s. 10d.ob.*
In Bills, Bonds, and Other Good Debts Due and Owing to the Testator, *155li.*
Summe Totall of This Inventary is—*183li. 3s. 2d.ob.*
[Exhibited October (*sic*) 1670.]

67.—Nathaniell Campyon of Writtle, husbandman. 22 April 1671.

IN THE HALL—One table, one ioyne stoole, one ioyne forme, foure chaires, one litle table, one presse Cupboard, one spitt, one dripping pan, two Cobirons, one paire of tongs, one paire of trammells, two pewter Dishes, foure little sasers with other implements, *1li. 11s.*

IN THE PARLOR—One ioyned bedsteadle with the Curtaines, one featherbed, one boulster, one old Coverlid, *2li.* 10*s.* 4*d.*; one little table, one presse Cupboard, foure hutches, two chaires, one ioyne stoole with other implements, 1*li.* 15*s.*

IN THE CHAMBER OVER THE PARLOR—One ioyne bedsteadle, one flockebed, three feather pillowes, one Coverlid, one paire of course towen sheetes, 1*li.* 3*s.* 4*d.*; three hutches, one box, 8*s.*; foure bushells of oates & pease, 9*s.*

IN THE MILKE HOUSE—One Cheese presse, one Chirne, one stan, two cheese moates, three shelves, one forme, one kneadinge troffe, one brasse pott, one brasse Kettle, one skillett with [cut away], 1*li.*

IN THE BUTTERY—One brewing tub, three beere vessells, one beere stall, two shelves, one[1] wollin wheeles with other implements, 15*s.*

IN THE CHAMBER OVER THE BUTTERY—Two sithes, two sickells, one picke ex, with other Lumber, 10*s.*

IN THE ENTRY—One Leade, 13*s.* 4*d.*

IN THE BARNE—Two bushells of wheate, one little Jag of straw, ten fanns of Chaffe, one bushell, one fann, 15*s.*

IN THE STABLE—One mare, one mare Colt, one gelt nag, 5*li.* 10*s.*; one Carte saddle, one paire of thilbells, one paire of boddy harnis, two bitt halters, two barkings, one pannell, one bridle, three Collers, two pitchforkes, one shovell, one spade, with other implements, 10*s.*

IN THE HAY HOUSE—Aboute eight hundred of hay, 8*s.*; two plow beames, one paire of Dunge Cart shaftes, 4*s.*

IN THE YARDS—One loade Carte, 2*li.*; one old Dunge Carte, 6*s.* 8*d.*; one plow, one paire of harrowes, one grinstone, 16*s.*; one Loade of rounde wood, with a little small wood, 12*s.*; one sow hogg, 15*s.*

His Waring Apar [torn away], and Moeny in his purse, 1*li.* 5*s.*
The total sum—23*li.* 16*s.* 8*d.*
[Appraisers—Abraham Brecknocke, Richard Horsenaile.]
[Exhibited 6 (May) 1671; endorsed, 'Martha Campions Inventory 1671'.]

68.—John Woolward of Roxwell. 20 October 1671.

IN THE HALL—One Cubboard, one long table, one forme, five Rush Chaires, four old Cushions valued att 18*s.*; Two Cobirons, one Spitt, fire shovell & tongs, one Cleaver & Shreding knife, one paire of tramells, & warming pan, 8*s.*

IN THE PARLOUR—One Bedstead, one Bed, two Boulsters, three Pillows, one Blankett, one Coverlid, one paire of sheets, Curtaines & valences, 2*li.*; three old Hutchess, one old Box, 6*s.*

IN THE PARLOUR CHAMBER—One old Tub, & woolen Reele, 4*s.*

IN THE HALL CHAMBER—Two flock Beds, two Borded Bedsteads, two Coverlids, two Boulsters, one old Blankett, one Pillow, one paire of sheets, 1*li.* 10*s.*; One Table, one forme, one old Hutch, one old trunk, 5*s.*

[1] (?)two, overwritten.

IN THE DAIRY—Two old Brase Kettles, two Skelletts, three Pewter Dishes, one Chees Press with the rest of the utensells thereunto belonging valued att 1*li.* 10*s.*

IN THE BUTTREY—Two Barrells, 2 small tubes, 2 Kemnells, a drinke stall, one saw, three old axes, two Billes, one Bush Hooke, 2 old spads, 12*s.*

IN THE KITCHIN—One Kettle, one tub, one Kemnell, one Dresser, one Hogstub, Lyletch & troph, syth & snath, 1*li.* 2*s.*

The wood in the yard, 6*s.*
The sheepe & lambs, 4*li.* 10*s.*; Two Cowes & two Calves, 3*li.* 10*s.*; one Mare, 1*li.*
One long Cart, 1*li.* 10*s.*; One paire of Harrowes, 2*s.* 6*d.*

IN THE STABLE—on Querne, 2 paire of plow harnis, one Cart sadle, 3*s.*
[Total—19*li.* 16*s.* 6*d.*]
[Appraisers—Henry Bright, Junior, Andrew Gladen.]
[Exhibited 21 October 1671.]

69.—Daniel Leonard of Writtle. 27 February 1671. See Plate XIV.

IN THE HALL—One Cubord & cubord Cloth, 12*s.*; one letle table & frame, one Joynt Stool, fower old Chaires & 2 formes, 4*s.*; one pair of Andireons, fyre shovell & 2 pair of Tongs, 1 pair of Creps, one pair of tramells with implements, 5*s.*; two Spits, & a grid ireon & a Ketle, 4*s.*; one Boughting Mill & a Meale Tubb, 4*s.*

IN THE PARLOR—One Table, & frame, with one forme, five Cushins, three wicker Chaires, 12*s.*; one letle table, two Boxes & a Chist, 8*s.*; twelve puter dishes, 6 porringers, two Candlesticks, with other implements, 1*li.* 10*s.*

IN THE CHAMBER OVER THE PARLOR—Two feather beds, 2 feather bolstars, two flock bolstars, 2 pillowes, two Bedsteads with Curtans & Vallance, 5*li.*; one Table, one Box, 2 old Chests, with a pair of Andireons, Tongs, & implements, 8*s.*

IN THE KITCHIN—One Small Copper, 2 Ketles, one brass pott, & one Ireon pott, 1*li.* 10*s.*; one Kneading trough, a meale tubb, one old boule, thre Tubbs, thre beere vessells, 3 Keeleers, with other implements, 1*li.*

IN THE CHAMBERS—One Ireon Beame & Scales, two halfe hundred Waights, Some Small waights, one wooden beame, 18*s.*; fifty Cheses great & Small, 2*li.* 10*s.*; one old Table, a peece of Leather with Several other Small implements, 1*li.*

IN THE SHOPP—One old Counter, three meate Tubbs, one old Chist, one Set of Boxes, one pair of Scales, five dozen of Candles, with other implements, 2*li.*; three Baggs with some nailes in them, one flitch of Bacon, 12*s.*

IN THE YEARD—One grind stone, & lie-trough, severall peces of bords & plancks, one load of fire wood, with other Small things, 1*li.*

In redy Money & wearing aparill, 1*li.*
Some Totall—20*li.* 17*s.*
[Appraisers—William Garrat, John Cooke. Exhibited 30 March 1672.]

70.—Alexander Reynoldson of Writtle, grocer. 28 February 1671.

IN THE HALL—One drawing Table & 5 stooles, 1*li.*; one Table-chaire, 2*s.*; one Cupboard & one deske, 7*s.*; one Keep, 4*s.*; 5 chaires, 2 old stooles, and a little Table, and a book shelfe, 9*s.*; 2 spits, 2 smoothing Irons, one Grid-iron, one paire of Tongs, one firepan, one paire of Trammels, one paire of Cobirons, 7*s.*; six Cushions, 4*s.*

IN THE BUTTERY—2 Brasse Potts, one iron Pott, 3 Brasse Kittles, three brasse skilletts, one old Copper, 2*li.* 8*s.*; one Kneading Trough, Shelves, & other Implements in the same place, 4*s.*

IN THE SHOP—One old Hutch, five Tubs, 14*s.*

Nine Pewter Dishes, one Bason, 2 Porringers, two Candlesticks, one Flaggon, 1*li.* 2*s.*

ATT MR BERESFORD'S—One Bedstead, 6s. 8d.

IN THE CHAMBER OVER THE HALL—One Chair, 1*s.* 6*d.*; one old pair of Virginalls, 5*s.*; one Truncke, 2*s.* 6*d.*; one Livery Cupboard with a Carpet, & one Box, 6*s.* 8*d.*; two good Hutches, 12*s.*; one old Hutch, 1*s.*; one old Bedstead, 2*s.* 6*d.*; one Feather Bed, one Bolster, five little Pillows, one old Rugge, 2*li.* 10*s.*; six pair of sheets, two paire of Holland Pillow Beeres, 2 other Pillow Beers, two Table Cloathes, one Dozen of Napkins, 2*li.* 10*s.*; one sett of Curtaines & Valliants, 2 pictures, & other little Implements, 12*s.*

IN THE NEXT CHAMBER—One Feather Bed, 3 Bolsters, 2 Blanckets, one Cover-lid, One sett of Curtaines, Valints, & Bedstead, 3*li.*, one Box with a Frame, together with other Implements in the same Roome, 4*s.*

IN THE NEXT CHAMBER—One Table & one Box, 2*s.* 6*d.*

AT THE WIDDOW WHITE'S—One old Table, 5*s.*

ATT MR JAMES HIS HOUSE—One high Presse, 1*li.*

ATT THE SAME PLACE—Two Counters, 10*s.*

One Cow & a Calfe—3*li.*; one old blinde horse, 10*s.*
His wareing Apparell, 1*li.*
Summe totall—24*li.* 2*s.* 8*d.* [should be 24*li.* 2*s.* 4*d.*]
[Appraisers—Thomas Bridgman, John Challice.]
[Exhibited 28 February 1671/2.]

71.—[See also No. 78.] Isaac Adames of Writtle, innholder. 30 March 1672.

IN THE HALL—One long Table, 2 Formes, Six Chayres, one Short Table, 16*s.*; one payre of Fire Irons, Fire Shovell & Tongs, Four Spits, two Dripping pans, 12*s.*; one Cubboard, one glasse Case, 5*s.*; twelve peeces of Pewter & Implements, 12*s.*

IN THE LITTLE PARLOUR—One Table, two Formes, 1 Chaire, 3*s.*

IN THE LITTLE BUTTERY—Foure Kettles & Skilletts, one Mustard Querne, a frying pann & other implements, 1*li.*; Two potts, one of Brasse, a little Table, 5*s.*

Chamber over the Entry—Two Bedds & Bedsteads, Curtaines & Valiance, one Chest, one Table, 1*li.* 10*s.*

In the Chamber over ye Buttery—One long Table, 2 Formes, one little [*sic*], one Chayre, two old Chests, 1*li.*; one Bedd & Bedstead, Curtaines & Valians & Covering, 3*li.*

In the Greate Chamber—Three Tables, Foure Formes, three Chaires, one old Chest, & implements, 10*s.*

In the Kitchen—Two Dresser boards, one old Kneading Trough, one lie Trough, and some Smale implements, 10*s.*

In the Bruehouse—Two old Coppers, Six brueing Tubbs, one Cowler with some implements, 3*li.*

In the yard—One Sow & pigs, wood, & implements, 2*li.*

Weareing Cloathes & Ready Money—12*s.*
Summa Totall' 15*li.* 15*s.*
[Appraisers—William Garratt, John Cooke. Exhibited 30 July 1672.]

72.—John Stookes of Roxwell, labourer. 11 June 1672.

In the Hall—One Longe table, one Cuboard, one little Table, two Joyne stooles, two litle Stooles, four Chaires, one Iron Pott, with some other Impliments vallued, 1*li.*

In the Butrey—One greate Beatle, four small Skellets, one Scomer, five Pewter dishes, four Little Kettles, two Porringers, one Salt, one Kneading trough, two tubbs, two Barrells, one woollen wheele, with some other Lumber vallued, 2*li.* 10*s.*

In the Palor—One feather Bedd, one flock Bedd, one feather Boulster, one flock Boulster, two Pillows, one Cover Lett, two Blancketts, one halfe headed Bedstead, one paire of Sheets, one press Cuboard, five hutches, one box, one warming Pan Vallued, 2*li*. 12*s.*

Palor Chamber—One featherbed, one flockbed, two ould feather Bolsters, three feather Pillows, two Blancketts, one Cradle, one Lynen wheele, one tubb vallued, 1*li.* 5*s.*

Linine—Three paire of twoing sheets, two paire of pillow Beares, three table Cloathes, two towells valued, 13*s.* 4*d.*
One acre of Pease, 1*li.*; eight Bushells of Wheate, 1*li.*
Wood in the yard, 5*s.*; One Pigg, 5*s.*; The Grasse, 4*s.*
His warring Apparrell—1*li.*; Money—9*li.* 10*s.*
Summa totalis—21*li.* 4*s.* 4*d.*
[Appraisers—William Crush, John Bouttell, Ezeckiah Godsafe.]
[Exhibited 17 June 1672.]

73.—Robert Hilliard of Writtle, bricklayer. 29 July 1672.

In the Parlor—Two Chists, two Boxes, and one Joynt stoole, 10*s.*

In ye Hall—Three Chaires, one letle Table, and some other Small implements, 3*s.*; one pair of Tramills, one pair of Andireons, fyre Shovelle & Tongs, & one Spitt, 3*s.* 4*d.*

IN YE BUTTREY—One letle old Dreaping pan, one pale, a forme, & other implements, 1*s.* 6*d.*; Two Beere Vessells, Three Brass Ketles, Three Skillits, one frying pan, with other Lumber, 1*li.* 4*s.*; Three Small peauter dishes, 1*s.* 6*d.*

IN THE CHAMBER OVER THE HALL—One Wainscot Chist, 5*s.*; one bedstead, flock bed & bolstar, with blancket & Covering, 15*s.*; Three pair of Sheets, 6 Napkins, & Some other old Lyning, 13*s.* 4*d.*

IN YE CHAMBER OVER THE PARLOR—Two old Bedsteads, one feather bed, one flock bed with Mats, Cords, blanckets, Coverings, with implements, 1*li.* 10*s.*

IN THE WORK-HOUSE & IN THE YEARD—One Kneading-trough, one Tubb, one Woll-whele, with his Tooles and other implements, 13*s.* 4*d.*; Two brewing Tubbs & a hen-coope, 2*s.* 6*d.*; for some Wood in the yeard, 5*s.*

Wearing Clothes, 15*s.*
Some Totall—7*li.* 2*s.* 6*d.*
[Appraisers—Mathew Maning, William Garrat. Exhibited 31 July 1672.]

74.—Abraham Brecknock of Writtle, yeoman. 25 September 1672.

IN THE HALL—One drawing table, 6 ioint stooles, and a forme, and a Bible, 2*li.*; One presse-cubbord, another wainscot cubbord, and all the wainscot about the Hall, & the long bench ioyning to the wainscot, 7*li.* 10*s.*; Three chaires, 6 cushions, & other implements, 1*li.*

IN THE PARLOR—One bedstead, one featherbed, & bolsters, & pillowes, & coverings, & curtaines & vallions, & window curtaines, 8*li.*; One cubbord, one trucclebed, a paire of andirons, fire shovell & tongs, two chaires, & three stooles, and other implements, 3*li.* 5*s.*

IN THE PARLOR CHAMBER—One bedstead, one featherbed, & bolsters, and pillowes, & coverings, and curtaines and vallions, and three chests, & other implements, 8*li.*

IN THE HALL CHAMBER—One bedstead, two featherbeds, bolsters and coverings, one great chest, and one ioint cubbord, & other implements, 8*li.*

IN THE KITCHIN CHAMBER—One bedstead, one truccle-bed, two featherbeds and coverings, one paire of curtaines and vallions, five chests, and other implements, 9*li.* 10*s.*

IN THE CHEESE-CHAMBER—Seavenscore cheeses, 14*li.*

IN THE MILKE-HOUSE—One cheese-presse, one stand, two churnes, two tubs, other milke vessell, some shelves, and other implements, 3*li.*

IN THE KITCHIN—One table and bench about it, one forme, one cubbord, and three chaires, and one dresser bord and shelves, 1*li.*; Three dozen of peuter dishes, 6*li.*; One peuter flagon, 10*s.*; A paire of peauter candlesticks, foure porringers, & other small peuter, 1*li.*; Nine brasse kettles, foure brasse pots, & five skillets, 6*li.*; One birding-piece, one musket, & sword, 18*s.*; Two dripping-pans, one iack, foure spits, two paire of trammells, and other implements, 3*li.* 6*s.* 8*d.*

IN THE BUTTERY—Ten hogsheads, *3li.* *6s.* *8d.*; foure leatherne bottles, & other implements, 13*s.* 4*d.*

IN THE BREWHOUSE—Two leads, *3li.*; One fatting-tub, 1*li.* 10*s.*; Two meashing-tubs, one cooler, & other brewing vessells, & a querne, & other implements, 2*li.*;

One silver boule, & ten silver spoones, 7*li.*
A paire of holland sheets, and three holland pillowbeares, 3*li.* 10*s.*; Sixe paire of flaxen sheets, 4*li.* 10*s.*; Eighteene paire of towing sheets, 7*li.* 4*s.*; Ten table-cloths, & three dozen and halfe of napkins, 5*li.* 17*s.*; Towells, and other small linnen, 2*li.*
His wearing apparrell & money in his purse, 20*li.*

IN THE MALT-HOUSE—One Cisterne, 5*li.*; One haire, 1*li.*; A paire of scales & weights, and three Dew-rakes, 1*li.*

IN THE MEN'S CHAMBER—Two flock-beds, two borded bedsteads, coverings, & three bolsters, 3*li.*

IN THE CORNE-CHAMBER—Three seame and halfe of old wheat, 5*li.* 5*s.*; Three seame of malt, 3*li.*; Two seame of bullimung, 1*li.* 10*s.*; One seame of old pease, 1*li.* 4*s.*

IN THE BARNE—Twenty seame of wheat, 30*li.*; Thirty seame of barly, 30*li.*; Thirty seame of old barly, 32*li.*; Three seame of pease, 3*li.* 12*s.*; Fortie load of Hay old and new, 60*li.*

IN THE STABLE—Sixteene sacks, a skrew, & two bushells, 2*li.* 12*s.*; Cart-harnesse & plough-harnesse, 3*li.* 13*s.* 4*d.*; Foure cart-robes, 10*s.*

IN THE CART-HOUSE—One wagon, 6*li.* 13*s.* 4*d.*; Two long carts, 7*li.*; Two dung-carts, 7*li.*; Three ploughs with their irons, 1*li.* 10*s.*; Foure paire of harrowes, 1*li.* 6*s.* 8*d.*; One wheele-barrow, 5*s.*

IN THE FIELDS—Foure horses, 16*s.*; Three more horses, 8*s.*; Eight bullocks, 30*li.*; Foure bullocks, 15*li.* 15*s.*; Nine fat bullocks, 40*li.* 10*s.*; Sixeteene smaller bullocks, 48*li.*; Five fatting Cowes, and a Bull, 19*li.* 10*s.*; Eleaven milch cowes & three calves, 41*li.* 10*s.*; One & thirty sheepe, 13*li.* 19*s.*; Eight hogs, 8*li.*; Eight store-pigs, 3*li.* 12*s.*; Threescore acres of fallow—72*li.*

The totall summe is—644*li.* 12*s.*
[Appraisers—William Bright of High Ongar, William Baker of Blackmore.]
[Exhibited 5 Oct. 1673.]

75.—An Inventory of y[e] Goods & Chattles of John Draper of Writtle in y[e] Countie of Essex yeoman lately Deceased taken by us Thomas Bridgman & Henry Bullen the second day of January 1672, which saide goods (as well within dores as without) were given & bequeathed by the aforsaid John Draper in his last will & Testamente unto his foure younger Daughters, vizt: Rebecca Draper, Elizabeth, Martha & Susanna Draper, to be equally devided amongst them.

IN YE HALL—One long Table plank, 2 Tressells, 1 Benchboard, 3 little lowe Tables, 1 long forme, 7*s.*; One great Chayre, 6 smale Chayres, & One standinge old Press, 8*s.*; Five Spitts & one Iron Drippen pan, 6*s.*; Two paire of potthookes, 1 Scummer, 1 firepan, 1 basting ladle, 1 paire of little tongs, I fleshforke, 1 Cleaver, 2 shreddinge knives, 3 Cloth irons, 2 brass coale dishes, 2 little brass morters, & 1 pestle, 8*s.*; Two Tramells, 1 fire Shovell, two peuter beakers, 1 peuter Tankerd, 1 halfe pint pott, 1 peuter Chamber pott, 2 peuter spones, & one brasse Candlestik, 1*li.*; One hanginge glass & 1 Peile, 2*s.*; One Dozen of Candle, 4*s.* 6*d.*; Two paire of Brass Scales, 1*s.* 6*d.*

IN THE PARLOR—One Joyne standinge bedsted, 1 Featherbed, 1 strawbed & Matt upon it, 2 feather bolsters, 3 feather pillowes, 1 blankett, 1 red Rugg, Curtaines & vallents of strip't Linsy wolsey, 4*li.* 2*s.*; Three Chaires, 1*s.* 6*d.*; One Livery Cupboard of Juniper & strip't Cloth, 4*s.*; One long Table, 7 Joynestooles & bench board, one wiker Chaire, 1 Joyne inlaid Chaire, 15*s.*; one great Chest & 2 little Chests, 5*s*; One standinge Presse Cupboard & Lynsy wolsey Cloth, & ye Table Carpett in it, 19*s.*; Thirteene smale peuter dishes. 2 peuter Candlestickes, 1 peuter bason, 3 peuter salts, Cupbord, 1 forme, & 16 Trenchers, 2*s.*

IN YE PARLOR CHAMBER—One Joine standinge bedsted, one new Featherbed & bolster, strawbed & Matt, two tikeinge pillowes, 2 blanketts, 2 old Darnix Coverings & one new one, 3*li.* 10*s.*; One plank forme, & one hutch, 1*s.* 6*d.*

IN YE ENTRY CHAMBER—Twelve Cheeses, 15*s.*; Three bushells of Mault, & one bushell measure, 9*s.*

IN YE HALL-CHAMBER—One Joine bedsted & featherbed, 2 feather Bolsters, strawbed & Matt, 1 blankett, & one wollen Coverlett, 3*li.;* One Table & 4 Joynestooles, 6*s.*; Two Joine Chests, 7*s.;* Two Cobirons, 1*s.*

IN YE SHOPP-CHAMBER—One Trundle bedsted, & ye Still y^e of it is in ye hall [*sic*], 4*s.*

The Linnen in sundry Places—Three paire of Flaxen Sheets, 1*li.* 10*s.*; Foure paire of Towen sheets, 1*li.* 8*s.*; Three paire of Coarse sheets, 18*s.*; Six flaxen pillowebeers & 1 holland one, 13*s.*; Five coarse Pillowbeers, 7*s.* Halfe a dozen coarse Napkins, 1*s.* 6*d.*; One dozen of Napkins wrought with white, & one dozen of blew milded napkins, 12*s.*; Two Table Clothes, one long, & one short & fring'd, 6*s.*; Two Coarse table Clothes, 2*s.*

IN YE BUTTERY—Two halfe Hogsteads & two little Barells, 7*s.*; Three warminge pans, 6*s.*; Two little Kettles, 3 larger Kettles, 2 brasse potts, 1 brasse lidd, 1 Iron pott, 1 payre of potthookes, 2*li.*; One brasse fryeinge pan, 2*s.* 6*d.*; One Coule, 1 powdringe Tubb, & 5 other Tubbs, 1*li.* 5*s.*; Three Skilletts, one of them potbrasse, & a mustard quern, 6*s.*; One Trifoote, 1 Iron Cobiron, one flaskett, & one Baskett, 4*s.* 6*d.*

IN YE SHOPP—Two new sackes & 3 old Sackes, 8*s.*; One Kneadinge Trough, 2 mealetubbs, and one forme, 5*s.*; One Iron Beame, Scales & weights, 10*s.* Three seives, 1 bakers Baskett, one Peck, halfe peck, & quarter, 2*s.*

IN YE OUT HOUSE—Two Ladders, 2*s.* 6*d.*

IN YE YARD—Three loads of wood & loggs, 1*li.* 10*s.*; One & Twenty Sheepe, 6*li.*; Fowre hives of Bees, 1*li.*

[Total]—42*li.* 17*s.* [should be 38*li.* 5*s.*]
[Exhibited 22 July 1673.]

76.—Widow Poole. 10 February 1672.

One feather Bed [1 b[o]lster, 3 pillows, deleted], 2*li.*
One blacke scarfe, one green aperen, 5*s.*
One flocke bead, 3*s.*
4 petecoats, one wastcoate, 1*li.*; one hatt, 3*s.*
8 puter dishes, 2 butter dishes, 3 porringers, 4 litle sacers, 2 litle plats, 3 salts, 1 Candle sticke, 1 dozen of spoones, in all Comes to, 1*li.*
A percell of small Course linin, 10*s.*; 3 payre of sheets, 2 table Cloaths, 1*li.* 6*s.*; 6 napkins, 2 pillow beares, 6*s.*; one Coverlid, 1 blankett, 12*s.*
2 huches, one trunke, 7*s.*
1 silver ring 2*s.*; 2 ould bibles, 6*s.*
1 brush, 2 litle round boxes, 1*s.*; 1 litle box, locke & key, 1*s.*; on rotten bedstidle, 1*s.*
Som ould petecoats, & bodys, & hatt, wastcoate, 5*s.*
Som is, 8*li.* 8*s.* Itam in money, 40*li.*
This is a True Inventary Taken of the goods of Goody Poole Decesed as above, Wittness our hands—Thomas Bridgman, Richard James.
[Exhibited 16 April 1673.]

77.—Thomas Osburne of Writtle, yeoman. 24 February 1672.

IN THE HALL—One Cobiron, 1 Tramell, 5 Spitts, 2 Drippen pans, 2 Brass basting ladles, 2 Chayres, 1 long table & 2 formes, 1 smale Ovall Table, & a round Table, 1 Livory board & Darnix Cloth & 2 Cusheons upon it, 1 long Darnix Carpitt, & 5 Cushions, 2*li.* 10*s.*

IN YE PARLOR—One long Table, 7 Joyne Stooles, 3 smale Joyne stooles, & one smale Table, 2 great joyne Chairs, 2 blew Cloth Chaires, 1 Livory board & greene & greene [*sic*] Cloth, 2 Tent stich Cusheons upon it, 2 paire of Cobirons, 1 Cloth presse, 2 Joyne Hutches, 1 Glass Case, 4 Cusheons, 1 standinge Joine Bed with Darnix Curtains & vallents, 2 featherbeds, 2 Pillowes, one blankett, 1 Red Rugg, & 1 Trundlebedsted, 10*li.*

IN YE KITCHEN—One planck Table & tressell-frame, 1 long forme, 1 old press, 4 old Chaires, 1 wicker chaire, 1 glass case, 2 Joynestooles, 2 Tramells, 1 gridiron, 1 round spitt, 2 brass morters, 1 warminge pan, 1 paire of Cobirons, fire shovell, Tongs, & Bellows, 1*li.* 10*s.*

IN YE MILKHOUSE & SINK HOUSE—One smale Copper, 1 Cheespresse, 1 Cherne, 2 old Kimnells, 3 Cheesmotes, 3 smale Kettles, 1 Scummer, 4 plank formes, 1 powdring trough & poudring Tubb, 1 stand Tubb, 2 other Kimnells, & shelves, 3*li.* 10*s.*

IN YE BUTTERY—Three Hogsheads, 5 smale vessells, 3 smale Kettles, 2 skilletts, 3 brass potts, 2 warming pans, 1 great Jack to drinke in, 3*li.*

IN YE BREWHOUSE—One Brewinge Copper, 2 Tubbs, 2 Coules, 1 Trough, 1 Kneadinge Trough, & other Lumber, *2li. 5s.*

IN YE KITTCHEN CHAMBER—One Joyne Bedsted & old vallents, 2 feather bedds, 2 feather bolsters, 1 blankett, 1 old Coveringe, 1 greene Rugg & Darnix Coveringe, 1 Table & 3 joyne stooles, one Cabenett, 1 Juniper Chist, 1 Trunk with ironplates, 2 other Chests, 3 Chaires, 1 paire of Cobirons, fire shovell & Tongs, & 1 standing press, *8li.*

IN YE SINKHOUSE CHAMBER—Three feather bedds, 4 bolsters, 3 pillows, four blanketts, 2 old Coverings, 1 standinge bedsted, 1 halfe heded bed, 1 grate for seacoale, 1 Joyne stoole, 1 Chaire, *7li.*

IN YE HALL-CHAMBER—Two boarded Beds, 2 flockbedds, 1 plank Tressell, & 1 Chaire, *1li.*

IN YE LITTLE CHAMBER OVER PART OF YE HALL—One halfe headed Joyne bed, 1 featherbed, two blanketts, 1 old rugg, 2 feather bolsters, & 1 Joyne Hutch, *2li.*

IN YE PARLOR CHAMBER—One Joyne bed with Curtaines & freinge, 2 featherbeds, 2 feather bolsters, 3 Rushia Chaires, 1 Joyne Chest, 3 greene Chaires, 1 plaine Hutch, 1 long Table & Joyne forme, 2 Joyne Stooles, one Chaire with turn'd pins, *9li.*

IN YE BREWHOUSE CHAMBER—Fleese wool, *3li.*

Linnen—Fifteene paire of sheets, 1 dozen of pillowbeers, 6 Tablecloths, 6 dozen of napkins, & other smale linnen, *12li.*
One silver bowle, 6 silver spoones, *3li. 10s.*
Peuter—Peuter, *5li.*
Five Horses & ye Harnesse, *12li.*; One old wagon, 1 Tumbrell, ploughs, Harrowes, & other Implements of Husbandry, *4li.*
Eighteene Acres of wheat, *16li.*; Twenty Acres of Barly, *7li.*; foure Acres of pease, *3li.*; Thirtysix Acres of Oats, *12li.*
Eleven Cowes, *27li. 10s.*; Fourty sheepe, *13li. 6s. 8d.*; Ten store piggs, *2li. 10s.*
Wearinge apparell & mony in his purse, *5li.*
Summa totalis—*175li. 11s. 8d.*
[Appraisers—Edmund Sterne, Thomas Bridgeman, William Poole.]
[Exhibited 5 (*sic*) February 1672.]

78.—[Copy, on paper, of No. 71.]

79.—Francis Taverner of Writtle, yeoman. 25 January 1673.

ATT MORE HALL IN THE KITCHIN—One Cupboard, One Table, two dresser boards, one bench, one Forme, three shelves, one keepe, one Muskett, one paire of Racks, one fire-iron, & two Gunns, *1li. 8s. 6d.*; Eighteene pewter dishes, two Candlesticks, one salt sell, two chamber potts, one Bason, three pye plates, three sawcers, sixe porringers, & one Flaggon, *3li. 10s.*; Three horse-baskets, & a wantye, foure Brasse potts, foure skilletts, two Kettells, one chafeinge dish, two Scummers, one ladle, one iron-pott, one frying pan, & a clever, *3li. 8s.*; fiveteene scaines of wollen yarne, *4s.*

IN THE GREAT BUTTERY—Five hoggs-heads, three beere stalls, two foorms, one meale-tubb, one funnell, one small tubb, one leather Bottle, 3*li.*; Two shelves, Sixe wooden dishes, one drippinge pan, earthen ware & other lumber, 6*s.* 8*d.*

IN THE BREWE-HOUSE—Two Coppers, three great tubbs, three smaller tubbs, a Cooler, one Bowle, one Kneedinge troffe, two sives, one dresser, foure little tubbs, & one peele, 6*li.* 5*s.*

IN THE MILKE HOUSE—One Cheese presse, two stanns, one milke tubb, five kimnells, five cheese moats, three cheese breads, two churms, foure shelves, one forme, one powdringe tubb, earthen ware, & other lumber, Sixe pailes, & a pestle & mortar, 4*li.* 16*s.* 8*d.*

IN THE LITTLE BUTTERY—Foure shelves, & other lumber, 5*s.*

IN THE HALL—Two great Tables, two small tables, two benches, two joynt stooles, seven chaires, one range, two trammells, fire forke, fire shovell & tongs, two gridirons, two iron hooks, a toasting iron, a fire iron, a paire of andirons, foure spitts, one dripping pann, one jack, a rack, & lumber, 6*li.* 5*s.*

IN THE CLOSSETT UNDER THE STAIRES—One halfe hoggshead, one Runlett, a butter firkin, a table, a Beerestall, a paire of Scoales & a beame, & two shelves, 15*s.*

IN THE PARLOR—One drawinge Table, two side tables, three joynt stooles, sixe leather chaires, seven Cushions, one foarme, a great chaire, two turkye worke stooles, two chaires, two greene stooles, three Carpetts, two paire of andirons, firepan, & tongs, & other lumber, 5*li.*

IN THE OLDE PARLOR—One bedstid, Curtains & vallance, one featherbed, a bolster, two pillows, two blanketts & a Coverlidde, a still, fire-shovell & tongs, foure chaires, two little tables, a glasse Case, three dozen of trenchers, one boxe, one shrapnett, & other small things, 7*li.* 10*s.*

IN YE MAYDS CHAMBER—Two bedstedds, one paire of Curtains & Vallance, one bed, one bolster, a blankett & Coverlidd, 3*li.* 10*s.*

IN THE ROOME OVER YE OLDE PARLOR—One bedstidd, Curtains & Vallance, one flockbed, blanketts & Coverlid, one table, & other things, 3*li:*

IN THE CHAMBER OVER THE GREAT PARLOR—One bedstidd, Curtains & Vallance, one bed, two bolstors, three pillows, three blanketts, one Coverlid, three paire of andirons, fire shovell & tongs, three cloth stooles, one glasse Case, two chests, a little table & a Carpett, 7*li.* 10*s.*

IN THE STAIRE CASE—A great presse, 1*li.*

IN THE HALL-CHAMBER—One bedstid, Curtains & Vallance, one bed, one bolster, three pillows, one blankett, a greene Rugge, One great chest, one boxe, a chest of drawers, one table-Cupboard, one liverye Cupboard, sixe leather chaires, one great arm'd chaire, one trunke, two warmeinge panns, fire shovell & tongs, a paire of andirons, and other things, 14*li.* 15*s.*; Twentye paire of flaxen sheets, a long table-cloth, one diaper tablecloth, one dozen & halfe of diaper napkins, seven dozen of flaxen napkins, seven flaxen table-cloths, tenn paire of towen sheets, seven paire of pillowbeers, halfe a dozen of towells, windowe Curtains, & a looking-glasse, 6*li.* 18*s.* 6*d.*

In the newe Gallerye—One bedstid, bed & bolster, two blanketts & a Coverlidd, 4*li.* 10*s.* 6*d.*

In the olde Gallerye—One bedstid, bed & bolster, two blanketts, & Coverlidd, & other lumber, 4*li.*

In the Garrett—Beanes & pease, a small bagge of hopps, & a Cradle, 4*li.*

In the Cheesechamber—Sixe score cheeses wayinge about thirtye leade, 15*li.*; A cheese table, & si[d]e Saddle, 5*s.*

In the Yarde—Sixe horses, and Colts, 12*li.*; Eleven Cows & a Bull, 37*li.* 10*s.*; One Sowe & Eleven store piggs, 4*li.* 17*s.*; One Fatt Cowe & a Bull, 7*li.* 10*s.*; Five Cowe-Racks, 1*li.* 5*s.*; Tenne Scotch Cows, Threescore & eighteene Sheepe, 36*li.*

In the Oxe house—Sixe Fatt Bullocks, 37*li.*

In the stable—Foure horses, two Mares, two saddles, two bridls, one pannell, one pillion, Cart harnesse & furniture for the horses, ropes, & other utensells, 31*li.*

In the Cart-house—One Waggon, two dunge Carts, two plows, & theire implements, one dewe rake, & one paire of harrows, 11*li.* 10*s.*

In the Barns—One Fanne, one Castinge-shovell, one barne-cloth, twelve sacks, one tubb, & other instruments, 1*li.* 16*s.*

In the Kell-house—One haire-cloth, a fire-rake, one malt shovell, 1*li.* 10*s.*

In the hay-house—Thirtye loade of hay, 30*li.*

In the wheate Barne—Twelve bushells of wheate, and five seame of pease, 8*li.* 6*s.*

In the Barly-barne—Sixe-teene seame of Barlye, and seventeene seame of Oats, 28*li.*;

Eighteene Acres of ground sowen with wheate, 42*li.*; Thirteene Acres of Barly-land, 14*li.* 6*s.*; Two Acres of Each land, & Foure & twenty Acres of Eaches uppon the first Cropp, 5*li.* 4*s.*; The growths of Marehall Wood & Highland grove, 70*li.*

In the malt-chamber—Sixe bushells of Malt, tenn bushells of teares, & tenn bushells of Oats, 2*li.* 5*s.*

An Inventory of the Goods & Chattells of the said Francis Taverner att his Farme called Reads taken by the said John Clarke & Thomas Crow Jan. 27th Anno Domini 1673.

In the Hall—One fire shovell, one paire of tongs, a paire of Andirons, one trammell, fower chaires, two tables, two foorms, & a dresser, 1*li.* 6*s.*

In the Parlor—Six bushells of wheate, two sithes, an iron pitch, a spade, one bushell, one peck, two butter basketts, one flaskett, one woollen-wheele, a sive, a plow share, a Reele, 2*li.* 13*s.* 6*d.*

In the Mayds chamber—One bedstid, bed, blankett, bolster, & Coverlid, 1*li.* 5*s.*

IN THE MANS-CHAMBER—One bedstid, bed, blankett, & Coverlid, 1*li.* 5*s.*

IN THE BUTTERY—Three hogs-heads, one little Vessell, two shelves, one tunnell, a leather bottle, a paire of scoles & wayts, a beerestall, wooden dishes, & earthen ware, 1*li.* 16*s.* 8*d.*

IN THE KITCHIN—One Copper, foure tubbs, one Kneedinge troff, one cheese-presse, one dresser, & other lumber, one iron pott, one fryinge pan, one brasse pott, one skillet, one Kettle, 4*li.* 16*s.*

IN YE DAYRY—One stann, one churme, sixe Kimnells, foure cheese-moats, one cheese-bread, one Cowle, two payles, one dresser & foure shelves, 2*li.* 4*s.*

IN THE CHEESE CHAMBER—Seventye cheeses at Eleven Leade or thereabouts, 5*li.* 10*s.*

IN THE CORNE BARNS—Foureteene seame of Barly & twenty seame of Oats, 27*li.* 8*s.*; Twentye seame of wheate, 48*li.* A screene, casting shovell, fann, & other implements, 8*s.*

IN SEVERALL BARNS—Foure & thirty loade of hay, 34*li.*

IN YE STABLE—Foure horses, a blind mare, & furniture for the horses, 12*li.* 4*s.*

IN THE CARTHOUSE—One Cart, one plowe, one paire of old harrows, 2*li.* 15*s.*

IN THE YARDE—Twentye Cows & a Bull, foureteene piggs, 59*li.* 14*s.*; Fourescore & Eleven sheepe, 24*li.*

Thirtye eight Acres of land sowen with wheate, 65*li.* 17*s.* 4*d.*; Three Acres of Barly land, one Acre of tilt, 4*li.* 2*s.*

His wareinge apparell, 10*li.*; In reddy monyes in the house att his death—12*li.*

The whole Inventory of both Farms amounts to 809*li.* 12*s.* [should be 810*li.* 7*s.*]

[Appraisers—John Clarke, Thomas Crowe.] [Exhibited 14 March 1673/4.]

80.—Christopher Perry of Roxwell, yeoman. 10 February 1673.

IN THE HALLE—One Long Table, One Long Forme, Two Little Tables, One Old Cupbord, One Short Forme, Fowre Chaires, Five Cushins, a Glase Case, Two Musketts & Bandeleeres, One Sword, Fowre Spitts, One Dripin pann, a payre of Cobbirons, One Fyreshovell and Tonges, Two payre of Tranells, one other Chaire, Fowre Cushins, and Other Implements, 2*li.* 19*s.* 6*d.*

IN THE KITCHIN—One Kneding Troufe, One Table, and Other Implements, 5*s.* 6*d.*

IN THE BUTTERY—Two Barrills, Two Small Vessells, One Troufe, an Old Churne, and other Implements, 18*s.* 4*d.*

IN ONE OTHER BUTTERY—Three Hoggsheads, One Tunell, Three Old Kettles, a Bakeing Pann, three Old Posnetts, Two Leatherne Bottles, One Skimmer, a basting Ladle, and Six Small Pewter Dishes, 2*li.* 10*s.* 6*d.*

IN THE MILKE HOUSE—One Cheise Presse, One Stand, One Milke Tubb, Two Formes, Twenty pound Off Leadon Waites, Milke vessells, Cheise Mootes, and Other Implements, 1*li.* 10*s.*

IN THE CHAMBER OVER THE HALL—One Old Table, 6*s.* 8*d.*

IN THE CHAMBER OVER THE BUTTERY AND MILKEHOUSE—One Feather Beed, One Feather Boulster, Two Feather Pillowes, One Flock Boulster, Two Coverlitts, One Blankett, One Cupbord, Three Chestes, One Joyned Beedstedle, and Other Implements, 4*li.* 13*s.* 4*d.*

In Linin—Two paire off Flaxen Sheetes, Fve Towin sheetes, Fowre Table Clothes, Fowrteene Napkins, Fowre Pillowbeires, 2*li.* 11*s.*

IN THE CHAMBER OVER THE KITCHIN—One Bedsteddle, One Flock Beed and Boulster, One Blankett, One Covering, One Table, One Chest, 1*li.* 13*s.* 4*d.*

IN THE CHAMBER OVER THE PARLOR—One Joyned Beedstedle, Vallians and Curtaines, One Feather Beed, One Flock Beed, One Coverlett, One Chest, and One Short Table, 5*li.* 10*s.*

IN THE MAULTHOUSE AND GRAMERY—Five Bushells of Whete, Fower quarters of Mault, Two bushells of Barly, Tenn Bushells of Peease, and a Little parcell of Wool, 8*li.* 6*s.* 8*d.*

One Lead, on Sesterne, in the Maulthouse, 6*li.*
The Bruing vessells in the Bruehouse, 1*li.* 10*s.*
In Wheete in the Barne—eight quarters, 19*li.* 4*s.*; In Barly in the Barne—Fifteene qrs., 18*li.* 15*s.*

IN THE STABLE—One old Gelt Horse and Harnice, and all the utensells of Husbandrey, as Bills, Axes, Roopes, Spades, Shovells, and Mathookes, 3*li.*

Hay in the Barne, and on a small Cock, 6*li.*

IN THE CARTEHOUSE—One Old Loode Carte, One Old Dunkart, Plow, Harrowes, and Ladders, 3*li.* 10*s.*

IN THE YARDES—Three Cowes, and Sixteene Sheepe, & sixe Piggs, 14*li.*

In Tenn Acres of Wheete Sowne, with the Fallow, Seed, and Reent of the Land, 20*li.*; In Sixe acres of Land Fallowed for Barley and the reent of the Land, 8*li.* 2*s.*
Weareing Apparrell, and Money in the Testators Purse, 3*li.*
Sum' Totall' of this Inventory is—131*li.* 5*s.* 10*d.*
[Appraisers—Henry Bright, Thomas Cheveley.]
[Exhibited 14 March 1673/4.]

81.—Henry Clarke of Writtle. 12 March 1673.

Three Cows valewed at nine pounds, 9*li.*; 1 bullock, fifty shillings, 2*li.* 10*s.*; a welch farrow Cow, thirty shilings, 1*li.* 10*s.*; 4 sheep, twenty shillings, 1*li.*; 2 piggs, sixteen shillings, 16*s.*
Hay, three pounds, 3*li.*; 4 bushells of wheat, twenty fowre shillings, 1*li.* 4*s.*

IN THE TWO CHAMBERS—Houshold Goods valewed at 2*li.* 10*s.*

In the Parlor—Goods valewed at 4*li.*

In the Hall—Goods valewed at forty shillings, 2*li.*

In the Milkehowse—Goods valewed at forty shillings, 2*li.*

In the Buttery—Goods valewed at twenty shillings, 1*li.*
The wearing Apparrell of the said Henry Clarke, 3*li.* 10*s.*
An ould Dung Cart, 5*s.*
the totall sum'—34*li.* 5*s.*
[Appraisers—Richard Horsnayle, John Bannester.]
[Exhibited 14 March 1673/4.]

82.—Henry Grouse[1] of Writtle, miller. 21 May 1674.

At The stayers hed—Three owld chests, One owld bedsted, and one owld boulster and pillow, 13*s.*

In The chamber Over the shop—One Joyn bedsted, with fether bed, boulster, And pillow, one blancket, and coverlet, and Curtains and vallants, one long table and frame, One foram, one littell chest, one chayer, 1*li.* 15*s.*

In the chamber over the hall—One Joyn bedsted, with fether bed, boulster, Blanket, coverlet, and curtains and Vallants, two payer of ould sheetes, One Joyne chest, two littel stouls, one wicker chayer, A leven [eleven] peuter Disshes, One littell bason, with other small peces, 3*li.* 15*s.*

In the hall:—One short table and frame, three ould Joyn stouls, one ould cubbert, fower chayers, one payer of cobirons, one fier shovell and tongs, one payer of tramells, one payer of bellows, Two iron driping pans, two spits, one bras collender, one coal dish, Two littel Morters, 1*li.* 19*s.* 6*d.*

In the littell buttry by the hall—Three bras ketells, fower bras skillets, One Iron pot, one pouldring tub, 1*li.*

In the shop—Three bruing tubs, one kneading Trof and lid, and other ould lumber, 15*s.*
His wearing clothes, and mony in his purs, 15*s.*
[Total—10*li.* 12*s.* 6*d.*]
[Appraisers—John Watts, John Cooke. Exhibited 14 March 1673/4.]

83.—Edward George of Writtle, yeoman. 11 July 1674.

In ye Hall—One Table & frame, & 6 Stooles, 17*s.*; one one greate Chist, 8*s.*; one letle Low Stoole, 8*d.*; five Chaires, & one rush stoole, 4*s.*; Two spitts, one brass morter, one brass Chafeing dish, one Cleaver, 6*s.* 8*d.*; one pair of Andireons, fire Shovell & tongs, one Trunk, & a Cole-dish, 4*s.*; two letle glass-cases, one Lanthorne, with other Small implements, 2*s.* 6*d.*

In ye Parlor—One Press Cubard, 10*s.*; 1 Chist, 2 Bowes, a trunck, feather bed & bolster, one Warmingpan, 2 Ireon Wedges, 5*s.*; Three pair of Flaxen sheets, 1*li.* 16*s.*; one pair of old Canvis Sheets, 4*s.*; Two course Table clothes, 3*s.*; Fower flaxen pillowbeers, one board cloth, fower Towills, & some other small lining, 8*s.*; one pair of Small Stilliers, 3*s.*

[1] Endorsed 'He: Groues [i.e. Groves] Inventory'.

LITLE PARLOR—One flock bed, & Bedstead, thre old blanckits with Matt and Cord, 5*s.*; one trapp-reele, & one Wheele, 5*s.*

PARLOR NEXT YE BUTREY—One Bedstead, Matt and Chord, 6*s.*; one Box, one Chair, one runlett, & implements, 4*s.*

IN YE BUTREY—Three old hogsheads, 2 Barrills, two Beerestalls, a table, with other lumber, 14*s.*; one Leather botle, one frying pann, and two Ireon potts, 13*s.*

CHAMBER OVER YE BUTREY—One flock bed, and two blanckits, 1*li.* 2*s.*; one old bedstead, with matt & Cord, 2*s.*; one Casting-shovell, 1*s.* 6*d.*; one Box, one baskitt, Some old Ireon, with some other Lumber, 8*s.*; Three pair of flaxen Sheets, 2*li.* 5*s.*; five flaxen Napkins, one board-cloth, and Six course Napkins, 15*s.*

IN YE DARY—One Cheese press, 5 Cheese-moats, five Boules, one Cherne, one powdering tubb, one letle Coule, two dressers, one Chese stand, three pailes, with other implements, 1*li.* 15*s.*

IN YE KITCHEN—One Copper Ketle, one Ketle, one stoole, one block, one washing tubb, 1*li.* 15*s.*; one Ketle; 4 Brass Skillits, one pott, 1*li.* 2*s.*; 17 pewter dishes, 2 porringers, one plate, & two Saucers, 2*li.* 10*s.*

CHAMBER OVER YE KITCHIN—Forty Seaven Cheeses, 2*li.* 10*s.*; twenty fleeces of Wooll, 1*li.* 5*s.*

IN YE BREWHOUSE—Fower tubbs & a coule, one old Cherne, a Kneading trough, with implements, 2*li.* 10*s.*

IN YE YEARD & GROUND—Seaven Cowes & 2 heafers, 27*li.*; one feild containing by estimacion 7 Acres Barly, 17*li.* 10*s.*; one Waggon & a dung-cart, 12*li.*; fower store-hoggs, 2*li.*; Six horses and Mares, 20*li.*; one Grindstone, 6 Cow-cribbs, one pair of old Waggon Wheeles, 2 Ladders, one Lie-trough, with some other Lumber, 15*s.*; two ploughs, & 2 pair of Ha[rrows], 1*li.* 10*s.*; one feild of Wheat con[taining] by Estimacion 7 Acres at 3*li.* 10*s.*, 24*li.* 10*s.*; The halfe part of [illegible] Wooll feild, 3½ Acres at 50*s.*, 8*li.* 15*s.*; Thirty Sheepe and Lambs, 10*li.* 10*s.*; Eaight Acres of grass at 30*s.*, 12*li.*; Eaighteene Acres of Oats and Pease, 22*li.* 10*s.*

In recoverable debts—25*li.*
In redy Money, & wearing apparell—3*li.*
Some Totall—215*li.* 0*s.* 8*d.* [should be 215*li* 9*s.* 4*d.*]
[Appraiser—William Garrat. Exhibited 24 October 1674.]

84.—Henry Evans of Writtle, husbandman. 21 January 1674.

IN THE HALL—One Cubard, 8*s.*; one Table, and six Stooles, 10*s.*; Two litle Spitts, 1*s.*; Seaven peces of pewter, 9*s.*; one Kneading trough, 2*s.* 6*d.*; one forme, and two low stooles, 3*s.*; one warming pan, & a old Ketle, one prass pott, with some implements, 15*s.*

IN THE PARLOR—One feather bed, one bolstor, 2 pillows, one Covering, Bedstead, & Matt, &c., 2*li.* 10*s.*; one Chist, and thre Boxes, 8*s.*; Two Barrills, 2 Tubbs, & berestall, 6*s.* 8*d.*; one Ireon pott, a frying pan, a pair of Andireons, tongs, & other Small things, 7*s.*

IN THE CHAMBER—One Bedstead, a flock bed, 2 bolstors, one old rugg, 9*s.*; one old Chist, 6*d.*; one trap-reele, 1*s.*
In redy money, wearing apparell & lining, 2*li.*
[Total]—8*li.* 10*s.* 8*d.*
[Appraisers—William Garrat, Thomas Bridgman.]

85.—William Boosey of Writtle, yeoman. 14 June 1675.

IN THE HALL—One Longe Table, one Forme, 2 Cubboards, 9 Chaires, one stoole, one Jak, 2 Musketts, bandeleires, sourd and a headpeece, 2 Tramells, 2 Cobirons, Fireshowell and Tongs, one Fyreforke, 5 old Cushins, sume Bookes, and other Implements, 3*li.* 10*s.* 3*d.*

IN THE PARLER—Three Tables & formes, one Cubbord, 4 Chaires, 8 stooles, 4 Cushins, 2 payre of Cobbirons, a Fireshowell and Tongs, a payre of bellowes, and other Implements, 2*li.* 17*s.* 4*d.*

IN THE KITCHIN—One old Table, one Forme, 3 Spitts, 6 Tubbs, Twoe Troofes, 3 Kettels, 3 Ladels, 2 brase poots, one Iron pott, 3 skilletts, 2 payles, 2 pare of Tramells, one payre of Tongs, one peeile, Dishes and Spoones, and other Implements, 3*li.* 11*s.* 6*d.*

IN THE MILKE HOUSE—One Old Table, one Cheise presse, one pouldering Tubbe, 3 Churnes, Twoe stands, 4 Milke vessells, 4 sives, 6 Cheise Mootes, one Trofe, 3 Cheese breads, one Cubbord or keepe, a stone Morter, one Musterd quearne, Earthen poots and pans, and other Implements, with a pestell & Morter, 3*li.* 3*s.* 4*d.*

IN THE BUTTERYES—5 barrells, one Old Chest, 4 Hoggsheads, a payre of Windinge blades, and a Wheele, Twoe Letherne Bottells, 4 Beire stalls, Twoe Tinells [?tunnels], one Frying pann, one Gridgiron, and other Implements, 3*li.* 4*s.* 4*d.*

In pewter—3*li.*

IN THE HALLE CHAMBER—Twoe Bedstedles, One Trundle bedstedle, 3 Feather Beeds, 4 fether Bolsters, 4 Flok boulsters, one Flock Beed, 3 Coverletts, one Rugg, 5 Chests, one Boxe, one blankett, 6 Fether pillowes, Curtaines and Vallians, and other Implements, 8*li.* 3*s.* 4*d.*

IN THE CHAMBER OVER THE PARLOR—One Joyned Bedstedle, one halfehedded bedstedle, One Feather Bed, one Flock beed, one Feather Boulster, One Coverlett, 2 blanketts, Curtaines and vallians and Curtaine roods, one press Cubbord, one Chest, 2 stooles, one wicer Chaire, an Old settle, one payre of Cobirons, a payre of Tongs, 7*li.* 7*s.* 6*d.*

IN THE CHAMBER OVER THE KITCHIN—In 4 stone and 10*li.* of wooll, in 18 bus. of Maulteane [malting] barly, one pillion and pillion Cloth, one side saddle, scoles and waites, and other Implements of Husbandry, 6*li.* 10*s.*

IN THE CHAMBER OVER THE MILKHOUSE—2 beedstedles, 2 flock beeds, 3 Feather Boulsters, one Flock boulstere, 2 blankett, 2 Kiverletts, one forme, one hopbagg, 7 Basketts, one hundred and a halfe of hopps with the Baggs, 6*li.*

In Limin [linen] & Fine Hollon Sheetes—5 payre of Towin sheetes, one Dyeper Table Cloth, 6 Dyeper Napkins, Three Table Cloths, 2 Dousen and Eight Napkins, 6 Towells, 6 payre of pillowbeires, and other Course Linnin aboute the House, 4*li.* 9*s.* 6*d.*

In One Old Sillver Guilt Boule, 2*li.*

IN THE MAULTHOUSE—One old Quearne, One Screine, one bushell, 5 sithes, one peeck, one halfe peck, 2 Dewrakes, 1*li.* 10*s.* 8*d.*

IN THE WORKEHOUSE—In 30^ty bushells of Coole, 29[?]qrs. of Horse Corne, one Sider presse with Divers other Implements and Tooles of Husbandry, 3*li.* 5*s.* 6*d.*

IN THE WHEATE BARNE—Fiftie one qrs. of Wheate, 30*li.*

IN THE STABLE—4 Stoone horses, one Old Gilt Horse, there Harnice & Roopes, & Implements of husbandry—35*li.* 10*s.*

IN THE YARDS—6 Milshe Kine, 6 small Welsh Steires, 9 Hoggs, 2 Sowes, one Boore, and 10 small piggs, Cowracks, and hoggetrouves, with other Implements & 3 Ladders, 39*li.* 17*s.*

IN THE FEILDS AND FELLEWES—33 sheep & 21 Lambs, 16*li.* 10*s.*

IN THE CARTEHOUSE—One Old Waggon, one Old Loode Carte, One Dungcarte, one Dungcart Coope, 2 payre of Harrowes, one ploue and the Irons, One wheele barrow, 14*li.* 15*s.* 10*d.*

In Timber and Wood in the yards and feilds—4*li.* 10*s.*
In three Roodes of Hoppground with an old stook of Pooles thereon, 6*li.*
In 43 Acres of Wheate and Barly, 143*li.* 6*s.* 8*d.*; In 21 Acres and a halfe of peease & 2 acres of Grase, 43*li.*; In 30 Acres of Leesse Land with the halfe yeares Reent where of 21 acres was Twice Fallowed and 9 acres but once Fellowed, 18*li.* 4*s.*; for 8 acres and ahalfe of Land belonging to Grayes Farme Once Fallowed, 1*li.* 14*s.*
Spirate Debts Due and Owing to the Testator—5*li.*
In Weareing Apparrell and Money in his purse—6*li.* 6*s.* 6*d.*
Summ' Totall'—423*li.* 8*s.* 3*d.* [should be 423*li.* 7*s.* 3*d.*].
[Appraisers—John Boosey, John Boosey (*sic*), Thomas Cheveley.]
[Exhibited 7 December 1675.]

86.—William Crush of Roxwell, yeoman. 6 November 1675.

YIN THE HALLE—2 tables, 3 formes, 2 Joynt stooles, 4 Chaires, one Cubard, one Jacke, fiere shovell and tonges, 2 Cobeiarnes, 2 tranneles, one large byble, one paire of bellece, 2*li.* 13*s.* 4*d.*

YIN THE PALLER—One fether bead, 2 fether boulsters, one blankeet, one Coverlid, one beedsted, Curtaines and Vallance, ad mate and Roodes [and mat and rods], one preese, one livoury Cubard, one small table, one large table, 2 stooles, 3 Chaires, 6 Cushings, 2 staipe [?striped] Carpeets, a paire of tonnges, a paire of Doges, a dixnary, 6*li.* 13*s.*

YIN THE DARY—One stane, one Charne, one poudering tube, and sume other small thinges, 15*s.*

YIN THE BUTTREE—One Cheese preese, 2 driping panes, 3 spittes, a gride-iarne, a small table, an ould troofe, one Yiarne poote, ad hukes [and hooks], and sume other od thinges at 1*li.* 11*s.* 2*d.*

YIN THE LITTELL BUTREY—3 small fessels, and a drinke stall, 10*s.* 6*d.*

YIN THE PALLER CHAMBER—One fether bead and boulster, 2 pillows, 3 blankets, a greene wosteed Rouge [rug], 2 beadsteeds, one mate, one Corde, and Rodes, 4 huches, one Chest, 2 Chaires, a paire of doges, and fire shovell, 5*li.* 5*s.* 4*d.*

yin linninge—7 paire of sheetes, 6 pillobeares, 4 table Cloathes, 4 dusen of napkins, with other small Linings, 7*li.* 11*s.*

YIN THE HALL CHAMBER—2 fether beades and boulsters, 4 pillowes, 2 beadstedes, 2 mates, 2 Cordes, 2 Chestes, 4*li.*

YIN THE CHEESE CHAMBER—For Cheses, and a lucking glase [looking-glass], 2*li.* 1*s.* 4*d.*

For peutore—1*li.* 15*s.*

YIN THE MAIDES CHAMBER—One small fether bead and boulster, 2 blankeets, 1*li.*

YIN THE FOLKES CHAMBER—One flocke bead and boulster, ad fether pillowe, 2 wheeles, 1*li.* 1*s.* 4*d.*; for a large foulling peece, 1*li.* [torn away], for a small Copen [copper], 3 brase [torn away], a brase poote, 3 skillits, 3*li.* 13*s.* 4*d.*

YIN THE SMALL BEARE BUTTREY—2 hogsheds, 6 tubes, a funnell, a quarne, a moulding plonke, a mustard mille, a Drinke stalle, a kneding trofe, with sume other od small thinges, 2*li.* 1*s.* 6*d.*

YIN THE CORNE CHAMBER—3 wedges, a leddon waite, a pair of scalles, with other lumber, 13*s.* 4*d.*

For 2 laders and a dew Racke, 6*s.*; for the waggine, 2 dungcarts, ad a ould bucke of a Carte, 7*li.* 10*s.*

For 3 hooges, 6 pigges, 5*li.* 8*s.*; for 2 horses, 5*li.*; 10 sheepe, 3*li.* 6*s.* 8*d.*; one Cowe at 1*li.* 13*s.* 4*d.*

For haye, 4*li.* 10*s.*

For plowes, and horse harnes, and harrowes, and Roapes, sadle, and sadle and bridle, and [?]halters, 1*li.* 2*s.*

For wheate and barly in the barne, 50*li.*; for pease, 1*li.*

For sackes, and screene, and bushell, and forkes, and shoveles, and spades, and other nesecary thinges, and fanes, 1*li.* 12*s.*

For waring Clothes, 3*li.*; Money in his purse—2*li.*; Munny owing to him—13*li.* 7*s.*

[Original not totalled; the sums as shown above amount to—142*li.* 0*s.* 2*d.*]

[Appraisers—Thomas Crush, John Nash. Exhibited 7 December 1675.]

87.—Henry Palmer of Writtle. 9 November 1675.

2 Cowes, 6*li.* 10*s.*; For hay, 1*li.* 10*s.*; wood, 14*s.*

One Poridgpott, 10*s.*; 3 kettls, 2 skillits, one bras pan, one Worminpan, 15*s.*;

one Morter, 2*s*. 6*d*.; 8 pewter dishes, one kandellstik, one salt, one bottle, 14*s*.
One table & forme, 5*s*.; one Coblard, 1*s*. 6*d*.; 4 Chayers, 3 plonks, 2 payles, 6*s*. 6*d*.; one Grinstoon, one Fryin pan, one slice, one pair Tranels, 3*s*. 6*d*.; one pair Cobirns, one spitt, 4*s*.
2 billes, 2 wedges, 2 exes, one mad hook [mattock], one fan, 4*s*.
For erthin warr, 2*s*.; one Chern, 2 trays, and dishes, 5*s*.; 3 shelves, 2 formes, 2*s*.; one powdaring tubb, 10*s*.; 5 tubbs, one stand, 10*s*.; 2 barrels, one knedin trove, 6*s*. 6*d*.; one swill tube, 1*s*.
3 Chest, 7*s*. 6*d*.; one bedd, and all belongin to it, 1*li*. 6*s*.; one trundle bedstidle, & Cradl, 4*s*.
Linnig, 6*s*.
For the Chees and butter, 1*li*. 6*s*.; For honey, 5*s*.
For a sack and bagg, 2*s*. 6*d*.; 3 baskels, 2*s*. 4*d*.; 2 pitchforks, one lader, and one Grinstoon, 2*s*.; scools and Wayts, 1*s*. 6*d*.
For warin Clothes, & mony in his pocket, 10*s*.
[Total]—17*li*. 18*s*. 10*d*. [should be 18*li*. 9*s*. 4*d*.]
[Appraisers—Hue (Hugh) Greene, John Burrowes.]
[Exhibited 7 December 1675, by John Robinson and John Harries.]

88.—Robert Douset of Writtle, husbandman. 1 December 1675.

IN YE PARLOR CHAMBER—One flock bed, one bedstead, two feather pillowes, & aboulstar, one Blankcet & a Covering, Mat & Cord, 1*li*.; 2 Chests, 2 Boxes, 2 formes, and two Joynt stooles, one letle table, with other implements, 12*s*.; Thre pair of Sheetes, one Table-cloth, 2 pair of pillowbers, 12 Napkins, & some other broken linen, 1*li*. 5*s*.

IN YE PARLOR—One feather bed & Bedstead, Green say Curtans & Vallance, one green Rug, 2 Blanckets, 2 feather Pillowes, & a flock bolster, Matt & Cord, 3*li*. 10*s*.; one old Cubard, one little Chest, one Chair, & Severall peces of Earthen wair, with Small implements, 6*s*. 8*d*.

IN YE HALL—One Table & frame, 2 Short formes, 6 Chaires, one litle Cubard, one bench, fower Cushions, & other lumber, 1*li*.; Thre Spitts, 2 gridireons, one Cleaver, & a Hatchet, a pair of Andireons, Tramils, 5*s*.

IN YE BUTREY—Fower Ketles, 3 Skillits, one Skumer, two Ireon pots, a frying pan, 2*li*.; fower bere vessells, & beere stall, Two tubbs, 3 keelers, one Chese-stand, one powthering tubb, & other Lumber, 1*li*. 10*s*.; one Kneading trough, 2*s*. 6*d*.; 12 peeces of peauter severall sorts, 10*s*.

IN YE CHAMBER OVER YE BUTREY—One flockbed, & bedstead, a pair of sheets, one Covering, 2 formes, one Saw, with other implements of Husbandry, 1*li*.; fowcr Sacks, with some small things, 5*s*.

In redy Money & wearing aparrill, 15*s*.

IN YE BARN—One parcell of Wheat Un-thrashd, 5*li*.

Eleaven Sheepe and Lambs, 2*li*. 15*s*.
Some Tot'—21*li*. 16*s*. 2*d*.
[Appraisers—William Garrat, Jonathan Sapford.]
[Exhibited 14 (December) 1675.]

89.—Mathew Woollard of Writtle. 4 December 1675.

IN YE HALL—One Cubard, 2 Tables, one Joynt stoole, 2 formes, 4 stooles, 4 Chaires, 4 Cushions with some other Small things, 15*s.*; one gridireon, a fyre shovele & tongs, 1*s.* 6*d.*

IN YE BUTRY—Fower pewter dishes, 2 Ketles, one warming pan, a pastey peele, & dreaping pan, 14*s.*; 2 Barrells, 2 letle tubbs, one old pot, & a frying pan, 5*s.*

IN YE CHAMBER—Two Beds, & Bedsteads, with Curtains & vallanes, Coverings, & all things belonging to them 5*li.*; one Table-Chair, one Chist, & a Trunck with some other implements, 10*s.*

For Some Linen, redy money, & wearing aparell, 14*li.* 5*s.*
[Total]—21*li.* 10*s.* 6*d.*
[Appraisers—William Garrat, Matthew Maning.]
[Exhibited 14 December 1675, by Elizabeth Woolward, widow.]

90.—[Heading torn away, but Inventory endorsed: 'Willia' Finch his Inventary.']

[ta]ble, seaven Joyned stools, and two Hutches, 1*li.* 4*s.*

In Linnen—A dozen and halfe of napkins, 2 table cloths, 6 pair of sheets, and 6 pillowbeers, 3*li.* 5*s.*

IN THE CHAMBER OVER THE MILKHOUSE—One Flock bed, and some ordinary moveables, 1*li.* 7*s.* 6*d.*

IN THE DAYRY—A cheese presse, milk stand, shelves, and other triffles, 10*s.*

IN THE BUTTERY—3 barrells, and some old tubs, 15*s.*; 3 kettles, an old Kopper, and 6 pewter dishes, 3*li.* 5*s.*

IN THE CHAMBER OVER THE HALL—For corn sacks, wooll &c., [?]10*s.*

The Livestock—3 Cows, 3 hoggs, a horse, and a mare, [?]15*li.*; for 14 Sheep and Lambs, [illegible], a cart, harrows, plough[?]taise, and chain, [?]3*li.*
For 3 acres and ½ of wheat, 10*li.* 10s.; For 7 acres of barly, [?]8*li.* 5*s.*; For an acre and ½ of pease, [illegible][1], For 4 acres and ½ of [?]Fetches; For the Hay.
His clothes and money in his purse.
For the Anvill; For the Bellows; For the coles.
The working tools, 1*li.*; The new Iron, 1*li.*
[Not totalled, but a sum on the *verso* amounts to 67*li.* 8*s.* 6*d.*]
[Appraisers—Phillip Richmond, Richard Reeves, Thomas Reynolds.]
[Exhibited 7 December 1675.]

[1] If the calculation on the *verso* is the value of the goods mentioned in the Inventory, the sum of this and the next six items amounts to 4*li.* 10*s.*

NOTE

Except for proper names and at the beginning of lines, capital letters have been disregarded in the remainder of the transcripts.

91.—John Dockley of Writtle, husbandman. 24 January 1675/6.

In the hall—One cubard & two joynt stools, 3*s.*; one table & a forme, 5*s.*; thre old chaires, 1*s.*; one spit, a dreaping-pan, one pair of tongs & fire shovel, 2*s.*

Parlor—One flock bed & bedstead, one covering with mat & cord, 20*s.*; thre chists, & 2 boxes, 10*s.*; one cubard, & some implements, 6*s.* 8*d.*; eaight peeces of pewter, 8*s.*

Chamber—Two old flock beds, and bedsteads, with coverings, 16*s.*; one old forme with implements, 1*s.*; one old pair of hand scales & some small waights, 1*s.* 6*d.*

Buttrey—Thre ketles, 3 skillits, 2 brass potts, one barrell, one kneading-trough, with other Lumber, 25*s.*

Yeard—One grindstone, thre beatles & 6 wedges, one spade, 2 axes, & other tooles, 10*s.*; thre old tubbs, & some wood with other implements, 10*s.*

In wearing clothes, & money, 30*s.*
Some Totall—7*li.* 10*s.* [should be 7*li.* 9*s.* 2*d.*]

On same sheet: John Dockley, junior.

In the hall—One table & forme, 7*s.*; one old chest, 2*s.* 3*d.*

Parlor—One chest, and his wearing apparell, 1*li.* 4*s.*; one brass pott, one brass ketle, one old chair, &c., 12*s.*
In redy money, 25*li.*
[Total]—27*li.* 5*s.* 3*d.*
[Appraisers for both inventories—William Garrat, Matthew Maning.]
[Exhibited 30 March 1676.]

92.—John Buredg of Roxwell. 28 February 1675/6.

In the hall—One tabell, two farmes [forms], four chayers, a glass-case, a benchboard, 2 spits, 2 cobiorns, a payer tramels, one warming pann, fier-shovell and tongs, and three wedges, a clever and shreding knife, two smothing iornes, gridiorn, and bellous, and other implements, 2*li.* 0*s.* 6*d.*

In the parlour—One bedstedl, one fetherbed, one flock bed, one fether bolster, one flock bolster, 2 pillowes, one coverlet, one blanket, one pres cubbert, one chest, 6*li.*

In the buttry—Three barells, four tubes, a cubberd, three bottls, one frying pann, 5 ketls, 4 skillits, one bras pot, 2 basting ladls, a stand, 5*li.* 2*s.*

In the chamber over the hall—One chayer, a whell and a rell, three sacks, a trunk, a trundl bedstedl, 2 sivefs [sieves], 17*s.* 6*d.*

In the chamber over the parlour—One halfheaded bedstedl, one fether bed, one fether bolster, two fether pillowes, one coverlet, two blankets, 3 chests, 2 boxes, one chayer, one joynstoall, one basen, six peweter dishes, a dosin of pewetr spones, 2 candlesticks, one morter, one pestel, one peuter saltseller, one flagone, three peweter sacsers, one payer of flaxon shets, 4 payer of toinge shets, 2 holland pillowberes, 3 flaxon pillowbers, one t[?]oing pillowbere, 10 flaxon napkins, 2 flaxon tabl cloths, one towell, and his wearing clothes, 13*li.* 10*s.*

IN HIS YARD—One pige, and wood, 1*li.* 16*s.*

One bond of thirty pound, 30*li.*
the Wholl summ is—59*li.* 6*s.*
[Appraisers—Edward Allin, Lorance Beadl. Exhibited 6 April 1676.]

93.—John Sapsford of Writtle, yeoman. 19 April 1676.

IN THE HALL—Two long tables, two formes, one ould levery cubard, 3 rush chaires, six cushins, one spining wheele, one glass-case, with some implements, 1*li.* 10*s.*

IN THE PARLOR—One long table & frame with darnix carpet, one side table and carpett, one bedstead, curtans & vallance, one trundle bed & things belonging to it, one pair of andireons, & thre chaires, 7*li.*

IN THE BUTREY—One old table, a chest, one fann, a beere vessell with some implements, 10*s.*

CHAMBER OVER THE PARLOR—One bed and bedstead, with searge curtans & vallance, one worsted rug, thre blanckets, 6 chaires & stooles, 7*li.*; 11 leather chaires, 2*li.* 4*s.*; one side table & carpet, one childs basket, a pair andireons & a lookinglass, 15*s.*; one chist wherin is 10 pair of sheets, one table cloth, one pair of pillowbeeres, & a callico sidebord cloth, 6*li.* 13*s.* 4*d.*

IN THE CLOSET—One box, 4 broken silver spoones, one chair, with some other small things, 12*s.*

CHESE-CHAMBER—63 cheses, & one cheseboard, 2*li.*

CHAMBER OVER THE HALL—One chist of drawers, one dozen of diaper napkins, one table cloth, with 2 cubard clothes, 1*li.* 10*s.*; one dozen of flaxen napkins, one dozon of course napkins, 2 long & 2 short table-clothes, with other things, 1*li.*; one bed & bedstead, with darnix curtans & vallance, a trundle bed, & a chist, 2*li.* 15*s.*

CHAMBER OVER THE BUTREY—One bedstead, 3 ould chists, one pair of bellowes, a pair of creepers, with some other lumber, 10*s.*

SERVANTS CHAMBER—One old fether bed, & boulstar, 1*li.*; one flock bed, & other lumber, 10*s.*

IN THE BUTREY—26 peeces & dishes of peauter, 2*li.* 10*s.*; one table & frame, 2 beere vessels, a buter baskitt, with other implements, 10*s.*

BUTREY NEXT THE KITCHIN—One pair of scales, some lead & iron waights, 14 sacks, 2 tubbs, five beere-vessells & implements, 2*li.* 12*s.*

KITCHIN—Thre brass potts, 5 ketles, 2 skillits, one iron dreaping pan, one brass morter & pestile, 3*li.*; 4 joynt stooles, one litle table, one sitle, one cubord, 3 rush chaires, 2 spits, a pair of andireons, fire shovell & tongs, 1*li.* 5*s.*

IN THE DARY—One chese press, 2 chernes, 2 chese-stands, 6 chese-moats, 9 trayes & keelers, one planckbord, 5 sives, with other implements, 2*li.*

BREWHOUSE—2 leads, *2li.*; 5 brewing tubbs, one cooler, one kneading trough, *1li. 10s.*

IN THE GATE-HOUSE—One capon-coope, 2 pair of Harrowes, & other things belonging to husbandry, *1li. 10s.*

GATE-HOUSE CHAMBER—Two quarters of malt, *2li.*; sives, ridles, &c. implements, *5s.*

IN THE YEARD & UPON THE GROUND—Twelve weather shepe, *3li. 12s.*; 30 sheepe & lambs, *12li.*; one stack of barley & pease, *8li.*; one sow and piggs, & 7 store hoggs, *5li. 10s.*

IN THE BARNE—One parcell of wheat thrasht & unthrasht, 30 quarters by estimation, *37li. 10s.*; one screne for corne, 2 fannes, & other implements, *12s.*; a hayre, *13s. 4d.*

IN THE YEARE [YEARD] MORE—Eaight cowes & 4 calves, *32li.*; two weanells, *2li.*; thre 2 yeare old cattle, *7li.*; five horses, & furniture, *35li.*; one waggan, *5li.*; one load cart, *2li.*; one dung-cart, *10s.*; 12 load of hay by estimation, *9li.*

Upon a bond due from John Staine, principal & intrist, *25li. 12s.*
On a morgage due from Nathaniel Adams, *72li. 19s.*
35 acres of fallow, *7li.*; 56 acres & 3 roods of wheat & barley fallowed land, at *46s.* an acre, *130li. 13s. 4d.*; 21 acres of other corn, pease, barly, & bullung, *21li.*
In redy money, & wearing apparill, *60li.*
The full Inventory is—*532li. 3s.*, less *60li.* To be deducted out of this for rent now due, *472li. 3s.*
[Appraisers—Henry Bright, sen., John Taverner, Henry Bright, jun.]
[Exhibited 22 April 1676.]

94.—Goods and chattells 'at the farme Called the lordsheep.[1] 15 June 1676.

IN THE HALL—2 formes, 2 geine [joined] stooles, 2 round tabells, 5 carpeets, windskott [wainscot] and seattell, 2 chaiers, 4 cushings, 2 cobirons, 2 speets, 1 dripenpan with sum other small things, *2li. 12s.*

IN THE PARLER—2 featherbeades, 1 strawbead, 2 bousters, 2 pillowes, 2 cuerlins, 1 blancket, 1 bedstead, curtins and vallanc, 1 trundell bedsted, *5li. 10s.*; 1 long tabell, 1 squeare-tabell, 7 joyne stooles, 4 chayers, 1 livrey cuberd, 1 prese, 2 hutches, 1 settell and panited [painted] cloath, 3 cuberd clothes, 4 cushings, 1 box, 1 glas cas, 2 curtins and curtinrodes, 1 glas judg [jug], 1 flower pott, *4li. 12s.*

IN THE PARLER CLOSETT—1 hutch, 6 shelves, 1 cheast of drawers, 1 pasty peell, 1 peybord, 1 pecke, 1 box and other small things, *11s.*

IN THE PARLER CHAMBER—1 ginebedsted, curtens and vallanc, 1 fetherbead, 3 boulsters, 5 pillowes, 1 cuierlett, *5li.*; 1 chest, 1 hutch, 7 chayers, 1 geyne stoole, 1 tabell, 1 forme, 2 cushings, *1li. 15s.*

[1] Endorsed: Widow Osborne's Inventory. [Mary Osburne was buried at Writtle, 26 April 1676.]

IN THE KITCHIN—2 dusen and 3 puter dishes, 2 dusen puter spoones, 1 puter flagon, 3 puter canstickes, 2 tinn canstick, 2 puter bowels and sum small things, *2li.* 15*s.* 4*d.*; six bras kettls, 4 bras skilits, 3 poots, 3*li.* 1*s.*; 3 spicts, 3 shredinknives, 1 box iron, 2 payr of tramels, 1 bare of yron, 2 kobrons, 1 yron firshovell and tongs, 2 gridyrons, 1 warmin pan, 2 payr of potthooks, 1*li.* 4*s.* 4*d.*; 1 tabele, 1 forme, 2 benches, 1 cuberd, 3 shelves, 2 glaskaces, 2 morters and pesells, 6 chayers, 1*li.* 3*s.* 6*d.*

IN THE BUTREY—3 hogsheads, 1 fringe pan, 2 shelves, 1 musterd quarne, a flex wheell, 1*li.* 4*s.* 6*d.*

IN THE KITCHIN CHAMBER—2 beadcs, 2 bolstors, 2 kivrins, 2 pillowes, 1 bedsted, 4*li.*; 2 chestes, 1 chest of drawers, 1 hutch, 1 cullerd, 1 tabell, 6 ginestooles, 1 box, 3 chayers, 1 trunck, 5*li.* 5*s.*; 13 payer of toingsheets, 4 payer of flexin sheets, 1 castingsheet, 2 dusen and half of dieper napkins, 4 dusen of flex and toing napkings, 3 dieper tabellkloaths, 3 flexen tabell-klothes, 1 hollon sheett, 8 pillibers, 2 towells, 12*li.* 12*s.*; 1 silvertanker, 2 cups, 10 spoones, 7*li.*

IN THE SINCKHOUS CHAMBER—1 featherbead, 1 flockebead, 2 bedsteds, 1 ruge, 1 blanckote, 1 tabell, 1 forme, 1 ginestoole, 2 featherbolsters, 2 flock-bolsters, 3*li.* 2*s.*

IN THE CHES CHAMBER—19, 1 tabell, 5 shellfes and sum ould stuf, 1*li.* 12*s.*

IN THE HALL CHAMBER—2 borded bedstedes, 1 featherbead, 1 strawbead, 3 blankotes and other ould lumber, 1*li.* 15*s.*

IN THE LITELL CHAMBER OVER THER HALL—1 bedsted, 2 chayers, 1 stoole, 1 payer of rakes, 10*s.*

IN THE YRON CHAMBER—Wooll and old yron and ould stufe, 2*li.* 4*s.*

IN THE BREWHOUSE—1 copper, 1 measintub, 1 kneading troth, 2 tubes, 1 coulder, 1 tunnell, 1 peell, 3 sives, 3*li.* 1*s.*

IN THE STRONGBEERE BUTREY—4 barrells, 2 drinkestalls, 4 shelves, 1 dusen and halfe of trinchers, 1*li.* 0*s.* 6*d.*

IN THE DAYREY—5 chesemotes, 1 stand, 1 pouderintub, 1 kimnill, 1 coull, 1 troath, 2 dressers, 5 shealves, 1*li.* 18*s.* 6*d.*

IN THE SINCK HOUS—1 leade, 1 cheespres, 1 charne, 4 payles, dishes and spoones and ould stufe, 2*li.* 2*s.* 6*d.*

The land upon the first crope is 47 acors at 1*li.* 17*s.* 4*d.* the acor; the land upon the second crope is 27 acors at 15*s.* 2*d.* the acore; for harrowing 13*s.* 4*d.* which is in all, 99*li.* 9*s.* 10*d.*
6 cowes, 1 bull, 21 sheep, 14 stores, 37*li.* 8*s.*
1 wagon, 1 long carte, 1 dung carte, 6*li.*
The wheate in the barne, 18 quarters, 21*li.* 12*s.*
For hay, 18 load, 20*li.* 5*s.*
4 horse and furnituer and 1 meare, 11*li.*
1 quarter peas and beanes, 1*li.*
Harrowes, plowes, fanes, 1 skrue, 1 bushell, 2 panyards, 10 ould sacks, 1 pannell and other working tooles and lumber, 2*li.* 5*s.*

Clothes and redey money, 5*li.*
More 10 quarters drest, 12*li.*
3 calves at 18*s.* a peece, 2*li.* 14*s.*
[Total]—294*li.* 5*s.*
[Appraisers—John Clarke, Thomas Gray, Thomas Crow.]
[Exhibited 2 September 1676, by Thomas Osburne, son.]

95.—Phillip Monke the elder, of Roxwell, husbandman. 28 December, 1676.

IN THE HALL—One long table, one bench board, 3 rush chaires, a little table, a spitt, a paire of cobirons, fire shovell & tongs, a smoothing iron with some other small utensells valued att 12*s.*

IN THE PARLOUR—One high bedstead, one feather bed, one feather boulster, two pillows, 2 blanketts, one olde press cubboard, two huttches, a trundle bed with the things belonging to itt, three pewterdishes, two chaires valued att 2*li.* 16*s.*

IN THE MILKEHOUSE—Three tubbs, three kimnells, a great troffe, a cherne, a seme, 3 shelves, 8*s.*

IN THE BUTTREY—One iron pott, three kettles, 2 barrells with some other small things, 1*li.* 2*s.*

IN THE CHAMBER OVER THE PARLOUR—Tenn bushells of barley, two bushells of wheat, one old tubb and a board, 1*li.* 15*s.*

IN THE CHAMBER OVER THE HALL—One borded beadstead with the things belonging to itt, one old hutch, a chaire, three bushells of oates, 2 bushells of pease, 1*li.* 3*s.*

IN THE CHAMBER OVER THE BUTTREY—One iron beame with a paire of scalls with some other small things valued att 7*s.*

IN THE BARNE—6 shock of wheat and a small cant of barley, a old bushell, 1*li.* 16*s.*

IN THE STABLE—One horse, a mare, 2 colts, with the harness, 3*li.*

IN THE MILLHOUSE—The mill with two old hutches valued at 2*li.* 10*s.*

Two cowes, 4*li.* 10*s.*; two piggs, 10*s.*; A long cart, 2*li.* 10*s.*
12 bushell of oats att his Chambr in Chelmsford, 1*li.*
26 sheep valued att 6*li.*; Hay in the barne, 1*li.* 10*s.*; Plow & plow irons, 4*s.*; The corne on the ground, 15*s.*
His weareing apparell, 6*s.*
[Total]—32*li.* 14*s.*
[Appraisers—Hezekiah Godsafe, William Man.]
[Exhibited 31 January 1676/7.]

'The words which Phillip Monke spake some small time Before he Departed as to the settling of his worldly estate was these, Thatt itt was his will and mind that his wiffe should have w[t] Stock and goods he left for to helpe maintaine her During her natureall life and w[t] part of the said Stock & goods should be left after his said wifes Decease should be equally Devided into three parts and his sone Phillip Monke to have one of them & the other two to be equally devided amongest his Daughters, Thesse words were spoken in the p'sence of Prissilla Elson, Sarah White & Mary Hawkins.'

96.—William Eree, of Writtle, blacksmith. 28 May 1677.

IN THE HALL—One long table and frame, two benches & 7 joint stools, 1*li.* 4*s.*; one cubard, thre rush chairs & one coach-box, 12*s.*; thre cobireons, 2 pair of tongs, 2 fire-shoveles, 4 spitts, one dreaping pan, one chafeing dish, one cullinder, a cleaver, one gridireon, one tosting iron, with other implements, 1*li.*; one short table, one letle trunck, a morter & pestile, 6*s.* 8*d.*; one warming pan, one box of drawers, & a smoothing iron, 3*s.*; a parcell of earthen ware and twenty fower glass bottles, 5*s.*; one jack with the waights, 9*s.*

IN THE PARLOR—One table, one forme, 3 joynt stooles, one elbow chair, & one litle chair, 15*s.*; one cubart & a wainscot chist, 1*li.*; one feather bed, bedstead, darnix curtans & vallance, one rug, one blancket, one boulstar, 2 pillowes, a trundle bedstead, matts, cords, &c., belonging, 3*li.* 10*s.*; 2 glass-cases & 4 cushins, 2*s.*; 14 dishes of peauter, one basin, 3 sawcers, 3 pewter potts, 2 candlesticks, 2 poringers, one boule, a salt, & other small things, 1*li.* 10*s.*

IN THE BUTREY—One table & frame, one powdering tub, one pasty pann, one trevit, & other implements, 12*s.*; one cider press, one cubard, 2 hogsheads, 2 other small vessells, 2 beere-stalls, 2 shelves, & some earthen potts, 1*li.*; one great brass kettle, 2 other brass kettles, 2 iron potts, 3 brass potts, 4 skillitts, a brass frying pan, & implements, 3*li.* 15*s.*

IN THE KITCHIN—One small lead or brass furnace, one skillitt, one kneading trough, one pair of tramills, one pair of tongs, with other small things, 1*li.* 5*s.*; nine brewing tubbs, one tunnill, 2 formes, with lumber, 1*li.* 10*s.*

CHAMBER OVER THE BUTREY—Two ould chists, one boarded bedstead, one old flockbed, one blancket, one coverlet, & 4 sacks, 15*s.*

CHAMBER OVER THE PARLOR—Two featherbeds, two flockbeds, 3 bedsteads, 2 coverlets, 3 blanckets, gren say curtans & vallance, one other pair of ould curtans, 4 bolstars, 4 pillowes, with matts, cords, & things belonging, 5*li.*; three chists & 3 boxes, 12*s.*; 18 pair of sheetes, six table napkins, two board clothes, 6 towills and 6 pillowberes, with other linen, 8*li.* 2*s.* 6*d.*

CHAMBER OVER THE SHOPP—One long table with trussells, one saddle, one pillion, a chese-rack, 2 tubbs, one wicker chair, 4 baskits, one peck and a halfe peck measure, one iron-pitch, & 2 pitch-forks, 1*li.*; one parcle of wood, 11*s.* 10*d.*

In redy money and wearing apparrill, 4*li.*
Some Totall of ye Inventory—39*li.*
[Appraisers—Edmond Stearne, William Garrat.]
[Exhibited 27 September 1677.]

97.—Henry Duke, of Writtle, yeoman. 26 September 1677.

IN THE HALL—One jack, 3 irons dripping panns, 3 spitts, 3 paire of andirons with brasse heads, fier shovell & tongs, 2*li.* 5*s.*; one presse cubbord, one joyned table, 3 joyned stooles, one forme, 8 chusshoons, 4 chaires, one litle table, with other implements, 1*li.* 10*s.*; the bible & [other] litle bookes, 3*s.* 4*d.*

In the parlor—One joyned bedd steddle, two feather bedds, two feather bolsters, three blanketts, one greene rugg, curtaines & vallances, 4*li.* 10*s.*; one joyned table, one forme, one livery cubbord, one presse cubbord, 6 leather chayres, two old stooles, one carpett, with other implements, 1*li.* 10*s.*

In the kitchin—3 tubbs, one kneding trough, one stand, one chayre, 10*s.*; the brasse, two leades, two potts, 4 kettles, one warmeing pann, one old skimmer, with other implements, 2*li.* 10*s.*

In the milkehouse—Two charnes, 5 shelves, 2 planks, the milke vessells & other implements, 10*s.*

In the buttery—One chessepresse, 2 hoggs heades & other implements 7*s.*

In the old parlor—2 bolsters, one beddsteddle, the scales & weights & other implements, one livery table, 10*s.*

In the chamber over the buttery—One joyned bedsteddle, two feather bedds, 3 feather bolsters, 2 pillowes, coverlett & blankett, two chests, 2 livery cubbords & other implements, 4*li.*; the pewter—24 peeces, 2*li.* 10*s.*

In the chamber over the parlor—The linnen—8 payre of sheetes flax & tow, 3 dosen of flaxen & towen napkins, 3 board clothes, 6 payre of flaxen pillowbeeres & other small linnen, 4*li.* 10*s.*; one joyned bed steddle, one trundle bedd, [illegible] feather bedds, 3 bolsters, 2 blanketts, one coverlett, one pillow, 2 tables, 3 chests, one truncke & other implements, 4*li.* 10*s.*; 3 pillowes, one coverlett, one payre of curtaines, 1*li.*

4 cowes, one heifer, 12 sheepe, 4 piggs, one old horse, 19*li.*

One old cart, one payre of harrowes, one screw, one bushell, one caveing sive & other implements, 1*li.*

The fallow & seed, 2*li.* 9*s.* 6*d.*

For a cow & a calfe, 5*li.*

Bills, bonds & desperate debts with his weareing apparell & money in his purse, 5*li.*

Summa totalis—63*li.* 4*s.* 10*s.*

[Appraisers—John Wallis, John Nash.]

[Exhibited 27 September 1677, by Margaret Duke, widow and administratrix.]

98.—Richard Bridgman, of Writtle, gardener. 26 September 1677.

In the hall—One table and thre joynt stooles, two letle side tables, two ould chaires, 9*s.*; five cobireons, 2 warming-panns, one jack, one chafeing-dish, one gridireon, a smoothing ireon, 2 fireshovells, one pair of tongs, with other small things, 13*s.* 4*d.*; thre spitts and two pair of tramills, 5*s.*

In the parlor—One court cubard, 5 chaires, 4 joynt stooles, one letle tables, a forme, with some potts & glasses & 2 candlesticks, 1*li.*

In the letle butrey—Two small beere barrills, one ould table, a joynt stoole, & a letle beere stall, 5*s.*

In the other butrey—Six ould beere barrills, one powthering tubb, 2 beere stalls, one joynt stoole, one cuberd, with other small implements, 12*s.*;

4 kettles, two letle brass potts, seaven skillits, one fryingpan, one chafeing dish, two brass candlesticks, with some other small things, 1*li.* 10*s.*; 15 small dishes and other peeces of peauter, 18*s.*

IN THE CHAMBER OVER THE SHOPP—One feather bed and boulstar, one bedstead with green say curtans and vallance, 2 ould blanckets & an ould rugg with matt & cord, 2*li.* 10*s.*; one press cubard, thre joynt stooles, thre chaires, one letle ould table with severall glasses & other implements, 15*s.*; one ould chist, 2*s.*

IN THE CHAMBER OVER THE HALL—One ould table and thre joynt stooles, two chists, one wicker chair, one ould trunck, 7*s.*; twelve glass quart bottles, 2*s.* 6*d.*; one bedstead, one letle featherbed & a flock boulstor & a pillow, 15*s.*

IN THE CHAMBER OVER THE PARLOR—One bedstead with old darnix curtans, one feather bed & boulstar, 2 pillowes, one blanckett & a coverlitt, 1*li.* 15*s.*; two ould trunks, 3 stooles & a box, 6*s.* 8*d.*; one old sea chest, 1*s.* 6*d.*; one letle trundle bed & bedstead, one rug, six sacks, one screene, with other lumber, 1*li.*; six pair of sheets, one dozen & a halfe of napkins, 6 pillow-beeres, thre table clothes, 3 towills & some other small lining, 2*li.*

IN THE SHOPP—Earthen ware severall potts & panns, &c., 7*s.*; tow counters with severall empty cask, 5*s.*; a nest of drawers & 5 shelves, 5*s.*; seaven peeces & remnants of severall sorts of cloth by estimation 40 ells, 2*li.*; pitch & tarr, with some other wares, 5*s.*; 3 pair of scales and waights, one pestile & morter, with severall lumber, 5*s.*; 3 pair of bodies, 2 flanill wastcoats, 6 pair of cource stockings with some remnants of fustian, tapes & filliting, 15*s.*

IN THE KITCHIN & BREWHOUSE—Eaight brewing tubbs of severall sorts with the beere stall & formes, 1*li.*; one old kettle, a kneading trough with severall other implements & lumber, 10*s.*; one lie-trough & leach, 2*s.* 6*d.*

IN THE YEARD & UPON THE GROUND—18 cowcumber-glasses, 9*s.*; one parcle of hay, 6*s.*; 2 spades, one shovill, a mattock, one grindstone, severall parcells of wood and other lumber, 10*s.*

One horss sadle & bridle, 2*li.* 10*s.*
In redy money and wearing aparill, 2*li.*
Somme Totall—*26li.* 16*s.* 6*d.*
[Appraisers—William Garrat, Edmond Stearne.]
[Exhibited 27 September 1677.]

99.—Edward George, of Writtle, yeoman. 27 September 1677.

IN THE HALL—One table and six joynt stooles, six chaires, one great chist, one cradle & a childs chaire, 1*li.* 5*s.*; one pair of andireons, fyre shovell and tongs, one pair of bellowes, tow spitts, and other small implements, 15*s.*

IN THE BUTTREY—Thre hogsheads, one halfe hogshead and two letle barrills, 16*s.*; one ireon pott, one letle table, two beere stalls with some small things, 9*s.*; two kettles, 5 skillitts, 1 dreaping pann, one cullinder, 3 other lattin panns, one leather bottle, 1*li.* 15*s.*

IN THE PARLOR—One bed and bedstead, one boulstar, greene linsey woollsey curtans & vallance, two blanckets, one green rugg, 5*li.*; one wainscott cubard, one chist, two boxes, one trunck & a warming pan, 1*li.*; 26 dishes and other peeces of pewter, 3*li.*; 9 pair of sheetes, two table clothes, one dozen of napkins, 6 towills & other linen, 5*li.*; one silver bowle, 3*li.*

IN THE CHAMBER OVER THE BUTTREY—Bedstead, one covering & a blanckett, 1*li.* 10*s.*; two chists, one wollin & one lining wheele, and some other implements, 10*s.*

IN THE KITCHIN AND DARY—One cheese-press, 1 chirne & stand, 5 cheese moats, one chese-bred, 4 boules and other things in the dary, 2*li.* 10*s.*; 85 cheeses waighing by estimation 240 lbs, 3*li.*; one small copper, 5 brewing tubbs, one kneading trough, 2 formes, one lie-trough, with severall other implements, 2*li.* 10*s.*

IN THE BARNES & STABLE—One parcell of barley by estimation 30 quarters, 30*li.*; a parcell of wheat by estimation 10 quarters, 15*li.*; a parcell of bullimung, 12*li.*; 18 load of hay by estimation, 18*li.*; one screene, one fann, one bushill, 8 sacks and other things belonging to the barne, 2*li.*

IN THE YEARD & UPON THE GROUND—One waggan, one dung-cart, one plough, one pair of harrowes, rakes, forkes, &c., 7*li.* 10*s.*; six horses, & their harness & furniture, 30*li.* 10*s.*; fower cowes, young & ould, 14*li.*; 5 sheepe, and three lambs, 2*li.* 10*s.*; 4 hoggs, one sow, and 5 piggs, 5*li.* 10*s.*

In redy money and wearing apparill, 5*li.*
Tene acres of fallow, 15*li.*
[Total]—189*li.*
[Appraisers—William Garrat, Thomas Crow.]
[Exhibited 27 September 1677.]

100.—[Blank] Bonington.[1] [No date.]

For two cous six, 6*li.*[2]

For a node [an old] bead stetel and a node teck and two blancoets, 1*s.*; two bostors [blank]; for a round tabul and a node tabul, 5*s.*; for two chists, 7*s.*; for [?c]eattel, 13*s.*; for a bracpot, 6*s.*
For his funarall charg three, 3*li.* 1*s.*[2]
[Total—7*li.* 12*s.*] [No appraisers.]

101.—Richard Wolfe of Roxwell. 24 September 1678.

IN THE HALL—A longe table & frame, six joyned stooles, two presse cubboards, a sideboard table, thre rush chairs, and a paire of cobirons, 2*li.* 18*s.*

IN THE PARLOUR—A longe table & frame and two formes, two leather chaires and a greene chaier, a rush chaire, a table carpett, a paire of cobirons, fire shovell and tongs, 2*li.* 4*s.*

[1] A John Bonington was buried at Writtle, 24 December 1676.
'Aninvetorie of sich goods as were my gran fathers.'

[2] Presumably correct; an exceptionally illiterate inventory.

IN THE LITLE CLOSET—Some woole, 15*s*.

IN THE LITLE PARLOUR—A table & frame, three joyned stooles, a carpet, a leather chaire, a rush chaire, a small stoole, two cushions, a paire of cobirons, 14*s*.

IN THE BUTTERY—A pipe, three hogsheads, a barrell & some other small things, 1*li*. 10*s*.

IN THE KITCHINGE—A table upon tressels, a forme, a litle tubb, a bench, a cubboard, fowre shelves, one joyned stoole, a forme, seven old rush chaires, two spitts, a jack with the weights, some smothing irons, fire shovell, tonges and bellows, tramels, three dripinge pans, with some small things, 1*li*. 14*s*.

In brasse—Five brasse kettles, two brass pots, foure skilletts & a friing pan, 2*li*. 5*s*.

In pewter—Six and thirty peeces, 1*li*. 10*s*.

IN THE LITLE BUTTERY—Fowre barrels, two drinck stals, fowre shelves and other implements, 11*s*.

IN THE BOWTINGE HOUSE—A kneadinge troafe, three shelves, a drinck stall, a stand, a powdringe tub and other small things, 11*s*.

IN THE BREWHOUSE—Two pane [pan] hangers, a malt querne, seven tubs, an old hogshead, and some small things, 4*li*. 10*s*. 6*d*.

IN THE MILKEHOUSE—A leaden vessell, two chernes, a cheese presse, a stand, three tubs, a cheese bread, six pailes, six trays, some cheese moates, three shelves, a forme with some earthen ware & some small things, 4*li*. 2*s*. 6*d*.; butter in the milkhouse, 1*li*. 15*s*.

IN THE CHAMBER OVER THE KITCHINGE—A bedstedle, curtains & valence, a featherbed and bolster, three pillows, a paire of curtains & valence in a chest, a livery cubboard with a carpet, two cushions, two stooles, two chests, two blankits, and a coverlett, 5*li*. 5*s*.

IN THE CHAMBER OVER THE ENTRY—A bedstedle, curtaines and valence, two feather beds, one bolster, three pillows, two blancketts and a coverlet, a chest of drawers, a trunck, fowre chests, a small box, and other small things, 5*li*. 4*s*.; two coverlets & a red rugg, 1*li*. 4*s*.

IN THE CHAMBER OVER THE BOWTINGE HOUSE—A halfe headed bedstead, a featherbed and two bolsters and two blanketts, a litle box, and a stoole, 1*li*. 12*s*.

IN THE SERVANTS CHAMBER—Two bedstedles, fowre blanketts, two flock beds and two bolsters, 1*li*. 5*s*.

In linninge—Eight paire of towen sheets, fowre course table cloathes, 5 course pillowbeers, six course towels, sixe paire of flaxen sheets, six paire of flaxen pillowbeers, six flaxen and towen table cloathes, three dozen of flaxen, table napkins, two dozen of towen table napkins, three flaxen towells, three holland pillow beers, one calaco cubboard cloth, & some other small peeces of linninge, 9*li*. 7*s*. 4*d*.

In plate—Eight silver spoones and a silver salt, 2*li*. 8*s*.

In the maids chamber—The bedstedles with the beddinge thereon, *2li.* 4*s.*

In the garrett—Ten bushels of oates, 12*s.*

In the cheese chamber—The cheese, there beinge six score cheeses at 2*s.* the cheese, 12*li.*

In the barne—The barly there, 45*li.*; the pease, 18*li.*; the burnt wheate there, 4*li.*
The hay cocks & hay in the house, 16*li.*

In the yards—One wageon with the wheeles, one longe cart, three dung carts with there shod wheeles and another paire of spare wheeles, 19*li.*; seven hoggs and six piggs, 9*li.* 18*s.*

In the stable—Seven horses with there firniture for plow and cart, ropes, winchpins, pitchforks, plows and harrows with shovels & other implements of husbandry, 41*li.*
Ten cowes and a bull, 38*li.*; in sheepe, thirty yeare old Norfolke, 10*li.* 10*s.*; fifty Norfolke lambs, 8*li.* 11*s.* 8*d.*
Two hairs on the kills [kilns], a few coabs [cobbs] and ten sackes, scoles & weights, 1*li.* 15*s.*
Twelve bags of old hops, 17*li.*; new hopps unbagged, 60*li.*; the hoppoales on the ground, 45*li.*
The tilt upon the ground being 49 acres is 26*li.* 10*s.*, and the rent of it at 10*s.* per acre is 24*li.* 10*s.*, which is in all, 51*li.*
The poweltrey in the yard, 1*li.*
The testators waringe apparrell and mony in his purse, 10*li.*
In good debts, 61*li.* 15*s.*; in desparate debts, 1*li.* 10*s.*; in redy mony, 100*li.*
Sume totall is—625*li.* 1*s.*
[Appraisers—Thomas Crush, Kellam Broune, Mathew Nightingle.]
[Exhibited 7 December 1678 by Ann Woolfe, widow.]

102.—Edmund Turnidge of Roxwell. 7 November 1678.

In the hall—A paire of skalles and wayts belonging to the scalles enough to wey a C. & sixteene pounds, two axes, a hatchett, a iron punch, a winch for a grinstone, four bills, a grubing axe, a pair of garden shears, a hand saw, and iron to stand before the fire, four logg wegges, two hammers, two spitts, a iron driping pann, a gridiron, a little beef forke, a peel, fire shovell & tongs, a pair of iron tay pins, three wimbles, three shaves, goug, a pacer, two smothing irons, three chopping knives, six chushings, one paire of tramells, three stooles, three rush chaires, a salt box, a hower glass, valued att 2*li.* 4*s.* 8*d.*

In the parlour—A press cubbord, a paire of bellows and a armed rush chaire, 12*s.* 6*d.*

In the passage out of the parlour and the little clossett by itt—A tinning driping pan, a lain seive & six barrells with some other utensells, 10*s.* 2*d.*

IN THE BUTTREY—One hoggshead, five little barrells, three brass kettles, four skilletts, a brass pott, six wooden dishes, two wooden platters, a wooden tunell, a iron frying pann, two lanthornes, four little shelves, two leather bottles, two drinke stalls, a short forme with sume other imployments, *2li.* 0*s.* 6*d.*

IN THE DAIRY—Nine small cheese motes, three chese breds, one stand, a little cherne, a powdering tubb, three kemnells, five bowles, two and twenty dishes & a halfe of butter, a musterd querne, some earthen dishes, ten shelves & boards, three formes, two trevetts, a parcell of baccon hookes, *2li.* 17*s.*

IN THE PARLOUR CHAMBER—Two joyne stooles, one chair, two bench boards, a stand to sett a basson on, 5*s.* 6*d.*

IN THE CLOSSETT NEXT THE HALL CHAMBER—Eight basketts, three little shelves, two dozen of trenchers, a little wooden pasty plate, two halfe inch boards, two little skillets, two old sithes, two bushells of aples with some other imployments & three dishes, 15*s.* 4*d.*

IN THE MANS CHAMBER—A woolen wheele & old linnen wheele, a sadle & pillion, a brome hooke & pickaxe and old troph, a little short forme, 6*s.*

IN THE KITCHIN—A kneading troph, three pailes, five porridg dishes, a wooden platter, a peele, a fire forke, two seives, 8*s.*

IN THE HOUSE WHERE THE HOGS TUBB STANDS—Two swill pailes, a swill tubb, a mattock, two spades, a shovell, a dung forke, 7*s.* 6*d.*

IN THE MAULT HOUSE—Thirteene tubbs, a scop, a chickins coop, a leaden sesterne, 5*li.* 1*s.*

IN THE KELL-HOUSE—The haire on the kell [kiln], 8*s.*

IN THE MAULT·CHAMBER—Six corne sacks, a bushell and a fann, a paire of winch pins, two shovells, one dew rake head, a troph, 2 bords, a forme, three seame of malt, and some other utensells, 3*li.* 13*s.* 4*d.*

IN THE CHEESE CHAMBER—Six scoore and eleaven cheese, 9*li.* 18*s.*; nine pitch forkes, two pease hookes, a table to lay cheeses on & 2 boards, 2 bushells of seed beans, two iron racks, one cart strake, one hanging shelfe, one corne seive, a bee hive, a old box, and one old hutch, 1*li.* 3*s.* 4*d.*

IN THE PEASE BARNE—Two long ladders, a paire of harrows, two pitch forkes, a fann & two ridles, four cow soles, a corne rake and a cutting knife, a mow of hay & the hay in the upper barne, 9*li.* 3*s.* 4*d.*

IN THE WHEAT BARNE—A mowe of wheat, a little cant of barley, a skreene, a fann, 2 corne rakes, one forke, a casting shovell, a caveing seive, a short ladder, 23*li.* 13*s.* 4*d.*; a grinstone & troph, a ly troph & ly lecth, 3*s.* 4*d.*

IN THE STABLE—One old querne, a pair of fetters, a old chaff seive, 3*s.* 4*d.*
Three small horses, 9*li.*
The plow irons & plow & a old wheele barrow and a ladder, 9*s.*
Five milch cowes, 16*li.* 13*s.* 4*d.*; nine sheep & eight lambs, 5*li.* 9*s.* 6*d.*; three hoggs and a parcell of pease to fatt them, 6*li.*

His weareing apparell and money in his purse, 2*li.* 10*s.*
[Total]—160*li.* 16*s.* [should be 103*li.* 16*s.*]
[Appraisers—Henry Bright, Richard Thorowgood.]
[Exhibited 17 December 1678.]

103.—John Putto of Writtle [miller]. 27 February 1678/9.

In the hall—1 great press, 1 littell tabell, 1 bench and bench bord, 1 joyne chayer, 4 other chayers, 2 joyn stooles, 1 foulingpeece, a payr of bellowes, 1 jack, 4 cobyrons, fier shovell and tongs, 1 sword, 2 trammells, bookes, 4*li.*

In the parlor—I featherbed, a flockbed, 1 joyne bedsted, curtins and vallenc, 2 blancots, 1 kivren, 2 boulsters, 2 pillowes, 3 chayers, 2 huches, 1 livrey cubbord, and other small things, 5*li.* 10*s.* 6*d.*

In the best chamber—1 dowen bed, 1 featherbed, 2 boulsters, 2 pillows, 2 blancots, 1 rudg, 1 bedsted and curtins, 7*li.*; tenn payer of sheets, 2 dusson of napkins, 3 tabell clothes, 3 cheasts, 1 huch, 1 trunck, 1 tabell, 5 joyn stools, 3 payr of cobyrons, 2 fiershovells, 1 payr of tongs, 1 payr of bellowes, 1 flexwhell, 6*li.* 14*s.* 6*d.*; 1 clock, 1*li.* 10*s.*

In the chamber over the hall—1 featherbed, 2 blancots, 1 civerlitt, 1 rudg, 1 boulster, 1 pillow, 1 bedsted, 1 trundellbedsted, 1 tabell, 1 prese, 1 cheast, 1 huch, 1 chayr, 2 formes, 5*li.*

In the mill chamber—1 bed, 2 boulsters, 1 blancott, 1 coverlitt, 1 cornhuch and other small things, 1*li.* 10*s.*

In the buttree—3 hogsheds, 1 barrell, 1 berestall, 1 keep, 1*li.* 11*s.* 6*d.*

In the dayrey—2 charnes, 1 stand, 1 [c]hesspres, 8 ceesmouts, 2 chesbreds, 5 boules, 2 firkins, 1 pouderin tub, dressers and shelves, 1 tray and small things, 2*li.* 3*s.*

In the briuehous—2 coppers, 5 kettells, 5 skillittes, 3 bras potes, 1 yron pott, 3 payr of potthoks, 6 spitts, 3 grigyrones, 1 frying pan, fier sovell and tongs, 1 dusen an halfe puter dishes, 6 spoons, 1 bacon [bason], 1 flagon, 1 candellstick, 4 silver spones, 9*li.*; 10 tubes, 1 knedingtroth, 3 sives, 2 payles, 1 pelle, 2*li.*

In the stabell—1 horse, 1 sadell, 1 bridell, 1 panell, 1 cartsadell, 1 coller, 3 pidgs, 6*li.* 7*s.*

1 Carte, 3*li.*

3 cokes of hay, 16*li.*

In the windmill—1 payer of stones, 2 brases, 1 gabellrop cloath, 1 hammer, 9*li.* 14*s.*

The watermill—1 payer of stones, beame skole and waits, 3 brases, 2 towell huches, nettes and sackes, millbills, gabellrope, 1 crow, 1 sledghamer, 1 grinston, 1 bushell, 1 half bushell, 13*li.* 5*s.*

Warring aparrell and redy money, 3*li.*
[Total]—97*li.* 5*s.* 6*d.*
[Appraisers—John Clarke, Thomas Crow, Henry Trapes, George Hunte.]
[Exhibited 7 March 1678/9 by Anne, widow and administratrix.]

104.—William Carnell. 6 March 1678/9.

IN THE CHAMBER ON THE CROSSE—Twentie paier of knaves, 3*li.* 5*s.*; five and twentie extries, 1*li.* 17*s.* 6*d.*; twentie paier of sharfes, 1*li.* 13*s.* 4*d.*; fowre paier of fore wastes for waggons, 10*s.*; five paier of hind wastes, 10*s.*; twelve paier of middle peeces for waggons, 12*s.*; fowerteene paier of tonges, 14*s.*; harrow bares and sharpe bares & carte ladder bares, six doz., 9*s.*; fowre plough handles, 1*s.* 4*d.*; tenn plough beames, 1*li.*; carte rounds eight paier, 8*s.*; ould lumber, 10*s.*

UPPON THE GREENE—Fower loade & 11 foote of Pollenger timber and timber topps, 4*li.* 5*s.*; one loade and three quarters of principall timber, 3*li.* 10*s.*; three hundred fowre score and one foote of ploncks, 3*li.* 15*s.* 2*d.*; jeyse and slabs, 1*li.* 1*s.*; fier logges, 10*s.*; a carriage and wheeles, 4*li.*

IN THE YARDE—Tenn trann of longe and shorte spokes, 4*li.* 10*s.*; sixteene trann of felleyes, 4*li.* 10*s.*; five bundles of harte lath, 10*s.*; fowre bundles of splints, 4*s.*; lumber, 1*li.*; a grinstone, 3*s.*; reparation stoufe & logges, 13*s.*; tyle, 1*li.* 4*s.*; eight oake boards, 8*s.*

IN THE SHOPP—Fower paier and one of hinde wheeles for waggons, 4*li.* 10*s.*; twoo paier of fore wheeles, 1*li.* 10*s.*; wheelebarrow wheeles, 6*s.*; rave pinns & whipple trees, 4*s.*; three paier of harrowes, 10*s.*; waggon blocks and old lumber, 2*li.*; workinge tooles, 2*li.*

IN THE HALL—One table, fowre joyned stooles, six chayres, one paier of cobirons, spitts and other trifelinge thinge, 1*li.* 10*s.*

IN THE PARLOR—A fether bedd & bolster with rugg & blancketts & andirons and other things, 4*li.* 2*s.*

IN THE CHAMBER OVER THE HALL—A bedd & furniture thereunto belonginge, twoo hutches & a trunke, 2*li.* 3*s.*

IN THE CHAMBER OVER THE PARLOR—Twoo bedds & furniture belonginge to one of them and linnen, an old hutch & a trunke & a box, 5*li.* 6*s.*

IN THE KITCHEN—Pewter, brasse, brewing vessells, a leade, a table & other things, 3*li.* 5*s.*

IN THE BUTTERY—Three hoggsheds, 7*s.* 6*d.*

IN THE MEALE HOWSE—Twoo hoggsheads & a kilderkin, kneadeinge trough & other things, 10*s.*; seaven hundred of brick, 14*s.*

IN THE HOGGS COURTE—Twoo hoggs & twoo piggs, 3*li.* 2*s.*
Wareinge apparell & money in his pockett, 2*li.* 11*s.* 6*d.*
[Total]—76*li.* 4*s.* 4*d.*
[Appraisers—John Inman, Thomas Perry.]
[Exhibited 28 March 1679.]

105.—James Carr. 25 March 1679.

IN THE HALL—Two tables, one forme, foure joynd stooles, foure chaires, two paire of trammells, one paire of andirons, one spitt, one paire of tonges, one fire pan, one gridgiron, one paire of bellowes, one cupboard, 1*li.* 6*s.*

IN THE PARLOR—One kneading troffe, three barrells, one beere stall, three kettles, one brasse pott, one iron pott, one warminge pan, one skillett, one tub, one paire of scoles, three waites, three sives, foure wedges, two sawes, two plowchaines, one shaine, one counter, one double hooke with other old iron, one leather botte, 3*li.* 1*s.*

IN THE MILKE HOUSE—One cheese presse, seaven pewter dishes, one chirne, one fryinge pan, one trevett, 1*li.* 2*s.*

IN THE BUTTERY—One spade, one shovell, two payles, one broome hooke, one mathooke, one bill, one ax, one fan, one caving sive with other ymplyments, 1*li.*

IN THE CHAMBER OVER THE MILKEHOUSE—One feather bed, one feather boulster, one flocke boulster, one pillow, one blanket, one coverlid, one bedsteadle & curtaynes, 3*li.*; one featherbed, one boulster, three pillows, one coverlid, one bedsteedle, 1*li.* 10*s.*; two chists, one box, one trunke, two paire of sheetes, six napkins, 1*li.* 8*s.*

IN THE CHAMBER OVER THE HALL—Three seame of wheate, eighteene bushells of barly, five bushells of pease, one bushell and a halfe of bullymon, two ridles, one halfe bushell, one pecke, one sacke, one bag, one sive, 9*li.* 10*s.*

IN THE STABLE—One mare, one colt, three paire of plowharnis, one paire of boddy harnis, one carte saddle, one paire of thatbands, two leather collers, one pannell, one bridle with other ympliments, 5*li.* 10*s.*

IN THE YARD—Three cowes, 8*li.* 10*s.*; nine sheepe, one hogg, 2*li.* 10*s.*; one carte and rowle, 1*li.* 5*s.*

Three acres of barly land, 3*li.*; two acres of pease, one acre of wheate, 1*li.* 14*s.*; hay, straw & chaffe, 2*li.*
His waringe clothes & money in his purse, 2*li.*
Sume is—48*li.* 6*s.*
[Appraisers—John Robinson, Thomas Crow.]
[Exhibited 20 (*sic*) March 1679.]

106.—Thomas Hills, of Writtle. 24 April 1679.

IN THE HALL—Two litle leads, 2 brasse kettles, one brasse pott, one skillett, fier shovell & tongs, one payre of trammells & other implements, 1*li.* 12*s.*; the pewter, 5 smale dishes, 2 old candlesticks, one pewter pott, 10*s.*

IN THE PARLOR—One halfe headed bedsteddle, one presse cubbord, one coverlett, 3 hutches, one warmeing pann & other implements, 1*li.* 2*s.*; the linnen, 5 payre of sheets, 1*li.*

IN THE CHAMBER OVER THE PARLOR—One old bedsteddle, one old feather bedd, one old flockebedd, 2 old hutches & other old implements, 1*li.* 10*s.*

IN THE BUTTERY—2 hoggsheads, one halfe hoggshead, 3 tubbs & other implements, 2*li.*

IN THE CHAMBER OVER THE BUTTERY—The corne in the house, 2*li.* 4*s.*; other smale implements, 1*li.*

IN THE MILKE HOUSE—One cheese presse, one charne, one stand & other implements, 15*s.*; 2 bruing tubbs, scales & weights & other implements, 1*li.*

3 cowes & the hay, 2 store piggs, 10*li.*; 2 mares & 4 sheep, 2 lambs & the harneis, 5*li.*
One load cart, one dung cart, one plough & harrowes, 3*li.*
3 acres of wheate, 7*li.* 10*s.*
His wareing apparell, bonds, bills & desperate debts & money in his purse, 6*li.*
Sum'—44*li.* 9*s.* [should be 44*li.* 3*s.*]
[Appraisers—John Robinson, Hugh Greene. Exhibited 25 April 1679.]

107.—Richard Bedwell of Roxwell. 26 June 1679.

The goods in the house, 5*s.*; one cow, 2*li.* 10*s.*; one pigge, 10*s.*; thee [?]haye, 1*li.* 5*s.*; the wheat upon the ground, 3*li.* 5*s.*; the pease upon the grown, 15*s.*
His wearing cloathes and his mony, 13*s.* 4*d.*
[Total—9*li.* 3*s.* 4*d.*]
[Appraisers—Weston Eve, Edward Turnidge.]
[Exhibited 16 December 1679, by Mary Bedwell, widow.]

On *verso.*

An Acount of ye Goods that Richard Bedwell sould in his Liffe Tyme as Followith viz.

on tubb & one drinke stole to John Joslin.
one bedd, one payer of tramils, and payer of tonges, one grate kittle to John Kolpape.
one kitle, one postnett, one table to Edward Turnidg of Cury Green.
one wheele to Will Lewis of Keves gren.
one cubard to Abreham Day.
One spade to Will Fowgin.
one trouel & one hamer to Philipe Dagnit.
one Forme to goodman Vinton.
one Poridg Poot to John Sach his wife.
one griiron & one blankit to John Sach.
one Lather botle to Ed Tomson.

107A.—(on same sheet as No. 107).

An acount of ye goods that are in ye widdow Bedwell House.

IN THE HALL—One little table, one forme, 2 chayers, one little cubord, 6*s.* 8*d.*

IN THE BUTTREY—One old kettle, one barell, one tub, one knedin bole, 7*s.*

IN THE CHAMBER—One old bed, one chest, 1*li.* 1*s.* 4*d.*
[Total—1*li.* 15*s.* Appraiser—Thomas Bright.]

108.—Peter Bradley of Writtle. 27 August 1679.

In the hall—One old table, one bench board, one setle, one forme, one kneading trough, 2 andirons, 3 old chayres, fier shovell & tongs, 2 andirons, 3 spitts with other implements, 2 payre of trammells, 1*li.*

In the chamber over the hall—One old bedsteddle, 2 old feather bedds, one flock bedd, two blanketts, 2 pillowes, 2 feather bolsters, 4 hutches & other implements, one old coverlett, 3*li.*

In the parlor—One old jonyed bedsteddle, 2 feather bedds, 3 feather bolsters, one coverlett, 3 hutches, one litle table, one trundle bedd, one presse cuboord, 2 joyned stooles, 6*li.*

In the chamber over the parlor—One lead of cheese with other implements, 12*s.*

In the milke house—One stand, 3 bowles, 2 charnes, one cheese presse, 4 cheese mootes with other implements, 1*li.*

In the buttery—One meashing tubb, one keeler, one drink stale, one fatt, 2 hogsheads, one barrell with other implements, 1*li.*

In the chamber over the buttery—Two old flock bedds, one feather bolster, 2 pillowes, one flock bolster, one borded bedsteddle, 3 old hutches with other implements, 10*s.*

In the mault house—One lead, one cisterne, one old haire cloath & other implements, 3*li.*

The brasse—4 kettles, one warmeing pann, 2 brasse potts, 3 posnets & other implements, 1*li.* 10*s.*
The pewter—13 smale dishes, 13*s.* 4*d.*
The linnen—3 flaxen sheets, 4 payre of old twoen sheetes, 4 table clothes, 2 napkins, 4 pillow beeres, 2 casting sheetes, 2*li.* 10*s.*
Two mares, one colt & the harneis, 4*li.*
One load cart, 3*li.*; one dung cart, 1*li.* 10*s.*; one plough and plough irons, one payre of harrowes, 15*s.*
3 cowes, 4*li.* 10*s.*; 3 hoggs, 1*li.* 10*s.*; 30 sheep & lambs, 4*li.* 10*s.*
The corne in the barne, being barley, oates and peese, 15*li.*
His weareing apparell, bonds, bills & desperate debts & money in his purse, 10*li.*
The fallow—2*li.* 12*s.*
The wodd in the yard, 1*li.* 10*s.*
Hay in the barne & other houses, 5*li.*; the hay & straw in ortyard, 1*li.*
The mill quorne & grinstone, 10*s.*
Summa totalis—74*li.* 2*s.* 4*d.* [should be 76*li.* 2*s.* 4*d.*]
[Appraisers—John Pond, William Bird, John Wallis.]
[Exhibited 20 October 1679.]

109.—Thomas Peach of Roxwell, yeoman. 29 September 1679. See Plate VII.

In the hall—On table, 5 stooles, 6 chaires, firshouell, tongs, spits & other small things, 2*li.*

IN THE PARLOUR—Two press cubbards, on table, 1*li.* 10*s.*

IN THE CHAMBER OUER THE PARLOR—On doune bed with furniture belonging to it, 2 cheastes, on trunke, 20 payer of sheetes, 3 dozen of napkins, 3 table cloaths & other small things, 21*li.*

IN THE CHAMBER OUER THE HALL—On fether bed with furniture belonging to it; 4 cheastes & other small things, 6*li.* 15*s.*

IN THE CHAMBER OUER THE ENTRI—On fether bed with furniture, on table, on siluer boule, 12 siluer spones, 14*li.* 13*s.*

IN THE CHAMBER OUER THE BUTTERI—On bed with furniture belonging to it, 2*li.* 10*s.*

IN THE BUTTERY—Six barrells, brass & peuter, & other things, 7*li.* 18*s.*

IN THE KICHIN & DARY—On leade, bruing uessells & dary uessells & cheses & other small things, 7*li.* 18*s.* 6*d.*

The corne & hay in the barns & hayhous, 30*li.* 6*s.* 8*d.*
Fouer horse & 2 coults, 8*li.*; thre cous, 2 heffers, 9*li.*; tuelue shepe, 3*li.*; fouer hoggs, 3*li.* 4*s.*
On waggon, on long carte & tumbriell, plow & harrows, 9*li.*
His waring apparill & monny in his purs, 20*li.*
Sum tottall—146*li.* 15*s.* 2*d.*
[Appraisers—Josiah Pepper, Alexandar Chalke.]
[Exhibited, 20 October 1679, by Henry Peach, son and administrator.]

110.—Mathew Harris of Writtle. 6 October 1679.

IN THE HALL—Two joyned tables, one forme, three chaires, one jacke, three spitts, one fire shovell and tongs, one paire of cobirons, one paire of bellowes, one paire of tramells with other implyments, 2*li.*

IN THE PARLOR—Foure feather beds, foure boulsters, two pillowes, two bedsteads, one chiste, one halfe-cupboarde, three old coverlids, three blankets, with other implyments, 8*li.*

IN THE CHAMBER OVER THE PARLOR—One featherbed with rug and blankets, curtaines & vallens, one table, two formes, one presse, one livery cupboard, one hutch, 6*li.* 5*s.*; six paire of sheetes, two paire of pillowbeeres, with other small linen, 4*li.*

IN THE CHAMBER OVER THE HALL—One bed and bedsteade with curtaines & vallens, one rug and blanket, one bouster, three chists with other things, 3*li.* 3*s.* 4*d.*

IN THE CHAMBER OVER THE KITCHIN—Twenty bushells of barly, foure bushells of wheate, three lead of cheese, one litle parcell of welch wooll, five sacks with other ymplyments, 4*li.* 13*s.* 4*d.*

IN THE BUTTERY—Three hogsheads, three litle vessells, foure tubs with other small things, 1*li.* 5*s.*

IN THE KITCHIN—One kneadingtroffe, one dresserboard, one tub, two payles with other ymplyments, 15*s.*; one leade, three kettles, three schillets, 2*li.* 6*s.*; ten pewter dishes, 1*li.*

IN THE MILKEHOUSE—One cheese presse, two stands, two keelers, one chirne with other implyments, 15*s.*

IN THE BARNE—Twelve quarters of wheate, 18*li.*; nine quarters of barly with other implyments, 8*li.* 2*s.*

IN THE YARDS—One stacke of pease and oates, 4*li.*; one litle peese of an old cocke of hay and one cocke of new hay, 3*li.*; one loadecarte, one tumbrill, one paire of harrows, and one plow, 3*li.* 15*s.*

Five cows, foure bollocks, two wennells, 20*li.* 3*s.* 4*d.*; seaven sheepe, 1*li.* 4*s.*; foure hogs, one sow and seaven pigs, 5*li.*

IN THE STABLE—Two mares and three colts, 6*li.*; old cartharnis & plowharnis with other ymplyments, 6*s.* 8*d.*

Wearing aparell with money in his purse, 2*li.*
[Total]—160*li.* 14*s.* 8*d.* [should be 105*li.* 13*s.* 8*d.*]
[Appraisers—John Nash, Richard Horsenayle.]
[Exhibited, 16 December 1679, by Elizabeth Harris, widow and administratrix.]
[A list of testator's debts is given which include 14 sums of money (no details) ranging from 70*li.* 19*s.* 5*d.* to 8*s.*, 'for shooing and Iron Work, 1*li.* 1*s.* 10*d.*', and for funeral charges, 3*li.* The total of these debts is 105*li.* 4*s.* 3*d.*]

111.—Samuel Woolfe of Writtle, gentleman. 4 November 1678.

IN THE HALL—One drawing table , six joyned stooles, one livery cubbord, one little table, five smale chaires, one clocke, one sword, two pistolls, one fowling peece, six cushins, one skreene, two spitts, one gridgiron, one toetcing iron, one bench cubbord, one payre of cobirons, a payre of tramells, fire shovell & tongs with other implements, 4*li.* 17*s.* 6*d.*

IN THE PARLOUR—One drawing table, six joyned stooles, one livery cubbord, one carpett, one cubbord cloath, seven chayres, eight cushins, one long stoole, one sword, one payre of doggs, fire shovell & tongs, 4*li.* 5*s.* 4*d.*

IN THE KITCHIN—One smale table, two shelves, one bench, one kneading trough, one copper, three skilletts, three kettles, one spitt, eight greate & smale tubs, a payre tramells with other implements, 5*li.* 12*s.* 10*d.*

IN THE MILKE HOUSE—Nine milke vessells, one lead, one stand, three tubbs, one churne, one cheesepresse, six cheese moots & breades, two payles, a payre of butter scooles & waits & other implements, 2*li.* 16*s.* 5*d.*

IN THE TWO BUTTERYS—[torn away] one side boarde cubbord, two shelves, [torn away] one candlesticke, one [torn away] pott, two tinn candlesticks, one case of knives, two basketts, foure dozen of trenchers, one pewter cullender, one bason, one sadle, one pewter [*sic*], one musterd box, fower porringers, one dozen of spoones, two hogsheads, five barrells, one wooden peeler, 4*li.* 18*s.* 3*d.*

IN THE CHAMBER OVER THE HALL—One featherbed, one bolster, two pillows, two blanketts, one rugg, curtens & valiens, one bedstedle & curtain rodds, two chayres, one little round table & table cloath, one payre of cobirons, a payre of bellows, one looking glasse with other smale implements in ye study, 10*li.* 2*s.* 6*d.*

In the chamber over the parlour—Two bedstedles, two feather bedds, two bolsters, two pillows, five blanketts, two coverledds, curtens & valians to one bedd & curten rods, two trunks, two chests, one chayre, three boxes, one old sword, 8*li.* 18*s.* 6*d.*

In linnen—One & twenty payre of sheetes, foure & twenty pillowbers, foure table cloathes, five cubbord cloathes, foure dozen & a halfe of napkins, foure towells, & course linnen about ye house, 11*li.* 0*s.* 6*d.*
In plate—One silver tankerd, ten silver spoones, one silver cupp, 10*li.* 6*s.* 8*d.*

In the chamber over the buttery—Two feather bedds, two bolsters, six blanketts, one bedstedle & trundle bedstedle, two hutches, one box, two iron waights, one little table, one chayre, & one flaskett, 6*li.* 15*s.*

In the garrett—In two heapes of woole, 2*li.* 10*s.*

In the cheese chamber—In fowerscore & one cheeses, 6*li.* 1*s.* 4*d.*

In the servants chamber—One feather bedd, two feather bolsters, on flock bedd, fowre blanketts, two low bedstedles, two basketts with other implements, 3*li.* 10*s.*

In the grainary—In all sorts of corne alsoe twelve sacks, one old fann, one ridle, one seede pecke, one bushell, one ould skreene & three shovells, 6*li.* 6s. 8*d.*; fowerteene quarters of mault, 16*li.*

In the cart house—One wagon, two dung carts, two payre of harrows, two ploughs with there irons, one wheelbarrow, three dewrakes, 12*li.*

Three smale hay cocks of flowen hay in the feilds, 5*li.*; twenty loads of hay in the two hay houses, 15*li.*
[Norfolke sheep and lambs, torn away], 55*li.*

In the yards—Nine cows, one bull, nine wenell calves, ten hoggs & nine piggs, one long ladder, one hoggtubb & one hogg trough, 50*li.*

In the stable—Five horses, one mare, one colt, horses harnesse, koopes, spades, bills, axes, mathookes, shovells, iron, pitch, two sawes with other implements of husbandry, 34*li.* 2*s.* 8*d.*

3 heiffer bullocks, 9*li.*

In the barne—Wheat & rye, 50*li.*; barly, 21*li.*; pease, oates & beans, 17*li.* 10*s.*

Thirty acres of wheate sowen, 53*li.*; seven acres of land tylled for barly & ten acres harrowed for oates, 15*li.*
Eleven young bullocks, 18*li.*
In debts dew & owing to the intestate, 10*li.* 10*s.*; desperate debts owing to the intestate, 8*li.* 13*s.* 4*d.*
Ready mony in the intestates purse & his wearing apparrell, 8*li.* 3*s.* 4*d.*
Summe Totall—486*li.* 0*s.* 10*d.*
[Appraisers—Thomas Cheveley, John Woolfe.]
[Exhibited, 10 November 1678 and 12 April 1679, by Elizabeth Woolfe, widow.]

112.—William Norden. 8 December 1679.

THE INWARD CHAMBER—1*s.*

IN THE NEXT CHAMBER—1 bed, furniture & chest, 2*li.* 0*s.* 2*d.*; for a parsell cheese, 3*li.* 12*s.* 10*d.*

IN THE HALL—2 cuberds, 4 joyne stooles, one table, 4 chaires, 1 warminge pan, 1 brasse morter, 1 cradle, 3 pewter dishes, & triffles, 1*li.* 5*s.* 5*d.*

IN THE BUTTRIE—2 vessells, 2 tubs, 1 brass pott, 2 skilletts, 5*s.* 5*d.*

IN THE SHOPP—Severall triffles, 11*s.*

IN THE PALER—1 pair cobirons, firepan & tongs with a glasse case, 3*s.* 4*d.*

IN THE BAKEHOUSE—1 brasse kettle with moulding boards & kneding troffe, 4*s.* 4*d.*

IN THE MEALE HOUSE—Meale, corne, scole & wayts, 2*li.* 9*s.* 6*d.*

A horse & a pigg, 2*li.* 10*s.* 3*d.*
Wood in the yeard, 3*li.* 1*s.* 3*d.*
His wearning cloths and monye, 17*s.* 9*d.*
[Total]—17*li.* 2*s.* 3*d.*
[Appraisers—William Walker, John Stradlinge.]
[Exhibited, 12 December 1679, by Clementia Norden, widow and administratrix.]

113.—William Webb of Roxwell. 8 March 1679/80.

IN THE HALL—To bench bords, on livery cobord, to spits, on drepen pan, to payerbells, on gregen, to cobbons, to chayers, to joyn stolls, outher implyments, 2*li.*

IN THE PALOR—On tabell, on forme, on stoll, on press cobord, on cop, shelfe, to barells, on whell, stand, and outher empliments, 2*li.* 5*s.* 4*d.*

IN THE HALL CHAMBER—To fetherbeds, to coverleds, on joyn bedstedell, on payer certens, on trondell bed, on tabell, cobord, on halfe heded bedstedl, on ould huch, 3 bolstors, on straue mate, 5*li.* 10*s.*

IN THE PALLER CHAMBER—4 huches, on tabell, on bedsted, on payer of certens & valants, on fether bed, on bolstor, on coverled, 5*li.* 15*s.*

IN THE KECHEN—On dreserbord, on tube, on meall tube, on nerden troath, to bruen tubs, on swell tube, to kelers, outher emplerments, 15*s.*

IN THE MELK HOUS—On ches pres, on churme, on puderen tube, on troath to salt baken, on mostord quarn, 6 shelfes and outher empliments & to barells, 15*s.* 9*d.*; on coper small, 3 ketells, one skelet, 3*li.* 13*s.*; puter deshes, 6, 13*s.* 4*d.*

Thre cous, on buloke, 9*li.*
Wheate in the barne, 5*li.*; barly 8 quarters, 6*li.* 4*s.*; haye, 3*li.*; pease, 3*li.* 10*s.*
Waren parell and moni in his porss, 3*li.*
On long carte and dong carte, on plou, on payer horroes, 3*li.*

[Total]—55*li.* 1*s.* 7*d.* [should be 54*li.* 1*s.* 5*d.*]
[Appraisers—Philip Richman, Simon Hudson.]
[Exhibited 7 August 1680 by John Webb, brother and administrator.]
[Dets oing oute of this (?)invitori therty on pounds. Charges of berian mother and son eaight pounds.]

114.—William Luckin of Roxwell. 1679.

Too coues and a bolloke and the hay, 8*li.*; three shepe and too piges, 1*li.* 16*s.*

IN THE PALER—One joine bedsted withe curtines and and [*sic*] valants, one fether bed, too bolerteres, one rug, coverlid, one blanket, 3*li.* 10*s.*; one liverry coberd, one schest, one box, 10*s.*; four joyn stoles, one chayer, too cossines, one bras candel sticke and a fewe triffelling thinges, 15*s.*

IN THE CHAMBER OVER THE PALER—One half heded bedsted with the thinges belongin to it, 2*li.* 5*s.*; too old huches and a too or three triffilling thinges, 5*s.* 6*d.*

IN THE CHAMBER OVER THE HALL—One trondel bed with the thinges belong to it, 15*s.*; fouer payer of flexen shets and too payer of toing shetes, too tabel cloes and a dosen of napkines and a littel other smal linnen, 3*li.*; one chest, one old huch, too peuter candelstickes, six small dishes and a faue smal puter thinges besides, 1*li.* 11*s.* 6*d.*; one bushel of wheat, 4*s.* 2*d.*

IN THE CHES CHAMBER—12 smal sheses and a too or three old bordes, 15*s.*

IN THE DARRY—Three citteles, too skillets, one stan, one bole, one tray, and a feue smal things be side, 2*li.*

IN THE HALL—One pres cobberd, too smal tabeles, six chayers, 3 joyn stoles, 2 spites, one warming pan, one chaffin dish, one tramel, one fire shovel, one payer of tonges, one gridiron, one payer of belles, one payer of cobbirnes, one morter and pessel, 2*li.* 3*s.* 9*d.*; one bybel, 1*li.* 6*s.*

IN THE BOTTERRI—One porrige pot, one friing pan, and too barriles, 10*s.*

IN THE CICHIN—Too old tooles, one coller, one coule, one ches pres, one chern, too ches mootes, and one bred, 14*s.*

His werring cloes and his money in his pocket, 1*li.*
[Total]—31*li.* 0*s.* 11*d.*
[Appraisers—William Bird, Edward Sandford.]
[Exhibited 7 August 1680 by Margaret Luckin, widow and administratrix.]

115.—William Pissey of Roxwell. 13 May 1680.

IN THE HALL—Two old tables, six joyned stooles, one press cuboord, one bench bord, five old chaires, two cushions, 1*li.* 10*s.* 3*d.*; a paire of small cobirons, a paire of tramells, fire shovell & tongs, a iron to lay before the fire, 6*s.* 3*d.*; a warming pan, a spitt, a lock iron, a cleaver, a paire of bellowes, & a tinn lanthorne with with other imployments, 6*s.* 9*d.*

IN THE PARLOUR—One joyned chest, one bedsteadle, two small shelves, two glass casses, 1*li.* 0*s.* 9*d.*; two old bibles with some other books, 4*s.* 6*d.*

IN THE BUTTREY—Four brass kettles and a brass pott, three skellets, two basting ladles, one scumer and a frying pann, a paire of potthookes, *2li.* 13*s.* 9*d.*; three barrells, three tubbs, one kemnell, 15*s.* 6*d.*; a trevett, three bouldishes, two old trayes, halfe a dozen small dishes, three small shelves, three meale firkins, a hop seive, a tining dripping [pan] with some other small tining things, 5*s.* 2*d.*; a spade, a shovell, a mattocke with some other utensels of husbandrie and some imployments belonging to the buttrey, 11*s.* 5*d.*

IN THE CHAMBER OVER THE HALL—One feather bedd, one feather boulster, two pillows, a coverlid and two blanketts, 2*li.* 15*s.*; one little table, one joyne stoole, three little stooles, a deale chest, two boxes, 6*s.*

IN THE CHAMBER OVER THE PARLOUR—Five paire of sheets, two old pillow beers, two old table cloathes, two old napkins, two old towells, 1*li.* 13*s.* 6*d.*; seaven pewter dishes, a pewter chamber pott, four porringers, two sawcers, two small salts, 10*s.* 9*d.*

A powdering tubb, one old hutch, three old sickles, a paire of sheares, two paire of scalles with sixteen pound of leaden wayte with some old iron, 11*s.* 2*d.*

Three bushells & a halfe of wheat, 10*s.* 6*d.*

A midle of a side of baccon with some pork in the powdering tubb, 4*s.* 6*d.*

IN THE BARNE—A fann, a caveing seive, a coller & harness, a old pannell, two seives, one ridle, one seed peck, two ould sackes with other imployments, 11*s.* 6*d.*

A acre of barley on the ground, 2*li.* 7*s.*

One old horse, 1*li.*; four sheep and three lambs, 1*li.* 4*s.*; one sow hogg, 13*s.* 6*d.*

His weareing apparell and money in his purse, 1*li.* 10*s.*

[Total—21*li.* 11*s.* 9*d.*]

[Appraisers—Richard Thorowgood, Simon Burrell.]

[Exhibited 1 October 1680 by William Peissey, son and administrator.]

116.—Nathan Wad[e] of Roxwell. [Glover] 29 November 1680.

IN THE HALL—One tabell, one forme, one bench and one cubburd, one round tabell, five chayeres, one payer of coboyrrnes, fire pann and tonges, one tramell, belles and sault box, 1*li.*

IN THE PARLER—One tabell, four joyned stooles, one bench, one cuburd, 2 hutches, 3 boxes, one glas case, one feather beed, one boulster, 2 pillowes, one coverlet, 2 blankets, one beedsted, curtens and vallente, one payer of coboyrenes and tonges, 2 chayeres, 5*li.*

IN THE PARLER CHAMBER—One feather beed, one boulster, one pillow, one coverlet, 2 blankets, one bedsted with old curtens, one flock bed, one boulster, one pillow, one old coverlet, one blanket, half heded beedsted, one old hutch, 3*li.*

IN THE CHAMBER OVER THE HALL—2 old flock beeds, 2 boulsters, one blanket, 2 coverlets, 2 beedsteds, 1*li.*

IN THE WOLL CHAMBER—A parcell of flees woll and lames woll and bay woll and cows woll, 4*li.* 10*s.*

IN THE CHEES CHAMBER—A few small cheeses, 10*s.*

IN THE CITCHEN—One dreser boord, one kneeding trofe, one bench bord, one meashing tub and 3 other small tubs, one small copper, 2 small cettels, 3 posnets, one small bras pot, one oyron pot, 3*li.*

IN THE DAYRE—One chees pres, one charne, one milke stand with milke vesels and chees moots, 11*s.*

IN THE LITELL BUTTREY—2 small beer vessels, one side planke, one small cubbard, one poudering tub, 2 shelves, 8*s.*

IN THE GREAT BUTTREY—One beer stall, 2 beer veseles, one old coop, one basket, 6*s.*

IN THE SHOEPE—One allaming trof, 2 old tubes, one shop bor[d], one stake and witch, 4 payer of sheeres, and sum small quantity of leather and gloves, 2*li.*

IN THE STABELL—One olde mare with bridell and panell, 1*li.* 5*s.*

IN THE BARNE—Wheate and hay with sum other implements for husbandre, 2*li.*

3 cowes, one sow, and 4 small pigs, 7*li.*
One akere of wheat, one akere of land, one plowed for barley, 1*li.* 16*s.*
The linnen—7 payer of sheets, 18 napkines, 4 tabell clothes, 9 pillobeers, 6 towels, one casting sheet, 3*li.*
The pewter—6 small dishes, one pot, 2 candell stikes, one small pewter tankard, 6 spoones, 13*s.* 4*d.*
His waring apparell and muney in his purs, 1*li.* 5*s.*
Sume Totales—38*li.* 4*s.* 4*d.*
[Appraisers—Hesepyah Godsuf,[1] Philip Munke.]
[Exhibited 9 July 1681 by Lydia Wade, widow and administratrix.]

117.—Francis Quy of Roxwell. 30 April 1681.

IN THE HALL—One long table and forme with other small implements, 1*li.* 1*s.* 9*d.*

IN THE PARLER—Two press cubards, five piuter dishes, eight spoones, a cupp & a drippin pann & two joyne stooles, one chayer and one table with other implements, 2*li.* 1*s.*

IN THE PARLER CHAMBER—One bedd and all that belongith to itt, 3*li*: 17*s.* 6*d.*; thre hutches, one table, two boxes, one trunke, and a forme, 17*s.*

IN THE HALL CHAMBER—One bedd and all that belongith to it, 4*li.* 8*s.*; one table, one whell, 5*s.* 6*d.*

IN THE SHOP CHAMBER—One halfe haded bedsted and a flock bedd and all that belongith to itt and some other implements, 1*li.* 4*s.*; eight payer of sheets, one dozen of napkins and two payer of pillow bers, two table cloths with other small linne cloth, 3*li.* 10*s.*

[1] Named as Henry Gadsuf in the heading to this inventory.

IN THE LITTLE BUTRE—Six kittls, fouer skillets, one brass friing pann with other implements, *3li.*

IN THE GRATE BUTRE—One poridg poot, fouer beere vesels with other small implements, 16*s.*

IN THE SHOP—Fouer peeces of lather, two seates, one cuting bord, eight dozen of lasts and all other shop tooles with other small implements, 3*li.* 6*s.* 6*d.*

WITHOUT DORES—One grinstone, six breuing tubbs, and two load of wood, 2*li.*; one hogg, 12*s.*

His waring apparill with his money in pockit, 3*li.*
Som Totall is—29*li.* 19*s.* 3*d.*
[Appraisers—William Boosey, John Sach. Exhibited 19 July 1681.]

118.—John Beadel the elder. 12 May 1681.

IN THE HALL—One joine tabel, 6 stouls, one joyne cubord, one littel tabel, 5 chries, 2 smuthing irrons, 1 gridiron, 1 spit, 1 firepan, 1 payre of tongs, 2 cobirons, 1 payer of bellows and other implements, 1*li.* 4*s.* 6*d.*

IN THE PALLER—One fether bed and bedsted, 2 boussters, 4 pilloows, 1 coverlid, 2 blankets, 2 huces, 2 bokes, 1 cuberd, 1 littele tabel, 2*li.* 10*s.*

IN THE BEST CHAMBER—1 flocke bed, 1 bolster, 1 bedsted, 1 coverlid, 1 blanket, 2 huches, 3 shets, 10 napkins, one tabele clothe, 4 pillowbers, 1*li.* 5*s.* 6*d.*

IN THE CORNE CHAMBER—2 seame and a hafe of wheate, 3*li.* 13*s.* 4*d.*

IN THE BUTTERY—2 tubes, 2 barrels, 3 brase kittells, 3 scillits, 1 brase pot, 6 peuter dicshes, 1 candelsticke, 1 porringer, 2*li.* 0*s.* 6*d.*

IN THE SHOPE—1 kneding troufe, 2 formes and his working toulls, 8*s.*

IN THE STABEL—One mare, 2 panells, 2 bridells, 1 sacke and other inplements, 2 forkes, 3*li.*

IN THE CARTTHOUSE—1 carte, 1 whelbarow, 1 quarne, 2 laders, 1 payre of harrows, 1 fan, 1 caveing sive, 1 ridel, 1*li.* 15*s.* 4*d.*

2 hogs of backon, 2*li.* 8*s.* 4*d.*; 1 horse, 1*li.*; 1 grinding stone, 3*s.*; 1 pige, 6*s.* 6*d.*

His wearing parllel and mony in his purse, 1*li.*
[Total]—20*li.* 8*s.* [should be 20*li.* 15*s.*]
[Appraisers—Edmund Sterne, Thomas Crow.]
[Exhibited 19 July 1681, by Elizabeth, widow of John Beadle.]

119.—Jereimah Westwood of Beamanoats, Writtle. 21 May 1681. See Plate XIV.

IN THE HALL—1 tabell, 1 livrey cubord, 1 press, 2 stooles, 3 formes, 2 chayers, 1 settell, 1 still, 2 cobyrons, 4 musquits, 1 sword, 1 pair of bandallers, 1 boxyron, 3 sickells, 4 cushins, 2*li.* 4*s.* 7*d.*

IN THE PARLER—1 bedsted, curtines an vallanc, 2 feather beds, 3 boulsters, 1 coverlett, 4 blankoots, 6 payer of sheets, 2 dusen of napkins, 5 paier of pillobers, 3 towells, 2 tabell cloathes, 1 settell, 1 paier of tongs, 1 silver cupe, 3 silver spoons, 1 bed pan, 10*li.* 9*s.* 6*d.*

IN THE HALL CHAMBER—2 bedsteds, 1 flockbed, 2 flockboulsters, 1 featherbed, 2 boulsters, 2 pillowes, 4 blankets, 1 rug, 1 coverlitt, curtens and valenc, 2 huches, 2 chayers, 2*li.* 13*s.* 6*d.*

IN PARLER CHAMBER—1 bedsted, 1 trundellbed, 1 featherbed, 1 flockbed, 2 boulsters, 2 pillows, curtins an vallanc, 2 coverlitts, 3 blancots, 1 flockbed, 1 flockboulster, 1 pillow, 5 leather chayers, 1 wickerchayer, 1 cheast, 1 tabell, 1 paire of cobyrons, wooll, 1 payre of sheets, 5*li.* 17*s.* 6*d.*

IN THE BUTREY CHAMBER—1 bedsted, 1 flockbed, 1 tub, 1 wheell, 1 reel, 1 logsaw, 2 duerakes, 4 peashooks, 4 cornrakes, 2 meadrakes, 1 capens coope, 1 bromehooke an other small implments, 17*s.* 6*d.*

IN THE BUTREY—3 hogsheds, 1 littell vesell, 2 tubes, 3 troves, 1 kimnell, 1 tray, 1 leather bottell, 2 tunnells, 2 sives, 1 flasket, 1 rush baskett, 1*li.* 19*s.* 6*d.*

IN THE LITTELL BUTREY—3 halfe hogsheds, 3 tubs, 2 formes, 4 shelves, 1 cubord, 17*s.*

IN THE KITCHIN—15 puter dishes, 1 puter flagon, 2 puter candellstikes, 4 puter chamberpotes, 1 puter cup, 4 porringers, 4 sasers, 4 plates, 1 tinpudingpan, 3 tinplates, 2 braspots, 1 yronpott, 3 skilites, 3 kettells, 1 broadpan, 2 chafindishes, 1 skumer, 3 spites, 2 dripinpans, 1 jack, 1 bras ladell, 1 gun, 1 paire of cobyrons, 1 paier of tongs, 1 gridyron, 1 tosting yron, 2 yron bars, 2 paire of tramils, severall waites, 1 bibell, 1 ouerglas, 1 lanthorn, 1 paier of skooles, 1 long tabell, 1 litell tabell, 2 formes, 2 chayers, 1 cubbord, 1 bench, 1 yrontrevett, 1 warmingpan, 4 shelves, 1 paier of bellowes, 4 cushins, 1 culinder and other small implments, 5*li.* 12*s.* 8*d.*

IN THE KICHINCHAMBER—1 bedsted, 1 flockbed, 2 boulsters, 1 pillow, 5 paier of sheetes, 2 paire of pillowbers, 3 tabelkloathes, 5 towells, 1 maultquarne, 12 sakes, 1 beame and skooles, 6 wedges, 2 roops, 1 bushell, 1 fan and sum small implments, 3*li.* 11*s.* 1*d.*

IN THE DAIRY—2 charmes, 1 stand, 3 bowels, 3 pails, 5 shellves, 1 pasteypell, 1 morter an pestel, 3 formes and other implments and earthen weare, 14*s.*

IN THE BRUHOUS—2 coppers, 1 chespres, 1 stand, 7 tubes, 12 chesmottes, 2 chesbreads, 1 sive, 1 friing pan, 4*li.* 3*s.* 6*d.*

IN THE CHESSE CHAMBER—68 cheses, 5 chese tabels, 3 shelves, 2*li.* 17*s.* 6*d.*

IN THE GARRETT—7 quarters rey at 2 shillings the bushell, 5*li.* 12*s.*

IN THE WHEATBARNE—20 quarters wheat at 4 shilling the bushell, 32*li.*

IN THE OTEBARNE—1 quarter otes, 12*s.*

6 horse, 30*li.*; harnis, 1*li.* 10*s.*
4 lode of hay at 30 shilling the lode, 6*li.*
1 wagon, 5*li.*; 2 dungcartes, 2*li.* 10*s.*; harrowes and laders, 6*s.*; 2 spades, 1 shovell, 2 exes, 2 bills, 1 matock, 5*s.*
8 cowes at 3 pounds the cow, 24*li.*; 10 hoges, 5*li.*; sheep and lams, 21*li.*

Plowes and plowyrons, 1 rowell, 10*s.*
36 acors of wheat, 45*li.*; 14 acors of barley, 17*li.* 10*s.*; 7 acors of peas, 3*li.* 10*s.*; 8 acors ots, 4*li.*; the first tilth of 48 acors fallow, 9*li.* 12*s.*
Waring aparrell an redey money, 15*li.*
Sum is—270*li.* 14*s.* 10*d.*
[Appraisers—John Clarke, John Taverner.]
[Exhibited at Chelmsford 22 July 1681, by Joseph Westwood, son and executor.]

120.—William Page of Writtle. 31 May 1681.

In the hall—One table and three joynt stooles, 2 chaires & a letle table, 10*s.*; one pair of cob-ireons, one spitt, one fyre-shovell, one dreaping pan, a fyre-shovell, 1 pair bellows, one warming pan, a frying pan, & thre bottles, 10*s.*

In the buttrey—One hogshead & a halfe hogshead, one beerestall, one tunnill, one kneading trough, two tubes, one old cubord & a forme, 1*li.* 10*s.*; two kettles, one skillet, one porridg pott, one peauter dish with some other implements, 1*li.* 10*s.*; three whole flitches of bacon and some other peeces of bacon, 4*li.*

In the shopp—2 woollen wheeles, one trench, one spade & a mattack, one shovell with some other implements, 15*s.*

In the chamber—One bedstead, one featherbed, 2 pillows, one bolstar, 2 blanckets, one rugg, & one box, 2*li.* 10*s.*; 2 pair of sheets & 6 napkins, 15*s.*

In redy money & wearing apparell, 10*li.*
[Total]—22*li.*
[Appraisers—William Garrat, John Cooke.]
[Exhibited 19 July 1681 by Elizabeth Page, widow and executrix.]

121.—John Chalke of Writtle, yeoman. 21 July 1681.

In the parlour—One long table, eighteene joined stooles, one litle table, a livery cupboard, two chaires, a wicker chaire, a clock & weights, 2*li.* 10*s.*

In the hall—One long table, two wainscott formes, two old presse cupboards, a litle table chaire, one other chaire, a wainscott forme, two old chaires, jack & weights, three iron dripping panns, six spitts, two paire of trammells, two paire of cobirons, a paire of bellowes, a gridiron, a fender, two smoothing irons, 4*li.* 10*s.*; two old musketts, a pike, an old pistoll, a fouleing peice, a sword and bandlears, 1*li.* 1*s.*

In the litle parlor—One wainscott bedsteadle, matt & cord, curtaines & vallientts, a straw bed, two feather bedds, two feather boulsters, three feather pillowes, two blanckets, two coverings, an old chaire, a stoole, a litle table, a leatherne meale bagg, a corne sive, an old saddle, 6*li.* 2*s.*

In the litle chamber—One wainscott bedsteadle, matt & cord, a feather bed & boulster, six old feather pillowes, foure old blancketts, one covering, a stoole & two hutches, 3*li.*

IN THE CHAMBER OVER THE PARLOR—One wainscott bedsteadle, matt & cord, curtaines & vallientts, three feather bedds, two feather pillowes, two feather boulsters, two blanckets, one covering, one other wainscott bedstead, a wainscott chaire, a cupboard presse, a chest, a deale presse, two old swords, 10*li.*

IN THE CHAMBER OVER THE HALL—One halfe headed bedsteadle, a trundle bedstead, three old hutches & other lumber, & a parcell of mault, 4*li.*

IN THE CHAMBER OVER THE DERRY—A halfe headed bedstead, matt & cord, one old blanckett, a parcell of old iron, a bushell weight in lead & other lumber, a table, a chaire, a stoole, 1*li.* 6*s.*

IN THE BUTTERY—A beere stall & three vessells, a paire of wooden scales, & other lumber, 12*s.*

IN THE KITCHIN—A lead, a breweing tubb & stall, two kimnells, a kneading trough, two sives, a lye tubb & a lye latch, an iron peele, a paire of trammells, a paire of cobirons, 3*li.* 5*s.*

IN THE DERRY—A lead, a dresser board, a cheese presse, eight cheese moulds, two churnes, a stand, two coolers, two bowles, two cheese breads, a kimnell, three earthen creame potts, & other lumber, 3*li.*

IN THE DISH BUTTERY—Three brasse potts, foure brasse kettles, three skilletts, a warming pann, a frying pann, a lanthorne, a beefe forke, two brasse candlesticks, a copper pan, & other lumber, 4*li.* 10*s.*

IN THE LITLE BUTTERY—A beere stall, two barrells & one hoggshead, a litle cupboard, a parcell of hoppes, & other lumber, 1*li.* 10*s.*

The pewter, 4*li.*; the lynnen, 5*li.*

IN THE MAULTHOUSE—A corne skreene, two dew rakes, foure bundles of lath, five gate posts, seaven hundred of brick & tiles, 1*li.* 17*s.*

IN THE YARD—Two dung carts & a load cart, 5*li.*; a parcel of gysts & ploncķes, 6*li.* 15*s.*

IN THE BARNES—The hay, 7*li.*; five cowes & a bull, 14*li.*

One silver bowle, 2*li.* 10*s.*
In good debts, 146*li.*
His weareing apparell and ready money in his purse, 145*li.*
Summe totall'—382*li.* 8*s.*
[Appraisers—Symon Hudson, John Wolfe of Hatfield Peverel.]
[Exhibited 10 November 1681 by John Skelton grandson and administrator of John Chalk.]

122.—Mary Wilks of Writtle, widow. 1 October 1681.

An oaken wainscott box, 2*s.* 6*d.*; a trunke of linnen haveing two paire of sheets, two dosen of napkins, two table cloathes & other linnen in it, 2*li.*; a smal box with foure payre of sheets & two paire of pillow beers in it, 2*li.* 13*s.* 6*d.*; two gold rings, 1*li.* 1*s.* 6*d.*; one great hutch with a set of striped linsey woolsey curtaines & vallance, three payre of coarse sheets, some pewter & other things in it, 2*li.* 17*s.* 9*d.*; five old stooles & one old chayre covered

with velvet, 12*s*.; a long wainscoat box with a payre of old sheets & other linnen in it; a smal table & a forme, 18*s*. 4*d*.; one hanging presse, one smal brasse kettle, one skillet, one dripping pann, & other implements, 15*s*. 2*d*.; two old featherbeds, two blankets, one covering, & one old bedsteadle, 3*li*. 15*s*.
Ready money, 17*li*. 5*s*. 6*d*.; Wearing apparrel, 6*li*.
Sum—38*li*. 1*s*. 9*d*. [should be 38*li*. 1*s*. 3*d*.]
[Appraisers—Thomas Hanbury, John Elletson.]
[Exhibited 9 December 1681.]

123.—John Duke of Writtle, yeoman. 18 November 1681.

IN STOO MARSHESS three cowes, 10*li*.; too olde cowes, 4*li*.; a bull stag, a bullchin and a bud, 4*li*.; six runts, 21*li*.; nine runts, 23*li*.; twelfe shepe, 3*li*. 5*s*.

AT WRITTLE—Too steers, 6*li*. 10*s*.; five cowes and a kallf, 10*li*.; too cowes, 5*li*.; three loade of hay, 4*li*. 10*s*.; too loade of hay, 2*li*.

IN THE BARNE—Wheate, 4*li*.; barly, 6*li*.

One oulde carte, 1*li*.; one horss, and too ladders and other implements, 5*li*.
Nine shepe, 2*li*. 5*s*.; too cowes, 5*li*.; a kallf, 14*s*.

IN HIS CHAMBER AT BILLERREKE—Five seame of molt at one pound six shillings per seame, 6*li*. 10*s*.

IN HIS CHAMBER AT CHELMESFORD—Too seame of mot at one pound fower shillings per seame, 2*li*. 8*s*.

Three seame and a half of wheate redde thrashed, 4*li*. 18*s*.
One downe bead and som other things, 5*li*.
His warring aparrill & money in his purs, 2*li*.
Billes & Bonds and desperate debts, 60*li*.
The sum totall is—198*li*.
[Appraisers—Thomas Crow, William Burde.]
[Exhibited 19 December 1681 by Henry Duke, brother and administrator.]

124.—Edward Huttly of Roxwell. 8 March 1681/2.

IN THE HALL—2 tables, 4 formes, 3 chairs, 2 joint stools, one payer of smale cobirons, fire shovel and tonges, 1*li*. 2*s*. 9*d*.

IN THE PARLOUR—One bedsted, curtains and vallance, fether bedd, feather bolster, 2 feather pillows, one [?]coverlet, [?]one blankett, 3*li*. 7*s*. 6*d*.; 2 hutches, one trunk, one little table, 4 rush chairs, 13*s*. 6*d*.

IN THE HALL CHAMBER—One bedsted, one one [*sic*] feather bedd, one feather boulster, one feather pillows, one ould coverlitt, 3 ould blankets, one matt, 2*li*. 0*s*. 9*d*.; 2 hutches, one forme, 5*s*.

IN THE PARLOUR CHAMBER—One bedsted with curtaines and vallance, one feathr bedd, 2 feather boulsters, 5 feather pillous, one coverlitt, one blanket, one matt, 5*li*. 2*s*. 3*d*.; one presse cobbord, one joint hutch, one trunk, one hutch, 1*li*. 6*s*. 6*d*.; one wicker chaire, one cloose stoole, 4 ould chairs, one little leggt table, and sume other smale things, 13*s*. 4*d*.

IN THE CHAMBER OVER THE BUTTERY—One bedsted, one feathearbedd, 2 blanketts, 2 fether bolsters, one matt, 1*li.* 6*s.* 8*d.*

The cheeses in the chamber, 2*li.* 12*s.* 6*d.*
One sidesaddle, scales and waights, one still, a few ould hops, 2*li.* 0*s.* 4*d.*
In linning—Eaighteene paire of sheets, 3 dosen of table napkins, 12 boord cloaths, 11 pillowbeers, 9*li.* 15*s.* 6*d.*
In plate—One silver tanker, 6 silver spoons, 4*li.* 5*s.*

IN THE BREWHOUSE—2 brass leads, 3*li.* 2*s.* 6*d.*; 2 brass potts, 2 brass kettles, 3*li.* 1*s.* 6*d.*; one mault querne, 1*li.* 15*s.*; 2 tubs, one coule, 2 kimnells, 1 hogstub, with other implements, 1*li.* 1*s.* 6*d.*

IN THE KITCHING—One table, one payer of cobirons, 2 paier of tramels, fier shovel & tongs, one foulling peece, with other implements, 1*li.* 10*s.* 6*d.*

In pewter—24 dishes, one pewter flagon, 2*li.* 8*s.* 6*d.*
The testatars wearing apparell and mony in his purse, 5*li.*
Summe total—52*li.* 11*s.* 1*d.*
[Appraisers—Simon Burrel, Matthew Nightingal.]
[Exhibited 19 December 1681 (*sic*).]

125.—Caleb Carter of Writtle, yeoman. 19 June 1682.

IN THE HALL—One table & forme, one bench, five chaires, one little table & a forme, two spitts, one gridiron, bellowes, fyre shovell & tongs, with some other small implements, 1*li.* 2*s.*

IN THE PARLOR—One feather bed with curtans & vallance, two pillows, & other things belonging unto it, 3*li.*; one chist, two chaires, one hogshead and one barrill, two hutches, a butter baskitt, and a warming-pan & other small things, 19*s.*

IN THE CHAMBER—One beame & scailes, two chaires, one parcell of wooll, & some other lumber, 1*li.*

IN THE ENTREY—One copper, one brewing-tubb, two pailes, one stand, two wash-pailes, 1*li.* 5*s.*

IN THE BUTTREY—One brass kettle, one cherne, a pair of baskitts, & a chese-stand, 14*s.*; fower ireon wedges, two mattocks, six tubbs, & some other implements, 13*s.*; one kneading trough, one brass pott, three skillitts, two peauter dishes, one pestill & morter, & other small things, 1*li.* 3*s.*

IN THE CHAMBER OVER THE HALL—Twenty five cheses, two sacks, one flitch of bacon, one corne shovill, one bushill, one halfe pick, two pannills, & a shelfe, 1*li.* 6*s.*

IN THE CHAMBER OVER THE BUTTREY—Severall old lumber & od things, 5*s.*

IN THE BARNE—One plough and chaine, one fann, two lathers, and one caifeing sive, 9*s.*

IN THE STABLE—Two mares and two colts with their harness, 6*li.*

IN THE YEARD AND UPON THE GROUND—One tumbrill and one load cart, 1*li.* 10*s.*; two acres & a halfe of wheat at 20*s.* an acre, 2*li.* 10*s.*; oates, beanes & barly growing, 2*li.* 10*s.*; grass growing upon the ground severall places,

4*li.*; fower cowes and one calfe, 12*li.*; three store hoggs, 1*li.* 10*s.*; three acres of fallow, 1*li.* 5*s.*; eight sheepe and a lambe, 2*li.*

In redy money & wearing apparill, 10*s.*

Poultrey, geese and henns, 12*s.*

The full some of this Inventory is—46*li.* 3*s.*

[Appraisers—William Garrat, Christopher Perrey.]

[Exhibited 3 October 1684 by Susanna Carter, widow and executrix.]

Debts that are owing to severall people.

To halfe a years rent	7*li.*		
Servants wages, taxes, & funerall charges	5*li.*		
Owing to Tho: Bridgman	5*li.*	7*s.*	
To Wm. Poole		3*s.*	1½*d.*
Charges in sickness & nursing	8*li.*	5*s.*	
	25*li.*	15*s.*	1½*d.*
Caleb Carter's goods, all debts paid is	20*li.*	7*s.*	10½*d.*

126.—John Nash of Writtle. 5 August 1682.

In the hall—To tables, one cubert, one payer of cobirons, to chaiers, to formes, to stooles, 1*li.* 15*s.*

In the parler—The bed, 5*li.*; thre tables, sixteene chayers and stools, 3*li.*

In the kichin—One table, one cubert, to guns, five spets, one dripinpan, one payer of cobiorns, one payer of tramls, six chayers and other impliments, 4*li.* 10*s.*

In the buttri—Six beere vessels, a tunnel, and other impliments, 1*li.* 15*s.*

In the wash-house—Five ketls, five skillits, one lead, thre poots, one cheese pres, six moots, five payles, to coper poots and othe impliments, 5*li.*

In the milk house—Thre churns, to stans, five milke vesels, fower tubs, a friing pan and other impliments, 2*li.* 12*s.*

In the bruhouse—One coper, five tubs, one kneding trofe and others impliments, 4*li.* 1*s.* 6*d.*

In the best chamber—The beed and all belonging to it, one chest, to tables and a forme, one chest of drawers, six stooles, to chayers, 9*li.*

In the chamber over the hall—A parsel of wool, one huch, thre wheeles, one reele, to creadls, scals and waits, and others impliments, 2*li.* 13*s.* 4*d.*

In the corne chamber—Thre seame of oats, to seame six bushels of malt, and other implyments, 6*li.* 8*s.*

In the chamber over the kichin—One bed, one table, fouer chests, to cuberds, one box, fier shovel and tongs, thre chayers, one payer of beles, and other impliments, 6*li.* 5*s.* 6*d.*

In the chamber over the wash house—Thre beeds, thre huchis, fower boxis, and other impliments, 7*li.* 6*s.*; the cheese and bearers, 7*li.* 10*s.*

IN THE SARVANTS CHAMBER—To beds, one trunke, *2li.* 1*s.* 6*d.*

IN THE MOLT CHAMBER—Seven seame ry, and thirteene seame of wheate, *25li.* 5*s.* 8*d.*

Sixteene cowes and a bull, 50*li.*
The new hay, and an old cock, 26*li.*
Aleven horse and coults, 35*li.* 15*s.*
One wagin, to load carts, and to dung carts, plowes and harrowes, 28*li.*
Fower hefers and a yeare ould bullock, 13*li.*; sheep and lames, 23*li.* 5*s.*; aleven hoogs, and one sow, and alevin pigs, 15*li.*
The sakes and bushels, one skreene, and other impliments 3*li.*
Fifty acurs of wheate, 100*li.*; twenty acurs of barly, 52*li.*; [?]nintene acurs of oates, 35*li.*; fifty and eight acurs of fallow, 58*li.*
The peuter and pleat, 7*li.*
Twenty seven paier of sheets and a casting sheete, ten paier of pillobeers, six talle close and six dusen of napkins, 20*li.*
Six load of hay at Margetin, 5*li.*
Wearing clots and muny in his purse, 10*li.*
[Total]—573*li.* 3*s.* 6*d.* [should be 575*li.* 3*s.* 6*d.*]
[Appraisers—William Crush, Thomas Crow, Edmund Thombes.]
[Exhibited 15 May 1683 by Sarah Nash, widow and executrix.]

127.—William Craig of Roxwell. 6 June 1683.

1 piece broun cloath contented 53 ells at 8*d.*, 1*li.* 15*s.* 4*d.*; 7 pieces [brown cloth], 111¾ ells at 7¾*d.*, 3*li.* 12*s.* 2¼*d.*; 2 pieces white tecklenbers, 15 ells at 8¼*d.*, 10*s.* 3¾*d.*; 2 pieces hammells, 19¼ ells at 6*d.*, 9*s.* 7½*d.*; 3 pieces brod blew, 39½ yds at 9½*d.*, 1*li.* 11*s.* 3¼*d.*, 2 pieces [broad blue], 20½ yds. at 8½*d.*, 14*s.* 6¼*d.*; 5 pieces nar[row blue], 96 yds at 5¾*d.*, 2*li.* 6*s.*; 2 pieces germanie hold, 19¾ ells at 13*d.*, 1*li.* 1*s.* 4¾*d.*, 3 pieces roulls, 23¾ ells at 6*d.*, 11*s.* 10½*d.*; 1 piece launs, 6*s.* 6*d.*; 2 pieces [lawn], 7¾ yds at 10*d.*, 6*s.* 5½*d.*, 2 pieces [lawn], 12¼ yds at 15*d.*, 15*s.* 3¾*d.*; 1 piece brod [lawn], 6¾ yds at 22*d.*, 12*s.* 4½*d.*, 1 piece mores calico, 2 yds at 20*d.*, 3*s.* 4*d.*; 2 pieces scots clo: 6¼ at 10½*d.*, 5*s.* 5½*d.*; a piece hold, 3 ells at 2*s.* 8*d.*, 8*s.*; 1 piece [hold], 2½ ells at 2*s.* 4*d.*, 5*s.* 10*d.*; a remnant [of hold], 1*s.*; 1 piece [of hold], 6¼ ells at 2*s.*, 12*s.* 6*d.*; 1 piece [of hold], 8 ells at 20*d.*, 13*s.* 4*d.*; 1 piece [of hold], 7⅛ ells at 3*s.* 9*d.*, 1*li.* 6*s.* 8½*d.*; 1 piece whittisecklinbers lying at Bockin, 22¼ ells at 8¼*d.*, 15*s.* 3½*d.* Total—19*li.* 4*s.* 7½*d.* [All indexed under *Cloths in variety.*]

Ane accompt of the countrie debt of the deceast William Craig drawn owt of his book—

Impremis due by goodman Howkey in Writtle,	1*s.*	5*d.*
mor by goodman Houchen in Dinmow,	1*s.*	0*d.*
mor by goodie Winson in Baddow magna	5*s.*	9*d.*
mor by goodie Stains in Dannbury	3*s.*	5*d.*
mor by goodie Sipiy in Dinmow	2*s.*	0*d.*
mor by goodie Haws in Little Badow	2*s.*	9*d.*
mor by his mother	1*s.*	2*d.*

mor by goodi Crab in Dinmow	4*s.*	0*d.*
mor by goodman Priery in Much Eshen	2*s.*	7*d.*
mor by goodie Allis in Writtle	2*s.*	6*d.*
mor by goodie Hirish for cloath ther	2*s.*	1*d.*
mor by Thomas Stains in Takley	5*s.*	7½*d.*
mor by Goodie Champion in Farsteed	6*s.*	0*d.*
mor by goodie Solles one Berry Green	5*s.*	0*d.*
mor by goodie Rickett in Nithell Cross	3*s.*	1*d.*
mor by goodie Roberts in Spellbrook	5*s.*	6*d.*
mor by goodie Brown in Spellbrook	5*s.*	6*d.*
mor by goodie Browns sister	1*s.*	4*d.*
mor by one other of hir sisters		6*d.*
mor by goodie Wood in Chickney	8*s.*	9*d.*
more by goodie Wailett in Dinmow	1*s.*	9*d.*
mor by goodie Warner in Dinmow	2*s.*	0*d.*
mor by goodie Cranfich in Rittle		6*d.*
mor by goodie Cobbs in Springfield	1*s.*	8*d.*

[Total]—3*li.* 15*s.* 10½*d.*

Money that he hade lying by him when he died is	5*li.*	13*s.*	6*d.*
The goods one the other page comes to	19*li.*	4*s.*	7½*d.*
	28*li.*	14*s.*	0*d.*

[Appraisers—James White, George Anderson.]
[Exhibited at Chelmsford 20 July 1683 by John Allison.]

128.—Edmund Sterne of Skiggs Farm, Writtle, 7 September 1683.

IN THE HALL—One joyned cupboard, two tables, 18*s.*; 1 joynd forme & 3 joyned stooles & an old forme, 3 rush chaires and a joyned chair, 1 hanging cupboard, 12*s.*; 2 paire of cobirons, 2 pair of tramells, 1 gridiron, 1 salt box, 4 spitts, one pair of bellows, & 1 gun, 14*s.* 6*d.*

IN THE PARLOUR—1 feather bed, 1 straw bed, 2 blanketts, 2 coverletts, curtains & vallents, a joynd bedstedd, 2*li.* 10*s.*; 10 pair of sheets, 2 dozen of napkins, 4 table clothes, 6 towels, 3 pair of pillowbers, 2*li.* 15*s.*; 1 table, 6 joynt stooles, a joynt form, 1 carpett, 1 little table & a carpett, 4 cusshions, 1 joyned cupboard, 1*li.* 5*s.*; 8 silver spoons, 1 silver bowl, 1 silver porringer, 4*li,*; 1 chest, 2 hutches, 1 box, 1 desk, 4 joynd chaires, 2 rush chaires, 1 wicker chair, & a glass case, 1 bible, 1 halbirde, 1 pair of cobirons, 1 pair of tongs, 1 pair of bellows, 1*li.* 7*s.*

IN THE HALL CHAMBER—1 joyned bedsted, 2 feather beds, 1 flock bed, 1 straw bed, 2 blanketts, 1 coverlett, 3 bolsters, 3 pillows, 2 little bedsteds, 1 pair of curtains, 2*li.* 10*s.*

IN THE PARLOUR CHAMBER—1 little table & a library, 1 hutch, 1 trunck, 4*s.*

IN FALLING DOOR CHAMBER—1 halfe headed bedsted, 1 feather bed, 1 straw bed, 1 bolster, 2 pillows, 2 blankets, a coverlett, curtaines & vallents, 3 hutches, other small implements, 1*li.* 5*s.*

IN THE CHEESE CHAMBER—Cheese, 3*li.* 10*s.*; 2 long tables & a forme, a hutch, & other implements, 5*s.*

IN THE SERVANTS CHAMBER—2 bedsteds, 1 flock bed, 2 blankets, 1 hutch, 5*s.*

IN THE BUTERY—1 hogshead, 1 barrell, 1 tunnell, & other implements, 8*s.*

IN THE MEAL HOUSE—An old quern, & a kneading troffe, & other implements, 6*s.* 6*d.*

IN THE DAIRY—1 copper, 1 cheese press, 2 stans, 2 churns, seven chimnels, 8 chees motes, 2 cheese breds, 2*li.* 9*s.*; 2 formes, 4 shelves, 2 pailes, 1 tray, two butter pots, 1 powdering tub, 10*s.*

IN THE KITCHIN—20 pewter dishes, 4 plates, 1 pasty plate, 1 bason, 2 flagons, 2 candlesticks, 1 bed pan, 3 sacers, 2 salts, 3 chamber pots, 2*li.* 10*s.*; 1 coper, 2 kettles, 4 brass pots, 3 skillets, 7 tubs & a hogstub, 4 brass candlesticks, one brass chaffeing dish, 1 pasty pan, 1 drippin pan, 1 cullender & other implements, 4*li.* 2*s.*

IN THE PARLOUR CLOSET—1 hogshead, 5 other vessels, 1 powdering tub, 1 keep, 3 boxes, 1 beer stale, 1 forme, 1*li.* 5*s.*

Wheate, 34*li.*; rye, 24*li.*; oates, 16*li.*; barley, 18*li.*; hay in the barnes & yards, 21 loades, 18*li.*
1 wagon, 2 tumbrills, 1 cart buck, 2 plowes, 1 paire of harrowes. & other implements of husbandry, 9*li.* 10*s.*; scrue & bushell, 8 sacks, a ½ bushell, shovel, 1*li.* 8*s.*
Follow, 44*li.* 10*s.*
50 sheep & lambs, 14*li.*; 5 hogs, 2 sows, 12 piggs, 8*li.*; 7 horses & mares & furniture, 14*li.*; 6 cowes, 3 weanel calves, 15*li.*
For wareing apparell & money in pocketts, 10*li.*
[Total]—259*li.* 19*s.*
[Appraisers—John Clarke, Henry Shettleworth.]
[Exhibited 19 January 1683/4 by Daniel Sterne, son.]

129.—William Poole the elder, of Writtle, blacksmith. 7 August 1684.

IN THE CHAMBER OVER THE HALL—One chist, & 2 bedsteads, 4*s.*; two old bedsteads, three chists, & a little parcel of wool, 1*li.* 10*s.*

IN THE PARLOR—One feather bed & bedstead, one flock bed, two pillows, and a bolstar, 2*li.*; one table & frame, two joynt stooles, one forme, & one chist, 18*s.*

IN THE HALL—Two old tables & frames, one forme, three stooles, two brass kettles & one ireon kettle, one brass candlestick, & a morter & pestell, one cubard, one old chair, a pair of cobireons, a spit, & some other small things, and three old skillets, 1*li.* 13*s.*; fower pair of sheets & other linen, 1*li.*

IN THE BUTTREY—Two hogsheads & two halfe hogsheads, one powdering tubb, one old cubard, one brass pott, six peauter dishes, & one old warming pan, & a frying pan, 1*li.* 7*s.*

IN THE SHOPP—Twenty five barrs of new ireon waighing 8 cwt and a halfe at 14*s.* per hundred waight, 5*li.* 19*s.*; twelve streaks of old ireon, one pair of bellowes, one slick-trough, three old gloomes *al's* anvills, hamers, tongs and other tooles with severall other peeces of old ireon, eleaven pair of hanges, one pair of eyes for gates, three pair of fork tines, tenn dozen of new hors-shooes, two box moulds, one beame, scales & waights, with other implements, 6*li.*

IN THE YEARD—Fower chalder of coales, 3*li.*; one grindston & trough, one swill-tubb, one small cock of hay, one old cart, some fyre-wood & other lumber, 1*li.* 10*s.*

Eight ewes and lambs at 8*s.* a cupple, 1*li.* 12*s.*; one mare & colt 1*li.* 5*s.*; one hogg, 14*s.*

IN THE KITCHIN—Five brewing tubbs, one old trough to salt bacon in, one kneading trough, one coule, one paire of old malt quarnes, one little copper, & other small things, 1*li.* 6*s.*

IN THE BARNE—The barly which grew on halfe an acre of land, 1*li.* 10*s.*

IN THE STABLE—A parcell of old hay, a cart saddle, one pair of harness, two flaggen collers, 10*s.*

Redy money, 7*li.* 2*s.* 6*d.*
Wearing apparell, 1*li.* 10*s.*
Debts recoverable and desperate, 10*li.*
Some totall of this Inventory—50*li.* 10*s.* 6*d.*
[Appraisers—John Stradlinge, William Garrat.]
[Exhibited 11 August 1684 by William Poole, executor.]

130.—John Taverner of Writtle. 1 September 1684.

IN THE HALL—One table, one forme, one press cubord, seaven rush chaires, one little table, a jack, four spitts, three small dripping pans, the tramell, a paire of cobirons, fire shovell & tongs, with some other small imployments, 2*li.* 15*s.* 3*d.*

IN THE PARLOUR—One feather bed & bedstadle, rugg, blanketts, curttains & valences, 5*li.*; one chest of drawers, 5 chaires, 2 stooles, a box, a paire of cobirons, fire shovells & tongs, one livery table, 1*li.* 0*s.* 6*d.*

IN THE BUTTREY NEXT THE HALL—One hoggshead, one barrell, 2 killderkins, eight pewter dishes, one pasty pann & plate, drinke stall, & other imployments, 1*li.* 12*s.* 2*d.*

IN THE SMALL BEARE BUTTREY—Four hoggsheads, one barrell, one killderkin, three small old kettles, 3 skillets, 2 pailes, with some other small imployments, 2*li.* 5*s.* 4*d.*

IN THE DAIRY—One planke with tressells, two cherns, 3 boules, 2 cheese moots, one chees bred, four kemnells, two powdering tubbs, 5 shelves, beame & scalls, with some other small imployments, 1*li.* 7*s.* 9*d.*

IN THE PARLOUR CHAMBER—One feather bed and bedstedle with the materialls belonginge to itt, two joyn chests, one trunke, four stooles, 2 chaires, 2 small boxes, a small looking glasse, 4*li.* 1*s.* 7*d.*

IN THE CHAMBER OVER THE BUTTREY—One halfe headed bedsteadle, bed and blanketts, one chaire, 1*li.* 9*s.* 6*d.*

IN THE SARVANTS CHAMBER—One feather bed, one flock bed, two halfe headed bedsteadles, 2*li.* 10*s.*

IN THE CHEESE CHAMBER—One table & tressells, 5 shelves, one trundle bedsteadle, a linen wheel, three score small cheeses, 5*li.* 8*s.* 3*d.*

IN THE CHAMBER OVER THE DAIRY—5 quarters of old oates, 12 bushells of old wheat, with some other small imployments, 5*li.* 8*s.* 10*d.*

IN THE KITCHIN & BREWHOUSE—2 leads, one meashing tubb, 3 other tubbs, one stand, one cooler, a cheespress, and a tropth, a little table & forme, one dresserboard, one querne, 2 swill tubbs, a capons coop, two kneading trophes, a trephett, with some other implements, 6*li.* 8*s.* 5*d.*

The linen—4 paire of flaxen sheets, 5 paire of ordinary sheets, 5 paire of pillowbeers, halfe a dozen of table cloathes, 3 dozen of napkins, & halfe a dozen of towells, 5*li.* 17*s.* 6*d.*
40 acres of wheat, 20*li.*; 12 acres of peas, 18*li.*; a percell of beany corn & tares, 4*li.*; the oates in the barne to thresh, 6*li.*; the hay in the house, 15*li.*; 24 acres of barley, 60*li.*
8 milch cowes, 18*li.*; 6 Welsh heifers, 11*li.*; 10 Welsh heifers which are fatt, 30*li.*; 9 hoggs, 6 shots, a sow & 8 small piggs, 12*li.*; 6 score sheep & lambs, 36*li.*; 7 horses, 30*li.*; 3 colts, 4*li.*
Collors & harness with the rest of the furniture belonging to them, 3*li.*
2 waggons, 2 dung carts, plows, harrows, with the rest of the things belonging to them, 14*li.*
Two old cocks of hay, 11*li.*
54 acres of fallow, 40*li.*
His wearing apparell & mony in his purse, 3*li.* 4*s.* 2*d.*
Summa totalis—370*li.* 9*s.* 3*d.* [should be 380*li.* 9*s.* 3*d.*]
[Appraisers—Richard Horsnaile, gent., William Bird, gent.]
[Exhibited 28 March 1685 by Mary Taverner, widow and administratrix.]

131.—John Scoling of Writtle, husbandman. 4 October 1684.

IN THE HALL—Two tables, one forme, 2 spitts, one driping pan, 4 chaires, other small things, 18*s.*

IN THE PARLOR—One fether bed, one flock bed, one table, milke vessells, other small thinges, one presse, 3*li.* 10*s.*

IN THE BUTTERY—3 ketles, one chirne, one pott, 2 barrells, one cheese preese, other small thinges, 2*li.*

IN THE CHAMBER OVER THE HALL—One fether bed, one flocke bed, boster and pillows, 2 huchs, other small things, 2*li.*

IN THE CLOSETT—One fether bed, blanketts, and other thinges, 1*li.* 10*s.*

IN THE CHAMBER OVER THE PARLOR—3 huchs, ten peuter dishes, other small things, 1*li.*

IN THE CHEESE CHAMBER—4 score cheeses att 1*s.* 6*d.* the cheese, 6*li.*

Linnen—3 paire of flaxen sheets, 3 paire of twoin sheetes, other linn napkins, 3*li.*
Five ackers of wheat a 3 pound an ackre, 15*li.*
Wheat in the chamber, 1*li.* 10*s.*
Three ackers of barley, 4*li.* 10*s.*; oates and peese, 5 ackers, 5*li.*
Five horses and colllts, 7*li.*; seven cowes, the hay and straw, 20*li.*; one bull, one heifer, 2*li.* 10*s.*; fifteene sheepe, 5*li.*
One long cart, one dung cart, harrows and plow, dewe racke, 2*li.*; implements of husbandry, 5*li.*
Two hoggs, 2*li.*; six pigges 7*s.* a pesce, 2*li.* 2*s.*
Eight ackers of follow, 8*li.*
Wearing aparrell, money in his pocket, 20*li.*
[Total]—119*li.* 10*s.*
[Appraisers—William Daves, William Baker.]
[Exhibited 28 March 1685 by Dionisia, wife of John Marridge, daughter and executrix.]

132.—Henry Bright, senior, of Roxwell. 14 February 1684.

IN THE HALL—One longe table & forme, on little table & forme, six chaires, four cushions, one glascase, a paire of cobirons, fire shovell & tongs, a jack, & a clock, 4*li.* 17*s.* 6*d.*

IN THE PARLOUR—Two tables, a hutch, seaven Rush [Russian] leather chaires, a joynd chaire, a paire of cobirons, a paire of tonges, 2*li.* 4*s.* 6*d.*

IN THE KITCHIN—On little table, a kneading troph, four brass kettles, two brass potts, one iron pott, three skellets, one warming pan, a brass basone, one irone dripping pan, three spitts and a girdiron, a old cubbord, with some other things, 5*li.* 6*s.* 4*d.*

IN THE BREWHOUSE—Two leads, one meashing tubb & four other tubbs, 3 trophes, an old boule, 3*li.* 13*s.* 4*d.*

IN THE DAIRY—A cherne, a milke stand, one kemnell, four milke trayes, a chees-press, a poudering tubb, 6 cheese moots, 2 cheese breds, with some other small things, 1*li.* 10*s.* 9*d.*

IN THE SMALL BEARE BUTTREY—Four halfe hoggsheads, 1*li.* 0*s.* 10*d.*

IN THE STRONG BEARE BUTTREY—Three hoggsheads, a drinke stall, a frying pann, a flower tubb, with some other small things, 1*li.* 9*s.* 8*d.*

IN THE CHAMBER OVER THE HALL—One joyn bedsteadle, feather bed, with all belonging to itt, two chests, one livery cubord, one great joyn chair, one napkin press, two nedleworke cushions, 7*li.* 3*s.* 9*d.*

IN THE CLOSSET NEXT THE HALL CHAMBER—Sixteene cheeses with some other small things, 1*li.* 10*s.*

IN THE PARLOUR CHAMBER—One joyn bedsteadle, feather bed and all belonging to itt, one chest, one press cubbord, a wicker chaire, three cushions, 6*li.* 1*s.* 2*d.*

Linen—6*li.* 16*s.* 8*d.* Pewter—2*li.* 15*s.*

IN THE CHAMBER OVER THE KITCHIN—One halfe headed bedstedle, feather bed & all belonging to itt, one chaire table, one still, one joyn chaire, a paire of small cobirons, *3li. 6s. 8d.*

IN THE CHAMBER OVER THE BUTTREY—One joyne bedstedle, feather bed and all belonging to itt, two great chestes, with some other small things, *6li. 5s.*

IN THE MAULT HOUSE—Seaven seame of mault & barley, a paire of scalles and wayts with some other imployments of husbandrey, *10li. 5s.*; a leaden sesterne, *2li. 10s.*

Hay in the hay house, *4li.*

IN THE BARNE—3 seame & half of barley, *4li.*; 13 quaters of wheate, *28li.*; a screene, 2 fanes, a casting shovell, caveing seive, with some other imployments, *1li.*

13 [?]sackes, *1li. 6s.*

A load cart, dung cart, a pair of harrows, plow & all belonging to itt, *5li. 10s.*

Six cowes, one bull stagg, *17li. 10s.*; 4 store piggs, *2li.*

IN THE STABLE—One horse, one mare and colt, collers, harness, halters, belonging to them, *8li.*

5 sheep, *1li. 13s. 4d.*

His wearing apparrell, *6li.* Money in his purse, *13li.*

[Total]—*158li. 15s. 6d.*

[Appraisers—Thomas Crush, Richard Thorowgood.]

[Exhibited 28 March 1685 by Thomas Bright, son and executor.]

133.—Samuel Sumers, victualler, of Roxwell, 20 May 1685.

IN THE HAAL—One long teabel, one forme, 4 chaers, 2 coshons, 8 pewter dishes, 4 poringrs, 2 salts, one pewter candelstik, 2 spits, 2 dripinpans, one cool dish, one lock iorn, one foullin peese, one cool rack, and soum other small things, *2li. 6s. 8d.*

IN THE PARLER—One bed and that belongs to it, and other thing, *3li. 10s.*

IN THE CHAMBER OVR THE PALER—One fether bed and other things belongin to it, 3 hutches, and other small things, *3li. 1s.*

IN THE BEST CHAMBER—One fether bed and that belongs to it, and one long teabel, and sum other things, *5li. 1s.*

IN THE GARIT—2 flockbeds and the things belongin to it, *2li. 1s.*

IN THE BRWHOUS—One coper and other bras and bruing vesels, and other impelemits, *7li. 1s. 6d.*

IN THE BUTTREE—The cask and flagines and beer, *5li. 1s. 6d.*; hops, *14s.*

Linen—*2li. 15s.*

A horcmill and other impelemts in the mill hous, *1li. 3s. 4d.*

The wood in the yard, *2li.*

2 old cowes, *4li. 15s.*; 5 pigs, *2li. 10s.*; cart, *1li.*; 4 sheep, *1li.*

3 acers of wheat and barly, *5li.*
Waring aparill and mony in his pocket, *2li.*
The sum is—*50li.* 1*s.* [should be *51li.*]
[Appraisers—Simon Hudson, Hesekyah Godsaf, Isaac Reeve.]
[Exhibited 26 September 1685 by Mary Sumers, widow and administratrix.]

134.—Mark George of Writtle. 20 June 1685.

In the hall—One drawing table, two joyn'd forms, on little table with a drawer, one press cupbord, six chaires bottom'd with rushes, two low stooles, one paire of cobirons, fire shovell & tongs, two gridirons, one tramell, one plank, two spitts & an iron dripping pan, & a tin candlebox, and a payre of bellows, with other small implements, *2li.* 8*s.* 6*d.*

In the great parlour—One featherbed, bolster, curtaines & vallants, one blankett, one rugg, one leafe table, one bedsted, one deale chest, one livory board, one deale cupboard, five join'd stooles buffeded, *6li.* 1*s.* 2*d.*

In the little parlour—One flock bedsted & one bolster, two pillows, one deale box, with other implements, *1li.*

In the chamber over the buttery—Four spades, one shovell, 3 garden rakes, 3 howes, two trapps for foxes, one wire sieve, one tin watering pott, 1 bagg, 1 riddle, *2li.*

In the buttery—One hoggshead, two halfe hoggsheads, four barrells, *1li.* 16*s.*; seven dishes of peuter, one bason, one flagon, two porringers, four spoones, one copper pott, one brass frying pan, one chamber pott, & a pouldering tubb, & some smale implements, *1li.* 6*s.*

In the kitchen—One brass copper, one brass pott, four kettles, three brass skilletts, *3li.* 10*s.*; one meashing tubb, three other tubbs, one kneading trough, *1li.* 8*s.*

In the dayry—One stand, one chern, three pailes, one kimnell, one trey, five cheesmotes, & other implements, *1li.*; eight & twenty cheeses, *1li.*; one flitch of bacon, *1li.*

Beanes, pease & the nurcery, *4li.*
Two horses, *4li.*; three hoggs, *2li.* 8*s.*
One wagon, one tumbrell, plow & harrows, & horse harness, *5li.* 10*s.*
Linnen—Two paire of sheets, & 12 napkins, & one table cloth, *1li.* 10*s.*
Eleven acres of wheat, *22li.*; nine acres of barly, *31li.* 10*s.*; ten acres of fallow, *13li.*; ten acres of meadow, *10li.*
Six milch cowes, *16li.* 10*s.*
Wearing apparell & ready money, *3li.*
Summa totalis—*135li.* 17*s.* 8*d.*
[Appraisers—John Clarke, Thomas Crow.]
[Exhibited 26 September 1685 by Jane George, widow and administratrix.]

135.—John Holmes of Writtle, innholder. 28 December 1685.

In the hall—One joyne table, six stooles, 14*s.*; 9 old chairs, 8 old cusheons, 3*s.*; 4 paire of tongs, 1 paire of cobirons, two fire pans, 2 paire of tramells, 1 paire of bellows, 1 brass sconce, 3 candlesticks, 10*s.*

IN THE PARLOUR—One bedsted with curtains & vallants, 2 feather bedds, 2 bolsters, 3 pillowes, 1 rug, and 1 blankett, 4*li.* 10*s.*; 1 little table, 4 joyne stooles, 1 form, 2 old joyne press cupboards, 10*s.*

IN THE BEER-BUTTERY—3 full hogsheads, 3 empty hogsheads, 2 empty barrells, 2 beerestalls, 7*li.*

IN THE KITCHEN—Six spitts, 1 jack, 2 iron dripping pans, 3 tin pans, 1 warming pan, 2 tramells, 1 paire of cobirons, 1 gridiron, 1 paire of iron racks, 2 irons to lay before the fire, 1 pewter still, 1 glascase, one old cupboard, & other smal implements, 2*li.* 10*s.*

IN THE LARDER—36 pewter dishes great & small, 6 pewter candlesticks, 6 porringers, 6 saucers, 2 salts, 5 pewter chamber potts, 4*li.*; 1 keep, 1 pouldering tub, 1 kneading trough, 1 mustard-querne, 4 bowls, 1 tray, 4 wooden platers & other implements, 1*li.*; 2 brass potts, 3 pott skilletts, 4 brass skilletts, & 1 brass frying pan, 3*li.* 10*s.*

IN THE BREWHOUSE—2 coppers, tubbs & cooler as they stand, 10*li.*

IN THE SHOP—One table, & a parcell of hopps, 2*li.*

IN THE HALL CHAMBER—One joyne bed, curtains & vallants, 1 feather bed, 1 straw bed, 2 bolsters, 2 pillows, 1 rug, 2 blanketts, 3*li.* 10*s.*; 1 table, 7 stooles, 3 leather chairs, 1 joyn chair, 1 livery board, 1 cloth press, 1 pair of cobirons & 1 fire pan, 1 paire of bellows, & 1 cusheon, 2*li.*

IN THE KITCHEN CHAMBER—Two joyne beds, the one with curtains & vallants, the other with curtains & noe vallants, 2 feather beds, 4 bolsters, 4 pillows, 1 rugg, 1 coverlett, 4 blanketts, 7*li.*; 1 table, 2 stooles, 1 form, 4 chaires, 3 cusheons, and 1 carpett, 1*li.*

IN THE STARR CHAMBER—One joyn bed with curtains, 1 feather bed, 1 flock bed, 1 strawbed, 1 bolster, two blanketts, 1 coverlett, 2*li.*; 2 tables, 7 stooles, 1 joyn form, 1 livery board, 10*s.*; 16 bushels of wheate, 2*li.* 8*s.*

IN THE CHAMBER OVER THE BUTTERY—Three old hutches, 3 boxes, 1 livery cupboard, 10*s.*

IN THE PARLOUR CHAMBER—One joyne bedsted, 1 feather bed, 2 blankets, 2 bolsters, 1 coverlett, 2*li.*; 2 old chests, 1 old trunke, 2*s.*

Linnen—21 paire of sheets, 8*li.*; 13 paire of pillow-beers, 1*li.* 10*s.*; 1 long table cloth, 2 short ones, 1 dozen of napkins, 1*li.* 10*s.*
Plate—One silver bowle, 1 silver drinking cup, 2*li.* 10*s.*
Weareing apparell & ready money, 2*li.*
Summe totalis—72*li.* 17*s.*
[Appraisers—John Cooke, Thomas May.]
[Exhibited 27 February 1685/6, by Mary Holmes, widow and executrix.]

136.—Thomas Crush, the elder, of Dukes in Roxwell, gentleman. 10 July 1686.[1]

[1] This inventory, edited, with notes, by the Rev. E. G. Norris, is printed in *Essex Review*, vol. xv, pp. 169-75. Mr. Norris refers to the inventories in the chest at Writtle as covering the period 1627-1730; these documents were transferred to the Essex Record Office and are the subject of this book, but extend from 1635-1749. The earlier inventories are apparently lost.

IN THE HALL—One long table, one little table, eight joyne stooles, one long forme & two joyne formes, two chayers, one presse cubbord, one still, a payer of cobirons, one clock, with other small implements, 4*li.* 9*s.* 9*d.*

IN THE PARLOR—One drawing table, one little table, fourteene chayers, two payer of cobirons, a fire shovle, a paier of tonges, one side bord table, with other implements, 3*li.* 18*s.* 6*d.*

IN THE KITCHIN—One long table, one little forme, two joyen stooles, seven chayers, one table chaier, two couberds, a paier of cobirons, a fire shovel and tonges, one jack, two payer of tramels, eight spitts, three iron dripping pans, two gridirons, a paier of racks, a paier of andirons, one fire forke, two midling kettels, eight small kettles, fouer small brass potts, two iron potts with hookes, fouer brass candelsticks, two brass morters, two pestls, one brass skimer, two brass ladels, three warming panns, one coale dish, with other smale implements, 14*li.* 6*s.* 8*d.*

IN THE DARY—One brass leade, five skillits, three brass frying pans, a paier of brass skales, one cheese presse, one stand, one leaden milk vessell, two kemnels, two trayes, two tubbs, two cherns, five bouls, six cheese motes, two cheese breads, three formes, two cleavers, three milk pailes, small weights, and other implements belonging to the dary, 8*li.* 9*s.*

IN THE PANTREY—One little sid board table, one glass case, one pastie peele, a parcell of bookes, one settle, a lanthorne, with other small implements, 7*li.* 15*s.*

IN THE CHAMBER OVER THE HALL—Fouer feather beeds, three flockbeeds, six feather boulsters, one flock boulster, two joyne beedsteds, one halfe headed beedsted all with curtins and valiens, one greene rugg, two coverlids, five blankets, one pres cubbord, one joyne chest, one hutch, fouer chaiers, one little table, two deskes, two joyne stooles, one hutch, one trunke, one little forme, one close stoole, a carpet and a coubord cloath, and nine cussions, 25*li.* 9*s.* 6*d.*

IN THE CHAMBER OVER THE PARLOR—One joyne beedsted with curtins and valiens, one trundle beedsted, two feather beeds, two feather boulsters, two downe pillows, a green rugg, three blankets, an counter pane, one chest of drawers, one drawing table, two chayers, fouer stooles, one sidbord cubbord, two payer of cobirons, a fire shovle and tongs, a payer of bellows, two carpets, two window curtains, and a looking glass, 25*li.* 7*s.*

IN THE KITCHIN CHAMBER—One joyne beedsted with curtins and valliens, one feather beed, two feather boulsters, two down pillos, one coverlid, two blankets, one press cubboard, one little table, one liveri side table, one great hutch, three payer of cobirons, thirty six pewter dishes, one beed pann, one basson, six candlesticks, fouer chamber potts, a pasty plate with other small peices of pewter, twelve silver spoons, a silver tankard, two silver bouls, a salt, a porrenger and a silver cupp, a dozen of flax and other implements, 38*li.* 17*s.* 6*d.*

IN THE MILKHOUSE CHAMBER—One joyne beedsted with curtins and valins, one feather beed, two boulsters, two pillows, one coverlid, two blankets, one trundle beedsteed, one feather beed, two pillows, two blankets, two joyne chests, one old hutch, 8*li.* 11*s.*

The lining—Thirteene table cloaths, one payer of holland sheets, tenn payer of flaxen sheets, fourteene payer of towen sheets, one dozen of diaper napkins, fouer dozen of flaxen napkins, two dozen and a halfe of course napkins, seven payer of pillow beires, 30*li.* 8*s.* 2*d.*

IN THE LITTLE GARRETT—One trundle beedstedl, one feather beed, one blankett, one olde boulster, and a parcell of wooll, 3*li.* 6*s.*

IN THE CHEESE CHAMBER—A hundred cheeses, three hutches, and a pillion, 10*li.* 10*s.* 6*d.*

IN THE OTHER GARRETS—One hutch, two lyning wheeles, one woollen wheele, two payer of cobirons, and other olde lumber, 5*li.*

IN THE SERVANTS CHAMBER—Two borded beedstedls, one featherbeed, one flockbeed, two boulsters, fouer blankets, 3*li.* 11*s.* 6*d.*

IN THE LITTLE SELLER—Five hogsheads, two barrels, two beerestalls, pouldring tubb, one other tubb, and a kemnell, 2*li.* 6*s.*

IN THE GREAT SELLER—Three hogsheads, one pipe, one barrell, two beerestalls, one barrell, and a tunnell, a tub, 1*li.* 10*s.* 6*d.*

IN THE BREWHOUSE—One copper, one little leade, one mashing tubb and underback, one cooler, one coule, two tubbs, one sider presse and a trough, a payer of tramels, one iron oven lid, one peele, and other implements, 10*li.* 7*s.* 6*d.*

IN THE BOULTING HOUSE—One meale tubb, a kneding trough and other implements, 15*s.* 6*d.*

IN THE MALT CHAMBER—One hundred and fifteen quarters of malt, 115*li.*; and in hopps, 55*li.* 4*s.* 3*d.*; one screw, one bushell, and three shovels, tenn bushels of pease and a quarter of barly, twenty sacks, with other old houshold stuffe, 8*li.* 12*s.* 3*d.*

IN THE MALT HOUSE—One leaden sestone, skales and weights, 11*li.*

IN THE KELL HOUSE—One hayer, 2*li.*

IN THE BARNE AND CHAMBERS—Wheate thresht and unthresht fifty five quarters, 55*li.*; a screw, two fanns, fouer shovels, six rakes, and other threshing instruments, 1*li.* 4*s.* 6*d.*

The wheat upon the grownd, twenty six acres, 73*li.*; the barly upon the ground, thirty seven acres, 111*li.*; the pease and beans upon the ground, twelve acres, 30*li.*

IN THE HOP GARDEN—Twelve thousand of hop poles, 60*li.*; the cropp upon the ground, 150*li.*; sixty acres of fallow twice plowd, 40*li.* 15*s.*

Thirty loads of hay, 30*li.*

Five horses, 41*li.*; eleaven cowes, 44*li.*; thirty two sheep, 11*li.*; thirteene hoggs, 13*li.*

One waggon, one waggon buck with fore wheels, one loade carte, three duncarts, and a wheele barrow, 31*li.* 7*s.*; collers, halters, harness, and other

furniture belonging to the horses, 13*li.* 15*s.*; two plows with their irons, and two payer of harrows, 3*li.* 1*s.* 6*d.*
Forty bushels of coales, 1*li.*
One malt mill, 2*li.* 10*s.*
Tenn forkes, 3 spades, 2 shovels, two mathookes, two axes, two bills, with other implements of husbandry, 2*li.* 0*s.* 11*d.*
Due to the testator, 142*li.* 12*s.* 6*d.*
Five gold rings, 4*li.*
His wearing apparell and money in his purs, 30*li.*
[Total]—1338*li.* 13*s.* 2*d.* [should be 1287*li.* 2*s.* 6*d.*]
[Appraisers—Simon Burrell, Mathew Nightingale, Thomas Poole.]
[Exhibited 11 September 1686 by Thomas Crush, son and executor.]

137.—Thomas Foster of Roxwell. 4 September 1686.

In the hall—A long table, five joyne stools, a little table, a press cubord, three rush chaires, one settle, two small stools, one warming pan, a spitt, a lock iron, and one cobiron, a paire of tramells, a cleaver, with some other small imployments, 1*li.* 18*s.* 6*d.*

In the parlour—Tw joyne bedsteadles, one feather bed, two boulsters, two pillows, two blanketts, two coverletts, curtains & vallences, one little table, three old hutches, 5*li.* 3*s.* 6*d.*

In a little roome next the parlour—One halfe headed bedsteadle, one feather bed & boulster, one pillow, one coverlett, 2*li.* 1*s.* 7*d.*; one chest, one old hutch, & two boxes, 7*s.* 6*d.*; six paire of sheets, one dozen of napkines, two course table cloathes, four old pillow beers, 1*li.* 16*s.* 8*d.*

In the cheese chamber—Threescore and seaven little cheeses, 2*li.* 1*s.* 9*d.*; tw tubs, a hanging shelfe, a old linen wheel, & a little parcell of wheat, 1*li.* 10*s.*; a small parcell of woole, 8*s.* 4*d.*

In the milke house—One cheese press, one cherne, one old stand, one tub, a kemnell, a bowle, two earthen milke pans, 5 creame potts, 4 wooden dishes, 4 chees moots, one kneading troph, a little meal tub, a long form, 2 shelves, with some other small potts and dishes, 1*li.* 2*s.* 3*d.*

In the buttrey—One hogshead, three barrells, two leather bottles, two pailes, a tunell, a old drink stall, two paire of scalls and some small waitts, a frying pan, with some other small imployments, 1*li.* 1*s.* 5*d.*

In the room next the buttrey—Five old tubs, a form, a shelfe, one old lead, 2 settles, one morter and pessell, a scumer, a treavett, one little iron pott & pott hooks, with some other small things, 2*li.* 1*s.* 5*d.*; his husbandry tooles, 18*s.* 6*d.*; six old pewter dishes, 7*s.* 6*d.*

In the barne—One fan, a ridle, a old bushell, a caveing seive, four forkes, an old casting shovell, flayle & rake, 7*s.* 9*d.*

In the stable—One paire of body harness, one old coller, cart saddle and thyll bells, chaff seive, and seed peck, a pannell, one old sadle, with some other imployments, 10*s.*

IN THE CART HOUSE—Two old carts, a paire of harrows, a plow & plow irons, *2li.* 16*s.* 8*d.*

Three acres of wheat, 6*li.* 10*s.*; three acres & halfe of barley, 5*li.* 15*s.*; two acres of peason, 2*li.*; the hay, 2*li.* 17*s.* 6*d.*
A mare & colt, 2*li.* 10*s.*; three old cowes, 6*li.*; nine sheep, 3*li.*; two hoggs, 2*li.*
His wearing apparell and money in his purse, 3*li.*
[Total]—58*li.* 5*s.* 10*d.*
[Appraisers—Richard Thorowgood, Henry Bright.]
[Exhibited 11 September 1686, by John Foster, son and administrator.]

138.—John Ruskin of Writtle, sawyer. 13 December 1686.

Two hoggs and twelve bushells of pease, 4*li.*; a mare and colte, 3*li.*
One hogges coate, 10*s.*; an old hovell, 2*s.* 6*d.*
A parcell of hey, 3*s.*
Two pitt roles, 2*s.* One trough & one ladder, 1*s.* 6*d.* One slead, 1*s.*
Dew from ye Widd. Mariage, 1*li.*; dew from Adam Eve, 8*s.*; more debts dew, 3*li.* 5*s.* 6*d.*
Wood, 8*s.*
Summa totalis—13*li.* 1*s.* 6*d.*
[Appraisers—Hugh Green, Ezekiah Godsafe.]
[Exhibited 13 December 1686.]

139.—John Mariage. 10 January 1686/7. (Died 20 November 1686.)

Four hoars, 10*li.*; two coults, 2*li.*; the harnes and pannel, 1*li.*; five cous, 13*li.*; four pigs, 1*li.* 10*s.*; waggon cart, and harrous, and plow, 1*li.*; one and terty shep and lams, 6*li.* 16*s.*; four seme of ots, 2*li.*; to lode of haye, 2*li.*; three seme of wheat, 3*li.*; a boshe for and sacks, 8*s.*; fiv acaker of wheat, 6*li.* 5*s.*; four acrses of barle land, 3*li.* 12*s.*

IN THE HOAL—Too tablels, chaires and other emplemnts, 1*li.*

IN THE PARLER—Bed and bed stedel, bousters and pillous, 4*li.*

IN THE CHAMB OVRE THE HOAL—To half half [*sic*] hedded bedl with beds upon them, and other enpemnts, 3*li.*

IN THE DARY—Milk vesseles, cheone and a stand, and othr emppln'ments, 10*s.*

IN THE CHICHEN—Four cettels, a bras pot a[n]d Iron pot, 2*li.*

IN THE BUTTEY—Drink vesels and bruing ves & tub, and tenn peuter dishes, 2*li.* 5*s.*

Six paire of sets, to tables closs, and a dossen of napkins, 2*li.* 10*s.*
Waring aparrel and mony in his purse, 2*li.*
Sum is—70*li.* 16*s.* [should be 69*li.* 16*s.*]
[Appraisers—Richard Horsnayle, John Robinson.]
[Exhibited 1 June 1687 by Dionisia Dennis, widow and executrix.]

140.—Thomas Crow. 21 February 1686/7.

GRAINE. In the wheate barnes; in the one barne—15 quarters of wheate threshed & unthreshed at 28*s*. the quarter, 21*li.*

IN THE BARNE AT THE LITLE FARME—theshed, 3 quarters & a halfe at 28*s*. the quarter, 4*li.* 18*s*.

IN THE STABLE AT THE LITLE FARME—5 quarters unthreshed at 28*s*. the quarter, 7*li.*

IN THE OATE BARNE—Twenty two quarters of oates threshed & unthreshed at 10*s*. the quarter, 11*li.*

IN THE BARLY BARNE & THE GRAINERY—Twenty quarters of barly unthreshed at 21*s*. the quarter, 21*li.*; and 8 quarters 3 bushells threshed at 21*s*. the quarter, 8*li.* 15*s*. 6*d*.

HAYE—In the haycock, 20 load: in one barne, one load: in the cowhouse, one load: in all 22 load at 20*s*. the load, 22*li.*

LUMBER WITHOUT DORES—Two wagons, 2 carts, 3 plowes, 5 harrowes, 2 lathers with other things belonging to the plowes & lumber, 22*li.*

Cattell—Five Welch runts & 3 yearling calves, 18*li.*; eight cowes, 27*li.*; one farrow cow, 1 bull, 6 heiffers, 17*li.*; five small calves, 3*li.* 10*s*.; thirty sheepe at 9*s*. a sheepe, 13*li.* 10*s*.; twenty nine sheepe at 5*s*. 6*d*. a sheepe, 7*li.* 19*s*. 6*d*.; eight horses & one colt, with geeres & lumber in the stable, 42*li.* 10*s*.; nine shoates at 9*s*. a shoate, 4*li.* 1*s*.; two gilts at 15*s*. a gilt, 1*li.* 10*s*.; one sow with 10 small piggs, 1*li.* 10*s*.
Tilledg, Sowing, & Seed—30 akers of one tilt at 5*s*. the aker, 7*li.* 10*s*.; wheate sowne 2 quarters at 24*s*. the quarter, 2*li.* 8*s*.; for harrowing 8 akers of wheat at 18*d*. the aker, 12*s*.; more wheate sowne on 23 akers, 5 quarters 6 bushells at 24*s*. the quarter, 6*li.* 18*s*.; for sowing 31 akers at 12*d*. the aker is 1*li.* 11*s*.; for harrowing 10 akers before it was sowne, 10*s*.; for plowing 49 akers at 14*s*. the aker, 34*li.* 6*s*.; for the last yeares rent for the 49 akers at 10*s*. an aker att Michaelmas last, 24*li.* 10*s*.; for beanes sowed & for sowing them, 14*s*.; for more tilt, 4*li.* 12*s*.

OD THINGS IN THE BARNES—Two fanns, 1 screeine, 1 bushell, 1 siffe & sacks, 1*li.* 3*s*.; parcells of chaff, 10*s*.

MORE HAYE—In a cock & in the stable under the wheate at the Little farme, 3 load & halfe, 3*li.* 10*s*.

GOODS IN THE HOUSE. IN THE KITCHEN—Pewter 90*lbs*. at 7*d*. per pound, 2*li.* 12*s*. 6*d*.; one peuter still, 9*s*.; one brass pott, 5 skellets, 1 kitle, 1 ladle, 1 candlestick, 10*s*.; 3 spitts, 3 driping panns, 2 tin panns, 1 hoope, 1 copper pott, 10*s*.; 6 sickells, 1 iron pott, 1 iron kitle, 1 brass chaffen dish, 1 jack, 1 pair andirons, 1 od andiron, 1 fender, 1 warming pann, 1 shovell, 1 pair tongues, 2 pott hooks, 1 *li.*; 1 peale, 3 pailes, 1 mattocks, 1 frying pann, 2 leaden waits, 1 elboe chaire, 1 board, 5 mated chaires, 1 settle, 1 fowling peece, 1*li.* 10*s*.

IN THE BUTRIE—12 earthen potts & panns, 1 chirne, stick & lid, 1 table, 2 pair scailes, 1 frying pann, 1 kimnell, 1 tub, 1 boul, 1 board, 1*li.* 5*s*.

IN THE PANTRIE—[torn away], 1 chaire, [torn away], 1 quiene, a parcell of old iron, 2 tubes, pair scailes, & other lumber, 1*li.* 3*s.*

IN THE BEARE BUTRIE—5 hogsheads, 6 tubs, 4 barrells, 1 brass kitle, 1 siffe, 1 tunnell, 1 kimnell, 3*li.* 5*s.*; one grinding stone in the yard, 1*s.* 6*d.*

IN THE BREW-HOUSE—2 brass copers, 1 stall, 1 cover, 3*li.* 2*s.*

IN THE BOLTING HOUSE & ROOME JOYNING—2 planks, 1 kimnell, 2 siffes, 1 cheesepress, 5 cheesemoats, 2 tubs, 2 cheese breads, 1*li.* 3*s.* 6*d.*

IN THE MILK-HOUSE—3 dresers, 1 kimnell, 1 standing kimnell, 1 tub, 1 chirne, stick & lid, 2 firmes, 1 creame pott, 3 shelves, 18*s.*; 2 flitches of bacon, 16 stone at 2*s.* 4*d.* the stone, 1*li.* 17*s.* 4*d.*

IN THE BACK-HOUSE—1 malt quirne, 1 drag-rake, 1 coope, 1 firme, 1 tubb, parcell plow timber & other lumber, 1*li.* 10*s.*

IN THE MUSSICK ROOME—1 bedstedle, 1 [?]feather bed, 1 flock bolster, 1 coverlid, 1 pair sheets, 1 trunk, 1 chest, 1*li.*

IN THE CHAMBER OVER THE BUTRIE—One bedsted, 1 feather bed & bolster, 1 flock bolster, 2 feather pillows, 1 coverlid, 1 blanket, 1 pair sheets, 4 curtens, vallance, 2 chests, 1*li.* 15*s.*

IN THE CHAMBER OVER THE DRINK-HOUSE—Two bedstedles, 1 feather bed & bolster, 1 flock bed & bolster, 2 coverlids, 2 blankets, 2 pair sheets, 1 bedsted, 1*li.* 10*s.*

IN THE 2 CHAMBERS, MATTED & THE CHAMBER BETWEENE THEN—Two bushells of pease, ½ seame of oates, 1 bedsted, 5 curtens & vallence, 1 coverlid, 2 chests, 1 stoole, 2 chaires, 1 cubord, 70 cheeses, 4*li.* 17*s.*

IN THE NURSSERRY—One bedsted, 1 fether bed & 4 pillows, 1 flock bolster, 1 coverlid, 2 blankets, 4 curtens & vallance, 1 chest, 1 cubard, 1 stoole, 1 pair andirons. IN THE CLOSSET—1 trunk, 2 chests, 2*li.* 5*s.*

IN THE HALL—Two tables, 1 cubard, 3 joynt stooles, 1 chaire, 1 pair andirons, & beare in the barrells, 1*li.* 15*s.*

IN THE PARLOUR—One table, 1 cubard, 6 joynt stooles, 3 chaires, 1 pair andirons, 2 carpetts, 1 pair sheets, 1 pair pillobers, 1*li.* 15*s.*

One calfe sold, 1*li.* 2*s.* 6*d.*; twentie sheepe sold, 9*li.* 2*s.* 6*d.*
Parcell linen & plate, 6*li.* 10*s.*
The poultrie, 5*li.*
[Total]—400*li.* 6*s.* 10*d.*
[Appraisers—Richard Bridge, Richard Mitkolls, Thomas Stone.]
[Exhibited 1 March 1686/7.]

141.—Edward Allin, the elder, of Roxwell. 10 March 1686/7.

IN THE HALL—One long table, six joyne stooles, one litle table, one presse couberd, five chayers, one jack, one dripping pann, foure spitts, two pestles & morters, a payer of cobirons, a fire shovle and tonges, two swords, a glass case, one warming pan, one salt box, two payer of tramels, one gridiron, two little formes, one brass pott, one payer of pott hookes, one iron barr, one cleaver, with other small implements, 5*li.* 2*s.* 6*d.*

IN THE PARLOR—A paier of cobirons, a fire shovel, a chaier and a cushion, 12*s.* 6*d.*

IN THE LITLE BUTREY—Three half hogsheads, one little barrell, one beere-stall, two formes, one pouldring tubb, one dozen of glasse bottels, 1*li.* 5*s.* 6*d.*

IN THE PASSAGE—One little table, two chayers, one cushion, 5*s.* 6*d.*

IN THE GREAT BUTREY—Twenty pewter dishes, foure poringers, two pewter flagons, two saltes, one candlestick, nine brasse kettles, three skillits, one little brass pott, three brass skimers, one gridiron, one tunnell, two pailes, three shelves, two leather bottls, one mustard quarne, one cullender, dishes and spoones, one dozen of round trenchers, and a dozen of other trenchers, 5*li.* 7*s.* 10*d.*

IN THE CHAMBER OVER THE PARLOR—Three feather beds, one feather boulster, one pillow, one coverlid, five blankets, one joyne bedstdle with curtins and valiens, one livrie cubbord, three joyn chests, one joyne box, six joyne stooles, four cushion stooles, two chayers, two windo curtins, and a payer of cobirons, 11*li.* 19*s.* 6*d.*

The lining—Five flaxen sheets, foure dozen and one napkins, fourteene table cloaths, nine pillowbers, 8*li.* 3*s.* 6*d.*

IN THE CHAMBER OVER THE DARY—One joyne bedstedl with curtains and valiens, one feather bed, one flock boulster, one rugg, two blankets, one table, one trunke, one hutch, 3*li.* 8*s.* 10*d.*

IN THE KITCHIN CHAMBER—One flockbed and two hutches, 10*s.* 6*d.*

IN THE HALL CHAMBER—One long table and dormans, 10*s.*; nine and thirty cheeses, and two bushels of wheate, 3*li.* 5*s.*

IN THE BREWHOUSE—One brasse leade, one mashing tubb, foure other tubbs, 2*li.* 10*s.*

IN THE GREAT BUTTREY—Three hogsheads and a beerestall, 1*li.* 8*s.* 6*d.*

IN THE DARY—One cheese presse, two stands, two tubbs, one chern, foure cheese mots, a payer of skales and nine small weights, potts, and other small implements, 1*li.* 9*s.* 6*d.*

IN THE STABLE—Two horses with their furniture, 9*li.* 5*s.*

IN THE YARD—One cock of hay, 6*li.*

IN THE CARTHOUSE—One load carte, on duncarte, and one duncarte coope, 7*li.* 2*s.* 6*d.*

Three piggs—1*li.* 13*s.*
Two plowes and a payer of harrows, 1*li.*
One and twenty sheep, 7*li.*
Six acres of wheate sowen, 10*li.* 4*s.*; thirteene acres and a halfe of barly land ready to sow, 15*li.* 5*s.*; eight acres of pease sowen, 5*li.*
One bushell, on fann, one screw, eight sacks, three casting shovels, and other implements of husbandary, 2*li.*
Due to the testator—1*li.* 1*s.* 6*d.*
His wearing apparell and money in his purse, 3*li.* 15*s.*
Som totall is—117*li.* 4*s.* 10d. [should be 115*li.* 5*s.* 2*d.*]

[Appraisers—Mathew Nightingale, Isaac Reeve, of Chignal St. James.]
[Exhibited 30 April 1687 by Francis Allen, executor.]

142.—Richard Nutting of Writtle. 5 May 1687.

FOR GOODS IN THE HALL, 1*li.*;

GOODS IN THE PARLOR, with wearing apparell & mony pockett, 2*li.* 12*s.* 6*d.*;

GOODS IN THE PARLOR CHAMBER—1*li.* 1*s.* 6*d.*;

GOODS IN THE BUTTERRY—1*li.* 3*s.*;

GOODS IN THE DARY—5*s.*

GOODS IN THE MAULT HOOSE, 3*s.*

GOODS WITHOUTT DORES—2 cows, 1 calfe, 5*li.* 10*s.*; 3 hoggs, 1*li.* 10*s.*; 19 sheep and 15 lambs, 6*li.*

2 acers of wheat, 3*li.*; 3 acers of barly, 6*li.*; 2 acers of bullimoung, 1*li.* 10*s.*
Ye Just Sum is—29*li.* 15*s.*
[Appraisers—Jonathan Sapsford, Thomas White.]
[Exhibited 1 June 1687, by Sarah Nutting, widow and administratrix.]

143.—Elizabeth Clarke of Roxwell, widow. 12 May 1687.

IN THE HALL—One joyne table, one joyne forme, 4 joyne stools, two other small tables, one old press cubbord, 8 rush chaires, and one cup shelfe, 1*li.* 14*s.* 4*d.*; two spitts, one paire of cobirons, one slice, a paire of tramells, a gridiron, a paire of tongs, a paire of bellowes, one driping pan, with some other small things, 12*s.* 9*d.*; six cushions, one Bible, with some small bookes, 9*s.* 6*d.*

IN THE PARLOUR—One halfe headed bedstedle, one trundle bedstedle, one feather bed & bolster, two feather pillows, one coverlid, curtaines & vallences, 3*li.* 6*s.* 8*d.*; one livery cubord, a joyne chest, two little tables, one joyne stoole, two cubord cloathes, and a peice of new cloath, a old wicker chaire, one little paire of cobirons, fire shovell and tongs, 1*li.* 13*s.* 6*d.*

IN THE HALL CHAMBER—One joyne bedstedle, a flock bed and two boulsters, one straw bed and matt, curtaines and vallences, one old chest, a livery cubbord, a little table, two old chaires, one stoole, with other small things, 1*li.* 16*s.* 8*d.*; two old paire of flexen sheets, one paire of flexen pillowbeers, four paire of corse sheets, three corse pillowbeers, a diaper table cloath, two flexen table cloathes, two corse table cloathes, a dozen of old napkins, 2*li.* 14*s.* 6*d.*; six pewter dishes, 2 sawcers, 2 porringers, one pewter cup, a pewter basson, and a chamber pott, 15*s.* 9*d.*

IN THE CHAMBER OVER THE GREATE PARLOUR—One halfe headed bedstedle, a flockbed & bolster, three blanketts, a matt, two hutches, 2 boxes, one little forme, with other small things, 2*li.* 5*s.* 6*d.*

IN THE CHAMBER OVER THE LITTLE PARLOUR—One halfe headed bedstedle, a flockbed, two flock boulsters, two blanketts, 2 chaires, 2 stooles, 1*li.* 1*s.* 4*d.*

IN THE CHEESE CHAMBER—Seaven little cheeses, 4 shelves, a little barrell, with other imployments, 9*s.* 6*d.*

IN THE KITCHIN—A lead, three kettles, three skilletts, 2 warming pans, a chaffing dish, a frying pan, seaven small tubs, a kneading troph, a querne, a woolen wheele & reel, two seives with other imployments, 4*li.* 11*s.* 8*d.*

IN THE DAIRY—One stand, a cheese tubb, a cheese press, a cherne, a kemnell, 3 cheese motts, a cheese bred, a poudering troph, a powdering tubb, three pailes, scales and waites, six shelves, with some small things, 2*li.* 10*s.* 6*d.*

IN THE BUTTREY—One hogshead, 3 barrells, 2 drink stalls, one kemnell, 2 iron potts & one paire of potthooks, with some other imployments, 1*li.* 6*s.* 3*d.*

The wheat in the barne with the screene, bushell, fan, forks, casting shovell, and other imployments, 16*li.* 5*s.* 10*d.*
Barley in the barley barne, 3*li.* 10*s.*; Hay in the hay house, 1*li.* 10*s.*
Fowr horses, 10*li.*; collers & harness for plow and cartt, with the rest of husbandrey imployments, 2*li.* 2*s.* 9*d.*; a waggon, a dung cart, plow, and all belonginge to itt, a paire of harrows, 10*li.* 2*s.* 6*d.*
Corne growinge on the ground—11 acres of wheat, 16 acres of barley, 54*li.*; 14 acres of pease & bullimonge, 8*li.* 8*s.*; hoppole on the hop ground, 7*li.* 10*s.*
Five cows and calves, 16*li.* 13*s.* 4*d.*; a score of sheepe & lambs, 11*li.*; five hoggs, 3*li.*
Her weareing apparell & mony in her purse, 5*li.*
Summa totalis—174*li.* 10*s.* 10*d.*
[Appraisers—Richard Thorowgood, Symon Burrill.]
[Exhibited 1 June 1687 by Joseph Clarke, son and administrator.]

144.—Lidiah Wead [Wade]. 31 May 1687.

IN THE HALL—One cubard, 2 tables, five chayers, one payer of cobirons, one spite, tongs and fier pann, with other impliments, 11*s.* 6*d.*

IN THE PARLER—One bedd, beddsted, curtins and valints, and one boulste, 2*li.* 10*s.* 8*d.*; one table, 4 stooles, one cubard, two hutches, a payer of cob-irons, 19*s.* 6*d.*

IN THE PARLER CHAMBER—One bedd, beddstidle, thre boulsters, curtins & valyants, one chest, and a box, 1*li.* 4*s.* 10*d.*

IN THE LITLE CHAMBER—One bedd, beddsted, and 2 flock boulsters, and one pillow, one hutch, 15*s.* 7*d.*

IN THE PANTREY—Fouer barrills, one kneding troffe, 2 formes, 2 drink-stoles, one pail with other impliments, 10*s.* 2*d.*; seven piuter dishes, and 2 dripen panns, 6*s.* 8*d.*

IN THE BREW HOUSE—One litle lede, two kitles, 3 skilets, one potig pot, one worming pann, one chaffen dish, 4 tubs, with other implements, 1*li.* 5*s.* 3*d.*

IN THE DEREY—One chees press, one stand, 3 chese moats, one charme, with other impliment, 6*s*. 8*d*.

In lining—3 payer of sheets, 2 pillower beers, halfe a dozen napkins, one table cloth, 1*li*. 0*s*. 6*d*.
Warring apparill and money in pocket, 15*s*.
Some is—10*li*. 6*s*. 4*d*.
[Appraisers—Jonathan Sapsford, John Lord.]
[Exhibited 1 June 1687 by Nathan Wade, son and administrator.]

145.—Hezechiah Godsafe of Roxwell. 13 June 1687.

IN THE HALL—One table, one short forme, one joint stole, five old chaires, one payer of cobirons, one fire shovell & tongs, 1 payer of tramells, one spit, one dripping pan, with other implements, 1*li*. 4*s*. 10*d*.

IN THE PARLOUR—One press cubbord, one joint forme, one joint stoole, thre chaires, & one payer cobirons, 18*s*. 6*d*.

IN THE CHAMBER OVER THE HALL—One bedstedle with curtaines & vallance, one feather bed, two fether bolsters, one coverlide, one blanket, one trundle bedsted with a matt, thre hutches, two chaires, 3*li*. 17*s*. 6*d*.

The linen—One payer of flexen sheets & 9 corse sheets, 2 payer of pillow-beers, two table cloathes, 3 corse tuells, 1*li*. 16*s*. 6*d*.

IN THE CHAMBER OVER THE PARLOR—One old boardded bedsted, a fether bed, two fether pillows, one old coverlide, & a blankett, one halfe heded bedsted, one flock bed, 3 blankets, with a matt & cord, one chaire, one warming pan, 3*li*. 13*s*. 4*d*.

IN THE CHEESE CHAMBER—Thirty thre old cheeses, forty fower new cheeses, 3*li*. 6*s*.; the wooll, 1*li*. 1*s*. 8*d*.

IN THE MILKE HOUSE—One cheese press, one charne, one stan, one kimnell, with otheir milke vessells, fower cheese moutes, one cheese bred, 2 milke pailes, one frying pan, with other implyments, 1*li*. 17*s*. 9*d*.

IN THE BUTTEREY—Seaven pewter dishes, one pewter kandlesticke, six pewter spunes, one salt, two pewter kandell stickes, 2 porrengers, & a sawcer, fower barrell, & a drinke stall, two leather bottles, with other impliments, 1*li*. 16*s*. 4*d*.

IN THE CHAMBER OVER THE BUTTEREY—One flock [bed] & bolster, & 2 blanketts, with other implyments, 10*s*. 6*d*.

Wheate in the corne chamber—12 bushells, 10 soks, a busshell, 2 casting shovells & 2 fanns, 3*li*. 3*s*. 6*d*.
Malt in the chamber—2*li*. 15*s*.

IN THE KITCHIN—A brase leade, 3 brase kettells, one brase boyler, one brase pot, 2 brase scillets, one leadle, one scumer, 3*li*. 17*s*. 6*d*.; one hand quarne, a neaden trofe, six tubs, with seifes and other implyments, 1*li*. 10*s*. 6*d*.; scolees & waites, a sith, a cradell, a betell, & 4 wages, with other implyments of husbendry, 1*li*. 10*s*. 2*d*.

The corne upon the ground—Five acres of wheate, 12*li*. 6*s*.; five acres of

barley, 12*li.* 10*s.*; 7 acres pease & oates, 3*li.* 10*s.* 9*d.*; 7 cowes & 2 buds, 25*li.* 15*s.*; 45 shepe & lambs, 12*li.*; 3 horses, 15*li.*; 4 hoges, a sow, & 7 piges, 3*li.* 13*s.* 4*d.*
One loade cart, & one dung cart, 6*li.* 10*s.*; harnes, colors, holters, cart sadles, pannells, plow & harrows, 2*li.* 6*s.* 8*d.*
A loade of old hay, 2*li.*
Debts good and bad, 5*li.*
Whearing cloathes & money in his purse, 5*li.*
Sume totall is—138*li.* 11*s.* 4*d.*
[Appraisers—Simon Burrell, Mathew Nightingale.]
[Exhibited 5 November 1687 by Mary Godsafe, widow and administratrix.]
Due to the landlord for rent at Michaelmas last, 19*li.* 5*s.*
Due to the smith, 1*li.* 17*s.* 2*d.*
Funerall charges, 5*li.*
Due to Mary Stokes for wages, 1*li.* 10*s.*
Due to Mr. Butler for tithe, 10*s.*
Lords Rent, 5*s.* 10*d.*
Chimney money, 4*s.*
Total—28*li.* 12*s.* to be taken out of the inventory.

146.—Ann George, of Writtle, widow. 30 July 1687.

IN THE HALL—1 cubbord, 2 tables, 5 rush chayers, 3 cushions, 13*s.*; 2 payer of cobirons, 2 fier pans, 2 payer of tongs, 3 spitts, 2 slices, 1 grid-iron, 1 fier forke, 1 chafin dish, a pessell & morter, 1 jack & chaine, 1 lock iron with heaters & box, 1 payer of tramils, 1 payer of bellows, 1*li.* 10*s.*; a persell of earthen ware, 3*s.*; 1 wheele, 3*s.*; 1 tubb & 2 stooles, 1*s.*; and sum small implments, 1*s.* 6*d.*

IN THE HALL CHAMBER—1 bedstid with matt & corde, a sute of curtins & valiants, 1 feather bed, 1 flock bed, 2 feather bolsters, 1 feather pillow, 1 hutch, 1 forme, 2*li.* 2*s.* 6*d.*

IN THE LITTELL CHAMBER—A parsell of old lumber, 5*s.*

IN THE SHOP CHAMBER—1 bedstid with matt & corde, 1 feather bed, 3 blankits, 1 rugg, 1 bolster, 4 pillowes, with a sute of curtins & valiants, 3 rods, 3*li.*; 1 table & carpit, 6 gined stooles, 1 cubbord, 1 cubbord cloth, 2 hutches, 1 trunke, 2 stooles, 1 cushion, 1*li.* 18*s.*; 13 payer of sheets & a od sheete, 3*li.* 15*s.*; 3 dozins & 4 napkins, 16 pillow beers, 1*li.* 18*s.*; 10 table clothes, 6 towells, 16*s.*; 1 parsell of trenchers, 1 littell trunk, 1*s.* 6*d.*; 2 bibles & other small boks, 10*s.*

IN THE BUTTREY—3 barrills, 2 payles, 7 wooden dishes, 2 wooden tuniells, 3 sives, 10*s.*; 1 small copper, 2 kettels, 3 skillits, 1 worming pann, 1 frying pann, 1 culinder, 1 puding pann, 2 basting ladels, 1 driping pann, 1 brass pott, 1 iron pott, 1 payer of potthookes, 1 hand saw, 16*s.*; 1 kneading troughe, 2*s.* 6*d.*; and other small implements, 1*s.* 6*d.*

IN THE BREWHOUSE—4 tubs, 1 charne, 1 boushell, 1 fann, 1 payer of scales with a beame, 1 beer stall, and other small implements, 12*s.*

IN THE SHOP—1 corn hutch, 1 old hutch without a lid, 2 formes, 6*s.*; 1 parsell of sope, 1 parsell of gingerbread, and candels, 3*s.* 6*d.*; thread, tape, laces, & spindels & balls, 1*s.* 7*d.*; 8 waights, 1 payer of scales, 9*s.*; 3 small measuers with sum small implements, 1*s.* 6*d.*

84 pound of pewter at 6*d.* per lb., 2*li.* 2*s.*
1 parsell of wood, 12*s.*
Waring clothes & redey money, 12*li.* 13*s.* 4*d.*
Sum Totall—35*li.* 8*s.* 5*d.*
[Appraisers—John Clarke, John Cooke.]
[Exhibited 5 November 1687 by Josephine Westwood & Thomas Browne, executors.]

147.—Edward Sandford of Roxwell, yeoman. 20 October 1687.

IN THE HALL—One great table frame, & forme, a little table & carpett, one clock, eight chaires, foure spitts, cobirons, fire shovell, gridiron, cleavers, tongs, two hanging cubbords, two glass shelves, & earthen ware, a parcell of bookes, & other small implements of household, 4*li.*

IN THE PARLOR—A long table, the frame, six joyned stooles, a forme, a Spanish table, foure rush chaires, a joynd chaire, a side board cubbord, a glasse shelfe, a paire of cobirons & other small things, 2*li.* 15*s.*

IN THE KITCHIN—One jack, one spitt, one table, two old formes, fire irons and tramells, & other odd things & lumber, 10*s.*

IN THE DAYRY—One cheese press, two cheese tubbs, two stands, two chernes, six kimnells, three pailes, three trayes, & other implements belonging to the dayry, 3*li.*

IN THE MALTHOUSE—One kneading trough, three sives, eight tubbs, two woollen wheeles, another greate trough, a sydar press, & other old lumber, 2*li.* 10*s.*

IN THE SMALL BEER BUTTERIES—Six hogsheads, two drinke stalls, a hanging shelfe, three iron dripping panns, two iron porridge potts, thre sawes, two leather bottles, & other small implements, 3*li.* 5*s.*

IN THE STRONG BEER BUTTERY—Two drinke stalls, one hogshead, six other drinke vessells, a small table, some tinn ware, a hanging shelfe, a parcell of glasse bottles, a powdring tubb, potts, panns, & other implements of household, 2*li.* 10*s.*

IN THE HALL CHAMBER—One bedstead, feather bedd with the furniture, a large press cubbord, a side board, a paire of andirons, two joyned stooles, two chests, foure truncks, & other odd things, 9*li.*

IN THE CHAMBER OVER THE ENTRY—One bedd, bedstead with the furniture, foure chests, & other small things, 3*li.*

IN THE BUTTERY CHAMBER—One bedd, bedstead with the furniture, two chests, and other small matters, 5*li.*

IN THE MANNS SERVANTS CHAMBER—One boarded bedstead, one feather bedd, one flock bedd, with the furniture to them, 3*li.* 10*s.*

Linnen aboute the house, 6*li.*; brasse, 3*li.*; pewter, 2*li.*; a silver cup & 5 silver spoones, 3*li.* 10*s.*

IN THE MALT CHAMBER—A beame scoale, boards & weights, a parcell of wheate, and pease, & other old lumber, 2*li.*

IN THE KILLHOUSE—An old malt quarne, a parcell of old lumber, pitch forkes, sythes, rakes, spades, shovells, sacks, a skreene, a bushell measure, & other implements of husbandry, 2*li.* 10*s.*

IN THE CHEESE CHAMBER—A parcell of cheese, 12*li.*

IN THE BARLY BARNE—Barly in the straw, 40*li.*; pease in the straw, 16*li.*; oates in the straw, 7*li.*; bullimung in the straw, 3*li.*

IN THE WHEATE BARNE—Wheate in the straw, 40*li.*

IN THE HEYHOUSES & ELSWHERE—The hey, and hay & straw together, 16*li.*

IN THE CART HOUSE & YARDS—One waggon, one dung cart, a wheelebarrow, two pair of harrowes, plowes, and other implements of husbandry, 13*li.*

ABOUTE THE GROUNDS—Twenty foure weathers, 8*li.*; thirty sheepe & lambs, 9*li.*; thirty sheepe more, 6*li.*; three fatting hoggs, 3*li.*; eight hoggs, 10*li.*; six piggs, 1*li.* 10*s.*; tenn milch cowes, 30*li.*; seaven fatting beasts, 15*li.*; five horses, with the plow harnes & cartharnes, 25*li.*; foure and twenty acres of fallowes, 24*li.*

ATT FLAWNES FARME—A bedstead, flocke bedd, copper, & other lumber, 2*li.*; barly in the straw, 27*li.*; pease in the straw, 8*li.*; eleaven acres of fallow, 11*li.*

His wearing apparell & mony in his purse, 5*li.*
Summa totalis—389*li.* 10*s.*
[Appraisers—William Davies, Henry Bright.]
[Exhibited 5 November 1687 by Ann Sandford, widow and executrix.]

148.—William White of Writtle, yeoman. 29 October 1687.

IN THE HALL—One table & forme & one table leafe, one forme, 4 chayers, one payer of cobirons, two payer of tramils, one joyne stole, a payer of tonges, and a fier shovel & a paier of belowes, 1*li.* 1*s.*

IN THE PARLER—Two fether bedds, one beddsted, two boulsters, thre pillows, two blankets, one civering, mat & cord, 1*li.* 6*s.* 8*d.*; thre hutches, one litle table, one cubard, and a trunke, a warming pann, and a seve, 15*s.*

IN THE BUTREY—Two brass pots, tu brass kitls, one skilett, a basting leadl, & skimer, thre piuter dishes, two sasers, a piuter chamber pote, a pie plate, two smothing irons, and an ould kitle, 1*li.* 5*s.*; thre kilderkins, thre spits, two tubs, thr trayes, a peel, a poudering tub, and gridiron, 16*s.*

IN THALL CHAMBER—One halfe heded beddsted, one trundel beddsted, and one ould box, 3*s.* 4*d.*

In lining—Two payer of sheets, two touells, and one tabe cloth, 10*s.*

IN THE STABLE—One cart sadle, & thilbels, two payer of plow harnis, a mathock, two brome hockes, 6*s.*

IN THE CARTE HOUSE—One carte, one payer of harows, two laders, two forcks, one fann, a ridel, one grindston, and a seve, *3li.* 19*s.* 6*d.*

Thre accors and a halfe of whete growing, 5*li.* 5*s.*
One horse, 4*li.*; five piggs, 1*li.* 2*s.* 6*d.*; thre sheep, 12*s.*

IN THE BARNE—Ninten boshells of oats, 1*li.* 1*s.* 4*d.*; seven boshels of rey, 16*s.*; two boshels of whate, 6*s.*; thre wedges, and an axe, one dozen of trenchers, 3*s.*
Wearing apparil & money in pocket, 10*s.*
Som is—23*li.* 18*s.* 4*d.*
[Appraisers—John Robinson, Thomas (?)Sterhes.]
[Exhibited 5 November 1687 by Francis Bangs, creditor and administrator.]

149.—Thomas Cruch. 12 March 1687/8.

2 cowes and weanell, 7*li.* 10*s.*; 2 coalts & a mare, 7*li.* 10*s.*; a parcell of hey, 2*li.*; 11 sheepe and rames, 3*li.* 10*s.*; 1 hog, 18*s.*
5 seames of wheat, 5*li.*
2 ladders, 2 forkes, and a ould bushell, 2 rakes, 2*s.*
2 tables, one forme and bench board, 6 cheares, and 3 cheares more in the hall, 1*li.*; 2 spits, 1 ould dripping pan, and a scumer, and 2 candlesticks, and a few smale things, 6*s.*; 2 cobars, one shovell, a payre tongues, peale, and ould gridiarn, 2 payre tramells, 6*s.*
2 halfe hogsheads, and a tube, and a few smale [things] in the buttery, 14*s.*; cheese presse, stand, and cherne, 2 tubbs, and old boule, mo[torn away], 3 shelves, and other smale things, 1*li.*; an old lead, brasse kettle, 3 skilletts, and a brasse pot, warmin pan, 6 dishes puter, 1*li.* 10*s.*; old ax, fettars, and spad, 1*s.* 6*d.*; 2 ould payles, 1*s.*
Ould panell girt bridle, 1*s.*
1 bed & blanketts, 1*li.* 15*s.*; skreen, 5*s.*; bed, bedstid, 2 blanketts, boulstar & pillow, 4*li.*
His waring cloth and mony, 1*li.* 10*s.*
2 hutches, one box, and a cubard head, 8*s.*; 6 payre shetts, tabling, 3*li.*
Chese, 1*li.*
[Total]—43*li.* 7*s.* 6*d.*
[Exhibited 2 June 1688 by Elizabeth Crush, daughter.]
[Endorsed—That Elizabeth Crush will take all the above-mentioned goods as they are appraised and will pay to each of her sisters their share. Also, rough notes " regarding payment of 1*li.* 5*s.* 6*d.* being expenses in connection with the exhibition of this inventory.]

150.—'Laurance of Roxwell,'[1] carpenter. 4 May 1688.

IN THE HALL—One table, one forme, 4 little stooles, a bench & a board up at the side with a forme & dresser board, one press cubberd, a hanging cubboard, a table, & three chaires, 18*s.* 3*d.*; five pewter dishes, one pewter candellstick, one pewter flagon, pewter collender, with other impliments, with

[1] Endorsed: 'Laurance Beadle his Inventary.'

tin & pewter, 1*li.* 1*s.*; a paier of tongs, a fier shovell, a payer of cobirons, two tramells, & one spitt, a gridiron, & a payer of bellowes, with other impliments, 11*s.*

IN THE PERLOR—One bedstedle, with a bed & bolster, one coverlide, two blankets, one chest, with other impliments, 1*li.* 14*s.* 6*d.*

The linen—One payer of flaxen sheets, two payer of canvis sheets, five old sheets, 2 pillowbers, one fiaxen table cloath, with other impliments, 1*li.* 5*s.* 9*d.*

IN THE CHAMBER OVER THE PARLOR—One bedstedle, a trunke, two old hutches, & a box, 11*s.* 9*d.*

The wheate in the chamber—Two seame, 1*li.* 14*s.*

IN THE HALL CHAMBER—One livery cubboard, one table cubboard, & one chest, 12*s.*

IN THE BUTTERY—Two barrells, a kneading trofe, one drinke stall, three shevells, two seifes, with other impliments, 12*s.* 3*d.*

IN THE GREATE BUTTERY—The brass, one kettle, one boyler, four skilletts, one warmeing pan, a morter & pessell, a basting ladell, a scumer, & one kandellstick, 1*li.* 15*s.* 6*d.*; two barrells, & a powdering tub, two dringe stalls, a leather bottle, with other impliments, 1*li.* 4*s.* 7*d.*

IN THE KITCHIN—One copper, four tubs, a couler, & a cowl, & old drinke stalle, & old table, a forme, & three pailes, with other impliments, 2*li.* 7*s.* 11*d.*

1 acre of etch barley, 1*li.*
The tooles in the shope, 4*li.* 18*s.* 3*d.*
One hog, 12*s.* The wood in the yard, 1*li.* 11*s.*
His wearing apparell & money in his purse, 1*li.* 15*s.*
Sume totall is—23*li.* 4*s.* 9*d.* [should be 24*li.* 4*s.* 9*d.*],
[Appraisers—Simon Burrell, James Bedell.]
[Exhibited 16 February 1688/9.]

151.—Martha Radley of Writtle, widow. 14 February 1688/9.

IN THE KITCHIN—One table, four joyned stooles, an old press cubbord, foure rush chaires, two brass porridge potts, two old small brass kettles, two skilletts, two spitts, two dripping panns, two paire of trammells, fire irons, cobirons, gridiron, and other small things, 1*li.* 10*s.*

IN THE HALL—Two tables, tenn leather chaires, a sideboard cubbord, two formes, a settle, 3 old cushions, a glasse shelfe with some small things in it, & a rush chaire, 2*li.* 6*s.*

IN THE PARLOR—Two tables, six joyned stooles, a paire of cobirons, fire shovell and tongs, 1*li.* 15*s.*

IN THE PARLOR BUTTERIES—An old table leafe, & tresles, another table, a forme, two small drink vessells, & other old lumber, & two old carpetts, 10*s.*

IN THE STRONG BEERE BUTTERY—A halfe hogshead, two other small vessells, the trestle, three dozen of trenchers, a forme, potts, panns, glasses, a forme, & other implements, 10*s.*

IN THE SMALL BEERE BUTTERIES—Two hogsheads, & two other drinke vessells, foure leather bottles, a tunnell, the drinke stall, an old cubbord, a wooden beame, scoale boards & lines & severall weights, the horse basketts, & other lumber, 1*li.* 10*s.*

IN THE PARLOR CHAMBER—One feather bedd, one bolster, one blankett, valence and curtaines, coverletts, bedstead, matt & cord, one little table, . . . loam, six leather chaires, & stooles, two chests, and a paire of cobirons, 5*li.* 5*s.*

IN THE CHEESE CHAMBER—Three score & tenn cheeses greate & small, 3*li.* 10*s.*

IN THE CHAMBER OVER THE BUTTERIES—One old bedstead, valence & curtaines, a feather bedd, two feather bolsters, one pillow, two blanketts, & a coverlett, a trucle bedd, with an old feather bedd, bolster, and coverlett, matts & cords, two chests, & a box, 4*li.* 2*s.* 6*d.*

IN THE HALL CHAMBER—An old bestead, one feather bedd, three feather bolsters, three blanketts, one coverlett, matt & cord, a large chest of drawers, a little table, a looking glass, two old chests, & a painted callicoe cubbord cloath, 4*li.* 5*s.*

IN THE KITCHIN CHAMBER—Two old sorry bedsteads, two feather bedds, three bolsters, two old coverletts, foure blanketts, & some old things, 4*li.* 1*s.*; three score & one pound of pewter aboute the house, 1*li.* 15*s.*

IN THE BREWHOUSE—Two little leads, a brasse kettle, three large brewing tubbs, & trestle, five smaller tubbs, a kneading trough, & other things, 4*li.* 2*s.*

IN THE DAYRY—One cheese press, five cheese mootes, two cheese breads, one cherne, two milke stands, 4 trayes, a kimnell, a large wooden boll, a powdring tubb, formes, shelves, potts, panns, & other materialls in that office, 1*li.* 15*s.*

Linnen about the house—Twenty paire of towen sheetes, 5*li.*; two paire of flaxen sheetes, 1*li.*; two diaper table cloathes & a dozen of napkins to them, 19*s.*; one long flaxen table cloath, a short one & thirteen napkins, one long towen table cloath, & 3 short flaxen table cloaths, 1*li.* 5*s.*; a paire of holland pillow beeres, & 7 other paire, & some other odd peeces of linnen for the use of the house, 13*s.* 4*d.*

IN THE CORNE CHAMBER—A parcell of barly, 2*li.* 10*s.*; a parcell of oates, 2*li.*; a parcell of wheate, 1*li.*; sixteen corne sacks, 1*li.* 10*s.*; a bushell measure, a corne skreene, corne sickles, fanns, shovells, spades, pitchforkes, & other utensills of farming & husbandry, 13*s.* 6*d.*

IN THE BARNE—A parcell of wheate in the straw, 18*li.*; a parcell of pease in the straw, 5*li.* 8*s.*; a parcell of barly in the chaffe, 7*li.*

IN THE STABLE—Foure cart horses, with their collars, cart saddles, halters, cart harnes, & plow harnes, with other things, 12*li.* 5*s.*

IN THE YARDS—One waggon, two dung carts, a long cart, two paire of harrowes, two plowes with what belongs to them, 10*li.* 1*s.*; eight piggs and a sow, *4li.* *10s.*; a little cock of hay, & other parcells of hay aboute the outhouses, *11li.*

ABOUTE THE FEILDS—Eleaven Hoggrill sheepe, & thirteene ewes, *7li.* *10s.*; five cowes, a calfe, three heifers, & a bull, *22li.*; thirteene acres of wheate sowne, *19li.* *10s.*; twenty acres of land fallowed to be sowne with barley, *20li.*; eleaven acres of land sowne with pease, *4li.* *19s.*
Her wearing apparell & mony in her purse, *5li.*
In good debts oweing her, *27li.* *11s.* *6d.*
Summe—*221li.* *19s.* *10d.* [should be *228li.* *1s.* *10d.*].
[Appraisers—William Bird, Henry Bright.]
[Exhibited 17 February 1688/9, by Nathaniel Sapsford, son & administrator.]

152.—John Waylett, tanner, of Writtle. [Undated.][1]

IN THE HALL—One table, 4 stooles, 2 little tables, 9 chaires, 1 press cubard, 1 little hanging cubard, 1 jack, 7 spitts, 3 gridgirons, 3 cobirons, 1 frying pan, an iron to ly before the fire, 1 muskett, 1 payer of garden shares, 3 scummers, 1 pessell, 3 morter, 1 chaffing dish, 1 candle stick, one salt box, books, & other implements, *4li.* *3s.* *6d.*

IN THE PARLOR—6 stools, 1 drawing table, 1 table cloth, 8 chaires, 1 clock & case, 1 looking glass, 1 bedsteadle, 1 feather bed, 1 boulster, 1 coverled, blanketts, curtains, valliants & curtaine rodds, 1 side cubbard, 1 little table, 1 payer tongs, 1 payer cobirons, 1 worming pann, & other implements, *7li.* *16s.* *6d.*

IN THE CHAMBER OVER THE TUFFTHOUSE—One bedsteadle, 1 bed, 2 blanketts, curtains, valliants & rodds, 3 hutches, 1 cheess rack, & other implements, *15s.*

IN THE CHAMBER OVER THE PARLOR—One bedsteadle, 1 feather bed, 1 coverled, blanketts, curtains & valliants, 1 table, 3 stooles, 4 cushing stooles, 2 hutches, 2 trunks, 1 payer of brass cobirons, 1 payer of tongs, 1 fire pann, *3li.* *5s.*

IN THE CHAMBER OVER THE CHITCHIN—One halfe heded bedsteadle, 1 boulster, 1 coverled, 2 ould hutches, 1 box, & other implements, *1li.*

IN THE BEST BUTTERRY—One hodgsed, 1 barrell, 2 bear stalls, 1 leather bottle, 1 still, a persell of glass bottles, 1 powdering tubb, & other implements, *1li.*

IN THE SMALL BEARE BUTTERY—6 hodgseds, 1 tunnell, 1 lanthorne, 1 screane, & 2 drink stalls, *1li.* *3s.* *6d.*

IN THE LITTLE BUTTERRYS—One powdering tubb, trenchers, 2 trays, 2 bouldices, & other implements, *7s.*

IN THE PASSAGE—6 brass potts, 3 brass kettles, 4 brass skilletts, 1 frying pan, & 94 lbs of pewter, & other implements, *6li.* *1s.*

IN THE CHAMBER OVER THE BUTTERRYS—2 flock beds, blanketts, coverleds, 2 trundle bedsteadles, 1 cradle, & one ould hutch, *1li.*

[1] Will dated 2 Jan. 1688/9 [catalogue mark D/APwP1/4].

IN THE CHITCHIN—One copper, 1 cooller, 1 meashing tubb & other small tubbs, 2 chires, 1 payer of trammells, & other implements, *5li. 5s.*

IN THE TUFFT HOUSE—One stann, 1 meal hutch, 1 kneading troff, 1 meal bagg & sives, 1 sider troffe, 1 flaskett, 1 baskett, & 1 payle, *12s.*

The plate—6 silver spoons & one silver cupp, *2li. 4s.*
The linnen—12 payer of sheets, 4 dosen napkins, 12 table cloths, 12 pillow beers, 10 towells, & 4 cubbard cloths, *11li. 6s.*

IN THE STABLE & IN THE YARD—2 mares, 1 horse, 4 pannell, 1 rugg, 1 carte sadle, 1 brigle, 2 load of hey, 2 load of wood, *10li.*

Wareing apperrell & mony in pockett, *6li. 5s.*

THE STOCK IN THE YARD—12 score & 7 backs att *17li.* per score, *209li. 19s.*; 18 score & 5 hides att *11li.* per score, *200li. 15s.*; 21 dosen of skines hogg & calfe, *35li. 14s.*; haire shorte & longe, *5li.*; the baike allowed in for the tanning of the ware. 4 shoots, 2 wheelebarrows, 4 skeps, 2 beams, workeing knives, a grinstone, with a percell of wood, & some other lumber a bout the yarde, & a percell of horns, *3li. 10s.* More 22 bakes att *17s.* a peece, *18li. 14s.*; & 12 hides att *11s.* a peece, *6li. 12s.*

Booke debts good & badd, *15li. 5s.*
Summa Tottalis—*557li. 12s. 6d.*
[Appraisers—John Pond, Thomas Gray, John Hewes, sen., Jeremy May.]
[Exhibited 16 February 1688/9.]

153.—Mrs. Porter of Writtle. [Undated.]

IN THE HALL—A jack, a spit, a pair of standing andirons, a pair creepers, a hearth iron, a settle of wainscot, a form, *10s.*

IN THE PARLOUR—A pair of andirons with brass heads, a paire of tongs, a fire pan, bellows, a salt box, a table & sideboard, a cupboard press, a gridiron, a chafin dish, colender, candle box, 2 candle sticks, a box iron & 2 heaters, 2 wooden stools, 4 other stools, 5 chairs, a looking glass, *16s.*

IN THE KITCHING—A kneading trough & box in the buttry, a hang kettle, a tin pan, a brass scale, 2 skillits, a basting ladle, a sive, a frying pan, 2 porridg pots, 1 pair of pothooks, a dripping pan, 3 tubs & a lyeletch, a stool, a pail, 5 dishes little & great, a pye plate, 4 trenchards, a stall, a measure, a bill, *1li. 5s.*

IN THE BUTTRY—A kilderkin & 2 little vessels, a tunnel, a beer stall, 3 bottles, an old wodden peel, *5s.*

IN THE GARRETS—A wheel, a small cupboord table, a bead & hal[f]-headed bedsted, a mat & cord, a bolster, 2 blankets, & old rug, *1li. 2s.*

IN THE PARLOUR CHAMBER—A feather bead, bedsted, matt & cord, curtains & valannts, 2 bolster, 5 pillow, a old [h]utch, 1 old chair, a stool, a box, *3li.*; plate, *1li. 5s.*

Linning—7 sheets, 15 napkins, 4 pillow beers, 2 table cloaths, *10s.*
In all—*7li. 8s.* [should be *8li. 13s.*]
[Appraisers—Thomas Bridgman, Edmund Butler, jn.]
[Exhibited 27 April 1689 by Francis Porter, administrator.]

154.—Robert Sach of Writtle. 23 April 1689.

IN THE HALL—One long table, one press cubbord, five rush chaires, two spitts, one tin driping pan, a paire of cobirons, fire shovell and tongs, one iron pott, a paire of trammels, with some other small things, 2*li.* 1*s.* 6*d.*

IN THE PARLOUR—One joyne bedstedle, one feather bed, one feather boulster, two pillows, one coverlid, three blanketts, curtaines and valences, 6*li.* 10*s.*

IN THE BUTTREY—Three halfe hogsheads, one littell barrell, one kneading troph, two leather bottles, a woolen wheel & reele, with some other implements, 1*li.* 10*s.*

IN THE BREWHOUSE—One lead, three old tubes, with some other small things, 1*li.* 12*s.*

IN THE DAIRY—Two chernes, one old stand, five small cheese moots, a cheesbred, with other utensells, 10*s.*

IN THE KITCHIN—Three kettles, three skillets, one brase scumer, with some other implements of husbandry, 1*li.* 19*s.*

IN THE CHAMBER OVER THE HALL—One joyne bedstedle, one old flock bed, 2 pillows, two blanketts, curtains and valences, one little barrell, 1*li.* 6*s.* 8*d.*

IN THE CHAMBER OVER THE PARLOUR—Two halfe headed bedsteds, one feather bed & boulster, one flock bed, 3 old boulsters, two coverlids, two blanketts, three old hutches, one short forme, two rush chaires, 2*li.* 12*s.*

IN THE CHAMBER OVER THE KITCHIN—One old querne, two bushells of bullimong, 2 pitchforks, a great baskett, with some other small things, 15*s.*

The linen—Three towen sheets, one flexon sheet, one flexon table cloath, a dozen of twoen napkins, 1*li.* 10*s.*
The pewter—13*s.* 4*d.*
Nineteene small cheeses, 6*s.* 8*d.*
One long cart, one dung cart, one paire of harrows, a long lader, 5*li.*[1]

Five seame of bullimonge, 3*li.* 15*s.*; a parcell of pease on a stake, 5*li.*; wheate in the barne thershed and unthreshed, with the screen & other implements, 11*li.*
The horses, collers, & harness, 10*li.* 10*s.*; two cowes, 4*li.*; thirty sheep, 7*li.*
Nine acres of wheat sowen, 10*li.* 16*s.*; nine acres of barley sowen, 11*li.* 6*s.*; pease & bullimong sowen, 4*li.* 15*s.*
Three store hoggs, 2*li.* 5*s.*
Six acres of fallow, 1*li.* 4*s.*
Plow & plowirons, 5*s.*
His wearing apparell and money in his purse, 3*li.*
Summa totalis—100*li.* 2*s.* 2*d.* [should be 101*li.* 2*s.* 2*d.*]
[Appraisers—William Bird, Henry Bright.]
[Exhibited 28 December 1689 by John Sach, son and executor.]

[1] Altered from 4*li.* to 5*li.* but total not altered.

Endorsed:—
deates due March 25 1689

	li.	*s.*	*d.*
for rente	31	0	0
fenril charges	5	0	0
due to Thomas Seach	6	0	0
due to John Seach	10	0	0
due to William Pond	25	0	0
due to Fransis Reed		12	0
due to Jeames Hornsen		10	0
due to Henry Maget		5	0
due to Mr. Hortun		15	6
due to Mr. Horsnaile		10	0
due to the smith		10	0
	80	2	6

155.—William Hillyard of Writtle, 6 December 1689.

IN THE HALL—A longe table, seaven joyne stooles, two little tables, five rush chaires, fire shovell & tongs, a paire of cobirons, a jacke, with some other small things, 1*li.* 10*s.* 6*d.*

IN THE PARLOUR—One joyne bedstedle with curtaines & valences, a feather bed, a feather boulster, two pillows, one rugg, two blanketts, 4*li.* 10*s.*; one little table & old carpett, six rush chaires, one trundle bedstedle, with some other small things, 9*s.*

IN THE HALL CHAMBER—Two old joyne bedsedles with curtains and valences, two feather beds, one boulster, 2 pillows, two coverlids, 4 blanketts, 5*li.* 2*s.*; one old chest, a little hutch, a little box, 5*s.*

IN THE PARLOUR CHAMBER—One old livery cubord, one old table, with a few small cheeses, 13*s.* 4*d.*

IN THE DAIRY—One cheespress, a cherne, a short forme, three brass kettles, two skelletts, one brass pott, tenn small pewter dishes, a spitt, with some other small things, 2*li.* 12*s.* 6*d.*

IN THE BUTTREY—One old hogshead, six barrells, a forme, 2 drink stalls, 3 leather bottles, 17*s.*

IN THE KITCHIN—Four tubes, a kneading troph, and an old lead, 1*li.* 3*s.* 6*d.*

IN THE BUTTREY CHAMBER—One old flockbed, a paire of scalles, a halfe c wait, and old haire, a corne sitch, a dew rake, with some other small things, 1*li.* 10*s.*

The linen—2*li.*

The horse, & harness, & hay, 10*li.*; three cowes & a heifer, 9*li.*; eighteene ewes, 3*li.* 12*s.*; thirteene weathers, 3*li.* 18*s.*

A waggon, a long cart, a dung cart, plow & harrows, 13*li.* 0*s.* 6*d.*

A sowe & three pigs, 1*li.* 8*s.*

Barley in the barne, 13*li.*; wheat in the barne, 3*li.*; a parcell of pease & oates in the barne, 4*li.* 8*s.*; money received for a parcell of wheat sold, 5*li.* 14*s.*; 10 acres of wheat upon the ground, 15*li.*; 7 acres of fallow for barley, 7*li.*
His warring apparel & money in his purse, 5*li.*
Summa totalis—114*li.* 13*s.* 4*d.* Indebted out of this sume, 33*li.*
[Appraisers—William Bird, Henry Bright.]
[Exhibited 28 December 1689 by Frances Hilliard, widow, and Gabriel Hilliard, son, administrators.]

156.—Joseph Bonnington of Writtle, yeoman. 12 December 1689.

IN THE HALL OF HIS DWELLING HOUSE—Two tables, six joyned stooles, five rush chaires, two boarded chaires, a standing cubbord, a clocke, six cushions, a jack, two spitts, two dripping panns, a birding gunn, a large paire of cobirons, a smaller paire, fire shovell & tongs, two paire of trammells, some books, & other things, 4*li.* 2*s.* 6*d.*

IN THE PARLOR—A joyned bedstead, a feather bedd, a bolster, two blanketts, a coverlett, valence & curtaines, matt & cord, a long table, two formes, a small table, two joyned stooles, three turky workt chaires, two stooles, a paire of cobirons, a glass case, and other small implements there, with a press cubbord in the passage into the parlor, 6*li.* 15*s.*

IN THE LITTLE BUTTERY—Three kilderkins, a halfe hogshead, a drinke stall, a small table, three leather bottles, & other things, 1*li.* 8*s.*

IN THE PARLOR CHAMBER—A bedstead, a good feather bedd, two feather bolsters, three pillowes marked as the bedd, a yellow rugg with the valence & curtaines, two markt blanketts, a leafe table, window curtaines, two chests, two stooles, two rush chaires, a wicker chaire, a paire of brass cobirons, fire shovell and tongs, a wrought cushion, a looking glass, & other small things there, with a livery cubbord, & a small joyned chaire in the passage roome to the chambers, 8*li.* 5*s.*

IN THE LITTLE CHAMBER—A small parcell of oates, beanes, corne, and malt, 15*s.*

IN THE HALL CHAMBER—A joyned bedstead, a trundle bedstead, matts & cords, two feather bedds, three feather bolsters, nine feather pillowes, one coverlett, foure blanketts, an old suite of curtens, five chests, a deske, a bench-board, & all other small things there & in the passage to that chamber, 6*li.*

IN THE BUTTERY CHAMBER—A trundle bedstead, & halfe headed bedstead, one feather bedd, two feather bolsters, one flock bedd and bolster, two coverletts, three blanketts, & some old lumber, 3*li.*

IN THE CHEESE CHAMBER—An old table, severall cheese boards & shelves, seaventy five cheeses, a parcell of pease & of bullimung, two linnen wheeles, & other implements, 6*li.* 10*s.*

IN THE DAYRY—Two milke stands, two cherns, a cheese presse, six cheese mootes, one cheese bread, three kimnells, twelve potts & panns, a powdring tubb, a meale hutch, foure sives, the shelves, & other implements there, *2li.* 15*s.* 3*d.*

IN THE GREATE BUTTERY—One hogshead, two halfe hogsheads, a drinke stall, a large tunnell, a mustard quarne, a forme & shelves, earthen ware, wooden dishes, & other things, 1*li.* 10*s.*

IN THE BREWHOUSE & KITCHIN—One brassing brewing pann, another for the use of the dayry, two large brewing tubbs, five other tubbs with the tressles & other implements to the brewhouse, a weighing beame, scoale boards & weights, two old chests, and some other lumber, 5*li.* 1*s.* 3*d.*

Linnen aboute the house—Five paire of flaxen sheetes, one flaxen sheete more, two paire of pillow beeres one of holland the other of flaxen cloath, two flaxen table cloaths, & two dozen of flaxen napkins, a diaper napkin, a holland napkin, six course flaxen napkins, six towen napkins, five flaxen pillowbeers, two towen table cloathes, seaven paire of towen sheetes, eight paire of towen pillowbeers, six course towells, & some other small matters of linnen, 11*li.* 4*s.*
Three brass kettles, three brasse skilletts, two brass porridge potts, a frying pann, a brasse mortar, two scummers, & other small matters of brass, with a warming pann, & iron porridge pott, 2*li.* 11*s.*; 85*li.* weight of pewter att 8*d.* per *li.*, & a tinn pasty pann, 2*li.* 18*s.* 8*d.*

IN THE BARNES & ELSWHERE—A parcell of wheate in the straw, 23*li.* 6*s.*; a parcell of barly in the straw, 21*li.*; a parcell of pease in the straw, and a parcell of bullimung in the straw, 5*li.*; a parcell of hay, 8*li.*; a screene for corne, a fann, pitch forkes, rakes, shovells, spades, bushell measures, tenn old corne sacks, sawes, a malt quarne, iron wedges, and other implements & utensills of husbandry, 2*li.* 16*s.*

A waggon, a load cart, an old dung cart, a paire of harrowes, a plow & implements to them, 11*li.*
Three gelt horses, with the collars, & plow harness, cart harness, and other furniture to them, 13*li.* 10*s.* Two fatt hoggs, 2*li.* 15*s.*; six store piggs, 2*li.* 8*s.*; seaven cowes, 18*li.*; eighteen sheepe, 2*li.* 5*s.*
Tenn acres of land sowne with wheate, 15*li.*; ten acres of fallowed land layd up for barly, 10*li.*
Six silver spoones, 2*li.* 2*s.* 8*d.*
His wearing apparell and mony in his purse, 5*li.*
Totall summe is—204*li.* 18*s.* 2*d.* [should be 204*li.* 18*s.* 4*d.*]
[Appraisers—William Bird, Henry Turnidge. Exhibited 28 December 1689.]

157.—Henry Bullen of Writtle, yeoman. 14 December 1689.

IN THE HALL—One drawing table, & 4 joynt stools, 1*li.*; 8 chaires, & 3 pair of andirons, 15*s.*; one glass-case, 4 cushins, books, & a writing-desk, one levery table, & a clock, 3*li.*

IN THE PARLOR—Two drawing tables, 6 joynt stooles, one chist of drawers, one couch, one picture, & other implements, *2li.* 10*s.*; thre pair of andirons, fyre-shovell & tongs, & nyne chaires, 1*li.* 5*s.*

IN THE HALL-CHAMBER—One feather bed & bolstar, fower pillowes, one bedstead, chord and matt, two blanckets, & a rugg, *5li.*; one trundle bedstead & matt, one chist, one levery table, 5 chaires, 3 stooles, one box, & 2 truncks, *2li.*; two pair of andireons, two fyre shovells, 3 pair of tongs, & a pair of bellowes, 10*s.*

IN THE PARLOR CHAMBER—One feather bed & bolstar, one bedstead, curtans & vallance, 2 blanckets & a rug, *7li.*; one levery cubard, one table, twelve chaires, & 8 stools, & 2 lookinglasses, *2li.* 10*s.*

IN THE KITCHIN CHAMBER—One bedstead, curtans & vallance, two feather beds, 3 bolstars, one pair of sheets, 2 pillows, one blancket, & a coverlit, *3li.*; one levery table, 3 boxes, 2 chists, one arme-chair, 3 stooles, & one box, 1*li.* 4*s.*; one bedstead, curtans & vallance, two feather-beds, & one bolstar, *2li.* 10*s.*; one halfe-headed bedstead, one featherbed, two blanckets, one rugg, one trundlebed, two blanckets, & a coverlid, *2li.* 10*s.*; 3 chists, 2 truncks, 2 boxes, two cushins, & other small things, 1*li.*

IN THE KITCHIN & BUTREY—One table, 3 joynt stooles, 3 small tables, thre formes, one levery table, one glascase, tenn old chaires, 1*li.*; one cole-rack, fyre shovell & tongs, thre spitts, one jack, one fyre-fork, 3 cleavers, a pair of bellowes, & 2 dreaping pans, and one fouling peece, *2li.* 10*s.*; 22 peauter dishes, 2 flaggons, six plates, 3 candlesticks, 3 chamber potts, 2 warming pans, one bed pan, & a still, *3li.*; 5 brass kettles, 3 brass potts, 5 skillits, 2 chafeing dishes, 2 scumers, and one frying pan, *2li.*; two pastey plates, a tynn dreaping pan, severall other panns, & other implements, 10*s.*; one large table & frame, 15*s.*

IN THE WASH-HOUSE—Fower hogsheads, 4 barells, 2 ladles, one powthering tubb, one cowle, one stand, a kneading-trough, one lie-leach, & severall other small things, 1*li.* 14*s.*

Tenn paire of sheets, 6 pillowbeers, 4 dozen of table napkins, and 4 tableclothes, *6li.* 10*s.*
One small silver tanckard, two silver salts, 8 spoones, 3 poringers, & one tobacco-box, 12*li.*
In redy money & wearing apparill, *5li.*
In all—70*li.* 13*s.*
[Appraisers—John Clarke, John Tooke.]
[Exhibited 28 December 1689 by Elizabeth Bullen, widow and executrix.]

158.—John Clarke of Writtle, yeoman, died 3 January 1689/90. Inventory taken 27 January 1689/90.

IN THE HALL—Two ovell tables, six cane chayers, 3 old searge chayers, two rush chayers, one couch, one settell, one jack & chayne, one littell cobert, one clock, one looking glase, one glase case, one payer of stilliardes, one muskett, one [fowling] peese, two payer of cobirons, fier pann & tonges, one payer of bellowes, *4li.* 9*s.* 10*d.*

IN THE PARLER—One bedsted, matt & cordes, one fetherbed, one fethe boulster, two fether pillowes, two blankettes, one coverlett, one countopeane, one payer of curtaines & valiantes & cortaine roddes, one chest of drawers, one littell table, fower frames for chayers, one chayer, one littell stoole, two littell carpettes, *6li.* 10*s.* 4*d.*

IN THE CHAMBER OVER THE HALL—Two joyned bedstedes with mattes & cordes, one fetherbed, one fether bouster, two fethe pillowes, two flockbedes, two flock boulsters, one rugg, one coverlett, two blankettes, two payer of curtaines with valliantes & curtaine roddes, one pallet bedsted, three trunckes, one box, two joyned stooles, one hanging press, one littell peece of tapestrey, 7*li.* 15*s.* 8*d.*

The lining in the parler chamber—Twelve payer of sheetes, five payer of pillowbeeres, two dieper tableclothes, twelve dieper·napkins, five other table clothes, twentie fower course napkins, 4*li.* 14*s.*

IN THE MANES CHAMBER—Two bordede bedstedes, one flock bed, & boulster, one coverlett, one blankett, 15*s.* 6*d.*

Pleate—One silver tankerd, six silver spoones, & one silver salte, 12*li.*

IN THE KITCHING—One brewing copper, one littell copper, two brase kittelles, one iron porredge pott, one iron kittell, three skillettes, one jack, three spittes, one iron driping pann, one basting ladle, five brewing tubbes, one washing tubb, one tramill, 8*li.* 10*s.* 4*d.*

IN THE DARY—One charne & staffe, one stann, six small milke vessells, two payles, three dussen of trenchers & sum other wooden ware, one frying pann, one cheese press, two dreser bordes, eight pewter dishes, twentie nine plates, one cheese plate, three pewter poringer, one clover, one trough, one powdering tubb, three cheesemootes, & sum other pottes & pannes, 3*li.* 9*s.* 4*d.*

IN THE BUTTERY—Fower hodgeheades, two halfe hodgesheads, three barrells, one tunell, two lether bottells, three drinke stalles, 1*li.* 11*s.* 6*d.*

IN THE BOULTING HOUSE—One kneding trough, one land sive, one dreser bord, one old cubberd, & sum other small thinges, 5*s.* 6*d.*

IN THE FEILDES—Nine cowes, three steere bullockes, five heffer bullockes, one wenell calfe, 22*li.*

IN THE STABLE—Three gelte horses, & one stone horse, 12*li.*

IN THE FEILDES—Two gelt horses, one meare, & one sucking coult, 9*li.* 10*s.*; fiftie nouffolke sheepe, & twentie two norffolke lambes, 13*li.* 10*s.*

IN THE WHEAT BARNE—[Illegible] of wheat in the barne & the chamber, 40*li.*

IN THE BARLEY BEARNES—In the strawe & sum thresed, 54*li.*

Rye in the barne—9*li.*

One cock of haye—12*li.*; nine store pigges, 3*li.* 3*s.*; two old waggons, 6*li.* 5*s.*; one dung carte, & one dung carte coope, 3*li.*; the carte harnis, & plow harnis, 1*li.* 10*s.*; plowes & harrowes, & irones belonging the two plowes, two dewe rackes, three ladders, 1*li.* 10*s.* 6*d.*; two scres, two fannes, one bushell, two corne shovells, twelve sackes, fower pich forckes, 2*li.* 0*s.* 6*d.*

IN THE HOPGROUND—One parsell of hoppoles, two hopp piches, one iron spade, one shovell, one matthooke, seven wedges, one beetle, two acxes, one bill, 5*li.* 17*s.* 6*d.*

His weareing aparrell & money in his pockettes, 5*li.*

IN THE LONGE HOWES—One quarne & sum other small things, 1*li.*

For the rent & plowing of seventeene acres of barly land, 17*li.*; for the rent & plowing of twentie-seven acres of land for wheate & for the wheat to sowe the sayd land, 33*li.* 10*s.*

In money nine hundred pounds, 900*li.*

Sum Totall—1200*li.* 11*s.* 8*d.* [should be 1201*li.* 18*s.* 6*d.*].

[Appraisers—Francis Dorrington, Isaac Reeve, Joseph Herridge.]

[Exhibited 5 February 1689/90.]

159.—William Garrat of Writtle, gentleman. 30 January 1689/90.

IN THE HALL—One long table & another lesser one, & a folding table, five joynted stooles, a joyn'd chaire, a wooden arm'd chaire, & five other chaires, a little pewter cisterne & bason, a paire of iron racks, cobirons, fire shovell & tonges, & a jack, 1*li.* 18*s.*

IN A CLOSETT—Five pewter dishes, & one plate, 5*s.*

IN THE PARLOR—1 table, & 4 chaires, 10*s.*

IN THE CLOSETT—A cubbard, table, three leather chaires, a table leafe, two desks, a cutlace, & a frying pan, 8*s.*

ON THE STAIRE CASE—A looking glasse, & a clock, lines & weights, 15*s.*

IN THE HALL CHAMBER—A bedstead, curtaines & valents, a feather bed & bolster, one feather pillowe, one pair of sheetes, two blanketts & one old quelt, two tables, one old turky carpett, two leather chaires, & two leather stooles, one old sea chest, 5*li.*

IN THE CLOSETT IN THE CHAMBER—One folio Bible Cambridge print, one leaden hatt presse, one leather chaire, 10*s.*

Linnen in the chamber—1 paire of flaxen sheetes, 1 pair of callicoe sheetes, 1 long callicoe table cloth, 8*s.*

IN THE PARLOR CHAMBER—Two flock beds, two bolsters, a pillow & 2 blanketts, one sheete, a half headed bedstead, a still, a chest of drawers, an old barne cloth, & an old paire of window curtaines, 1*li.*

IN THE BUTTERY—2 hogsheads, & 4 half hogsheads, & a tunnell, 3 brasse skillettes, 1 cast brasse pott, one great brasse pott, 1*li.*

IN THE MEAL BUTTERY—2 meal tubbs, a little old cowle, a pair of scales & weights, an old pitch pan, & a watering pott, 10*s.*

IN THE ROOME OVER THE BUTTERY—A bushell, a skreene, a peck, a casting shovell, 3 sives, & a riddle, 15*s.*

IN THE KITCHIN—A mashing tubb, a working tubb, & eight other tubbs, a sider presse, a great copper, & a little copper, two pailes, a bed pan, & a chamber pott, 4*li.*

UPON THE HEDGE—Two pair of sheets, *2s.*

IN THE BARNE—One long ladder, two short ones, one wheel barrow, & one old cart, two rakes, & one forke, *10s.*

IN THE STABLE—One old horse, & saddle, & bridle, two forks, & one old pannell, one shovell, *6s.*

IN THE YARD—One old cow, & one heifer, *3li. 10s.*

[Total]—*21li. 7s.*
[Appraisers—John Cooke, William Greenwood.]
[Exhibited 1 February 1689/90.]

160.—John Webb of Roxwell, yeoman. 29 May 1690.

IN THE HALL—One long table, three joyne stools, a short forme, a little cubbord, six rush chaires, two spitts, a paire of cobirons, fire shovell & tongs, a paire of tramells, a brass mortter and pessell, a tininge dripping pann, with some other small things, *1li. 10s. 4d.*

IN THE PARLOUR—Two little tables, a press cubbord, two rush chaires, and a small glass case, *1li. 7s.*; eleaven pewter dishes, four porringers, four sawsers, halfe a dozen of pewter spoons, *1li. 4s. 9d.*

IN THE KITCHIN—One table & forme, a kneading troph, a meale tubb, five other tubbs, one cowle, with some other wooden dishes, *1li. 19s. 4d.*; a lead, three possnetts, a brass scumer, two kettles, one iron pott & pott hoocks, a paire of cobirons, and a paire of tramells, *3li. 19s. 5d.*; a spad, shovell, mattock, one axe, one bill, with some other implements of husbandrie, *6s. 8d.*

IN THE DAIRY—A cheespress, a stand, a cherne, milke boul, a powdering tubb, five shelves, a troph, tenn little cheeses, with some other small things, *1li. 4s.*

IN THE LITTLE BUTTREY—One halfe hogshead, two barrells, a drinke stalls, one wooden bottle, two shelves, *11s. 9d.*

IN THE GREAT BUTTERY—One hogshead, one halfe hogshead, two drinke stalls, *9s. 5d.*

IN THE CHAMBER OVER THE HALL—A joyne bedstedle, curtaines & valences, a feather bed and boulster, one pillow, two blanketts, and a coverlid, *3li.*; three hutches, a little cubbord, a paire of brass cobirons, a rush chaire, a fire shovell, with some other small things, *1li. 0s. 4d.*

IN A LITTLE CHAMBER OVER THE ENTREY—One halfe headed bedstedle, a feather bed and boulster, one blankett, two coverlids, *2li. 2s. 6d.*

IN THE CHAMBER OVER THE PARLOUR—A joyne bedstedle, curtaines & valuences, a feather bed & bolster, three feather pillows, two blanketts, and a rugg, *4li. 0s. 6d.*; a livery cubord, one chest, two hutches, a box, and three chaires, *1li. 6s. 8d.*

IN THE CHAMBER OVER THE KITCHIN—A short table, two woolen wheels & a reel, and five bushells of wheat, *1li. 4s. 6d.*

IN THE CHAMBER OVER THE DAIRY—A trundle bedstedle, flock bed & boulster, a paire of scalls and some small waites, 19*s.* 7*d.*

The linen—5*li.* 19*s.* 4*d.*

IN THE MAULTHOUSE—A leaden sesterne, four seame of mault, a seame of barley, three bushell of pease, a screen, a fann, a bushell, a ridle, and two mault shovell, 8*li.* 8*s.*

Horse & harness, 4*li.*; a old long cart & dunge cart, 2*li.* 10*s.*; two cowes, 4*li.* 10*s.*; eight ewes with their lambs, 2*li.*; two hoggs, 1*li.* 4*s.*; the plow, harrows & plow irons, 7*s.* 3*d.*
The corne growing upon the ground, 13*li.* 13*s.*
His weareing apparell & money in his purse, 4*li.* 10*s.*
Summa totalis is—73*li.* 9*s.* 4*d.* [should be 73*li.* 8*s.* 4*d.*]
[Appraisers—Simon Burrell, Edward Godsafe.]
[Exhibited 31 May 1690 by Theodosia Webb, widow and executrix.]
[Also a copy on parchment but with the second sum of money entered as 1*li.* 17*s.*; the total, however, is given as 73*li.* 9*s.* 4*d.*]

161.—Abraham Day of Roxwell. 31 May 1690.

IN THE HALL—One planck table, one little table, a settle, an armd chaire, a salt box, a short gun, a chaffin dish, a cleaver, one old lanthorne, 13*s.* 6*d.*

IN THE PARLOUR—One press cubbord, a glass case, eight pewter dishes, three pewter porringers, one pewter salt, a tining dripping pan, 2 tining pudding pans, a pewter tankard, 1*li.* 19*s.* 6*d.*

IN THE DAIRY—A cheespress, a cherne, a powdering tubb, two trays, a barrell & drink stall, a iron frying pan, a hand dish, 15*s.* 9*d.*

IN THE BUTTREY—A brass lead, a kettle and a skellett; one barrell, 2*li.* 0*s.* 8*d.*

IN THE CHAMBER OVER THE HALL—A halfe headed bedstedle, & curtaines & valences, a feather bed, two feather boulsters, one feather pillow, one blankett, one rugg, two huttches, 4*li.* 1*s.*; two pair of sheets, a short table cloath, 2 towells, one pillow beers, 5*s.* 6*d.*

Two sackes, 6 bushells of pease, 13*s.* 4*d.*; tools belonging to his trade, 1*li.* 10*s.* 6*d.*; his husbandrie tooles, 6*s.* 8*d.*
A cart buck, 13*s.* 4*d.*; a little mare, 1*li.*; 4 sheep & seaven lambs, 1*li.* 8*s.*; a cow, 2*li.* 10*s.*
The corne on the ground, 6*li.*
His wearinge apparell and mony in his purse, 3*li.* 10*s.*
[Total]—27*li.* 7*s.* 9*d.*
[Appraisers—Simon Burrell, Thomas Bright.]
[Exhibited 25 September 1690 by Abraham Day, son and administrator.]
[Endorsed—owing in detts by the said Abraham Day, 9*li.* 10*s.*]

162.—Richard Horsnaile of Writtle. 7 July 1690.

IN THE HALL—One press cubbard, on livery cubbard, on drawing table, on long table, 8 joyned stools, 2 armed chaires, 3 cushions, 2 short forms, 2*li.*

In the best chamber—One feather bed, 2 feather boulsters, 2 feather pilows, 2 pillow beers, 1 paier of sheets, 1 coverled, 1 rugg, a bedstedle, matte & cord, a paier of curtains & vallians, 1 joyned cubbard, 1 hutch, 1 armd chaier, 1 joyned stooll, 3*li.* 10*s.*

In the hall chamber—One feather bed, 2 feather boulsters, 2 feather pillows, 2 pillow beers, 1 pair of sheets, 3 blanketts, 4 old hutches, 1 old cubbard, 2 old leaves of a table, 2 little joyned stoolls, 1 little chaire, 1 old pewter dish, 4 pleats, 1 pewter cup, a parsell of cheese, with other implements, 3*li.* 5*s.*

In the midle chamber—One feather bed, 2 feather boulsters, 1 paier of sheets, one blanket, 1 coverled, bedstedle, matte & cord, 2 old cubbards, 2 old hutches, 2 old chaiers, 2*li.*

In the chamber over the kitchin—One feather bed, 1 feather boulster, 2 bedstedles, 2 matts & cords, 3 paier of sheets, 2 table cloths, 6 napkins, 2 livery cubbards, 2 old hutches, 1 old little trunke, 2*li.* 5*s.*

In the chamber over the dairy—One old bedstedle, matt & cord, 2 old hutches, 1 old trunk, 1 old settle, 1 wooden chaier, 1 old joyned stool, 5*s.*

In the chamber over the brewhouse—One small feather bed, 1 feather boulster, 2 pillows, matt & cord, & sume other implements, 1*li.*

In an old room—Sume old lumber, 2*s.* 6*d.*

In the kitchin—2 brass porridg potts, 2 iron porridg potts, 7 spitts, one jack & chaine, 2 grudgirons, 2 cobirons, 2 trammells, fire pann & tongs, 1 paier of bellows, 3 skillets, 18 peuter dishes, 2 pye pleats, 1 tinning pudding pan, 1 pesstle & morter, 1 old cubbard, 1 old table, 1 form, 4 chaiers, with other implements, 3*li.* 15*s.*

In the dairy—2 brass milke panns, 1 churn & staff, 2 way tubbs, 3 milk vessells, 4 cheess moots, 3 forms, & other implements, 15*s.*

In the brewhouse—2 brass leads, 1 meashing tubb, 4 other tubbs, 2 kettls, 2 pails, 1 chees press & a cheese stand, 1 trammell, & other implements, 2*li.* 15*s.*

In the strong beer buttery—2 hogsheads, 1 beer stall, 2*s.* 6*d.*

In the small beer buttery—2 hogsheads, 1 old beer stall, 1 meal chest, 1 kneading trough, 2 leather bottls, 5*s.*

In the mault house—One leaden cistern, a old haire cloth, a old mault quern, 3*li.*

In the mault chamber—Mault & wooll, 1 bushell, a screen, 12 old empty sacks, 2 old dew reaks, old iron, 6*li.* 2*s.* 6*d.*

In the stable—5 horses, 1 mare, 4 old collers, 4 paier of cart harnis, 5 paier of plow harnis, 5 bite halters, one cart sadle & thilbals, 1 old pannell & sturrips, 1 bridle, 16*li.*

Without doors in the yard—One waggon, 1 dung cart, 1 wheell barrow, 1 plow, a paier of old harrows, 6*li.*

In the feilds—Grass standing, 6*li.*; 4 acres of pease growing, 5*li.*; 6 acres of bullymong growing, 7*li.* 10*s.*; 14 acres of barly growing, 21*li.* 14*s.*; 16

acres of wheat growing, 30*li.*; faullow ground, 26 acres plowed twice at 8*s.* an acres, & 6 acres plowed once at 4*s.* an acres in all 32 acres, and for the rent of these 32 acres at 7*s.* & 6*d.* an acres in all it comes too, 23*li.* 12*s.*; hay made, 8*li.*

6 milch cowes, 18*li.*; 11 little Welch runts, 14*li.* 13*s.* 4*d.*; 43 Welch sheep & lambs, 8*li.* 12*s.*; 1 sow, 9 pigs, 4 sheats, 3*li.* 2*s.* 6*d.*
Wheat, 10*s.*
Wareing apparrell & mony in pockett, 2*li.* 10*s.*
Ye tottall—202*li.* 6*s.* 4*d.*
[Appraisers—John Wallington, Thomas Barker.]
[Exhibited 7 July 1690 by Mary Horsnaile, widow and administratrix.]

163.—Martha Meagle. 24 September 1690.

In the shop—One brass cettle, 2 scillets, 3 driping pans, one cullender, one frying pan, one cupbard, one form, a salt box, and 3 little tubs, and other wooding things, 1*li.*

In the hall—One long table, 6 joyntes stools, one press cubbard, a little table, 2 small stools, 6 chayers, 3 cuchins, 4 spits, 2 payers of cobirons, 2 fiar pans, three tramels, 3 payer of tongs, one gridiron, 2 iron racks, one pessel and morter, one candle box, a scons, smothing iron, a lanthor, and bellows, 3 candle sticks, 5 earthen dishes, four beer glasses, 2 mugs, and one jug, one iron driping pan, 2*li.* 9*s.* 6*d.*

In the buttery—2 small vessels, 2 beer stalls, one little form, one small cettle, a warming pan, a pot scillet, 6 peuter spoons, 2 porengers, 2 chafing dishes, 2 scimers, a basting ladle, one dosen of trenchers, 4 earthen dishes, 4 pots, and pans, 1*li.* 0*s.* 6*d.*

In the parlor—One feather-bed and bedstead, 2 boulster, 2 pillows, curtains and valyants, a rug and 3 blancets, one mat, one table, and 2 stools, one chayer, 6 small books, 3*li.* 10*s.*

In the chamber over the shop—One feather bed and bedstead, one flock bed and mat, 2 blancets, one cover lid, curtains and valyants, one table, and 3 stools, a livery cubbard, 3 chests, five small boxes, 5 chayers, a glass case and too glases, a cloth press, one payer of bellows, one peuter dish, 6 bed sticks, 12 payer of sheets, and 2 feather boulsters, 3 pewter chamber pots, ten pewter dishes, 2 pewter candlesticks, one flagon, 2 plates, 3 sasers, 6 payer of pillow beers, 2 dosen of napkins, 3 table clothes, one towel, 10*li.* 13*s.* 4*d.*

In the hall chamber—On feather bed and bedstead, one straw bed and mat, 2 feather boulster, 2 pillows, 2 blankets, one rug, curtains and valyands, one small table, 2 stools, 3 leather chayers, one joynt chayer, one livery cubbard and cubbard cloth, 4*li.* 14*s.* 7*d.*

Her wearing clothes and wearing linnen, 1*li.* 10*s.*

In the room over the buttery—6 pewter dishes, 2 pewter candle sticks, one flagon, 2 brass pots, and a brass cettle, a wicker chayer, a pilyon and cuchon, an old trunk, 1*li.* 10*s.*

IN THE CICHIN—One small copper, 8 little tubs, a kneading trough, and other thing which be long to the cichin, 1*li.* 10*s.* 6*d.*

Suma Totalis—27*li.* 8*s.* 5*d.*
[Appraisers—John Hubbard, Thomas May.]
[Exhibited 25 September 1690 by Thomas Meagle, son and administrator.]

164.—Robert Hawes of Roxwell, bricklayer. 25 March 1691. See Plate IX.

One feather bed, one feather boulster, one old couerlid, and one blankett, 1*li.* 15*s.*; two payer of olde sheets, three pillowbeers, two towels, one table cloath, 5*s.* 6*d.*; one olde hutch, 2*s.*; nine pounds of pewter, 5*s.* 3*d.*; one olde cubbord, 1*s.*; one leathern bottell, 1*s.* 6*d.*; his working tooles, 3*s.*; one paile, 1*s.*; one olde copper, 18*s.*; his wearing apparell and money in his purse, 5*s.*
[Total]—3*li.* 17*s.* 3*d.*
[Appraisers—Abraham Gaward, William King.]
[Exhibited 4 April 1691 by John Sach of Roxwell, administrator.]
['Upon the Copper there was borrowed by the said Robertt Hawes before he dyed 10*s.*']

165.—William Bird of Horsely Park in Writtle. 26 May 1691.

IN THE HALL—A drawing table, five joyned stooles, foure leather chaires, an old elbow chaire, a couch, a press cubbord, six cushions, two warming panns, two paire of cobirons, fire shovell & tongs, two pillions, and 2 pillion cloathes, & some other small matters, 4*li.* 10*s.*

IN THE PARLOR & CLOSETT—A large ovall table, a small ovall table, twelve cane chaires, a greate paire of brasse cobirons, fire shovell & tongs, a large looking glass, a chimney peece in colours, white window curtaines & rodds, & other odd things, 7*li.* 6*s.* 8*d.*

IN THE PANTRY—A small table, five calves leather chaires, a cloath elbow chaire, two cloath stooles, a small still, thirteen pewter dishes greate & small, a bed pann, a large pewter flaggon, two dozen of pewter plates, a pye plate, six dozen of glass bottles, 32 pewter spoones, & some other little parcells of pewter, a case of knives, white window curtaine & rodd, & other implements there, 5*li.* 5*s.*

IN THE PANTRY CHAMBER—One good feather bedd, a feather bolster, one pillow, a gray searge quilt, the like curtaines & valens, curtaine rodds, bedstead, & six searge chaires, white window curtaine & rodd, 8*li.* 10*s.*

IN THE PARLOR CHAMBER—One feather bedd, one feather bolster, two pillowes, a painted callicoe quilt, with redd cheyny curtaines & valens, white inward curtaines & valence & rodds, bedstead & bagis, a red damaske couch, a chest of drawers of olive wood, a looking glass the frame olive, a paire of cobirons, fire shovell & tongs & bellowes, a large silver boll, a small silver cupp, nine silver spoones, a lignum vite cup tip't with silver, white window curtaines & rodds, & the hangings of the roome, 40*li.*

In the garrett over the hall chamber—One feather bedd, two bolsters, a pillow, a greene rugg, green printed curtaines & valence & rodds, bedsted, matt & cord, & 8 green chaires, 7*li.*

In the garrett over the pantry & parlor chamber—A parcell of hopps of aboute 200 weight, two old elbow chaires, an old forme, a parcell of wooll, & other small things, 5*li.* 10*s.*

A clock & case in the stair case, 1*li.* 10*s.*

In the chamber over the buttery—One feather bed, bolster, pillow, darnix curtaines & valence, coverlett, bedstead, rodds, matt & cord, a trundle bedstead & hutch, 3*li.* 10*s.*

In the chamber over the hall—A feather bedd, bolster, old printed curtaines & valens, & coverlett, an old bedstead, rodds, matt & cord, a hanging press, one chest, 4 hutches, an old joyned box, close stoole, window curtaines & rodds, 2 rush chaires, & other odd things, 8*li.* 5*s.*

In the chamber over the kitchin—A feather bedd, two feather bolsters, one pillow, one blankett & coverlett, a joyn'd bedstead, curtaines, valens & rodds, matt & cord, two other good coverletts, a greate chest, three hutches, a box, & some other small matters, 6*li.* 13*s.* 4*d.*

In the old lofts—Some shelves, old iron, & other old lumber, 1*li.*

In the old garretts.—Two feather bedds, two bolsters, eight blanketts, two coverletts, a flock bed, one halfe headed bedstead, a trundle bedstead, a muskett, 2 old swords & other old lumber, 7*li.*

Linnen aboute the house—One dozen paire of flaxen sheetes, one dozen paire of towen sheetes, two diaper table cloathes, a dozen of diaper napkins, a dozen & halfe of course napkins, five paire of good flaxen pillow beers, 3 holland pillow beers, eleaven long table cloathes, two other of flaxen & tow, foure towells, foure long cubbord cloathes, two other table cloathes, and twelve towells, 25*li.* 6*s.* 8*d.*

In the kitchin—Two tables, a forme, five rush chaires, a hanging cubbord, a birding peece, three iron dripping panns, foure spitts, two cleavers, a turne spitt jack, an iron gate & tramells, a paire of cobirons, fire shovell & tongs, a greate paire of andernes, three lock irons, a nest of drawers, an iron porridge pott & hooks, foure leather bottles, a hopp pitch, thirteene pewter dishes, a copper pott, & severall other implements of household, 6*li.* 15*s.*

In the dayry—One cheese press, two milke stands, one cherne, one cheese tubb, 8 cheese mootes, three cheese breads, foure milk bolls, two traies, 3 kimnells, a frying pann, a gridiron, a powdring tubb, seaven shelves, severall potts, panns, & other implements belonging to the dayry, 4*li.*

In the brewhouse & backhouse—Two brewing coppers, seaven brass kettles, two brass porridge potts, six brass skilletts, brasse scumers & ladles, a mashing tubb, a guile fatt & cooler, & eight other brewing tubbs, a large cherne, an iron beame, scoale boards & weights, several pailes, tressles & dressers, and many other implements there, 15*li.*

In the boulting house—A kneading trough, a meale hutch, two formes, a bran tub, foure sives, a paire of trammells, & other small matters there, 1*li.*

IN THE BUTTERY—Six hogsheads, two butts, a tunnell with the drinke stalls, & other implements there, 4*li.*

IN THE CELLAR—Seaven hogsheads, five halfe hogsheads with the drinke stalls, an old joyned stoole, and other things there, 4*li.* 15*s.*

IN THE GRANARY & ELSWHERE—One hundred & fourescore quarters of malt, 126*li.*

IN THE BARNE—Twenty quarters of wheate, 20*li.*; pease in the straw, 1*li.* 16*s.*; a parcell of hay there, 2*li.*

IN & ABOUTE THE BARNE & CARTHOUSE—Three waggons, 21*li.*; three dung carts, 10*li.*; thre paire of harrowes, 15*s.*; two plowes, 12*s.*

IN THE YARDS, GROUNDS, STABLES, & CORNE CHAMBER—Eight milch cowes and a bull, 22*li.* 10*s.*; three sockling calves in the penn, 2*li.*; six quarters of oates, 2*li.* 14*s.*; foure quarters & halfe of pease, 3*li.* 12*s.*; the malt quarne, 1*li.*; eight store hoggs, 5*li.* 12*s.*; the cartharnes, collers & halters of the best furniture, the other cart harnes, and furniture, the plow harnes and what belongs to them, a corne hutch & padlock, bridles, sadles, & other things in the stable, 8*li.*; five horses and three mares, 33*li.*

The shovells, spades, mattocks, pitchforks, rakes, fanns, bushell measures, skreenes, timber chaine, sawes, wedges, & other implements & tooles of husbandry, with two and thirty corne sacks, 5*li.*

Fifteene acres of barly att 35*s.* per acre, 26*li.* 5*s.*

Foureteene runts, 38*li.*; twelve sheepe, sold, but undelivered, 6*li.*; seaventeene cowple of sheep & lambs, 5*li.* 19*s.*; twenty acres of wheate growing, 36*li.*; thirteen weathers, 6*li.*; thirteen fatting cowes & heifers, 30*li.*; six acres of oates groweing, 4*li.*; foure large runts, 18*li.*; five smaller runts, 11*li.* 10*s.*; tenn fatting cowes and heifers, 25*li.*; 24 acres of land once fallowed att 4*s.* per acre, 4*li.* 16*s.*; five acres of pease, 2*li.* 7*s.* 6*d.*

His wearing apparell & mony in his purse, 68*li.*

Totall summe is—676*li.* 5*s.* 2*d.* [should be 714*li.* 5*s.* 2*d.*]

[Appraisers—Henry Bright, Mathew Nightingale.]

[Exhibited 18 July 1691 by Abraham Brecknock, administrator.]

166.—George Bradford of Writtle, gardener. 2 October 1671.

Five rush chaires, 4*s.*; five joynt stooles, 6*s.*; two glass casses, one dustbaskett & old dripping pan, 2*s.*; five cushens, 5*s.*; one fetherbed & blankett, 2*li.*; one yellow rug, two blanckets, two pillows, one fether boulster, 2*li.*; one flockbed, two blanketts, 12*s.*; one steale of yellow curtains & vallyans, 1*li.* 5*s.*; one old coverlid, one old blanckett, two pillows, one castern, 10*s.*; two oaken desks, 8*s.*; twenty & two napkins, 14*s.*; one pair of sheets, two board cloaths, two pillabeers in a deale box, 18*s.*; three sheets, six napkins, six coars table cloaths, 15*s.*; three pair of sheets, one table cloath, & one towell, 1*li.* 7*s.*; ten pewter dishes, one pye plate, one chamber pot & bason, on bed pan, a still head, two little bowls, a beker, & other old pewter, 1*li.* 5*s.*; fower skillets, one morter, a warming pan, a brasse cover, a brasse basting ladle, two pair of tongs, one fier shovel, 18*s.*; two coppers, one brasse pot, one kettle, three skimmers, *2li.*; cheesefats, & a wooden platter, with a trevett, *1s. 6d.*; a spit, *1s.*; a looking glasse, *1s. 6d.*; two kettles, 1 skillet, a pewtre dish, & a parcel of lead, *13s.*; a parcell of books, *1li.*; a pewtre dish, green curtains & vallyans for a bed, & a pillion cloath, *1li. 7s.*; a great chest, *6s.*; a hutch, *2s. 6d.*; a livery table, *3s.*; a little paynted box & 3 wooden bowls, *1s. 2d.*; a joyne chaire, *2s.*; a gold ring, *16s.*; fower pair of sheets, *1li. 12s.*; 3 table cloaths, *5s.*; 9 napkins & a towel, *3s. 6d.*; a trunck, *2s.*; 3 swords, *3s.*; of these goods left in Goodman Lyllirs house the sum is *22li. 9s. 2d.*

Wood & lumber in Goodman Lyllirs yard, *16s.*; 268 foot of oaken boards at 5 farth' per foot, *12s.*; two placks, *2s.*; a beetle, 2 stumpers & an old hatch, *2s.*; a beerstall & a little form, *5s.*; a cheese presse, *4s.*; a sweell tub, *2s.*; a nother form, *1s.*; 2 tubs, *2s. 6d.*; a cowl, *2s. 6d.*; a hutch, *3s. 6d.*; an old bedstead, *2s.*; 2 bedmatts, *2s.*; a great forme, *2s. 6d.*; one joynt beadsteadle, *10s.*; a little barrel & two deale boxes, *2s.*; a parcell of old pales, *6s.*; a cover for a copper, & a little baskett, *10d.*; a pitchfork, & a chicken coop, *8d.*; a grinding stone, & hogstrough, & a chopping block, *5s.*; sum—*4li. 3s. 6d.*

Goods in Goodman Lyllirs kitchin—A pair of andirons, & a pair of cobirons, hooks, & a spitt, & 2 trammels, & a pitch, *10s.*; a great long table, *8s.*; a parcel of old iron, *2s. 6d.* (sold); a green rug, *8s.*; a bowlster, *3s.*; a linnen presse, *2s. 6d.*; two spades, a shovell, & a scoop, *2s. 6d.*; a little cubbord, *2s. 6d.*; a little falling table, *2s. 6d.* (sold); a close stoole, *5s.*; a joyn stoole, a saw, a frying pan, & a jack, *7s. 6d.*; a great bowl, *8d.*; fowr curtains & 3 rods, *7s. 6d.*; a green chayr, *1s.*; a little barrel, *1s. 6d.*; a bushel, a peck, & halfe a peck, *2s.* (sold); a tub, *2s. 6d.*; a spitt, *1s.* (sold); a great chair, *1s. 6d.*; another green chayr, *1s.*; an iron pot, *4s.*; a fetherbed, boulster, & a pillow, & an old castern, *2li.*; 2 sieves, *8d.*; an old blancket, *3s. 6d.*; a cubboard, *16s.*; a beadstead, *16s.*; sum—*5li. 13s.* [should be *7li. 12s. 10d.*].

In ready money, *11li. 15s.* Apparrell, *1li.*

Cloaths bequeathed Mr. Walker by Georg Bradford—Two black gowns, *2li.*; fower petticoats, *2li. 10s.*; one homemade gown, 4 petticoats, & muff, *1li. 1s.*; a gold ring, *1li. 1s.*; 6 shifts, *15s.*; small linnen, *6s.*; sum—*7li. 12s.*
[Not totalled—*54li. 12s. 6d.*]
[Appraisers—Michael Beresford, clerk, Richard James, Thomas Bridgman.]
[Exhibited 2 October 1671.]

167.—Hickguly Eve of Writtle, married man. 29 October 1691.

IN THE HALL—On long tabell, 4 joins stooles, half a dusson of chaires, a pair of cobirons, & a paire of tongs, & othere emplyments, *1li. 15s.*

IN THE PALLERE—One feathere bed, one bolstere, one coverlid, one blancoat, curtons & vallinantt, all thing belonging to it, *4li.*; on cobbered, two chest, a glasscass, *15s.*

IN THE CHAMBER OVER THE HALL—One feathere bed, on feathere bolstere, two pillows, one cuelering, on blankett, *2li.*; & all othere emplyments, *10s.*

IN THE CHAMBER OVER THE PALLER—An old huch, & othere emplyments, 10*s*.

IN THE CHEESS CHAMBER—All the cheesses there, 15*s*.

IN THE MILCKE HOUSE—A cheess presse, a charme, 4 milck vessell, & othere emplyments, 16*s*.

IN THE BUTTERY & KETCHEIN—On lead, tow kettell, 4 barrells, three tuds, a hand quarn & othere emplyments, 3*li.* 1*s*.; all the buttere, 7*s*.; tow paire of sheets & one odons [i.e. odd one], half a dussen of napkins, & sume othere smale lineing, 1*li.* 10*s*.

IN THE STABELL—Tow paire of carte harness, a pair of thillbell & cart sadell, 3 paire of plow harness & colleres, & othere tackelining, 14*s*.; on wagon, on old dun carte, on old plow, & a paire of harrows, 2*li.* 6*s*.; tow old mears, young gelt colt, 5*li.*; the cows, tow old cows, 4*li.* 10*s*.; a leaven sheep, 1*li.* 15*s*.; tow hoggs and 8 pigs, 4*li.* 11*s*.

IN THE BARNE—The wheat & barly, 4*li.* 10*s*.; the peass & bullymonge, 5*li.*

IN THE FILD—Five arkeres of folowrd wheat soen & the rent, 6*li.* 10*s*.; five akeres of barly land tilled twices & the rent of the land, 3*li.*
His wareing aparill & monnys in his pocketts, 3*li.*
The Sume In all—56*li.* 15*s*.
[Appraisers—William Becker, Daniel Hudson.]
[Exhibited 24 May 1692 by Elizabeth Eve, widow and administratrix.]

168.—Thomas Richards of Writtle, yeoman. [Undated.]

IN THE HALL—One long table and two fourms, one benche board, one little table, one joined cubert, one long forme, four chaires, one jack, three spits, two smoothing irons, two cobirons, fire shovell and a paire of tongs, one gridiron, one cleaver, one tramell, one glase case, with other smalle things, 2*li.* 5*s*.

IN THE PARLOR—One feather bed and one boulster, one bedsted with curtains and valiants, one flock boulster, one rugg, two blankets, one livery cubert, two leather chaires, 3*li.* 15*s*. 6*d*.

IN THE CHAMBER OVER THE PARLOR—One feather bed, two feather boulsters, one coverlid, one blanket, one bedsted and curtains, one flock bed, one bedsted, two pillows, one blanket, two greate chest, one smale chest, one deale box, 4*li.* 10*s*. 6*d*.

Linin—Five paire of course sheets and three flexen sheets, two flexen table cloath, one course table cloath, one course sheet, and four napkins, 2*li.* 6*s*. 8*d*.

IN THE CHAMBER OVER THE HALL—One cheese board, two tressells, one kilderkin, one beerstall, two sithes with snathes, two peasehookes, one bushell, one fan, one screne, one seed peck, two sives, three bushells of wheate and six bushells of barley, and some other smale things, 2*li.* 14*s*. 10*s*.

IN THE FOLKS CHAMBER—One flock bed, two flock boulsters, one coverlid, one blanket, one bedsted, one trundle bedsted, one wheelle, one reell, two dew rakes, two forkes, 1*li.* 5*s*.

IN THE DARY—One cheese prese, two churns, one stand, one powdering tub, one litle table, two tressells and shelves, two cheese moots, and the milk vesels, one musterd quarn, one brase morter, scales and weights, and other smale things, *2li.* 5*s.* 6*d.*

IN THE BOUTING HOUSE—One kneading trove, one meale chest, one capons coope, one ax, and two bills, one mathooke, one lanthorne, 12*s.*

IN THE BUTTREE—Two hogsheads, one half hogshead, one beerstall, one old table, two shelves, one little forme, one brase pot, one iron pot, two kettles, two skillets, one coalle dish, one frying pan, one warming pan, six pewter dishes, one pewter candlestick, one pewter salt, two andirons, one leather botle, and some other smale things, 3*li.* 9*s.* 6*d.*

IN THE KITCHIN—One brewing lead, three tubs, two cowls, one tunnell, one tap oze, one hop sive, one hogs tub, two pailes, one peele, one fire forke, one moulding board, one old stall at three pound (3*li.*), 3*li.* 10*s.*

IN THE MALTHOUSE—Seaven seame and a half of malt, 8*li.* 5*s.*; the malt tub, and quarne, and old haire, and one malt shovell, 1*li.* 16*s.*

IN THE CARTHOUSE—One old waggon, and one dungcart, 7*li.* 10*s.*

IN THE STABLE—Three old horse, 8li.; harnise, collers, and halters, thilbells and cart sadle, 1*li.* 19*s.* 6*d.*

Fourteen sheep and five lambs, 3*li.*; three cows and one calve, 5*li.* 15*s.*; five store piggs, 1*li.* 10*s.*
One plow, one paire of harrows, one roule, whipple trees, and all the plow irons, 1*li.* 2*s.*; five troughs, 7*s.*
Fifteen accres and a half of fallowland barley, 37*li.* 15*s.* 7*d.*; two accres of etche barley, 3*li.* 8*s.* 6*d.*; two accres of fallow land with wheate, 4*li.* 9*s.* 6*d.*; seaven accres of pease, 5*li.* 14*s.* 9*d.*
His wearing aparrell and ready money, 1*li.*
Summe tottall—117*li.* 17*s.* 4*d.* [should be 118*li.* 7*s.* 4*d.*].
[No appraisers' names given.]
[Exhibited 24 May 1692 by Joan Richards, widow and administratrix.]

169.—Joseph Clarke of Roxwell [grocer and draper]. 1 July 1692.

IN THE HALL—One long table, one litle table, one press cubbard, 3 stooles, one jack, & other things therto belonging, 2*li.* 3*s.* 4*d.*

IN THE CHAMBER OVER THE HALL—One bed & bedsted, curtains & vallance, &c: small things, 2*li.* 10*s.* 6*d.*

IN THE CHAMBER OVER THE KITTCHING—One bed & bedsted, curtaines & vallands, &c., one chest of drawers, one table, 6 chaires, & other small things in that roome, 5*li.* 2*s.* 6*d.*

IN THE CHAMBER OVER THE SHOP—One bed & bedsted, & a few od things, 18*s.* 3*d.*

IN THE BUTTERY & MEALE HOUSE—The vessells, & an old table, with some bone, & other small things, 1*li.* 10*s.* 8*d.*

IN THE KITCHING—One copper, some small matter of brass, the pewter about the house, & other small things, 3*li.* 3*s.* 4*d.*

IN & ABOUT THE STABLE—One old horse & saddle, & other small things, 2*li.* 10*s.*

IN THE YARD & ABOUT THE YARD—About two loads of wood fourty shillings, 2*li.*
The houshold linnen and other linnen about the house & belonging to him, 2*li.* 10*s.* 4*d.*
His wearing apparrell & money in the house, 8*li.* 10*s.*
Good debts owing that are sperat, 20*li.* 1*s.* 6½*d.*
Desperate debts, 25*li.* 7*s.* 4*d.*

GOODS IN THE SHOP—22 yds of Linsey at 12*d.*, 1*li.* 2*s.*; 6 yds ¾ of red cotton at 13*d.*, 7*s.*; 11 yds ¾ frize at 21*d.*, 1*li.* 0*s.* 7*d.*; 9 yds ½ of broad cullerd bayes at 20*d.*, 15*s.* 10*d.*; 15½ of cloath sarge at 21*d.*, 1*li.* 7*s.*; 8 yds ¼ of broad cloath at 5*s.* yd., 2*li.* 1*s.* 3*d.*; 25 yds of Kersy halfe thick at 21*d.*, 2*li.* 3*s.*; 18 yds of Kersy at 2*s.* yd., 1*li.* 16*s.*; 11 yds of broad cullerd bayes at 21*d.*, 19*s.* 3*d.*; 6 yds ½ of w^{tt} Manch' bayes at 14*d.*, 7*s.* 7*d.*; 5 yds ½ broad cloath in 2 remnants at 4*s.*, 1*li.* 2*s.*; 4 remnants of Linsy & flannell, &c., 10*s.*; remnants of sarge, 13*s.* 6*d.*; 2 peticoats of broad stripe, 8*s.*; some remnants of bangall & callicoe, 8*s.* 6*d.*; 70 yds of stuffes at 9*d.* yd., 2*li.* 12*s.* 6*d.*; 46 yds of crape at 7*d.*; 1*li.* 6*s.* 10*d.*; 12 yds ½ of strip'd Dunithy at 12*d.*, 12*s.* 6*d.*; 27 yds of fustion cullerd at 9*d.*, 1*li.* 0*s.* 3*d.*; 14 yds of w^{tt} narrow at 6½*d.*, 6*s.* 7*d.*; some od remnants, 6*s.* 8*d.*; 15 yds ½ of w^{tt} bayes at 18*d.* yd., 1*li.* 3*s.* 3*d.* Linnen: 17 ells of w^{tt} & browne harford at 9*d.*, 12*s.* 9*d.*; 17 yds of flaxen rowles at 6*d.* yd., 8*s.* 6*d.*; 21 yds of w^{tt} buckram at 8½d. yd., 14*s.* 10½*d.*; 35 yds of Hammeks browne at 3*d.*, 10*s.* 3*d.*; 7½ yds of broad blew at 10½*d.*, 6*s.* 5*d.*; 19 ells of canvas at 13*d.* per ell, 1*li.* 0*s.* 7*d.*; severall remnants, 8*s.*; 20 yds of rowle at 6*d.*, 10*s.* Haberdashery: tapes & fillittings w^{tt} & cullerd, 2*li.* 12*s.*; more bindings & tape with some thread, 15*s.*; pinns, laces & pack thread, 12*s.*; 6 pr. mens hose at 20*d.*, 10*s.*; 3 coats, 1*s.* 6*d.*; 8 pr. hose at 12*d.*, 8*s.*; 7 pr. at 12*d.*, 7*s.*; 8 pr. at 7*d.*, 4*s.* 8*d.*, 2 pr. at 2*s.*, 4*s.*; a parcell of silke, 4*s.*; buttons, 1*li.* 10*s.*; ribbins & ferritts, 15*s.*; golome & twist, 10*s.* Grocery: 6 lbs of pepper at 16*d.* lb., 8*s.*; powder & balls, 8*s.*; indigoe, 3 lbs. at 14*d.*, 3*s.* 6*d.*; stone blew & powder blew at 9*d.*, 9*d.*; spice of all sorts, 14*s.* 6*d.*; needles, 12*d.*; seeds, 12*d.*; cloathes & lonmigs ready made, 1*li.* 1*s.*; a remnant of red Kersy, 2*s.* 6*d.*; a parcell of hornes, 1*s.*; raysons, tobacco powder, &c., 1*li.* 10*s.*; mollosses & rossen, 5*s.*; oatmeale & mops, 3*s.*; hempe, bedlines & coard, &c., 1*li.* 5*s.*; corks & some od things, & a firkin of tarre, 10*s.*; w^{tt} starch halfe hundred, 10*s.*; w^{tt} sugar, 2*li.* 8*s.*; browne sugar, 5 cwt. at 34*s.*, 8*li.* 10*s.*; sugar po: 3 cwt. at 39*s.*, 5*li.* 17*s.*; nayles, shott & sope, 2*li.* 10*s.*; candles, bellowes, & mouse traps, 1*li.* 6*s.*; salt, about 12 bushells, 1*li.* 8*s.*; brandy, about 3 gallons at 3*s.* 8*d.*, 11*s.*; allom, pipes, bedlines & broomes, 1*li.* 11*s.* 6*d.*; for the boxes, shelves, scales & weights, 2*li.*
The somme totall is—145*li.* 8*s.* 2*d.*
[Appraisers not named.]
[Exhibited 22 August 1692 by Mary Clark, widow and administratrix.]

170.—Martha Force. [Undated.]

21 pound of puter, 14*s.*; one spit, to payer of coboyrnes, 2 payer of tounges, one fier pan, to fier shofles, one wicker chayer, 6*s.*; one round table, 1*s.* 6*d.*; one loung table and 6 stolles, 10*s.*; 4 huches, 8*s.*; one dosen of tranchers and 4 waytes, one touill, 1*s.* 6*d.*; 2 worminpanes, 3*s.*; one glascas, to olld boxes, one dripinpan, one littell table, 3*s.*; 2 wheles and a rell, one hobinoyrn, 4*s.* 6*d.*; 2 catels, one porrig pot, one skilet, 13*s.*; one fetherbed, 2 fether bolsters, one fether pilow, one payer of curtines and valantes and badsted and mat, one civerlid, 2 olld blackits, one flock bad, 2 payer of shetes, 2*li.* 10*s.*; 8 napkins, one bord cloth, 12*s.*; one pres cobard, 4*s.* 6*d.*
Total—6*li.* 11*s.*
[Appraisers—John Cocke, Thomas Rickner, William Greenwood, Thomas May.]
[Exhibited 28 December 1693, by Mary Force, sister and administratrix.]

171.—Henry May of Writtle, miller. 17 November 1693.

IN THE HALL—One longe table & 6 joynt stooles, 16*s.*; one little table, one forme, one press cubbard and cloth, 9*s.*; four chaires, 1 boxe of drawers, 6*s.*; one payer of belloues & 2 cobirons, 4*s.*; 2 payer of tongs, & 2 fire panns, 1*s.* 6*d.*; one beaf forke, & one cliver, 6*d.*; one smoothing iron, 3 heatters, & one little pessell & morter, 3*s.* 6*d.*; one jacke, one spitt, & 1 dripping pan, 4*s.* 6*d.*; one burding peece, 1 window curtaine & rodd, one worming pann, an iron to lay before the fire, 7*s.*; one tosting iron, one iron oven lidd, 1 payer of trammill, 2 pottige potts, 1 payer of pott hookes, 1 payer of iron rackes, 3 candlesticks, & one salt boxe, 12*s.* 6*d.*; the bookes, & 1 shelfe, & 1 sickle, 2*s.* 6*d.*

IN THE PARLOR—One longe table & forme, & four joynt stooles, 12*s.*; one press cubbard and cloth, one ould hutch, 1 chaire and 3 chussins, and 1 payer of cobiorns, 9*s.*

IN THE LOWER CLOSSETT—One powderring tubb, 8 glass bottles, sum earthen ware, & shelves, 5*s.*

IN THE LITTLE BUTTERRY—Four little vessells, 8*s.*

IN THE PARLOR CHAMBER—One bedsteadle with curtaines, valliants and rodds, one feather bed, one matt and corde, one feather boulster, 2 feather pillows, one payer of sheets, & one rugg, 5*li.* 10*s.*; one trundle bedsteadle and corde, one looking glasse, one glasse casse, 11*s.*; one greatt chest, one two armed chaire, 9*s.*; one round table ,one livery cubbard and cloth, 2 quilted stooles, & 2 leather chaires, 1*li.* 2*s.*; 2 payer of cobirons, 1 payer of tongs and shovell, 2 curtaines & 2 rodds, 8*s.*

IN THE CLOSSETT OVER THE HALL—Two barrells, 12 glasse bottles, 1 pewter flaggon, 12*s.*

IN THE CHAMBER OVER THE MILL—One bedsteadle, matt & corde, one feather bed, 2 feather boulsters, one feather pillow, one payer of sheetts, 1 payer of blanketts, & one coverlid, 3*li.*; one ould flex wheel, 1 ould hutch, & 2 ould boxes, 2*s.*

IN THE CHAMBER OVER THE HALL—One bedsteadle with curtaines, rodds and valliants, one feather bed, matt, corde, 2 feather pillows, 2 pillowbeers, one feather boulster, one flock boulster, one payer of sheetts, 1 blankett, and one rugg, 4*li.* 10*s.*; one trundle bedsteadle and corde, one hanging press, one ould chaire, 7*s.*; one chest, one hutch, 4 chushings, 2 leather chaires, 1 little looking glasse, 2 curtaine rodds, 4 curtaines, & one ould sworde, 12*s.*; one persell of boards, 12*s.* 6*d.*; 16 cheeses, 1*li.* 10*s.*

IN THE LITTLE CHAMBER OVER THE MILL—One ould bedsteadle with flock bed, and flock boulster, corde & matt, one ould blankett, 1 ould coverlid, & 2 ould tubbs, 8*s.*

IN THE GREAT BUTTERRY—Three brass kettles, 4 skilletts, 1 cole dish, 1 scummer, 1 basteing ladle, 2*li.* 5*s.*; all the pewter, 1*li.* 9*s.*; one tinn fish plate, 1 cullender, one pudding pann, and 1 poynt pott; & three sives, 2*s.*; two beare vessells, 4 tubbs, a stann, 1 galland vessell, 1 beare stalle, 15*s.*; one kneeding troffe, one pasty peele, 2 dosen of trenchers, and 1 iron seare, 5*s.*; 6 silver spoones, 1*li.* 10*s.*

The linnen—6 payer of flexen sheetts, 3*li.* 10*s.*; 6 payer of pillow bears, 1*li.* 4*s.*; 1 long flexen table cloth, and 1 dosen of napkinns, 1*li.* 6*s.*; 1 longe flexen table cloth & 1 dosen of napkinns, 1*li.* 2*s.*; 4 table clothes, 14*s.*; 18 towells & little board clothes, 9*s.*

IN THE MILL IF NOTT MY LORDS—One payer of cullen stones with spindle and ringe, 3 brasses, a cogg wheell, an axtree, 2 payer of trundles, 1 bredg wheell tree, 2 brays, 1 liter & trofe, & fatt, and hopper, and all things there unto belonging, 7*li.* 7*s.*

BELONGING TO THE PEEK MILL—One peek, one French stone, a spindle and wring, 2 brasses, 3 rowles, a gable and counter line, hopper, and fatt, and liter, and troffe, and all things there unto belonging, 5*li.* 6*s.*

IN THE MILL—13 peek bills, & two French bills, 7*s.*; a sheluch hammer, & a croe of iron, and a spileing chesscell, 3*s.* 6*d.*; three halfe hundred waits, one ¼ cwt. & small waits 23 *li.*, one beam, and 1 payer of scales, 1*li.*; 12 sacks, 12*s.*; 1 flew, & 1 fishing bray, & 1 riddle, 5*s.*; a parcell of edge tooles, 4*s.*; one lanthorne, one halfe bushel, and six ould tubbs, one halfe peck, one peck, and 2 tread plonkes, 5*s.*; coggs & staves, ruffle heaven, 1*li.* 5*s.*; 5 bushells of wheat, 1*li.* 18*s.*; 4 bushells of barly, 14*s.*

IN THE YARD—Ould plonkes, board, logges, & other wood, with timber and rowell board, 4*li.* 9*s.*

IN THE STABLE—2 horses, one mare, and mare coult, with 2 pannills, 1 saddle, 2 brideles, with hey, 1 forke, & 1 shovell, 6*li.*

Bonds, good and badd, 79*li.* 16*s.*; booke debts good and badd, 24*li.* 4*s.* 9½*d.*; reddy mony in the house, 4*li.* 17*s.*
His wareing apparell and mony in his pockett, 5*li.*
For ½ a years rent dew from Phillip Bright, Mickelmas 1693, 2*li.*; for rent dew from John Hawkin, Mickelmas (93), 10*s.*; some other debts good & badd, 7*li.* 18*s.* 11*d.*
Y^e Tottall—193*li.* 7*s.* 8½*d.*

[Appraisers—John Hall (miller at Chelmsford), Oliver Clayden (of Chelmsford), John Hurrell (of Writtle).]
[Exhibited 20 December 1693, by James Mays, guardian of Henry Mays of Writtle, a minor.]

172.—Simon Hudson of Writtle, yeoman. 2 December 1693.

IN THE HALL—One long table, one square table, one long forme, six joined stooles, seven chaires, one clock, one jack, three spits, & some other small things, 4*li.* 14*s.* 9*d.*

IN THE PARLOR—One drawing table, one little table, two joined chaires, seven leather chaires, two leather stooles, one pair of cobirons, with other small things, 2*li.* 13*s.* 10*d.*

IN THE CHAMBER OVER THE HALL—One joined bedsteed with curtans & vallence, one feather bed, one bolster, two pillowes, one livery cupboard, one box of drawers, one joined chest, 5 chaires, one pair of cobirons, & other small things, 4*li.* 12*s.* 2*d.*

IN THE CHAMBER OVER THE PARLOR—One bedsteed with curtains and vallence, one feather bed, 1 bolster, 2 pillows, 1 rugg & 2 blankets, one chest of drawers, one looking glass, one table, six chaires, one pair of cobirons, 7*li.* 13. 5*d.*

IN THE CLOSET—All the plate, bookes & other things, 9*li.* 7*s.* 6*d.*; all the linnen, 23*li.* 19*s.*

IN THE CHAMBER OVER THE PANTRY—One bedsteed with curtains and vallence, one feather bed, 2 bolsters, 2 pillows, 2 blankets, 1 clothe press, 2 joined chests, 2 hutches, 1 trunk, 4 boxes, with other small things, 6*li.* 4*s.* 6*d.*

IN THE CHEESE CHAMBER—All the cheese, 2 parcells of hopps, 1 parcell of wooll, & other lumbar, 6*li.* 4*s.* 6*d.*

IN THE GARRETS—One bedsteed, 3 flock beds with bolsters, coverlid & blankets, 3 hutches, 2 saddles, 1 pillion, 1 still, a parcell of old iron, & other lumbar, 5*li.* 5*s.*

IN THE PANTRY & BUTTERY—All the pewter, 5*li.* 8*s.* 6*d.*; all the brass, 4*li.* 2*s.* 6*d.*; 2 iron potts, 13*s.*; 2 cupboards, 3 barrells, 4 doz. bott[les], scoals, weights, shelves, & other implements, 3*li.* 4*s.* 6*d.*

IN THE SMALL BEER BUTTERY—One hoggshead, 2 barrells, one cupboard, & other lumbar, 1*li.* 14*s.* 1*d.*

IN THE MILK HOUSE—One cheesepress, 1 cherne, 1 stann, 1 powdering tubb, 3 hoggs of bacon, & other small things, 7*li.* 1*s.*

IN THE BREWHOUSE—2 coppers, 1 large pair of scoals & weights, all the brewing tubbs, & other implements, 5*li.* 3*s.*

IN THE STABLES—8 horses & furniture, 18*li.*; 4 cows, 12*li.* 10*s.*; 7 piggs, 2*li.* 15*s.*; 2 waggons, 1 cart, 1 dung cart coop, 1 new pair of wheels, 1 plow, 2 pair of harrows, & a wheell barrow, 18*li.* 10*s.*

IN THE BARNES—All the wheat, 21*li.*; all the barley, 21*li.*; all the peas, 3*li.*; all the hay, 5*li.* 10*s.*; 2 skreens, 2 fans, 13 sacks, 1 bushell, 3 shovels, with forks, rakes, & other utensils of husbandry, 3*li.*

IN THE CORNE CHAMBER—1 querne, 2 dewrakes, and other things, 2*li.* 8s.

22 acres of wheat upon the ground, 28*li.*; 17 acres of barly land, 12*li.*; all the hopp poles, 5*li.* 10*s.*
Debts good & bad, 40*li.* 5*s.*
Wearing cloathes & mony in his purse, 5*li.*
Summe—296*li.* 9*s.* 3*d.*
[Appraisers—Abraham Melbank, Simon Burrell.]
[Exhibited 30 December 1693, by Catharine Hudson, widow and administratrix.]

173.—Richard Clary of Writtle, yeoman. 14 February 1693/4.

IN THE HALL—One longe table, one forme, one little table, one ould pres cubbard, & one cubbard cloth, one salt boxe, 3 candle sticks, one jacke, 1 payer of bellowes, 1 payer of tonges, fire shovell, one payer of cupp cobirons, 7 chaires, one boxe of drawers, one shooeing iron, 4 weed hookes, one bench borde, & one houre glasse, one seaven pound weight & jacke chaine, 1*li.* 12*s.* 6*d.*; 4 flitches of bacon, & one peace of bacon, 2*li.* 14*s.*

IN THE PARLOR—One joynt bedsteadle, curtaines, rodds, matt & corde, one feather bed, one feather boulster, & one pillow, one flock boulster, & one straw bed, one coverlid, & 2 blanketts, 3*li.* 14*s.*; one longe table & 6 joynt stooles, one wicker chaire, one other rush chaire, 1*li.*; 2 livery cubbert tables, 8 glass bottles, one casting shovell, 6*s.*

IN THE PARLOR CLOSSETT—3 little shelves, 3 little vessells, 4*s.* 6*d.*

IN THE DARY—One little table, one forme, one cheese press, one milk stann, one charne & staffe, 6 shelves, 6 cheese motes, 5 cheese breds, 3 milke pann, 2 trayes, one hand dish, one friing pann, 2 sieves, 5 potts, one pann, & other impliments, and one butter baskett, 1*li.* 6*s.* 6*d.*

IN THE LITTLE BUTTERRY—One hogsed, 4 shelves, 5 potts, one firkin, and other small implyments, 8*s.*

IN THE GREAT BUTTERRY—Two hodgseds, one stall, one tunnell, one hopp sive, two tap hoses; one [*sic*] 4 dishes, & 1 dosen of trenchers, 12*s.*

IN THE KITTCHIN—7 tubbs, one swill tubb, one hogsed, & 2 stalls, one meash rule, 1*li.* 8*s.*; 3 pailes, one flaskett, one kneding troffe and forme, 6*s.* 6*d.*; one pottige pott & pott hookes, 3 skillittes, one kettle, 2 brass leads, and one oven lidd, 2*li.* 13*s.*

IN THE CHAMBER OVER THE KITCHIN—One bedsteadle, cord & matt, one flock bed, 2 boulsters, one feather pillow, 2 blanketts, 1 coverlid, & one payer of sheets, 1*li.* 10*s.*; one flock bed, one boulster, one pillow, 2 blanketts, 1 coverlid, and one payer of sheetts, 18*s.*

IN THE GARRETT—One ould hutch, 2 ginn pulles, and gable, one malt quarne, and plow timber, one sithe, 1*li.*

In the chamber over the hall—Two trundle bedsteadles & cords, 8*s.*; one press cubbard, 2 hutches, two chaires, two basketts, one ould trunke, tow little boxes, one settle, halfe a side of leather, 1*li.*; 4 payer of sheetts, 2 napkinns, 2 pillowbers, 2 towells, 2 table clothes, and another clothe, 1*li.*

In the chamber over the parlor—Tenn bushells of tears, 1*li.* 6*s.*; 5 sickells, one ridle, one plonke, & a persell of ould iron, 10*s.*; thirteen bushells of peason, 2*li.*

In the best chamber—Three payer of sheett, 3 pillow beers, 2 napkinns, & a little bag, 17*s.*; one bedsteadle, with curtaines, valliants, rodds and matt, one feather bed, 2 feather pillows, one feather boulster, one flock boulster, 2 blanketts, & one rugg, 4*li.*; one table, 4 stooles, one hand dish, 3 boulds, 2 dishes, another hand dish, one payer of scales, one pye peal, one wooden pessell, one chopping block, 8 trenchers, one pessell & morter, one stone judge [jug], 2 cream potts, 5 other potts, & one oile bottle, one nutmeg grater, one cheese racke, & one candle sticke, & boxe, 18*s.*; one mustard quarte [*sic*], one powdering tubb, 2 meale barrells, 1 little kimnell, 3 chairs, one pannill with gurts & foott stoole, 2 little boxes, one livery cubbert, one tray, one forme, 2 seives, one baskett, one flex wheell, 1*li.*; one worming pan, one fire shovell, one chafeing dish, one little payer of cobirons, one cup cobiron, one pease hooke, 2 hey forks, one hatchet, & 2 peeces of iron, 7*s.*; one hodgsed, & 1 stall, & another hodgsed, & 2 shelves, 9*s.*

In the little kitchin—4 skilletts, 1 kettle, 1 scummer, 1 brass pott, 1 pott lid, 13*s.*; one payer of irons to keep the fire up, 2*s.* 6*d.*; 3 tubbs, 1 coule, 1 empty caske, & one hand boule, 8*s.* 6*d.*; one keep, 2 hoggs troffes, one block, 2 coopes, one wheel, one longe [and] one shorte forme, 3 bords, & 2 stalls, 10*s.*; one matthak, one spade, one peckaxe, one grubing axe, one bill, & one forke, & one timber chaine, 15*s.*

In the stable—5 horses, 14*li.*; collerrs, haltors, & harnis both for plow & carte for one team being 2 setts and one pannill, 2*li.* 5*s.*; one shovell, 1 dung forke, 1 forke, 1 corne hutch, 2 chafe sives, 1 sead cobb, and one sive, 7*s.*

In the barne—6 seam of wheat, 18*li.*; 4 seam of barly, 5*li.* 4*s.*; 2 fanns, 2 sives, 2 forkes, a caving sive, 1 casting shovill, one bushell, & a ½ bushell, 2 rakes, 14*s.*

In the little barne—2 seam of peason, 2*li.* 12*s.*; one scrue, one ladder, 6*s.*; the hey, 6*li.*; the chafe, 5*s.*

In the carte house—2 plowes with shares, couluters, chaines and whipple trees, 1*li.*; 5 harrows, 1*li.* 5*s.*; the carrage, 1*li.*; the lode carte, 6*li.* 10*s.*; one waggon, 5*li.*; 2 dungcartes, one payer of wheells, 4*li.*; the ropes, & ladder, & winchpinns, 7*s.*

In the yarde—3 cribbs, one gate, one hoggs-trofe, 14 sacks, one racke, & 2 cows tyings, 2*li.* 5*s.*; one cribb, 2*s.*; 8 hoggs, 4*li.* 13*s.*; 17 sheep, 5*li.* 2*s.*; 3 cows, 12*li.*; one heffer, 2*li.*; 2 yearelinge budds, 2*li.* 7*s.* 6*d.*; one quarter of barly, & 2 bushells of tears, 1*li.* 11*s.*

IN THE FEILDS—16 acers of wheat, 40*li.*; 14 acers of peason, 12*li.* 12*s.*; 13 acers of barly land, 13*li.*

Ye Tottal—200*li.* 4*s.* 6*d.*
[Appraisers—John Arnold (of Chelmsford), Thomas Stoaks (of Ingatestone).]
[Exhibited 17 March 1693/4.]

174.—Abraham Brecknocke of Roxwell, yeoman. 15 February 1693/4.

IN THE HALL—One long table with dormers, a forme, a small table, six rush chaires, a joyned chaire, two small hanging cubbords, two glass shelves, foure spitts, a chaffing dish, a paire of cobirons, fire shovell & tongs, a paire of tramells, two gridirons, a box iron, a brass sconce, a small parcell of bookes, a brass candlestick, some little earthen ware, and several other implements there & in the closett, 3*li.* 15*s.*

IN THE PARLOR—A long table, six joyned stooles, a forme, foure chaires, a livery cubbord, a small glass shelfe, an old little table, a pair of cobirons, & other little matters, 2*li.* 10*s.*

IN THE BUTTERIES & ENTRY—Three hogsheads, a drinke stall, another hogshead, a halfe hogshead, a drinke stall, three iron wedges, foure wimbles, two hand bills, a hand saw, two axes, & other carpentry tooles, two sives, two long sawes, a large tunnell, two leather bottles, a copper drinking pott, two old iron dripping panns, a wine hogshead, another barrell, a paire of garden sheeres, two pillions, a butter baskett, with the shelves & severall other implements there & in the entry, 4*li.* 10*s.* 6*d.*

IN THE STRONG BEERE BUTTERY—One hogshead, three halfe hogsheads, a barrell, a drinke stall, a small old table, two other small drinke stalls, 3 shelves, two potts of butter, 3 of snett & grease, bottles, potts, panns, & other little matters, 2*li.* 19*s.*

IN THE KITCHIN—One old table, an old turne spitt jack, an iron peele, a dresser board, a bench board, two formes, 4 shelves, 2 paire of tramells, two brass brewing panns, three brass kettles, three brass porridge potts, an old iron one, seaven brasse skilletts, a brass scumer, a copper sawce pann, a cleaver, a brass mortar & pestle, a warming pann, a brass frying pann, a paire of iron racks, mattocks, spades, iron punch, wooden dishes, trenchers, drinke potts & pitchers, & severall other implements & matters there, 6*li.* 8*s.*

IN THE MALTHOUSE & KILNE HOUSE—One large mashing tubb, two stalls, six other tubbs, one old large tubb, one longe trough, two kneading troughs, two meale sives, a sider press, an old barrell, a malt quarne, three sythes with their kilter, & severall other matters, & lumber there, 4*li.* 10*s.*

IN THE DAYRY—One cheese presse, seaven cheese mootes, a cheese bread, two milke stands, two chernes, two cheese tubbs, five kimnells, two trayes, a poudring tubb, three great butter potts, a small weighing beame & scoale boards, six shelves, potts, panns, & severall other implements there, 3*li.* 10*s.*

IN THE HALL CHAMBER—One large feather bedd, two feather bolsters, two blanketts & coverletts, an old suite of curtaines & valens, with a bedstead & appurtenances to it, a large presse cubbord, a little table, two truncks, one chest, a joyned box, a paire of cobirons, a fire shovell, a curtaine for the window, & rodds, & other small matters there, 7*li.*

IN THE CHAMBER OVER THE ENTRY—One feather bedd & feather bolster, a coverlett, two blanketts, a boarded bedstead, & some other matters, 3*li.* 10*s.*

IN THE CHAMBER OVER THE STRONG BEERE BUTTERY—One feather bedd, a feather bolster, an old pillow, two coverletts, one blankett, an old bedstead, valens & curtaines, matt & cord, a chest, & two small stooles, 4*li.* 10*s.*

IN THE CHAMBER OVER THE SMALL BEERE BUTTERIES—A boarded bedstead, a trundle bedstead, one flock bedd, one old feather bedd, two flock bolsters, a coverlett, & two old blanketts, 1*li.* 15*s.*

IN THE CORNE CHAMBER—A parcell of barly of aboute seaven quarters, 10*li.*; a parcell of pease & beany corne of about 4 quarters; about 3 bushells of bullimong, aboute a quarter of tares, & aboute 4 bushells of ridlings of pease, 7*li.*

IN THE CHEESE CHAMBER— Fifteene lead of cheese, shelves, cheese boards, & an old box with leather in it, 9*li.*

IN THE STABLE, BARNES & OUTHOUSES—Two gelt horses, six horse collars, foure paire of cart harness, six pair of plow harness, two cart saddles, two paire of thill bells, foure bitt halters, an old saddle, a new pannell, two barlings, & severall other implements there, 7*li.*

Eight & thirty sheepe & lambs, 13*li.* 5*s.*; six large sheats or store piggs, 4*li.* 16*s.*; one waggon, two dung carts, & an old cart body, 13*li.* 10*s.*; tenn cowes, 42*li.* 10*s.*; wheate in the straw of aboute seaven quarters (as supposed), 22*li.* 8*s.*; a parcell of barly in the straw, in the chaffe, & in sackes of aboute six quarters, 9*li.*; bullimung in the straw about five quarters, 5*li.*; three quarters & two bushells of pease in sacks in the barne, 4*li.* 6*s.* 8*d.*; the hay in the outhouses & on a stack, 12*li.*; two plowes with their furniture, two paire of harrowes, one dew-rake, 2 hoggs tubbs, two ladders, 2*li.*; fifteene corne sacks, 1*li.*; two fanns, a corne skrew, a casting shovell with a bushell measure, pitchforkes, rakes, cart ropes, seed peck, & other implements & tooles of husbandry, 1*li.* 1*s.*; a parcell of chaffe, 10*s.*

In pewter—Forty pound weight, & a halfe of new pewter, 1*li.* 13*s.* 9*d.*; twenty pound weight, & a halfe of old pewter, 10*s.* 3*d.*

An iron weighing beame, scoall boards & weights, 1*li.*

In linnen—Twelve paire of sheetes, six pillowbeeres, six table cloathes, fifteene napkins, & six towells, 6*li.* 2*s.*

Thirteene acres & a halfe of barly land fallow, 13*li.* 10*s.*; seaventeene acres of land sowne with wheate, 29*li.* 16*s.*; six acres of land sowne with pease, 3*li.* 10*s.*

Thirty quarters of malt att Edward Turnidge's, 45*li.*; nineteene quarters of barly att Mr. Boosey's of Spurriers, 27*li.* 11*s.*

His wearing apparell, 6*li.*

In good debts oweing to him, 11*li.* 3*s.*; more in good debts oweing to him, 23*li.* 5*s.*

In ready monies in his purse, 80*li.* 19*s.*

A silver spoone, 8*s*.
Totall Sume is—453*li.* 12*s.* 2*d.* [should be 459*li.* 12*s.* 2*d.*].
[Appraisers—Mathew Nightingale, Henry Bright.]
[Exhibited 10 March 1693/4, by John Brecknock, administrator.]

175.—William Maggett of Writtle. 21 May 1694.

IN THE HALL—One longe table, one longe forme, one press cubard, one leather chaire, one 2 armed chaire, & 2 ould rush chaires, one little table, one dripping pan, spitt, one payer of cobirons, fire shovell & tonges, & one payer of bellowes, one salt boxe, one basteing ladle, one watering pott, with other small implyments, 1*li.* 1*s.* 6*d.*

IN THE BREW HOUSE—One lead, one meashing tubb, & 5 other tubbs, 1*li.*

IN THE BUTTERY—One kettle, 2 pottige potts with pott hookes, 2 pewter dishes, 1 skillett, 2 pasty panns, one hodgsed with 2 small vessells, a persell of earthen ware, & other implyments, & one fryin pan, 15*s.* 6*d.*

IN THE PARLOR—One bedsteadle with curtaines and rodds, one feather bed, one flock boulster, one trundle bedsteadle, 4 hutches, 2 tables, 2 joynt stooles, 2 warming panns, one powdering tubb, & 2 vessells, 5 pewter dishes, one pewter flaggon, one candlestick, one pewter cupp, 6 pewter spoones, & other implyments, 3*li.* 10*s.*; 5 payer of sheetts, 6 napkinns, 3 pillow bears, 3 table clothes, 1*li.* 5*s.*

IN THE CHAMBER OVER THE HALL—One bedsteadle with curtaines and valliants & rodds, one feather bed, two feather boulsters, with corde & matt, one rugg, 2 huttches, 2 tables, 1 forme, 1*li.* 7*s.* 6*d.*
Wareing apperrell & money in his pockett, 10*s.*
[Total]—9*li.* 9*s.* 6*d.*
[Appraisers—Edmund Butler, John Cooke.]
[Exhibited 16 June 1694.]

176.—John Crush of Roxwell. 14 June 1694. See Plate XI.

IN THE PARLOR CHAMBER—One bedsted, mat and cord, one trundle bedsted, 5 stript curtains and valiens, and curtaine rods, one feather bed, two boulsters, two pillows, three blankets, one ruge, one old feather pillow, 5 chests, and one box, three cushens, one chayer, two [illegible], 5*li.*

IN THE MAIDS CHAMBER—One feather boulster, two pillows, two trussells, 8*s.*

IN THE HALL CHAMBER—One bedsteed, a payer of greene curtains with rods, one trundle bedsted, one hutch, fouer payer of sheets, three table cloaths, six napkins, one siluer spoone, one looking glasse, two shurts, fiue pillowbers, fouer hankhers, fiue neckcloaths, 2*li.* 7*s.*

IN THE PARLOR—One bedsted, mat, cord and curtin rods, fiue stript curtings and valiens, two feather beds, one boulstr, two blankets, one couerlid, two tables, two stools, two carpets, one cubbord cloath, one press cubbord, one cort cubberd and cloath, one payer of curtin rods, one fire shouell, a payer of tongs, one chaier, one drinkstale, 5*li.*

IN THE MENS CHAMBER—One bedsted and flock bed, one pillow, fouer blankets, 14*s*.

IN THE HALL—Two tables, fouer forms, two joyne stools, one cubbord, two chayers, three cushions, a payer of cobirons, one forke, one fire pan, one paier of tonges, one jack, one wayt, two spitts, one warmin pan, two tramils, one hower glase and frame, and one skreen, 3*li.* 5*s*.

IN THE DRINK BUTREY—Two half hogsheads, one hanging shelf, one berestall, 8*s*.

IN THE SMALL BEERE BUTTREY—Two kettels, one skillit, one poridg pot, one dripping pan, a resting eiorn, 9 pewter dishes, fouer small pewter candle sticks, one frying pan, 2*li.* 9*s*.

Tenn bookes, 5*s*.
His wearing apparell and money in his purse, 1*li.* 16*s*.
Sum totall is—21*li.* 12*s*.
[Appraisers—Kellam Browne, Edward Boggas.]
[Exhibited 16 June 1694.]

177.—Joseph Westwood of Writtle, yeoman. 12 November 1694.

IN THE HALL—One long tables, 3 formes, one joined chaire, 6 other chaires, one smale cubbert, one jack, one round table, 2 cobbirons, fire shovell and tongs, one tramell, and bellowes, one brase chafindish, 2 fowling peeces, a box of drawers, a persell of books, and some other smale things, 3*li.* 17*s*. 6*d*.

IN THE PARLOUR—One bedsted with curtains and valliants, one coverlid, 2 blankets, one trundle bedsted, one featherbed, one flockbed, one feather bolster, 2 flock bolsters, one chest, 2 joined stools, with other smale things, 4*li.*

IN THE KITCHIN—2 brase coppers, 3 skillets, one kettle, 3 spitts, 2 dripping pans, one paire of cobbirons, fire pan and tongs, one tramell, 2 warming pans, and some earthen ware, 4*li.* 16*s*. 8*d*.

IN THE SMALE BEERE BUTTREE—4 hogsheads, one drinkestall, and the breewing tubs, and 2 leather bottles, 3*li.* 5*s*.

IN THE STRONG BEERE BUTTREE—4 barell and one drinkestall, one greate trough, 20 pewter dishes, one still, one duzen of plates, one pewter flaggon, one bedpan with some other smalle pewter, 2 duzen of trenchers, half a firkin of sope, with some other smale things, 6*li.* 12*s*. 2*d*.

IN THE DARY—One cheeseprese, 2 churnes, one stand, with the other milke vessells, 8 cheese moots, some earthenpotts, 8 shelves, one prese cubberd, one powdering tub, one flowr tub, 2 brase potts, one iron pot, 2 kettles, 2 skillets, 4 brase candle stiks, a brase cullender, with other smale things, 4*li.* 8*s*. 8*d*.

IN THE CHAMBER OVER THE HALL AND THE PARLOUR—2 bedsteads with curtains and valliants, 2 featherbeds, one flock bed, 4 feather bollsters, 2 coverlids, 6 blankets, 2 chest of drawers, one round table, one hanging prese, 6 leather chaires, 4 other chaires, 2 stooles, 3 paire of cobirons, one fire shovell and tongs, and bellows, one lookeing glase, one clocke, 17*li.* 6*s*. 2*d*.

In linin—8 paire of flaxen sheets, 8 paire of other sheets, 4 table cloathes, 3 dozen of napkins, 8 paire of pillowbeers, 3 cubbert cloathes, 3 corse table cloathes, 8 towells, 6 window curtains, 14*li.* 13*s.* 10*d.*

Two silver cupps, one silver porringer, four silver spoones, 4*li.* 15*s.*

IN THE CHAMBER OVER KITCHIN—One bedsted, curtains and valliants, one feather bed, one flock bed, one rugg, 2 blankets, one feather bolster, one flock boulster, one trundle bed, one flock bed, one coverlid, one blanket, one bolster, 6 paire of pillows, one prese cubberd, 3 joined chests, one other chest, one trunke, one settle, 7*li.* 8*s.* 10*d.*

IN THE FOLK CHAMBER—One bedsted, one trundle bedsted, one flock bed and boulster, one coberlid and blanket, one liverey cubbert, one settle, 18*s.* 8*d.*

IN THE CHEESE CHAMBER—90 cheeses, one meale trough, one kneading trough, one table, 4 shelves, 2 horse baskets, 2 skep baskets, a persell of hops, 6*li.* 10*s.* 10*d.*

Wheate in the barne and granary, 52*li.* 10*s.*; a stack of oats, 11*li.* 10*s.*; 16 sacks, one bushell, one fan, one shovell, one wire sive, one skreene, 2*li.* 15*s.*; two stacks of hay, 10*li.*

IN THE COWHOUSE—One malt quarne and cow tying, 1*li.*

IN THE CARTHOUSE—One waggon, 2 dungcarts, 12*li.*; one plow, one paire of harrows, 16*s.*

IN THE STABLE—4 horse, one mare, one colt, 11*li.* 10*s.*; the harnesse, collers and halters, 1*li.* 6*s.* 8*d.*

Six cowes, 19*li.* 10*s.*; 27 sheep, 9*li.*; one sow, and eight piggs, some old hop polls, 8*li.*
10 accres of wheate of fallow land, 16*li.* 16*s.* 8*d.*; 2 accres of etche wheate, 3*li.* 1*s.* 4*d.*; 8 accres of barley land, 6*li.* 13*s.* 4*d.*
Wareing cloaths and money in his pocket, 5*li.*
One beame and weights, spade and shovells, and other implements of husbandry, 2*li.* 3*s.* 4*d.*
[Total]—252*li.* 5*s.* 8*d.*
[Appraisers—William Boosey, Isaac Reeve.]
[Exhibited 5 July 1695, by Priscilla Westwood *alias* Reeve, widow and executrix.]

178.—Joseph Taverner of Writtle, butcher, 6 March 1694/5.

IN THE HALL—One little table, 2 leather chaires, fire shovell and tongs, one little chest without a cover, 2 shelves, with some other things, 5*s.*

IN THE PARLOUR—One old bedstead, a featherbed, two boulsters and one pillowe, two blanketts, and an old rugg, curtains & valence, one chest, & a box, 2 paire of sheets, 3 shirts, 3 capps, 3 neckcloths, one handkercheif, some wearing apparell, 1*li.*

IN THE BUTTERY—2 little vessels, a pannell & girt, an old bridle, a scraue, and earthen pan, 5*s.*

IN THE SHOP—A block, a hogs trough, a chaff sieve, & skillett, a warming pan, & some other lumber, 2*s*. 6*d*.

IN THE YARD—Foure geese & one gander, 10*s*.

In ready mony, 8*li*. 0*s*. 6*d*.; debts good and bad, 19*s*. 8*d*.
[Total]—11*li*. 2*s*. 8*d*.
[Appraisers—Thomas Bickner, Thomas May.]
[Exhibited 26 March 1694/5.]
[Also a copy on parchment not quite so detailed as that given above.]

179.—Thomas Dowset of Writtle, yeoman. 6 April 1696.

IN THE HALL—Won great bible, won longe table, won old pres cupboard with other odd implements, £1 10*s*.

IN THE PERLOR—Won feather bed, bedstead, table, & 2 or 3 old chairs, £2 10*s*.

IN THE BUTTERY—4 barrells, & bear stall, 10*s*.

IN THE DARY—& old chees press, chirn, stand, & milk pans, 5*s*.

IN THE CHAMBER OVER THE HALL—Won bed & bedstead, hutch, & trunke, with a little table, £2; won flock bed, & a old hutch, 5*s*.

IN THE CHAMBER OVER THE PERLOR—2 old [torn away], & old flock bed, & other odd implements, £1.

6 acres of oats, £6; 8 acres of wheat, £12; 3 acres of barley, £3; & old wagon & cart.; 4 [?]horss, £2.
A plow & harrows, 10*s*.; old harness & halters, 10*s*.
2 little cows, £4; 2 pigs, 10*s*.; 2 sheep, 10*s*.
[Total]—£39 10*s*.
[Appraisers—Joseph Springham, William Claxee.]
[Exhibited 4 June 1696, by Rebena Dowsett, widow and administratrix.]

180.—John Lord of Writtle, yeoman. 28 July 1696.

IN THE HALL—One longe table, one forme, one little table, 6 chaires, 5 spitts, 2 dripping panns, one salt boxe, one jacke, waite and lines, one boxe of drawers, 2 boxe irons, 2 heeters, 2 cobirons, one payer of tonges, one fire shovell, one cole dish, one gridgiron, one payer of trammells, one candle boxe, one fl[ou]er boxe, one payer of bellows, 3 candle sticks, and 10 little bookes, 1*li* 15*s*. 6*d*.

IN THE GREATT PARLOR—One longe table, one forme, one novill [oval] table, one little table, one forme, 6 leather chaires, one 2 armed chaire, 5 rush chaires, one payer of cobirons with greatt bras heads, one little payer of cobirons with bras heads, one payer of bellows, fire shovell & tonges, one little looking glass, one clock & waits and lines, 2 window curtaines, 3*li*. 7*s*. 6*d*.

IN THE BEST CHAMBER—One longe table, one forme, one novill table, 3 chaires, 2 cushinns, one greatt chest, one baskett, 2 window curtains, one bedsteadle with curtains, valliants, and rods, one feather bed, one flocke bed, one matt, one cord, 2 blanketts, one rugg, one boulster, 5*li*. 2*s*. 6*d*.

IN THE LITTLE CHAMBER OVER THE GREATT PARLOR—One bedsteadle, one feather bed, one blankett, one coverlid, one cole rack, one wicker chaier, 2 greatt basketts, 1*li.* 5*s.*

IN THE CHAMBER OVER THE HALL—One bedsteadle with curtaines and vallyants and rodds, one feather bed, one strawe bed, one blankett, one coverlid, 2 boulsters, one pillow, one trundle bed, one ould feather bed, 2 boulsters, one blankett, one coverlid, 4 huttches, and one joynt stoole, 2*li.* 10*s.*

IN THE CHAMBER OVER THE SELLER—One bedsteadle with curtaines, vailiants and rodds, one feather bed, one flock bed, one straw bed, 2 boulsters, 1 blankett, and one coverlid, one trundle bed, one feather bed, one straw bed, one boulster, 4 chaires, chests, one trunck, one longe table, one little table, 2 boxes, one payer of cobirons, with other small implyments, 3*li.* 10*s.*

The linnen—13 payer of sheetts, 6 payer of pillobers, 6 table clothes, 3 dosen ½ of napkinns, 6 towells, 7*li.* 10*s.*

IN THE LITTLE PARLOR—One longe table, 2 formes, one chaire, one press cubbard, 2 hallburds, & one trevett, 1*li.*

IN THE SHOPP—One ould bedsteadle, one flock bed, one blankett and coverlid, one bushell, one tubb, 2 sacks, one forme, and a little wooll, 12*s.*

IN THE PANTRE AND SMALL BUTTERRY—One barrill and stall, one powdering tub, one worming pan, 4 skillitts, 4 kettles, one pottige pott, and one iron pott, one payer of scales & weitts, one frying pan, one forme, 1*li.* 10*s.*

The pewter—dishs, plates, flaggons, other messers, 2*li.* 8*s.* 8*d.*

IN THE SELLER—8 hodgseds & 4 full of bear, one little barrill, 2 little tubbs, one tunnell, one leather bottle, 4 bear stalls, 1 dos: ½ bottles, 3 tillders, 10*li.*

IN THE BREWHOUSE—Two coppers, one meashing tubb, tap hose, one troffe, one working tubb, a cooller, 7 tubbs, a kneeding troffe, 6*li.*

IN THE YARDS—2 mares, 2 coults, 5*li.*; 20 shepp and lambs, 5*li.*; one ould waggon & dungcarte, 2*li.* 10*s.*; one load of hey, 1*li.*; horses, harnis, sadle and pannill, brigle an halters, 10*s.*; 6 piggs, 3*li.*; 2 hoggs troffes, 1*s.* 6*d.*

4 acers of wheat and rye, 3 acers of peasons, beans & oatts, 21*li.*
His wareing apperrell and mony in pockett, 3*li.*
[Total]—87*li.* 12*s.* 8*d.*
[Appraisers—John Hurrell, Richard Bridges.]
[Exhibited 21 December 1696, by Elizabeth Lord, widow.]

181.—Richard Bridges of Writtle. [1698.]

Hogs & piggs, £3 16*s.*; wheat, £19 10*s.*; wrye, £9 12*s.*; nine cows, £36; cauls, £4; score of drey sheep, £8 10*s.*; cuppels of sheep & lambs, £2 10*s.*; six horses, £15; horses, plow harnes, & cart harnes, £3 10*s.*; wagen, & carts, & plowes, & harrows, & ladders, £15 10*s.*; quarne, & weges, & mateck, & dewracke, £1 10*s.*; bushels, & fanns, & screen, & forks, & rackes, & sackes, £2.

Fourteene akers of wheat, £49; 27 akers of wrye, £40; seven akers of barly, £20; tenn akers of oates, £10; five akers of gras, £5.
Chichen and deary, £6.

HALL AND THE CLOSETT THAT BELONGS TO THE HALL, £3 10*s*.
PALLER, £2 10*s*.
SMALL BEERE BUTTERY, £1 10*s*.
STRONG BEERE BUTTERY, £2 15*s*.
THE MENS CHAMBER, £1 10*s*.
TWO ROUMS & THE CHEES CHAMBER, £12.
HALL CHAMBER, £3 10*s*.
THE BEST CHAMBER, £10

The linen, £6.
[Total]—£294 13*s*.
[Appraisers—John Sturgun, Isaac Sapsford. Exhibited 18 June 1698.]

182.—Thomas Bright of Roxwell. 2 June 1698.

IN THE HALL—Two old tables, two old formes, a jack, a paire of cobirons, & other the fire irons & other small matters, with a glass shelfe & some chaires, 1*li.*

IN THE PARLOR & CLOSETT—Two old tables, eight leather chaires, a paire of cobirons, & other small matters there, 1*li.*

IN THE HALL CHAMBER & CLOSETT—An old bedstead with the bedd & all that belongs to it, a press cubbord, five chests, a parcell of books, & other small things there, & an old clocke, 3*li.* 5*s*.

IN THE PARLOR CHAMBER—An old bedstead, two feather bedds, bolsters, & pillowes & other furniture to it, an old chest, & other small things, with a wicker chaire, 5*li.*

IN THE DAYRY & BUTTERY—A cheese press, a milke stand, & other vessells & things belonging to that office, with two hogsheads, 1*li.* 10*s*.

IN THE KITCHIN & BREWHOUSE—Two leads, three troughs, six tubbs, fire irons, & other old lumber & things there, 3*li.*

IN THE BUTTERY CHAMBER & GARRETT—An old bedstead, a feather bedd, bolster, & other furniture to it, an old chest, & other lumber there, 1*li.* 5*s*.

IN THE CHEESE CHAMBER—The cheese boards, powdring trough, & other small things there, 10*s*.

Holland & damask linnen (whereof his sister Taverner has already her halfe part), 3*li.*; the rest of the linnen, 2*li.*
Pewter & brass, 4*li.*
In plate—Five silver spoons, 1*li.* 5*s*.
His wearing apparell, & mony by him, 30*li.*

WITHOUT DORES & IN THE FEILDS—A parcell of wheate & barly, 15*li.*; one gelt horse, 3*li.*; a long cart, a dung cart, plowes, harrowes, a malt quarne, plow harness, & cart harness, corne skreen, shovells, spades, & other inplements & tooles of husbandry, 7*li.*; foureteen couple of sheepe & lambs, & 11 weathers, 11*li.*; two hoggs, 1*li.* 10*s*.; seaven cowes & a bull, 20*li.*

Five acres of groweing wheate & barly, & three acres of pease, 11*li.* 10*s.*
Total—125*li.* 15*s.*
[Appraisers—Thomas Sandford, Richard Woolfe.]
[Exhibited 18 June 1698.]

183.—Christopher Perry. 16 June 1698. [Died 10 May 1698.]

IN THE HALL—One table, one cubord, two formes, and two chayres, 10*s.*

IN THE KITCHING—Seaven pewter dishes, two spits, one dripping pan, fire shovell & tongs, one settle, five chaires, and other implements, 1*li.*

IN THE DARRY—One cheese-presse, five cheese mots, one stand, one chorne, two tunnils, and other nessessarys, 1*li.* 10*s.*

IN THE PANTRY—Two kitls, one porride pot, two skillits, and other small things, 1*li.* 10*s.*

IN THE BUTTERY—One halfe hogshead, two barrils, 10*s.*

IN THE BREWHOUSE—One copper, one meashing tub, & two other tubs, one mault quarn, 1*li.* 10*s.*

IN THE CHAMBER OVER THE KITCHIN—One fether bed, bedstead & the furniture, one table, one trunke, 3*li.*

IN THE CHAMBER OVER THE BUTTERY—One fether bed, & bedstead, with the furniture, 5*li.*

IN THE CHAMBER OVER THE DARRY—One flock bed, & bedstead, with other furniture, one table, on hutch, 1*li.* 10*s.*

The lininge, 2*li.* 10*s.*
Two cows, 5*li.*
His wearing close & monny in his pockit, 5*li.*
[Total]—28*li.* 10*s.*
[Appraisers—John Robinson, Zachary Browne. Exhibited 18 June 1698.]

184.—Thomas White. 30 June 1698.

IN THE HALL—Tow cubbords, tow tabells, 6 chairs, on form, tow paire of coberns, on gune, 3 spits, a worming pan, & sum small emplyments, 1*li.* 12*s.*

IN THE PALLERE—A feathere bed, tow bollsteres, tow pillow, on coverlid, on blankett, curtins & vallints, a hanging prees, tow chairs, on old chest, a small tabell, 2*li.* 13*s.*

IN THE BUTTERY—Tow halfe hogsheads, tow killderkins, tow stands, 4 small tub, on milck lead, tow kettells & a peice of one, 3 littell skillits, on porrig pot, & on old pot, a frying pan, 4 small peautere dichess, 3*li.*

IN THE CHAMBER OVER THE HALL—On feathere bed, on bollstere, tow blan-ckets, a small coverlid, tow chest, on form, a ging [joined] chaire, & other emplyments, 2*li.* 10*s.*

IN THE CHAMBER OVER THE PALLER—On sory bed, tow blankets, tow small chest, sum smale things, 1*li.*

IN THE BARN—On skrue, tow ridell, tow shuffells, on fan, on forke, on buchells, 10*s.*

IN THE STABELL—The collers, halters, harness, thibells, cart sadells, & small rops, 10*s.*

IN THE CART HOUSE—Tow old carts, on plow, on paire of harows, on dew racke, 2*li.* 10*s.*; on old horse, & a sory meare, 1*li.* 7*s.*; 6 sheep, & 6 sory lams, 2*li.*

4 or 5 paire of shetts with the rest of the lineine, 1*li.* 10*s.*
His waring cloaths & mony in his pocket, 1*li.*
Three akers & a halfe of wheat, 7*li.*; three akers of each wheat, 4*li.*; three akers & a halfe of barly, 5*li.*; tow akers & a halfe of peas, 3*li.* 10*s.*
The totall In all is—39*li.* 12*s.*
[Appraisers—Edward Jones, Daniel Hudson. Exhibited 19 April 1699.]

185.—John Aillett of Writtle, yeoman. 13 May 1699.

IN THE HALL—One long table, 2 little tables, and 2 formes, one press cubert, 5 chaires, 2 spitts, one iron dripping pan, 2 cobirons, fire pan and tongs, one fire fork, one tramell, with other small things, 2*li.* 5*s.*

IN THE CHAMBER OVER THE HALL—One joined bedsted, one trundle bedsted, one featherbed, one feather bollster, 2 blankets, one coverlid, curtains and valliants, one livery cubert, 2 tables, one joined chest, one glas case, 6 joined stooles, five chaires, one looking glass, 6*li.* 13*s.* 4*d.*

IN THE CHAMBER OVER THE DARY—3 old bedsteds, one featherbed, one flock bed, one old rug, one old coverlid, one joined chest, and three other chests, and 2 blanketts, 4*li.* 6*s.* 8*d.*

IN THE DARY—One cheese prese, one churne, one stand, 5 cheese moots, 2 brase kettles, 2 formes, shelves, and milk vesells, with some other smale things, 2*li.* 2*s.*

IN THE BUTTREE—One hogshead, 3 smaler vesells, two brass potts, 5 brass skilletts, 2 tubbs, one beerstall, one brass frying pan, with some other smale things, 4*li.* 2*s.* 6*d.*

IN THE KITCHIN—One brass copper, 5 brewing tubs, one kneading trough, one tub stall, and one tramell, 2 cobirons, scales and weights, with some other smale things, 4*li.* 1*s.* 6*d.*

IN THE CHEESE CHAMBER—Some cheesses, 2*li.* 5*s.*; one bottle, 6 wedges, and one saw, 12*s.*

IN THE BARNE—16 bushells of ry, 3*li.*; one load cart, 5*li.* 10*s.*; one bushell, one fan, forks, sacks, and one shovell, 13*s.* 4*d.*

IN THE STABLE—2 mares, collers, and harnes, 6*li.* 10*s.*; one plow, one paire of harrows, 13*s.* 4*d.*

IN THE YARDS—Four cows, 14*li.* 10*s.*; and three hoggs, 2*li.* 6*s.* 8*d.*

IN THE FIELDS—5 accres of wheate and ry, 12*li.* 10*s.*; 2 accres of barley, 3*li.* 15*s.*; 2 accres and a half of oats, 2*li.* 5*s.*; three sheep and three lambs,

1*li.* 6*s.* 8*d.*; one accre and a half of follow at Chelmsford, 1*li.* 1*s.*; 6 accres of follow at home, 3*li.* 12*s.*

Six paire of sheets, 2 paire of pillowbeers, and some other smale linin, 3*li.* 6*s.* 8*d.*

Twelve pewter dishes, one plate, one candlestick, 1*li.* 6*s.* 8*d.*
Wearing apparell and money in his purse, 2*li.* 10*s.*
[Total]—91*li.* 4*s.* 4*d.*
[Appraisers—William Boosey, Isaac Reeve.]
[Exhibited 12 August 1699, by Sara Aylett, administratrix.]

186.—John Lingood of Roxwell. 30 September 1699.

IN THE HALL—One long table, 2 formes, 4 chayres, one presse cupbard, one perror of tramells, one peory of cobirons, with others implements, 18*s.* 6*d.*

IN THE PARLOUR—One bed, one bedstead and all things belongin to it, 4 old hutches, one little table, one trunell bed, 2 blankets, one coverlid, £3 10*s.*

IN THE BUTTERY—3 barrells, 3 tobs, 2 old kittls, and other small things, £1 5*s.*

IN THE CHAMBER OVR THE HALL—One floke bed, bedstide, 2 old blankets, 2 hutches, 6 [torn away] puter diches, 4 perrer of sheettes, £1 2*s.* 6*d.*

A little moue of barly aboute 10 seme, £13.
7 akeres of fallo, £7; 3 horsses, £5 10*s.*; 2 hogges, £1 15*s.*; one old cart, one donk cart, plou and harrowes, £3 17*s.* 6*d.*; one sheepe, 2 lames, 12*s.*
Mony in his purse and wearing cloathes, 19*s.*
The sume totall is—£39 9*s.* [should be £39 9*s.* 6*d.*]
[Appraisers—Matthew Nightingale, Isaac Reeve.]
[Exhibited 9 October 1700, by Joseph Lingood, son and executor.]

187.—John Flacke of Roxwell. 27 April 1700.

IN THE HALL—One long table and frame, one forme, one little table, one press cupbord, five rush chayers, one payer of cobirons, fier shovel and tongs, one payer of bellows, one gridiron, one spit, and other smale things, 1*li.* 7*s.*

IN THE BREWHOUSE—One brass lead, six tubbs, one hoggshead, one tunell, and other smale things, 3*li.* 5*s.*

IN THE BOUTING HOUSE—One kneading trough, two brass potts, five brass kettles, two skillets, one frying pan, one barrell, one cheese press, two cheese mouts, fouer puter dishes, and other smale things, 4*li.*

IN THE MILKEHOUSE—Three milke bouls, one butter cherne, one stand, one barrell, three formes, and other small things, 1*li.*

IN THE CHAMBER OVER THE HALL—One beadsted, one fether badd, two fether boulsters, one rugg, one blanket, curtins and valiants, one trundle bedsted, one flock bed, two hutches, two boxes, one joynt stoole, 5*li.*

Fouer payer of sheets, one table cloath, 1*li.* 10*s.*

IN THE CHAMBER OVER THE PARLOR—Two hoggsheads, one barrell, one drinke stale, one payer of horss baskets, one roape, one payer of winch pinns, six little cheeses, one flitch of bacon, and other smale things, *2li.*

One logg beetle, five wedges, one chaine, 14*s.* 9*d.*; fouerteene bushels of wheat, 3*li.* 3*s.*; three quaters fouer bushels of malt, 4*li.* 11*s.*; fouer bushels of pease, 16*s.*; five bushels of oats, 8*s.* 9*d.*; fouer bushels of barly, 12*s.* 9*d.*

IN THE STABLE—Three horses, with their furniture for plow and carte, 7*li.* 10*s.*; one waggon, one long cart, two dung carts, one ould payer of wheeles, two payer of harrows, one plow with the iron worke, two dive rakes, 11*li.* 12*s.*; one malt quarne, 1*li.*; two cows, 4*li.* 15*s.*; fouer piggs, 1*li.* 14*s.*; eleven sheep, 3*li.* 17*s.*; one bushel, ten sacks, one skreene, two casting shovells, one riddle, one fann, forks, and raks, 1*li.* 7*s.*

Corne groing upon the land with the plowing and seed, twelve acers and three roods of wheat, 19*li.* 14*s.* 6*d.*; eaight acers of barly, 13*li.* 4*s.*; seven acers and halfe of pease, 5*li.* 8*s.* 9*d.*; two acers of oats, 1*li.* 14*s.*; for the rent of the land, 11*li.* 8*s.*; for plowing twelve acers of land one tillt, 2*li.* 8*s.*
Cutting and making up the wood in the yarde, 3*s.*
Nine hundred of hay, 18*s.*
His waring appariell and mony in his purss, 2*li.* 10*s.*
Sum Totall—117*li.* 11*s.* 6*d.*
[Appraisers—Matthew Nightingall, Thomas Reeve.]
[Exhibited 9 October 1700, by William Flacke, son and administrator.]

188.—Richard Maggett of Writtle, tailor. 31 October 1700.

IN THE HALL—One long table and forme, two little tables, four chayers, a glascase, 9*s.*; one kneading trough, one salt box, a half peck, three spitts, two dripping panns, two beef forks, a slice, a shreding knife, five candlesticks, two puding pans, an olde cubbord, two smothing irons, a cleaver, a warming pan, a pestle and morter, an hower glass, two dozin of trenchers, two pewter dishes, a pint measure, on quarter measure, two porrengers, a flower box, a pepper box, three hayforks, three hoes, a sithe, a payer of tramels, two cobirons, two payer of tongs, a fire shovell, a peele, a gridiron, 1*li.* 0*s.* 6*d.*

IN THE PARLOR—One press cubbord, one table, two joyn stools, one feather bed, one bedsted with curtains, two blankets, one huch, one livery cubbord, with other impliments, 1*li.* 15*s.*

IN THE CHAMBER OVER THE HALL—3 rundlets, one to hand [two-handled] saw, one bed and bedsted with the furniture thereunto belonging, one table, one chaier, one stand, one sithe, and cilter, 2*li.* 16*s.* 6*d.*

IN THE CHAMBER OVER THE SHOP—One bed and furniture, one hutch, 1*li.*

IN THE CHAMBER OVER THE PARLOR—One table cloath, three napkins, fouer payer of sheets, two olde huches, one trunke, and a screen, 1*li.* 12*s.*

IN THE SHOP—One livery cubord, two chests, three barls [barrels], a drink stall, four shovels, with other impliments, 15*s.*

In the butery—Two half hogsheads, a drink stall, two skillits, a little kettell, a skimer, a frying pan, two porridg pots, two sives, a boule, a cowle, a water pot, a bottle, and other implements, 1*li.*

In the kitchen—One littell brass lead, two kettls, scals and weights and beame, seven little tubbs, two pails, a sider press and forme, a shovel, a spade, one fann, two cobirons, a paier of tramels, a pitch pan, and other implements, 2*li.* 19*s.* 6*d.*

In the yard—One wheele barrow, a short lader, six planks, one old plow, a grindstone, and a sheep rack, 10*s.*

In book debts good and bad, 25*li.* 18*s.* 6*d.*
Sume is—39*li.* 16*s.*
[Appraisers—John Glascock, John Cooper.]
[Exhibited 27 December 1700, by Elizabeth Maggett, widow and administratrix. Also a copy on parchment.]

189.—Zachariah Day of Roxwell, blacksmith. 22 January 1705.

In the hall—One ovell table, six rush chaires, three hanging cubbords, a couch, a dresser, and form, a turn spitt jack, three driping pans, three spits, two beefe forkes, two shreding knives, a bras candle stick, and four iron candle stiks, one tin pasty pan, two druging boxes, a candle box, a morter and pessle, a cobiron, two creepers, a fire iron, a paire of bellows, fire shovell and tongs, two paire of tramels, a gridiron, a chaffin dish, a small percell of books, and some other small matters there, 4*li.* 1*s.* 3*d.*

In the parlor—One feather bedd, two feather bolsters, one pillow, three blankets, a quilt, a sute of curtaines and valence, a chest of drawers, one small ovell table, six rush chaires, a huch, three boxes, a small looking glase, a warmeing pan, and window curtaines there, 7*li.* 5*s.*

In the chamber over the parlor—A bedsted, a bolster, two pillows, a trunk, and ten cheeses, 1*li.* 1*s.* 9*d.*

In the chamber over the hall—Two feather beds, two feather bolsters, two blankets, a rugg, with curtains and valence, four huches, two chaires, with some other small impliments, 5*li.* 15*s.*

In the strong beere buttery—Three halfe hogsheads, a drink stall, seven flitches of backon in salt, a powdering tub, two brass boylers, a cheese press, two formes, four small tining pans, a culinder, three small trayes, and a few glass bottles, and some other small matters, 7*li.* 11*s.* 9*d.*

In the small beere buttery—Three hogsheads, a drink stall, an iron poridge pott, three brass kettles, six skillets, three brass ladles, a sauce pan, a suit [suet] strainer, an old wormeing pan, a scumer, a brass frieing pan, with poridge dish, trenchers, and other small matters, 3*li.* 10*s.*

Eaighteen pewter dishes and a duzen of plates, 2*li.* 12*s.*
Linnen about the house—Ten paire of sheets, foure paire of pillow beeres, a diaper table cloth, a duzen of diaper napkins and other table linen, with some towels, and a little other small linen, 5*li.* 5*s.*

IN THE BREWHOUSE & BAKE HOUSE—A brass brewing pan, two kittles, a mashing tub, eaight other tubs, a stall, a kneading trough, and meale tub, and three sives, with some other small matters, 4*li.* 13*s.*

IN THE CHAMBER OVER THE BUTTERIES—One feather bedd, two bolsters, and a coverlet, 2*li.* 1*s.* 6*d.*

IN THE BARNE—Three quarters and a halfe of wheate, 3*li.* 10*s.*; a quarter and a half of beanes, 1*li.* 7*s.* 6*d.*; three quarters of oates, 1*li.* 16*s.*; a bushell, six sacks, a screen and fan, two shovels, a caveing sive, two rakes, and two forks, 18*s.*; three load of hay, 3*li.*; a load cart, and wheele barow, 2*li.* 2*s.* 6*d.*

Sixteen store sheep, 3*li.* 10*s.*; two store hoggs, 1*li.* 4*s.*
Six acers of wheate groweing, 12*li.*
The stock in the shopp, 30*li.*; in booke debts, 25*li.* 5*s.* 6*d.*
His wareing aparell and money in his purse, 10*li.*
Summe Totall is—138*li.* 9*s.* 9*d.*
[Appraisers—John Bricknock, John Asser.]

190.—Elizabeth Eree of Writtle, widow. 6 March 1705/6.

IN THE HALL—One longe table, six joyned stooles, one table leafe, a press cupboard & falling table att the end and earthen ware upon the cupbords heads, a livery table, an old skreene, a glasscase with the implements, a joyned forme, four old chaires, three spitts, three paire of pothooks, four paire of cobirons, two trammells and iron barr, a fender, a gridiron, a paire of bellows, & other implements, 2*li.* 10*s.*

IN THE PARLOUR—One bedstead, curtaines, valents and rods, one feather bed and bolster and pillow, a paire of blankets, one rugg, bedmatt and cords, one press cupboard, a livery table, a falling table, two glasscases and implements, two looking glasses, two chaires, two stooles, one paire of bellows, and a candle box, & other implements, three window curtaines, & two rodds, 4*li.* 12*s.* 6*d.*

IN THE GREAT BUTTREY—Three beere vessells, two beerestalls, one table, one swill tub, and other wooden & earthen ware, one brass copper, two brass kettles, a bras pann, and two bras pottage potts, a brass cullender, a skimmer, a warming pan, a coale dish, three skilletts, two ladles, a brass potlid, a brass scone, one iron dripping pan, an iron pott & potthooke, one lanthorne, three tinn pans, & other implements, 3*li.* 3*s.* 10*d.*

IN THE LITTLE BUTTREY—Nine pewter dishes, one pewter bason, two plates, two porringers, two saucers, seaven pewter spoones, two pewter tankards, two pewter candlesticks, a candle cup, a flagon, a pewter cup, two salts, one frying pan, halfe a dozen plate trenchers, a drink stall, one powdring tub, earthen ware, & other implements, 1*li.* 1*s.* 7*d.*

IN THE CHAMBER OVER THE PARLOUR—One feather bed, bolster and pillow, one blankett, one rugg, one quilt, one bedsted, curtaines, valents and rods, one table, two joyned stooles, two chaires, two large chests, two trunks, three boxes, one cabinett, 4*li.* 18*s.*

In the midle chamber—Three large chests, a nest of drawers, one armed chaire, and other odd things, 6*s.* 4*d.*

In the little chamber—A trundle bedsted, a straw bed, a flock bolster, and two matts, a needing trough, and a long forme, and other lumber, 8*s.* 4*d.*

In the chamber over the hall—A paire of wooden scales and beame, a side bed, one sack, one bagg, a peck and a halfe peck, one old horse baskett, a paire of winch pins, and other odd things, 3*s.* 2*d.*

In the wood house—Three tubs, a tunnell, a ladder, and other lumber, 12*s.* 6*d.*

Linnen—three paire of sheets, fifteen napkins, & one table cloth, 1*li.* 17*s.* 6*d.*
Wearing apparrell and ready money, 2*li.*
The totall sume is—21*li.* 13*s.* 9*d.*
[Appraisers—Christopher Lingard, John Hubbard.]

191.—Richard Fuller of Writtle. 16 July 1706.

In the first chamber—One bed with furniture, two tables, four chaires, one looking glass, ij*li.* xv*s.* vj*d.*

In the second chamber—Bed and bedstead, with two old truncks, 1*li.* xvj*s.*

In the third chamber—One bed, one trunck, a cheese rack, 1*li.* 1*s.* vj*d.*

In the parlour—One bed, one table, one glass, one glasscase, four chaires, 1*li.* xv*s.* vj*d.*

In the hall—Six pewter dishes, six plates, two porringers, four shelves, twelve chests, two tables, one forme, four chaires, two stooles, a paire of racks, fire shovell and tongs, two trammills, two skilletts, one gridiron, one frying pan, three kettles, three spits, one dripping pan, one candle case, three candle sticks, one warming pan, one keve, one wheele, one cullinder, iiij*li.* viij*s.* v*d.*

In the buttery—Four vessells, four tubbs, one pottage pott, one funnill, a beere stall, ij*li.* vi*s.*

In the dairy—One cheese press, one churne, six milk panns, three cheese moults, one stand, xiij*s.*

Four cowes, vj*li;* thirteen sheep, ij*li.* ij*s.* iiij*d.*; two hoggs, 1*li.* xij*s.* vj*d.*
One cart, cart sadle, collar and fillbells, and cart roape & halter, 1*li.* xv*s.*
An acre of wheate, iij*li.*; an acre of pease, ij*li.*; for hay, iiij*li.*

In the cowhouse—Two forks, two rakes, two spades, one shovell, one mattack, pickax, and other od things, xij*s.* vj*d.*

Purse and apparrell, vij*li.*
Summa totalis—xlij*li.* xviij*s.* iij*d.*
[Appraisers—William Mandur, William Fuller.]
[Written on stamped parchment.]

192.—Henry Bright of Roxwell, yeoman. 15 April 1707.

IN THE HALL—A square table, one ovall table, an elbow chair, eight turky worked chairs, a couch, a pair of brass cobirons, and a pair of creepers, one tramell, a pair of bellows, fire shovell and tongs, with some other small matters, £3 5*s*.

IN THE PARLOUR—One long table, two formes, six leather chairs, one elbow chair, a pair of cobirons, with a few glass bottles, £1 5*s*. 6*d*.

IN THE HALL CHAMBER—One feather bed, a feather bolster, two pillows, two blanketts, a rug, curtain and vallens, a chest of drawers, one hutch, a trunk, with six leather chairs, and some other small matters, £4 1*s*. 9*d*.

IN THE PARLOR CHAMBER—Forty six cheeses, two tressles, four shelves, and a reel, £2 13*s*. 6*d*.; a clock, £1 10*s*.

IN THE CHAMBER OVER THE BUTTERYS—A feather bed, two feather bolsters, two blanketts, a pillow, rugg and coverlett, a bedstead, curtains and vallence, a side bed, three chests, a hutch, two boxes, a small looking glass, three window curtains and rods, with other small implements, £3 5*s*. 8*d*.

IN THE CHAMBER OVER THE KITCHIN—Two feather beds, three bolsters, three blanketts, two coverletts, bedsteads, curtains and vallens, a pair of cobirons, with some other odd things, £2 15*s*.

IN THE GARRETT—A feather bed, one bolster, three blanketts, a trundle bedstead, a pillion and cloth, and an old jack, £1 5*s*. 3*d*.

IN THE KITCHIN—One ovall table, a little square table, a press cupboard, five rush chairs, a brass pott, five brass kettles, four skilletts, a turne spitt jack, four spitts, two dripping panns, a scummer, a ladle, and slice, a cleaver, two shreding knives, a beefe fork, a morter and pestle, a warming pann, a tinn pasty pann, a tin pudding pann, three candlesticks, two pott irons, two pair of cobirons, fire shovell and tongs, a birding peece, porridge dishes and trenchers, with a small parcell of books, £7 4*s*. 9*d*.

IN THE STRONG BEER BUTTERY—Three half hogsheads, a barrell and drink stall, seventeen pewter dishes, a dozen of plates, two pewter candlesticks, two pie plates, a pair of stilliards, with some small implements, £5 17*s*. 6*d*.

IN THE SMALL BEER BUTTERY—Three hogsheads, a half hogshead, and a barrill, two drink stalls, a tunnell, a pair of winch pinns, £1 10*s*.

IN THE DAIRY—A cheese press, a cheese tubb, and milk stand, two churnes, six milk trayes, and six cheese moots, three cheese breds, seven butter potts, a frying pann, two porridge potts, a powdering tubb, three small bowles, two doxen of trenchars, with nine shelves, and some small earthen ware, £3 10*s*. 10*d*.

IN THE BREWHOUSE—Two coppers, a mashing tubb, with ten other tubbs, a kneading trough, and meale tub, a pair of garden sheers, three lives [*sic*], with some other small implements [no value given].

Linnen about the house—One pair of Holland sheets, four pair of flaxen sheets, five pair of other sheets, five pair of pillowbeers, a dammask table cloth, eight dammask napkins, two diaper tablecloths and eighteen diaper napkins, seven course table cloths, and sixteen course napkins, with towells, and some other small linnen, £10 16*s*. 6*d*.

IN THE MAULT HOUSE—A cisterne, a screen, a beetle and wedges, a hop-pitch, a crow, three spades, shovells, mattocks, bills, sawes, forkes, racks, with some other odd tools belonging to husbandry, and twenty corn sacks, £4 10*s*.

IN THE CORN CHAMBER—Three quarterns [*sic*] of oats, a quartern [*sic*] and an half of barley, and two old tubs, £3 8*s*. 6*d*.

IN THE BARNE—Eight quarters of wheate in sacks, 12 quarters in the straw as supposed, £20; a screen, bushell, and fann, with some other working tooles, 15*s*.

IN THE YARD, STABLE, HAYHOUSE & GROUND—Five cows & two calves, £13 5*s*.; four sheets or store piggs, £2 12*s*.; sixteen store sheep, £4 16*s*.; three load of hay, £4 10*s*.; cart harness, collers & plow harness with there furniture and what belongs to them, bridles, saddles, and odd things in the stable, £2 10*s*.; a malt quarne, £1 10*s*.

IN AND ABOUT THE COWHOUSE & CARTHOUS—A waggon, a load cart, two dung carts, boddyes, a wheele barrow, a plow, two pair of harrows, three ladders, £14 6*s*. 6*d*.

Eight acres of wheate growing, £9 12*s*.; eight acres of barley, £9 19*s*.; three acres of pease, £1 13*s*.; four acres of pease & oats, £2 10*s*.; one acre & half of white oats, 17*s*. 6*d*.; ten acres of fallow one tilt, £2.
His wearing apparell and money in his purse, £10.
Summa totalis—£157 5*s*. 9*d*.
[Appraisers—Richard Browne, John Asser. Exhibited 5 June 1707.]

193.—Robert Hilliard of Writtle, yeoman. 28 April 1708.

IN THE HALL—One long table, 4 joynt stools, 5 chaires rush ones, 1 payer of tongs, one fire shovell, 2 cobirons, one salt box, one payer of bellows, one chaffing dish, one warming pann, 2 spitts, one payer of tongs, one grid-iron, one clever, one lock iron, one pudding pann, one pessell and morter, 4 candle sticks, one glas casse, one candle sticke, one iron peall with small implyments, 1*li*.

IN THE BREWHOUSE AND BUTTERY—One copper, 2 pottig potts, 4 skillitt, one frying pann, two bras kettles, one hodgsed, one halfe hodgsed & two killderkinns, one flower tubb, one kneeding troff, and six brewing tubbs, one cullender, 3 sieves, two leather bottles, one lanthorne, dishes, and spoomes, with some eathen ware, one scummer, one dosen trenchers, 5*li*. 13*s*.

IN THE DARY—Two churns, one stann, two cimnills, one tray, 4 chees mootts, 3 payls, one payer of butter scales and waits, one cheese pres with smoe [*sic*], milke panns, and other eathenware, 1*li*. 0*s*. 6*d*.

IN THE PARLOR—One beadsteadle, with curtains and valliants and rodds, one feather bead, two boulsters, two pillows, 3 blanketts, and a curverlid, chaires, one huttch, one table, and window curtains, 5*li*. 15*s*.

All the pewter, 10*s*.

IN THE HALL CHAMBER—One bedsteadle, with curtains and vallyants and rods, one feather bed, two boulsters, one pillow, 3 blanketts, and a curverlid, one chaire, 3 hutches, 3 boxes, one forme, and matt and corde, 4*li.*

IN THE PARLOR CHAMBER—One halfe headed bedsteadle, one flock bed, one boulster, one blankett, one curverlid, one table, one pillion and cloth, one sithe, two sickles, 1*li.* 12*s.*

All the linnenn, 1*li.* 10*s.*

IN STABLE—Three payer of plow harnis, one payer of body harnis, 3 bitt halters, 3 hemping halters, one payer of thill bells, and one cart sadle, and three collers, one bridle, and one pannill, one shovell, one chaf sive, 10*s.*

IN THE BARNE—One fann, one bushell, one shovell, one flaie, 4 forke, and 4 rakes, & four sacks, 9*s.*

IN THE CART HOUSE—One waggon, one dungcarte, one payer of harrows, one plow, two ladders, one mattak, two axes, two bills, one spade, one beadle & wedges, 9*li.*

IN THE YARD—4 cows and two calves, 9*li.*; 2 horses and a coult, 4*li.*; 15 sheep and 13 lambs, 3*li.* 15*s.*; 2 sows, 1*li.*

6 acres of wheatt, 7*li.*; 4 acres of barly, 8*li.*; 6 acres of oatts, 6*li.*
Wareing appearrell and mony in pockett, 1*li.*
The Sum Totall—70*li.* 17*s.* [should be 70*li.* 14*s.* 6*d.*].
[Appraisers—Laurance Hilliard, William Clary (or Claree).]

194.—Henry Mansfeild of Roxwell, yeoman. 17 June 1708.

IN THE HALL—2 wheels, one kittle, one malt quarn, 2 small tubbs, one chair, one joyned stoole, with other things, 2*li.* 7*s.*

IN THE PARLOUR—One long table, 6 joyned stooles, one small table, 8 chairs, one press cupboard, 4 pewter dishes, one bed-pan, one pewter salt, one payer of cobirons, a payer of tongs, with other things, 2*li.* 16*s.*

IN THE OLD PARLOUR—2 dew rakes, one riddle, one sythe, 7*s.* 6*d.*

IN THE STRONG BEER BUTTERY—2 halfe hogs heads, one barrell, one kimnel, 14*s.*

IN THE PARLOUR CHAMBER—One feather bed, 2 blankets, 1 bolster, 2 pillows, one bedsted with curtains and valens, one livery cupboard, 4*li.*

IN THE MATTED CHAMBER—One bedsted with curtains & valens, 12*s.*

IN THE MAIDS CHAMBER—One feather bed, one bolster, one pillow, one blanket, one rugge, one bedsted, 2*li.* 10*s.*

IN THE KITCHIN CHAMBER—2 feather beds, 2 bolsters, 2 pillows, 5 blankets, one bedsted, one hutch, one box, 2 chairs, one joyned stoole, 6*li.* 10*s.*

IN THE MENS CHAMBER—2 flock beds, 3 blankets, 3 bolsters, 2 bedsteds, 3*li.* 2*s.*

IN THE KITCHING—One long table, 1 forme, 6 chairs, 1 joyned stoole, one payer of stilyerds, 1 jack, 2 spitts, 1 dripin pan, 1 pasty pan, 1 lock iron, 4 small pewter dishes and other small pewter, 2 kittles, 3 skillets, 1 payer of brasse scales, 1 gun, 1 payer of cobirons, 1 payer of tramels, one brasse pott, with other things, *3li.* 13*s.* 6*d.*

IN THE SMALL BEER BUTTERY—4 hoggs heads, 3 leather bottles, 1*li.* 11*s.*

IN THE MILK HOUSE—2 churns, 1 cheese press, 1 stand, 1 cheese tubb, one leaden vessell, 2 keelers, 1 tray, 1 powdering tubb, 8 cream potts, 6 cheese moots, 4 pails, with other things, 2*li.* 8*s.* 6*d.*

IN THE BREWHOUSE—One copper, six tubbs, 3*li.* 2*s.*

IN THE MEALE HOUSE—1 kneading trough, 2 sieves, 1 linin wheele, 1 reele, 7*s.*

IN THE CORN CHAMBER—1 screen, 2 fanns, 1 bushell, 20 sacks, 6 forks, 7 rakes, 6 pease hoocks, 3 shovels, 1 spade, 1 logg-beetle & wedges, with other things, 3*li.* 3*s.*

IN THE STABLE—6 horses and all their furniture, 20*li.*

IN THE HAY BARN—1 waggon, 1 cart body, 1 chain, 8*li.*

IN THE CART HOUSE—2 dung carts, 2 plows, 2 pair of harrows, 4*li.* 10*s.*

7 hogs, 4*li.* 11*s.*; 66 sheepe and lambs, 12*li.*; 33 drye sheepe, 9*li.*; all the wooll, 15*s.*; 8 cows, 26*li.*; 1 cow & calfe sold for 2*li.* 19*s.*
23 acres of wheat upon the ground, 51*li.* 15*s.*; 22 acres of barley, 44*li.*; 24 acres of pease & oates, 33*li.*; 14 acres of grasse, 14*li.*
All the linin, 3*li.* 7*s.* 6*d.*
Wearing clothes and money in his purse, 5*li.*
51 acres of fallowe, 53*li.* 11*s.*
Total—329*li.* 12*s.* [Appraisers—John Crush, Thomas Ellis.]

195.—Thomas Robjant of Writtle. 5 August 1708.

IN THE HALL—One long table, & cub[ert], & two small tabls, an form, & four small puter dishes, four puter poringers, one spit, with some other small things, 1*li.* 2*s.* 6*d.*

IN THE PALLER—One fether bed, & bolster, with curtins an valents, one samll [*sic*] table, three chars, two hutches, & [bed]stetel, coverlid, one blanket, & other small things, 2*li.*

IN THE DARY—Three kettell, one churnn, a chese press, one stan, a boilling pot, fring pann, and other small things there unto belonging, 1*li.* 6*s.* 8*d.*

IN THE BUTTRE—Four small vessells, a drink stall, an other small things, 10*s.*

IN THE KITCHIN—One coper, one neading trough, four small tubs, with other small thing, 14*s.*

IN THE CHAMBER OVER THE PALLER—Two old beds, & stedle, couerlids, an two blankets, one old chest, & linin, 2*li.*

IN THE CHAMBER OVER BUTRY—One old table, one floc bed, and a [?]setall, old lumber, 10*s.*

For the hay, 2*li.*

IN THE STABLE—One mare, an colt, with panell, an harnis, & other metearlls thereunto belonging, 3*li.* 5*s.*

IN THE CART HOUS—One old cart, an plow, 10*s.*

IN THE YARD—Three cows, forteen sheep and lambs, two pigs, 6*li.* 10*s.*
The corn upon the grownd, 4*li.* 10*s.*
His wareng aprill and mony in his pockett, 1*li.* 10*s.*
[Total]—26*li.* 8*s.* 2*d.* [Appraisers—John Baker, Laurance Robjant.]

196.—Joseph Herridge of Writtle. 8 August 1709.

IN THE STABLE—Four hors, £10.

IN THE YARD—Five cows, twnty two shep, £16 18*s.*

IN THE HOGSTY—Seven hogs, £3 10*s.*

IN THE FIELD—One plow, two payer of harows, 15*s.*

Fiften acears of whete upon the grond, £26 5*s.*; fourten acers of follow for barley, £14.

IN THE HALL—Two tabels, on cubord, two forms, five chayars, a payer of belles, with other emplyments, £1 2*s.* 6*d.*

IN THE GREAT PALER—One bed, two cubord, two tables, six chayares, with other empliments, £5 3*s.*

IN THE LITTLE PALER—On bed, one cbbord, two hutches, with other empliment, £2 10*s.*

IN THE BEST BEAR BUTARY—Four haf hogsed, and bear stalls, 16*s.*

IN THE SMALL BEAR BUTAREY—Fouar hogsed, two bear stalls, £1 2*s.*

IN THE DAREY—Two cetles, four skilits, one potedg pot, four puter dishes, one ches pres, one chirm, two celers, with other empliments, £1 10*s.*

IN THE BRUHOUS—Two copars, one meshin tub, three little tubs, two payls, £2 1*s.*

IN THE CHAMBERS—Two bed, one hutch, £2 5*s.*

Waring aparill, mony in the pockits, £1 5*s.*
One bible, 2*s.* 6*d.*
[Total]—£89 5*s.* [Appraisers—John Banistor, William Green.]

197.—John Nash of Roxwell. 20 January 1712/13.

His pockett money and waring cloathes, £iiij xv*s.*
9 acres of follow and for the rent of the land & sowing & seeding at £1 14*s.* per acre, £xv vj*s.*; for plowing 3 acres of each, xij*s.*
3 horses, & the harness in the stable, £vj; a wagon, & one plow, £v; 6 heaffers and two cowes, £xvj; 12 sheep and lambes, £iij x*s.*
Seven seame wheat, £x; 3 seame of barley, £ij xj*s.*

IN THE KITCHEN AND THE BREWHOUSE—One lead, 2 tubes, & other old lumber, £ij.

IN THE HALL—A long table, 3 spitts, & some pewter and other furniture, £ij j*s*.

IN THE PALAR—One bed, 1 chest, and a table, some linen, & other small things, £iij ij*s*.

IN THE SMALL BEER BUTTERY—2 vessells, brass, and other lumber, £j xiij*s*.

IN THE DARY—One churne, & stand, & a powdering tub, and other small things, 17*s*.

IN OTHER BUTTERY—3 vessells, & other things, 9*s*.

IN THE CHAMBER OVER THE HALL—One table, 1 bed, and other small things, £j xviij*s*.

IN THE CHAMBER OVER THE PALAR—2 bedes, and other small things, £ij iij*s*.

IN THE SERVANTS CHAMBER—An old bed, iiij*s*. vj*d*.

6 sackes and a fane, xij*s*.
Summa totalis—£lxxviij xiij*s*. vj*d*.
[Appraisers—John Glascock, Alexander Perkinson. Witnesses—John Mason, Thomas Winley. Exhibited 7 February 1712/13.]

198.—Richard Brown of Horsefrith Park, Writtle, yeoman. 4 June 1713.

IN THE DAIRY—Two milk leads, six [?]lanndles, one churn, one milk stand, one powdering tubb, & other utensills belonging to the dairy, ij*lb*.

IN THE BREWHOUSE—Two small coppers, one mashing tub, one cooler, & other brewing utensills, v*lb*.

IN THE BACKHOUSE—One milk lead, one milk kimdle, one kettle, one cheese press, & other old lumber, ij*lb*.

IN THE CELLER—Eight hogsheads, & two half hogsheads, & drink salls, & some bottles, ij*lb*.v*s*.

IN THE SMALL BEER BUTTERY—Five old hogsheads, & stall, j*lb*.v*s*.

IN THE KITCHEN—One jack, two spitts, two tammells, cobirons, fire shovell & tongs & bellowes, one old cubbard, & seven rush bottom chaires, j*lb*.x*s*.

IN THE PARLOUR—Twelve cain chaires, two tables, one looking glass, two brass andirons, & two pair of window curtaines, ij*lb*.xv*s*.

IN THE PANTRY—Twelve pewter dishes, three dozen of plates, one table, & six old chaires, ij*lb*.x*s*.

IN THE HALL—One wanscoat table, & four joynt stooles, six leather chaires, one square table, one clock, & 2 andirons, ij*lb*.xij*s*.vj*d*.

IN THE CHAMBER OVER THE PARLOUR—One old bed & blancketts & other furniture thereunto belonging, one chest of drawers, seven cain chaires, two red chaires & couch, one small table, one pair of andirons, tongs & fire shovell, two pair of window curtaines & hanging of the roome, vj*lb*.

OVER THE PANTRY—One bed, bedstead, curtaines & vallens, boulsters, & blancketts, & coverlid, one square table, & looking glass, six black chaires, v*lb*.

IN THE GARRETT OVER THE HALL CHAMBER—One bed, bedstead, curtaines & vallens, blancketts, & coverlid, two small tables, & nine old red chaires, iiij*lb.*

IN THE CHEESE CHAMBER—All the cheese & rack, ij*lb.*x*s.*

IN THE CHAMBER OVER THE HALL—One bedstead, feather bed, curtains & vallens, blancketts, and coverlid, one chest of drawers, four old chaires, & hanging press, all the linnin & plate, x*lb.*

IN THE CHAMBER OVER THE SMALL BEER BUTTERY—Two bedsteads, one feather bed, curtains & vallens, blancketts, & coverlid, & one old chair, & one stoole, ij*lb.*

IN THE CHAMBER OVER THE KITCHEN—One bedstead, bed, curtaines & vallens, blancketts & coverlid, & two old chaires, j*lb.*

OVER THE DAIRY—One half headed bedstead, two flock beds, & blancketts, j*lb.*

OVER THE BREWHOUSE—A small parcell of wool, weights & scales, & an old kneading hutch, xij*s.*vj*d.*

Sheep & lambs thirty eight couple, xix*lb.*; forty cowes & calves, Cxx*lb.*; sixteen dry cowes & one bull, xxxviij*lb.*v*s.*; one sow & tenn piggs, v*lb.*; four horses & their furniture, xxxiiij*lb.*viij*s.*; four small horses, & plow harniss, and bridle, and sadle, xij*lb.*; one breeding mare & two colts, xij*lb.*
Mowing ground forty & eight acres, xxxvj*lb.*; six acres of wheat, xviij*lb.*; fourteen acres of barley, xiiij*lb.*; fourteen acres of bullemon, xxj*lb.*

IN THE CART HOUSE—Three dung carts, three waggons, three pair of harrowes, two ladders, one roole [roller], plowes & gears, & other implements belonging to husbandry, xxiiij*lb.*xvij*s.*vj*d.*

IN THE MALT HOUSE—All the malt, a screen, a bushell, & wire for the kiln, some sacks, rackes, forks, & other implements belonging to husbandry, xlj*lb.*xiiij*s.*

IN THE BARNE—All the wheat, one fan, rake, shovell, & riddles, viij*lb.*

AT FITHLERS—Thirty & seven sheep, xj*lb.*ij*s.*; twenty four fatting cattle & one bull, lvj*lb.*v*s.*; one field of wheat & barley twelve acres, xlij*lb.*; one feild of wheat, oates & barley fourteen acres, xxix*lb.*xv*s.*; two feilds of bullemon twelve acres, xv*lb.*; twenty seven acres of mowing ground, xx*lb.*v*s.*; a cock of old damaged hay, iiij*lb.*

In money & bonds, Mlxxxv*lb.*; debts sperate, lxx*lb.*x*s.*; debts desperate, xxix*lb.*xij*s.*vj*d.*
His wearing apparell and money in his purse, lij*lb.*
Summa totalis—MDCCClxxij*lb.*xiiij*s.* [should be 1873*li.* 14*s.*]
[Appraisers—Richard Alger, Samuel Shettleworth. Exhibited 10 July 1713.]

199.—John Battle of Roxwell, 18 July 1713.

IN THE HALL—One long table, a little table, two joind formes, and one old chair, 9*s.*

IN THE PARLOR—One old feather bead, a feather bolster, a blanket and coverlet, an old joind bead stead, a pres cuboard, a little table, and three little stools, 1*li.* 15*s.* 6*d.*

IN THE HALL CHAMBER—One old bead stead, one bolster, a blanket, old curtaines, valiants and rods, three joind stools, and an old cubboard, 13*s.* 9*d.*

IN THE KITCHEN—Two old tables, four old cairs, a jak, three spitts, a dripin pan, seven pewter dishes with other small matters, ax, fire shovell, tongs, cobirons, and belles, 1*li.* 9*s.* 4*d.*

IN THE CAMBER OVER THE KITCHEN—One old feather bead, a flock bead, three old blankets, two bolsters, two old bead steads, four hutches, with a small box, 2*li.* 2*s.* 6*d.*

IN THE CHAMBER OVER THE BRUE HOUSE—A flock bead, bolster, one blanket, an old rugg, with an old bead stead, 17*s.* 6*d.*

IN THE BREW HOUSE—A bruing copper, an old mashing tubb, four small tubs, three sickles, with sume other small matters, 1*li.* 19*s.* 9*d.*

IN THE DARY—Two churns, a milk stan, two small whay tubs, three bowls, two cheese moates, an old frying pan, with some small earthen ware, 14*s.* 4*d.*

IN THE BUTTERY—One hoghead, two halfe hogheads, a drink stall, two old porredg pots, four small skillets, a madog, spade, a shovell, an old saw, three wedges, with some other small matters there, 1*li.* 9*s.* 7*d.*

IN THE STABLE—Two old horsses, a mare, three paire of harness, four collers, three bitt holters, barlines, cart sadle, and thill bels, with some other small matters, 10*li.* 7*s.* 6*d.*

IN THE BARNE—A screen, fan, bushell, and shovell, 7*s.* 6*d.*

IN THE CART HOUSS—An old waggon, a paire of dung cart wheeles, a plow, and harrows, 3*li.* 15*s.* 7*d.*

Four cows, 10*li.* 5*s.*; sixteen sheep, 3*li.* 17*s.* 6*d.*; four store pigs, 1*li.* 1*s.*
Wheate upon the ground, 10*li.* 5*s.*
In linen—Six paire of sheets, three pillow beers, six napkins, with some other small linen, 1*li.* 11*s.* 9*d.*
Sume totallis—53*li.* 2*s.* 1*d.*
[Appraisers—John Brecknock, John Goold. Exhibited 9 [*sic*] July 1713.]

200.—Edmond Butler of Writtle. 26 November 1713.

All the goods in the shop and warehows, £114 2*s.* 3*d.*
All the goods in the hall, £3 10*s.*
All the goods in the parllor, £4.
All the goods in the kitchin, £5 14*s.*
All the goods in the seller, £1 5*s.*
All the goods in the brewhows, £5 18*s.*
All the goods in the brewhows chamber, £2 10*s.*
All the goods in the parllor chamber, £8 5*s.*
All the goods in the shop chamber, £6 10*s.*
All the linnen £5.

All the goods in the hall chamber, £5 16*s.*
All the goods in the kitchin chamber, £3 16*s.*
All the goods in the garrit, £1 15*s.*
All the wheat on the ground, £4.
One mare, £4.
Old timber [and w]ood, £4.
All the silver pleat, £8.
Bills, bonds, and book debts, £74.
Some totales—£262 1*s.* 3*d.*
[Appraisers—Nathaniel Hurrill, Edmond Butler. Exhibited 1 April 1714.]

201.—Henry Isaacson of Roxwell. 4 January 1713/4.

In the hall—A drawing table, a little table, a forme, two stools, two chairs, a jack, four spitts, a dripping pan, a pasty pan, a bell mettel morter and pessell, two candle sticks, a wormeing pan, one tramell, cobirons, fire shovell, tongs, and bellows, wtih some other small matters, 2*li.* 2*s.* 9*d.*

In the parlor—A feather bead, one bolster, two pillows, a blanket, a rugg, bead steadle, and rods with curtains and valiance, a little table, five leather chairs, a glass case, a byble, with some other small books, 6*li.*

In the parlor chamber—A feather bead, two bolsters, two pillows, two blankets, a bead steadle with old curtains, valiance and curtain rods, two leather chairs, a little ovall table, a side board table, with some other little matters, 2*li.* 1*s.* 6*d.*

In the hall chamber—A feather bead, one bolster, two blankets, a rugg, bead steadle with rods, an old chest of drawers, a trunck, two hutches, a little box, a looking glas, cobirons, fire shovell and tongs, 3*li.* 17*s.* 9*d.*

In the buttery chamber—Eleven bushells of wheate, eleven bushels of barly, eaight bushels of beans, two chairs, a pillion, with a small parcell of old iron, 6*li.* 4*s.* 5*d.*

In the butteries—One half hoghead, two cilder kins, two drink stalls, two old pres cuboards, a little brass boyler, an iron poredg pott, one iron kettle, two skillets, six trenchers, with some other small matters, 1*li.* 12*s.* 9*d.*

In the dary—A chees press, a churn, a stan, a chees tubb, two little forms, five shelvs, three chees moats, a milk kimell, a milk paill, three earthen dishes, with other small matters of earthen ware, 1*li.* 9*s.* 4*d.*

In the kitchen—A little bruing copper, a meashing tubb, two cowls, five other tubbs, a kneading trough, a meale tub, two sivs, a table, and form, a hand quarn, two spads, a shovell, a saw, three wedges, a maddog, one ax, a bill, a tramell and cobirons, with a small parcell of plow timber there, 4*li.* 3*s.* 6*d.*

In the barne—Ten bushells of pease, 1*li.* 5*s.*; oates in the chafe and in the strow about eaight quarters as supposed, 4*li.* 16s.; four bushells of barly, 11*s.*; a screen, a caveing sive, a ridle, fan, and casting shovell, forks, and rakes, an old bushell, and a half peck, 13*s.* 5*d.*

IN THE STABLE—An old mare, four collers, two pair of plow harness, two bitt halter, barlins, a panell, cart sadle, and thill bells, 1*li.* 9*s.* 6*d.*

IN THE CART HOUSE—A load cart, a pair of harows, and a plow with whiple trees and chains, 4*li.*

Two load and a halfe of hay, 3*li.* 2*s.* 6*d.*; one old cow, 1*li.* 10*s.*

Three acers a halfe sowne of wheate, 6*li.* 16*s.* 6*d.*; three acers a roode of barly land fallow, 3*li.* 7*s.* 6*d.*

Three brass kettles, 2*li.*; in peuter one hundred waite, 2*li.* 10*s.*

In linen—Two pair of Holland sheets, one pair of flaxen sheets, and two pair of cours sheets, two table cloaths, twenty four napkins, with some other small linen, 2*li.*

Sume totallis—61*li.* 11*s.* 5*d.* [should be 61*li.* 13*s.* 5*d.*].

[Appraisers—Richard Woolfe, Bartholomew Wright.]

202.—Isaac Day of Roxwell, blacksmith. 28 February 1715.

IN THE HALL—Two tables, seven rush chairs, two cuboards, a little box of drawers, a jack, two spitts, two gridirons, one beefe fork, three cobirons, a pair of tramells, fire shovells, and tongs, a cleaver, a salt box, a pair of bellows, three patty pans, a box iron, four sickles, and a clock, with some other small matters, 5*li.* 12*s.* 6*d.*

IN THE PARLOR—A feather bead, two feather bolsters, one pillow, a quilt, two blankets, curtains and valiance, curtain rods, and beadstead, a chest of drawers, an ovell table, ten rush chairs, a looking glass, with a small matter of earthen ware, 10*li.* 9*s.* 6*d.*

IN THE CHAMBER OVER THE HALL—A feather bead, two bolsters, a coverlet, two blankets, curtains and valiance, beadstead and curtaine rods, two hutches, a trunck, two boxes, a hanging press, a little parcell of nails, with some other small things, 5*li.* 15*s.* 9*d.*

IN THE PARLOR CHAMBER—A feather bead, a bolster, two blankets, and a beadstead, 2*li.* 3*s.*

IN THE CHAMBER OVER THE BUTTERY—One old feather bead, two bolsters, four blankets, an old beadstead, two chairs, 1*li.* 15*s.* 3*d.*

IN THE STRONG BEER BUTTERY—Two halfe hogsheads, a barell, and drink stall, a powdering tub, a porke tub, a duzen of trenchers, two duzen of glass bottles, and a little earthen ware, 18*s.* 7*d.*

IN THE SMALL BEERE BUTTERY—Three hogsheads, two old pails, a tunell, and drink stall, 1*li.* 12*s.*

IN THE BREWHOUSE AND BAKE-HOUSE—A brewing coper, a mashing tub, eaight other small tubs, a kneading trough, and meale tub, 8*li.* 5*s.*

IN THE BARNE—Three quarters of wheate, five quarters of barly, a fan, a shovell, two raks, two forks, and three sacks, 9*li.* 3*s.* 6*d.*

IN THE SHOP—One anvell, a pair of bellows, working tools, iron and coales, 13*li.* 10*s.*

In brass and pewter—Two poredg pots, four skillets, a frying pan, a warme-ing pan, eaight pewter dishes, a duzen of plats, two pewter poringers, and a salt, 4*li.* 7*s.* 6*d.*

An acer and halfe of wheate, & two acers and a halfe of barly land, 5*li.*
In linine—twelve pair of sheets, two pair of pillow beers, one table cloth, two duzen napkins, 6*li.*
Three silver spoons, 1*li.* 5*s.*
Sixteen sheep and lambs, 3*li.*
In booke debts, 69*li.* 6*s.* 9*d.*
His wareing apparell & money in purss, 10*li.*
Sume totall—158*li.* 4*s.* 4*d.*
[Appraisers—Richard Woolfe, Matthew Flack.]

203.—William Long of Roxwell. 12 December 1716.

IN THE HALL—4 chaires, 2 tables, and a morter, 2 spitts, a settle, and a cubbard, & 3 candlesticks, & a pott iron, & a tosseing iron, & a looking glass, and a paire of bellowes, & a pair of cobbirones, and other small implements, £2.

IN THE KITCHING—2 coppers, 2 kettles, and 2 bellmeatle pottage potts, & 3 skillets, £4; 50 pound of pewter at eight pence a pound, £1 13*s.* 4*d.*

IN THE BRUEHOUSE—1 meatching tubb, one long wort tubb, & one cheese tubb, 7 more small [*sic*] and 2 pailes, £2 2*s.*; a cheese press, 3*s.*

IN THE DARY—2 charnes, & 2 standes, & 6 cheese moates, & 3 milk cimmells, & 4 creame potts, and 2 paire of small scales and waites, £2 2*s.* 6*d.*; for 9 weages weighed 56 pound & a beatle, 14*s.* 9*d.*

IN THE PALAR—8 chaires, & 2 tables, and a paire of cobbirons, £1 17*s.*

IN THE BUTTERY—4 hodgsheades, & one tunnell, & one butter baskett, & a pillion, & a pillion cloath, £1 10*s.*

IN THE STRONG BEER BUTTERY—One hodgshead, & 2 halfe hodgsheads, and 2 barrels, & 2 pottage potts, and a frying pan, & a press cobbard, & a leather bottle, & another bottle, £1 15*s.*

IN THE CHAMBER OVER THE PALAR—One bed & bolster, & 2 pillars, & 3 blanketts, & a coverlide, and curtaines and vallin, £7 5*s.*; two tables & 3 chaires, 9*s.*

IN THE CHAMBER OVER THE BUTTERY—One bed and bedstead, & curtaines and vallin, & a coverlide, and two blanketts, & a bolster, & piller, £3.

IN THE CHAMBER OVER THE HALL—One bed and bedstead, & curtaines & vallin, & 2 blanketts, & a coverlide, and 3 hutches, & a fire shovel, and tonges, & a pair of cobbirons, £4 6*s.*

IN THE CHAMBER OVER THE ENTERY—One bed, & 2 blanketts, & bolster, & one flock bed, & coverlid, £2 12*s.* 6*d.*; 8 pair of towing sheets, £4; 3 pair of flexing sheets, £2 5*s.*; 4 paire of pillerbeers, 12*s.* 6*d.*; 4 bord cloaths, 16*s.*; a dozen of napkings, 6*s.*

IN THE SERVANTS CHAMBER—Two flocks & bolster, £1 5*s.*

IN THE CARTHOUSE—One wagon, & 2 dung carts, and 3 harrows, and one plow, £10 1*s.* 6*d.*

IN THE STABLE—4 horses, £18; collers, and harness, & a cart sadle, with halters & barlings, & 3 panneles, & a shovel, & a seed peck, £2.

IN THE BARN—A bushel, and a fane, & a fork, & 2 shovels, & a corn scrine, & a kuting knife, 13*s*.; 12 sackes, £1 4*s*.

12 cowes, £41; 3 haffers, £6; 8 piggs, £3; a fat hogg, £1 11*s*. 6*d*.; 30 Norfolks lambes, £6.
14 load of new hay, £21; a cock of old hay, £2.
15 acres of wheat on the grown, £27 15*s*.; 12 acres of barly follow, £12.
10 seame of wheat, £18; 11 seame of barley, £9 17*s*.; straw, 10*s*.
Cheese in the Chamber, £3; a mault quarne, & a worming pan, £1.
His wearing cloaths and pockett money, £5.
The Total is—£254 2*s*. 7*d*. [should be £234 6*s*. 7*d*.].
[Appraisers—Bartholomew Wright, Samuel Shettleworth.]
[Note that Patience was the widow of William Long.]

204.—Stephen Chalke of Roxwell. 18 June 1717.

IN THE HALL—Two tables, a clock, five chaiers, & other implyments, £2 5*s*.

IN THE PARLER—Three huches, two cuberds, a spening wheele, and other implyments, 15*s*.

IN THE DEARY—One kettel, one cheesepres, milke vessels, and other implyments, £2 5*s*.

IN THE MEALE HOUSE—One knedingtrof, a frying pan, one barrell, and other implyments, 10*s*.

IN THE BEUTTERY—Two hole hogeseds, & eight half hogeseds, and other implyments, £2 5*s*.

IN THE KICHING—Two tables, one coper, three chaires, two cobirons, fier shovel & tongs, a jack, six tubes, three kettles, fower skellets, fifteen peuter dishes, twelf pleats, and other implyments, £6 5*s*.

IN THE PARLER CHAMBER—One feether bed, curtins, valyants, two blankets, one chest of drauers, six chaiers, one table, two cobeirons, fier shovle & tongs, £4 5*s*.

IN THE HALL CHAMBER—One feether bed, one hanginpres, two huches, three chaiers, & other implyments, £1 10*s*.

IN THE KICHING CHAMBER—One feether bed, blankets & curtins, one trundle bed, two chaiers, one huch, one trunk, tenn paier of sheetes, two paier of pillowbeares, three tableclothes, and twelf napkins, £5.

IN THE SARVANTS CHAMBER—One flocke bed, 15*s*.

IN THE CORNE CHAMBER—Twelf sackes, two shovels, two forkes, one beetle, three weges, two spades, & one matehock, £1 10*s*.

IN THE STABLE—Six horsses, harnes, collers, halters, and all other implyments belonging to them, £12 3*s*. 6*d*.

IN THE MALT CHAMBER—About twenty quarters of malt, one skren, & other implyments, £19 7*s*. 6*d*.

IN THE CARTE HOUSE—One waggion, one long carte, two dunge cartes, one chain, two plowes, & a paier of harrowes, £12.

IN THE COWE HOUSE—Six cowes, £15 10*s.*

Thirty nine cupple of sheepe & lames, £17; five hoges, £3.
Twenty seven ackers & three roods of wheat, £70; twenty eight ackers & a half of barly, £63 7*s.* 6*d.*; fower ackers of pease & teares, £6; the plowing of forty three ackers of fallow the first tilte, & nine ackers the second tilte, £10.
Reddy money & warring aparill, £10.
[Appraisers—John Crush, Richard Alger. Exhibited 29 June 1717.]
Debts owing to the deceased—due from Richard Stockes, £6 18*s.*; John Umfrey, £5; William Beard, £1 10*s.*; Mr Batman, £3 1*s.*; John Neale, £1.
[Total]—£283 2*s.* 6*d.*

205.—Francis Allin of Roxwell. 1718.

THE BEST CHAMBER—A bedd & furniture, £3; two tables, 6*s.*; two chests & linnin therein, £2 5*s.*; five chaires, 1*s.* 8*d.*

THE HALL CHAMBER—One bedd, £1; 1 old table, 2 old chaires, 1 old trunck, 1 side cupborad, 6*s.*; 1 paire cobb irons, 1 fire pan, 1 paire toungs, 4*s.*

THE KITCHIN CHAMBER—2 old bedds, 15*s.*

THE GARRETT—1 old bed, 2*s.*

THE HALL—22 plates, 11*s.*; 11 dishes, 15*s.*; 2 chamber potts, 1*s.* 6*d.*; 9 flaggons, 9*s.*; 3 porringers, 1*s.*; 1 cy [*sic*] plate & bason, 2*s.*; 1 quarter & ½ quarter measure, 6*d.*; 2 pewter candlesticks, 1*s.*; 1 tinn candle box, 6*d.*; 3 Bibles, 5*s.*; 1 jack & spitts, 5*s.*; 1 box iron, 1*s.*; 1 paire toungs, 1 fire pann, 2 gridd iron, 1 tramell, 2 cobb irons, 1 paire bellows, 4*s.*; 2 brass candlesticks, 1*s.*; muggs, 1*s.* 6*d.*; table, chaires, &c., 9*s.*

THE LONG PARLOUR—1 long table, 1 ovill table, 1 forme, 10 chairs, 13*s.* 4*d.*

THE KITCHIN—Scales & weights, 3*s.*; 1 meale binn & meale, 1*s.* 6*d.*; 3 kettles, £1 10*s.*; 2 boylers, 5*s.*; 2 warming panns, 2*s.*; 5 skillitts, 5*s.*; 2 pales, 2*s.*

THE BREWHOUSE—The office & utensills, £7 5*s.*

THE MALT CHAMBER—1 malt quarne, 10*s.*; malt & wheat on the floore, £3.

THE CELLER—14 hoggsheads, beerstall & five empty, £29 10*s.*; 3 doz. bottles full & empty, 12*s.*

THE YARD—Hay, £3 10*s.*; wood, £1 5*s.*

[Total]—£60 2*s.* 6*d.* [should be £60 1*s.* 6*d.*].
[Appraisers—Robert Mottram, Thomas Josleyne. Exhibited 20 May 1719.]
[Note made to the effect that 'In Debts about £10 0*s.* 0*d.*', but no indication at to whether owed or receivable by deceased.]

206.—Widdow Flack. 21 November 1719.

IN THE HALL—12 pewter dishis and 12 plates, 2*li.*; 2 tables, one coubard, and joynt stools, 2*li.*; 1 jack, 10*s.*; 3 spits, & driping pan, & the other implements belonging to the chimby, 10*s.*

IN THE PARLOW—The clock, *2li.*; [torn away], *2li.* 10*s.*; 2 tables, 3 hutchis, and other implements, *2li.*

IN THE BEST CHAMBER—2 beeds, 2 blankits, 1 quilt, pillers, & bolster, 10*li.*; 1 chest of drawers, 1*li.* 10*s.*; 6 pair sheets, 12 knaptings, and 2 tables cloathes, *2li.* 10*s.*; 2 tables, 12 chaers, and 1 looking glass, *2li.*

IN THE SARVANTS CHAMBER—1 beed, and trifels, *2li.*

IN THE BUTTERY—6 half hodgheads, and drink stols, 1*li.* 5*s.*

IN THE BRUHOUSE—1 coper, and bruing vessels, and kneading troufe, *2li.* 10*s.*

IN THE DARY—1 lettel frying pan, and pottage pot, 10*s.*; cheese press, and chern, and other implements, 15*s.*

IN THE MAIDS CHAMBER—1 beed, blankets, and sheets, 1*li.* 15*s.*

6 sacks, and horse baskets, & pillion, 10*s.*; a few small cheesis, 5*s.*
2 carts, 3*li.*; 2 pear of harrows, and plow, 15*s.*; harness belonging to the stalse, 15*s.*; quarn, 7*s.*; 1 grinstone & bellus, and anvil, and the rest of the things belongind to the shop, *2li.*
2 hodgs and 7 pigs, 3*li.*
1 screen, and fan, and bushels, and other things belonging to the barn, 12*s.*
3 cows, 4*li.* 10*s.*; 3 horses, 5*li.*; 20 Norfolk lambs, 3*li.* 10*s.*
8 seeme of barly, 8*li.*; corn that lyeth in the Widdow Bushes barn, *2li.* 10*s.*
8 acres of wheat sown, 12*li.*; 8 acres of barrly land, 8*li.*
Mony in pocet & wearing cloathes, 3*li.*
Sum is—81*li.* 19*s.* [should be 93*li.* 19*s.*].
[Appraisers—Edward Jones, Nathaniel Osborne.]

207.—Henry Turnidge of the Green Lane, Roxwell. 30 December 1719.

IN THE HALL—Two long tables & frames, two fourms, two joynt stools, four chairs, one press cupboard, four spitts, one drippin pan, two cleavers, two gridirons, two salt boxes, four sicles, one gun, two lock irons, four heaters, six hand irons, a morter and pestle, five candlesticks, a basting ladle of brass, a pair of cobirons, two tramells, a fire shovell, a pair of tongs, and other small things, £3 5*s.*

IN THE PARLOUR—A carved bedsted, a feather bed, two bolsters, five pillows, three blanketts, one quilt, a sett of curtain rods, a press cupboard, a clock & clock-case, a joynt hutch, an ovell table, two chiars, four stools, seven boxes, a pair of cobirons, a pair of tongs, a pair of bellows, a box full of books, a fire shovell, & other small things, £10 8*s.* 6*d.*

IN THE HALL CHAMBER—One bedsted, curtains & vallions, a feather bed, two bolsters, two pillows, three blanketts, two coverlids, a press cupboard, a hogshed, two hutches, a chair, a stool, a wheel, a pair of cobirons, and other small things, £3 0*s.* 6*d.*

IN THE PARLOUR CHAMBER—A flock bed, a trundle bedsted, two tables, two hutches, three boxes, a poudering tub, a hoop nett, two barrells, a saddle & pillion, & pillion-cloath, fourteen cheeses, four dozen of empty bottles, one fourm, a few garden beanes, & other small things, £2 1*s.* 6*d.*

DAIRY—A cheese press, two churns, one stann, three pails, three fourms, six cheese moats, seven butter potts, twelve milk pans, a pair of scales and weights, two dozen of trenchers, a hand bowl, two potts of butter, & other small things, £1 18*s.* 6*d.*

BUTTERY—Two hogsheads, one half hogshead, a cowl, two drink stalls, a form, a funnell, a leather bottle, & other small things, 16*s.* 6*d.*

DAIRY CHAMBER—A bedsted, a flock bed, one bolster, two blanketts, a wheel & reel, eleven beehives, a carding stock and carts [cards], a nobbing iron, 16*s.*

KITCHEN—A mashing tub, five other tubbs, a kneading trough, a brass lead, a little lead, a drink stall, and other small things, £2 6*s.* 6*d.*

Fourty two lbs. of pewter, £1 8*s.*; thirteen plates, 6*s.* 6*d.*

Brass—Two frying pans, one warming pan, one skimmer, six skilletts, three kettles, two brass pottage potts, £1 15*s.*

STABLES—Two horses, one mare, one colt, with furniture for plow & cart, a malt quarne, a pair of fetters, £11 15*s.*

MALT HOUSE & KILN—Thirty three harrow teeth, three bolts, and other old iron, five wagon clouts, two washers, a beetle, & five wedges, a new plow shear, a coulter, two bolts, a rack swiffle, ten forks, three dung forks, two spades, two lip'd shovells, six other shovells, four rakes, three axes, two bills, one mattock, two grubbing axes, two pease hooks, four sythes & snaths, one dung rake, two dew rakes, eight hogs yokes, three corn cradles, a hop pitch, a hair cloath, & other small things, £3 6*s.* 11*d.*

MALT CHAMBER—Three quaters or barly, £3 12*s.*

BARLY BARNE—Twenty quaters of barly upon the floor & to thrash, a caving sceive, £23 9*s.* 6*d.*

WHEAT BARNE—Twenty five quaters of wheat, a bushell, two fans, a wheat sceive, two riddles, eight sacks, £38 0*s.* 6*d.*

HAY BARNE—Two load & half of hay, £5.

CART HOUSE—A wagon, ropes, & winch pins, two carts, two plows & whippletrees, & chains, a pair of harrows, & other small things, £15 10*s.*

Peas upon the stack—Six quaters, £9 12*s.*

A wheel barrow, three ladders, a swill tub, a hogs trough, a grindstone, & winch, 18*s.*

Four cows, two two-year old bullocks, two wennell calves, £15; nineteen Norfolk lambs, £5 4*s.* 6*d.*; nine piggs, £4 10*s.*

Linin—twelve pair of sheets, fourteen table cloaths, eighteen pillow beers, a diaper table cloath & eight diaper napkins, sixteen towells, & two dozen of napkins, £22.

Sixteen acres sown with wheat plowd four whole tilths & a half, £15 4*s.*; four quaters of wheat for seed, £6 8*s.*; the heir [hire] of the land, £9 16*s.*; ten acres & half for barly plowd three whole tilths & half, £7 7*s.*; rent of the land, £6 9*s.* 6*d.*

Wearing apparell & monie in his purse, £5.

Total Sum—£236 5*s.* 5*d.*

[Appraisers—John Brecknock, Zachariah Bridges.]

208.—John Overill of Roxwell, miller. 14 January 1719/20.

MILL HOUSE—The milstones with the other old stone, a beam, scales and weights, milbills, spilling chisels, a cable, and counter-line, and hammer, a croo, a half bushell measure, six old sacks, a wheat hutch, a riddle, & other implyments, £4 13*s*. 8*d*.; three bushells of wheat meal, 10*s*. 6*d*.

HALL—Two tables, two little çoboards of drawers, a jack, three spitts, six chairs, three candlesticks, a lock iron, two heaters, two cobirons, a fire shovell, a pair of tongs, a gridiron, a chaffing dish, a pair of bellows, a warming pan, & other small things, £2 2*s*.

BEST CHAMBER—One bed and bedsted, two blanketts, one quilt, curtains and vallions, two bolsters, one oval table, four hutches, four chairs, a trunk, two boxes, a cupboard of drawers, and other small things, £6 8*s*.

MILL CHAMBER—One bed & bedsted, coverlid, blankett & matt, £2 10*s*.

BREWHOUSE—One copper, one mashing tub, two other tubs, £3 15*s*.

BUTTERYS—Two hogsheads, a kneading trough, a large kettle, a dish kettle, a boyler, a frying pan, three skilletts, a few trenchers, & other small things, £2 19*s*. 6*d*.

Pewter—Five dishes, one dozen & half of plates, £1 8*s*. 6*d*.
Linnen—Three pair of sheets, six pillowbeers, six napkins, a table cloath, & other linen, £2 10*s*.

STABLE—A mare, a pannell, a bridle, & other small things, £4.

Wearing apparell & monie in his purse, £3.
Total—£33 17*s*. 2*d*.
[Appraisers—Thomas Overill, Henry May.]

209.—John Brown of Little *alias* New Boyton Hall, Roxwell. 30 January 1719.

IN THE HALL—One long table, stools, chairs, and other materialls, £1 17*s*. 6*d*.

IN THE PARLOUR—One long table, stooles, chairs, cubbard, &c., £1 11*s*.

PARLOUR BUTTERY—Hogsheads, stalls, &c., 16*s*.

STRONG BEER BUTTERY—Beer vessells, stalls, &c., £2.

SMALL BEER BUTTERY—Hogsheads, stalls, and other small materialls, £1 11*s*.

THE PANTRY—An old hutch, fourm, powdering tub, and other small materialls, 11*s*.

THE KITCHIN—One long table, foorm, and other materialls, £1 5*s*.

THE BOULTING HOUSE—A large kneading trough, seives, earthen & wooden dishes, &c., 15*s*.

Brass and pewter, £4 2*s*. 6*d*.; potts, spitts, & brass kittles, £3 7*s*.

IN THE DAIRY—One stan, charns, cheese press, and other materialls, £3 15*s*.

IN THE BREWHOUSE—Two coppers, & other utensills, £6 0*s*. 6*d*.

In the workehouse—Beetles, wedges, spades, shovells, and other materialls, £2 15*s*.

Hall chamber—Table, chairs, bed & furniture, & clock, £4 10*s*. 6*d*.

Chamber over the porch—One bedstead, curtains, vallance, table, stools, chairs, & looking glass, 14*s*. 10*d*.

The maids chamber—Bed and furniture, £1 14*s*. 6*d*.

A spare chamber—2 bedsteads, 3 wheels, & reels, £1 0*s*. 6*d*.

Parlow chamber—One bed, curtains, & valliance, chest, drawrs, table, &c., £8 4*s*. 6*d*.

Servants chamber—Beds, blanketts, & coverlids, £2.

Kitchin chamber—Bed and bedstead, curtains, valliance, hutches, cloose stoole, &c., £3 7*s*. 6*d*.

In the C[torn away] chamber—Shovells, pease hooks, rakes, &c., £1 1*s*. 6*d*.

In the best stable—Four horses, & all the furniture for plow & cart, £33.

The little stable—Four horses, & all the furniture for plowing, with bridles, saddles, & pannells, &c., £12.

Cart houses—Three wagons, 2 carts, & wheelebarrow, 1 plow, £30.
Nine cows & a bull, £27; sow & piggs, £1 10*s*.; 10 store piggs, £7 10*s*.
3 shovells, 11 forks, 2 bushells, caveing scives, & fanns, 15*s*.; four dew rakes, & 3 ladders, quarne for malt, & cistern, 27 sacks, £4 10*s*.
40 Northfolks lambs, £9 5*s*.; 35 sheep, & a ramm, £12.; 3 colts, £6 5*s*.
Wheat in the barn & chamber, £132; barley, £34; oats & pease, £10 5*s*.; white pease and tares, £7; sowne upon the whole farme, wheat, £50; barly land plowing £27 6*s*.; pease & bullemung sown, £13 4*s*.; a cock of hay and hay in the barne, £16 11*s*.
[Total]—£487 1*s*. 4*d*.
[Appraisers—John Crush of Barnish [Berners] Roothing, Richard Alger of Leaden Roothing.]

210.—William Clary of Writtle. 18 June 1720.

In the hall—3 tables, one jack, a gun, a musket, 4 cobirons, 3 pair of tongs, one gridiron, a lock iron, a shreding knife, a candle box, a press cubbard, a box of drawers, a tramell, a warming pan, 2 chairs, & and other small things, 3 joint stools, £2 7*s*. 6*d*.

In the parlor—One feather bed, a bedstead, 2 boulsters, and curtins, 2 tables, 1 joint stool, 4 chairs, one cubbert, a pair of brass cobirons, & five sickels, £3 7*s*. 6*d*.

In the chamber over the parler—One bed and bedstead, a boulster, 2 pillows, & curtains, 2 blankets, a quilt, a chest of drawers, 4 chairs, a table, a smal pair of handirons, &c., £6.

In the chamber over the hall—A bedstead, & curtins, and 3 pillows, 4 hutches, 14*s*. 6*d*.

IN THE CHAMBER OVER THE BUTTERY—One feather bed, a boulster, a flock bed, and beadstead, £1 6*s*.

IN THE KICHING—2 coppers, 2 little kittles, 8 tubs, a coule, 3 pailes, a milk seive, a hop sive, &c., a tramel, a neading trofe, a cleaver, a forme, £5 14*s*. 6*d*.

IN THE DARY—A cheese press, 2 churms, a stand, 8 chese motes, 2 pair of scales & weights, a tray, a forme, pots and pans, a salt box, a powdring tub, a forme, 3 dressers, 2 shelfs, another tub, and other smal things, £1 13*s*.

IN THE OLD PARLER—A bed and bedstead, 2 boulsters, 2 blankets, £1 0*s*. 6*d*.

IN THE SMALL BEERE BUTTERY—3 hogsheds, 3 half hogsheds, drink stalls, &c., £1 2*s*.

IN THE STRONG BERE BUTTERY—6 skillits, a coale dish, 2 porridge pots, 7 pewter dishes, six plates, 2 formes, a driping pan, a frying pan, and a spit, trenchers, and small impliments, 2 hutches, £3 12*s*.

Lining, £2.

IN THE CORNE CHAMBER—A chaine, a pair of horse baskets, a chickin basket, 2 shovels, a bushele, a betle and 6 wedges, 2 flailes, a chaving sive, and old lumber, £2 1*s*.

Wool, £1 10*s*.

IN THE CHESE CHAMBER—19 cheses, 10*s*.

IN THE MAULT HOUSE—2 axes, 2 grubing axes, a mattock, a dung forck, a plow, 5 harrows, plow chain, a mault quarn, a sithe and things belonging to it, 8 sacks, forcks, & rakes, £2 10*s*.

IN THE STABLE—Collers, halters and harness, 2 shovels, a spade, pannell, 2 cart sadles, 2 bridles, £3 12*s*. 6*d*.

IN THE BARNES—A waggon, 3 ropes, 2 pair of winch pins, 2 ladders, £6; a plow, and chain, & slead, 10*s*.

IN THE CARTHOUSE—2 dung carts, a load cart, a whele barrow, £7 10*s*.

Corne—23 aceres of wheat, £64 8*s*.; 6 acers 3 roods of barley, £15 15*s*.; 1 acere and 3 roods of oats, £3; 12 aceres of tares and bullimong, £15; 3 acers of pease, £9; 8 acers of grase, £10.
Five cows, £17 15*s*.; three mares and one horse, £14; twentty couple of sheep and lambs, £11 15*s*.; four hogs, and five pigs, and eighteen geese, £6 10*s*.
Fallows, £18.
Wearing cloaths and pocket mony, £3.
[Total]—£232 5*s*. 6*d*. [should be £241 4*s*.].
[Appraisers not named. Exhibited 19 April 1721.]

211.—John Bridgman of Writtle, gardener. 18 November 1720.

His waring cloes an poket mony, 15*li*.

IN THE CHICHEN—on [?]gun, an meterels, 1*li*. 5*s*.; puter, 7*s*.; too payer of cobioyrns, 2*s*.

IN THE BREWHOUS—On coper, too cettles, 5 tubes, 1*li*. 10*s*.

IN THE PANTRY—7 vesels, an a beare stale, an table, 15*s.*

IN THE SMALL BEARE BUTREY—A drinke stal, 1*s.*

IN HIS LOGIN ROUME—Too beeds, an too beeds steds, a payer of toyngs, a shovel, 5*li.*

GOODS IN THE CHAMBER OVER THE BREWHOUS, 10*s.*

Hors, bridle, an sadle, 3*li.*
Trees an plants in the Croune Garden, 2*li.* 10*s.*; the stok in the hom [Home] garden, 5*li.*
[Total]—£35.
[Appraisers—Richard Bridgman, John Bird. Exhibited 19 April 1721.]

212.—William Flack of Writtle. 27 May 1721.

IN THE HALL—One long table, one oval table, one form, six chairs, a pair of cobirons, bellows, tongs, & other small usefull small things, £1 10*s.* 6*d.*

IN THE PARLOUR—One bedsted, & feather bed, a blanket, 2 pillows, two boxes, a trunk, a chair, & other small things, £3 6*s.*

IN THE BUTTRY—One hogshead, other small vessells, a mashing tub, & other small tubs, £2 12*s.*

IN THE DAIRY—A cheese press, stan, chirm, four cheesmoats, & other small things usefull in the said room, 15*s.*

IN THE PANTRY—A kneading trough, poudering tub, scales & weights & beam, & other smal things, 11*s.* 6*d.*

HALL CHAMBER—One bedsted, & feather bed, a bolster, a blanket, a rugg, 3 chairs, & other small things, £2 13*s.* 6*d.*

DAIRY CHAMBER—Three quarters of wheat, 2 bushells of pease, £3 5*s.*

Lining—Three pair of sheets, three pair of pillowbeers, three table cloaths, nine napkins, eight towells, £1 16*s.* 6*d.*
Brass—a pottage pot, frying pan, warming pan, four kettles, 2 skilletts, £3 1*s.* 6*d.*
Pewter—Nine dishes, two plates, a chamber pot, a porringer, & other small things, £1 4*s.*

A log beetle, 6 wedges, an axe, a bill, a fan, 2 old sacks, & other small things, 19*s.*
Two loads & ½ of old hay, £2 10*s.*; two store piggs, £1 8*s.*; four acres of grass, £3 10*s.*; one acre & rood of wheat, £1 16*s.* 9*d.*; one acre of barley, £1 3*s.*; two acres bullimong, £1 4*s.*

STABLE—Furniture for plow & cart for one horse, 5*s.*

A load cart, £3; three cows, two calves, £10; a mare, a colt, £4 5*s.*; a plough, a chain, 2*s.* 6*d.*
Wearing aparel & monie in his purse, £5.
Summa totalis—£55 18*s.* 9*d.*
[Appraisers—Zachariah Bridges, Thomas Wolfe.]

213.—John Freeman of Writtle, barber surgeon. 24 October 1721.

In ready mony, 92*li.*; in notes that are good, 26*li.* 10*s.*; in notes that are dubius, 29*li.*
The goods in the shop, [?]10*s.*
One pair of silver spurs, 1*li.*; fifteen shirts, 1 [torn away]s.
The shop lining, [torn away].
Two pair of bootes, 13*s.*
The wareing cloathes & mony in pocket, 8*li.* 8*s.*
Total—£173 2*s.* [An added note refers to [?]3*li.* 'due from Mr. Hubbard by Note'.]
[Appraisers—Thomas Horsnayle, John Sorrell.]

214.—Widow Hatchman of Writtle. 21 April 1722.

In the hall—A long tabale, & other utanshals, £1 10*s.*

In the parler—One bed, & other utanshals, £2 10*s.*

In the best chalmber—One bed, & other utanshals, £2.

In the hall chalmber—One bed, & other utanshals, £1 10*s.*

In the butterree—2 vesels, & a chespres, 12*s.*

In the brueing ofice—A smale coper, & other utanshals, £3.

In the dary—One churn, & other utanshals, £2.

Without dores—One cowe, & 2 piges, £3.

[Total]—£16 2*s.*
[Appraisers—Bartholomew Wright, Thomas Overill.]

215.—William Stookes. 21 April 1722.

In the holl—1 tabel, and a prescoberd, and other things, 10*s.*

In the paller—1 bed, and a huch, and other things, £3.

In the chamber—1 bed, and a char, £1 10*s.*

In the butry—2 veseles, and 3 small tubes, and a kettel, and other things, £1 5*s.*
[Total—£6 5*s.*]
[Appraisers—Bartholomew Wright, Thomas Overill.]
[Endorsed—'Mary ye Relict'.]

216.—John Herridge of Writtle, yeoman. 15 June 1723.

The Income of the Farme being paid by Mr Capell after, £10; ten acres three tilts, £6; 5 acres 4 tilts, £4; 5 acres 3 tilts, £3; one acre three tilts, 12*s.*; two acres three tilts, £1 18*s.*; 7 acres plowing, 10*s.*; rent of the followes, £10 15*s.*; 9 acres of wheat, £31; 9 acres of wheat, £22 1*s.*; 7 acres of wheat, £23 16*s.*; 17 acres of barly, £37 2*s.* 6*d.*; 7 acres of oates, £13 13*s.*; a small parcell of bullymong, £1 5*s.*; four acres of grass, £3.
8 cows, £20; 6 calves, £5 9*s.*; 53 sheep & lambs, £15; 5 horses, £25; 10 hoggs, 3 sows, 27 piggs, & 3 hogs troughs, £13 1*s.*

IN THE BARNE—The wheat, 1 screen, 1 caveing seive, 1 fann, 1 wire seive, 3 casting shovells, some rakes & forks, £13 18*s*.

IN THE CART HOUSE—2 waggons, 2 tumbrills, 1 wheel barrow, and one grindstone, £16 2*s*. 6*d*.

IN THE YARD—2 dew rakes, 1 water cart, 1 plow, five harrows, 3 ladders, 1 cock of old hay, & other odd things, £9 12*s*.

IN THE STABLE—All the cart & plow harness, 1 panell, 1 shovell, &c., £3 10*s*.

IN THE HALL—1 clock & case, 2 tables, 1 forme, 1 cupboard, 6 rush bottomed chairs, 1 old dresser board, 1 jack & weights, 3 spitts, 2 pair of andirons, 1 pair of bellows, 1 pair of brass candlesticks, snuffers & box, 1 fire shovell & tongs, 1 candle box, a pair of stillyards, 1 iron candlestick, 1 brass scumer, 1 brass ladle, 1 joynd stoole, 1 brass mortar, 1 box iron & heaters, 1 gun, 1 pair of tramells, 1 gridiron, & 1 chaffeing dish, £4 1*s*.

IN THE GREAT PARLOUR—1 bedsted with the furniture, 1 feather bed & bolster, 2 pillows, 1 quilt, 1 coverlett, 2 blanketts, 2 tables, 1 chest of drawers, 1 hanging cupboard, 9 rush bottom chaires, 1 pair of andirons, fire shovell & tongs, 1 small lookinglass, a parcell of earthen ware, 1 childs baskett, a parcell of small pictures, £5 14*s*. 6*d*.

IN THE LITTLE PARLOUR—1 bedsted, matt, cord, curtains & vallens, 1 blankett, 2 feather pillows, 1 warming pan, 2 hutches, 1 table, 1 box, 1 childs cradle & quilt, £1 16*s*. 6*d*.

IN THE CHAMBER OVER THE GREAT PARLOUR—2 halfe headed bedsteads, matts & cords, 2 feather beds, 3 bolsters, five blanketts, 1 pillow, 1 rugg, 1 coverlett, & 7 rush chairs, £5 12*s*. 4*d*.

IN THE CHAMBER OVER THE LITTLE PARLOUR—A parcell of tares & peese, & about 4 seam of oates, £3 13*s*.

IN THE CHEESE CHAMBER—A parcell of cheese, £1 3*s*.

IN THE CHAMBER OVER THE BUTTERY—17 sacks, 2 wire seives, 2 riddles, 1 pitch pann & brand, one basket, and some old lumber, £1 10*s*.

IN THE CHAMBER OVER THE DAIRY—One halfe headed bedsted, matt & cord, 1 flock bed, 1 feather bolster, 3 blanketts, and one coverlett, 16*s*.

IN THE BUTTERYS—5 holfe hog'ds, 4 hog'ds, 1 barrell churn, 2 small vessells, 1 tilder, 4 drink stalls, 1 large bottle, 1 tunnell, and one cutting knife, £3 9*s*.

IN THE DAIRY—1 stand, 2 churns, 2 keet[?les, or keelers], 1 tray, 2 milk pails, on jarr, one salt box, one seive, a parcell of earthen ware, one cheese tubb, three formes, one tin pann, sixteen pewter plates, six pewter dishes, one frying pann, one hand bowle, one peel, one powdering tubb, one large bowl, [not valued].

IN THE BREWHOUSE—One coppar copper, one brass copper, two brass kettles, three brass skilletts, two boylers, one meash tubb, eleaven other tubbs, one wort trough, one kneading trough, one cheese press, one peel, one table, one meal tubb, one paire of tramells, and two seives, £6 8*s*.

Seaven paire of ordinary sheets, and other household linnen, £3 10*s.*
Wearing apparrell & ready money, £3 10*s.*
Summa totalis—£313 13*s.* [Total of goods as transcribed, £331 8*s.* 4*d.*]
[Appraisers—John Stocker, Nathaniel Hurrell.]

217.—Abraham Boosey of Writtle. 22 July 1723.

IN THE HALL—1 round table, 1 square table, 1 clock, 1 jack, 2 cobirons, 6 chairs, a payer of tongs & fire shovell, 1 payer of stilyerds, 1 saw, & other things, 5*li.* 17*s.* 6*d.*

IN THE PARLOR—2 tables, 6 chairs, 2 cobirons, a fire shovell, window curtains, & other small things, 1*li.* 6*s.* 6*d.*

IN THE KITCHIN—2 coppers, 8 brewing tubbs, 3 pails, 1 cheese press, 1 cheese tubb, 1 small table, 1 dresser, & other small things, 4*li.* 10*s.*

IN THE DAIRY—2 churns, 1 powdering tubb, 1 stand, 3 keelers, 3 trayes, 4 cheese moots, some earthen ware, a payer of scales & weights, & other small things, 1*li.* 18*s.* 6*d.*

IN THE STRONG BEER BUTTERY—4 halfe hogsheads, 1 tunell, 2 dozen glass bottles, 1*li.* 7*s.*

IN THE SCULLERY—2 pottage potts, 1 kettle, 4 skillets, 1 warming pan, & other things, 2*li.* 13*s.*

IN THE SMALL BEER BUTTERY—2 hogsheads, 1 drink stall, 1 cupboard, and other small things, 1*li.*

IN THE PANTREY—1 frying pan, 1 tea kettle, 1 wire sieve, 1 table, stalls and shelves, & other small things, 1*li.* 0*s.* 6*d.*

IN THE CHAMBER OVER THE HALL—1 feather bed, with curtains & vallens and all belonging, 2 chests, 3 chairs, 1 table, and other small things, 2*li.* 15*s.*

IN THE CHAMBER OVER THE PARLOR—1 feather bed, 1 quilt, 1 bedsted with curtains and vallens, 2 pillows, 1 looking glass, 4*li.* 5*s.*

IN THE CHAMBER OVER THE PANTREY—1 feather bed & bedsted, 1 cradle, 1 small quilt, and other small things, 1*li.* 17*s.*

IN THE GARRETT—2 flock beds, 2 bedsteds & blankets, 1 flax wheele, 1*li.* 18*s.*

IN THE CHAMBER OVER THE DAIRY—Kneading trough, 1 wheel, 1 reele, two old tubbs, a payer of basketts, and other small things, 15*s.*

IN THE GRAINERY—1 screen, 2 fans, 1 bushell, 5 forcks, 2 pease hoocks, 2 spades, 1 ax, 2 shovells, 1 log-beetle & 2 wedges, 1 riddle, 8 sacks, one caveing sieve, and other small implements, 2*li.* 15*s.* 6*d.*

IN THE CARTHOUSE—1 waggon with a payer of ropes and winch pins, 2 dung carts, 2 payer of harrows, 1 plow, & plow irons, 12*li.*

IN THE STABLE—3 horses, 1 mare & colt, & all their furniture, 13*li.*

Nine cows & seven calves, 23*li.*; twenty eight sheepe, 7*li.*; a sow and nine piggs, 2*li.*; twenty nine geese, 1*li.* 14*s.*; small fowles, 13*s.* 4*d.*
Fourteen acres of wheat upon the ground, 49*li.*; five acres of barly, 14*li.*;

six acres of pease and oats, 6*li.*; sixteen acres of fallow plowed three times, 9*li.* 12*s.*
All the hey, 17*li.* 5*s.*
Pewter—11 dishes and 2 dozen plates, 2*li.* 9*s.*
All the linin,—7*li.*
Plate, ready money & wearing apparrell, 20*li.*
Summe Total—218*li.* 11*s.* 10*d.*
[Appraisers—William Lukin, John Crush.]

218.—Margaret Allen of Roxwell. 16 May 1724.

IN THE PARLOUR—1 shuffle board table, 1 oval table, 1 form, 9 old chaires, 1 sett of shuffle bord peices, £1.

IN THE HALL—2 tables, 4 joyn'd stools, 3 chaires, 1 pair of cobirns, 1 pair shovell & tongs, 1 pair bellows, 1 gridiron, 1 trammell, 1 hook, 4 spitts, 1 jack, 4 iron candlesticks, 2 brass candlesticks, 1 brass morter, 1 brass bowl, 1 wax candlestick, 10 pewter dishes, 1 bason, 1 pie plate, 2 chamber pots, 2 Winchester quarts, 5 [Winchester] pints, 1 quart wine measure, 1 halfe pint wine measure, 2 quarterns wine measure, 1 ½ quartern wine measure, 18 pewter plates, 1 funnell, 1 nest of drawers, 1 warming pan, £4 15*s* 6*d.*

IN THE CHAMBER OVER THE PARLOUR—1 bedstead, matt & cord, curtains and vallents, 1 feather bed, 1 bolster, 2 pillows, 1 blanket, 1 coverlid, 1 rugg, 2 tables, 4 leather chairs, 1 old hutch, £4 9*s.*

IN THE CHAMBER OVER THE HALL—1 bedstead, matt & cord, with old curtains, 1 feather bed, 1 bolster, 2 pillows, 1 blanket, 1 rugg, 3 chaires, 3 hutches, 1 pair iron doggs, 1 liverey cupboard, £2 5*s.*

IN THE CHAMBER OVER THE KITCHEN—2 old bedsteads, 1 pair of old curtains, 1 feather bed, 2 bolsters, 1 old flock bed, 3 old blankets, 1 old rugg, 1 broken chairs, 1 form, £2.

IN THE GARRETTS—2 old halfe headed bedsteads, 2 old flock beds, 1 feather bolster, with some peices of old blankets, 12*s.* 6*d.*

IN THE BUTTEREY—4 hoggsheads, 2 beer stalls, 3 dubble mugs, 2 single mugs, £2 5*s.*

IN THE BUTTEREY IN THE YARD—2 small butts, 4 hoggsheads, 1 halfe hoggshead, 3 beer stalls, 1 iron driping pan, 1 pipe iron, 2 wooden funnells, £3 12*s.*

IN THE BREWHOUSE—1 copper, 2 mashing tubs, 1 underback, 1 cooler, 3 wort tubbs, 1 hopp sive, 2 tap hoses, 2 jetts, 2 payls, 1 trough, 2 stalls with ye copper bars, £10 2*s.*

IN THE KITCHIN—1 cobiron, 1 old chest, 1 pair scales and beam, 4 leaden weights, 1 iron weight, 1 hoggshead, 1 beer stall, £1 2*s.*

IN THE BUTTEREY BEHIND THE KITCHIN—2 hoggsheads, 1 beer stall, 2 forms, 1 brass cock, 1 filter, 2 payls, 2 wash tubs, £1 7*s.*

Beer, £1 18*s.*
4 score fagetts & caredg, 13*s.*; 1 lode of rowin' woods & loges with caredg, 15*s.*

Total—£36 16*s*.
[Appraisers—J. Lea, Richard Raven. Probably witnesses to endorsement 1.]
Endorsements—1. 'June the 25th 1724. Rec'd then of John Simpson five and twenty pounds in parte for ye goods aforemenconed by order of Richd Raven. [Signed] Wm. Shipton.'
2. 'Jen ye 19th 1724/5. then Rec'ed of John Simpson ye sum of Leven pound sixteen shill: being in full for my Mother Allins Goods att ye Chaquer in Roxwell by me [Signed] Wm. Shipton, £17 16 0.'

219.—Abraham Gowan of Roxwell. 31 July 1725.

In the hall—One ould ould [*sic*] table, 2*s*.; two joynt stools, 1*s*.; three ould rush chayers, 1*s*.; one payer of iron cobirons, 1*s*. 6*d*.; one ould jack, & a payer of flat irons, 4*s*.

In the kitchin—One ould copper, £1; to bruing tubes, 10*s*.; 2 skelletts, 1*s*.; brace & puter [brass and pewter], £1 2*s*. 6*d*.; 3 iron candelsteackes, 6*d*.; the other utensills, 2*s*. 6*d*.

In the buttery—5 ould vesels, 10*s*.

In the best chamber—One ould fether bed, 1 boutster, 2 pillows, 1 coverled, 1 bedstitell & curtings, £4; 5 ould chayers, 2*s*. 6*d*.; one payer of drayers, 4*s*.; 1 looking glase, 3*s*.

In the chamber over the shope—One ould fether bed, one boulster, 2 pilowes, 1 bedstitell, 2 pilowes, & curtings, £1 10*s*.; one ould chest, 2*s*. 6*d*.; 2 payer of window curtings, 2*s*. 6*d*.; whearing aparill, £1; one cloce stoole, 2*s*.; 6 lether chyers, 5*s*.

In the chamber att the stayer hed—One ould fether bed, & bedstitel, one boulster, & ruge, & 1 blankett, & curtings, £1 10*s*.; one ould chest, 2*s*. 6*d*.; one chayer, & 1 joynt stoole, 1*s*. 6*d*.; one ould clack, 10*s*.; one tubb, 1*s*.

In the poot chamber—One ould chest, 2*s*. 6*d*.

In the shope—Scales, waits, & other utensills, £15.

The lining—£1 2*s*. 6*d*.
Totall—£29 17*s*. 6*d*.
[Appraisers—John Perry, William Shipton.]

220.—Joseph Wollward of Writtle. 4 January 1724/5. See Plate XIII.

In the hall—One table, 2 joyned stooles, two puter dishes, 3 chayers, one lanthorn, one cubard, 12*s*. 6*d*.

In the butterry—One porrig pot, 2 cettles bras, one churn, one chespres, £1 3*s*.; one bere vessell, one tub, 6*s*.

In the parler chamber—Two beeds, 2 sorry bedsteds, 2 indeferant bolsters, 2 indeferant blankets, one pair of shets, three pillobers, £2.

In the barne—3 sakes, 2 forks, one wier sive, one riddle, one half bushell, 8*s*.

IN THE STABLE—A parcell of old hors takel, 8*s*.

One cart, one pair of harros, one plow whith whot belong to it, one deeu-rake, £2.
One hors, 2 cowes, £8.
[Total]—£14 17*s*. 6*d*.
[Appraisers—Samuel Shettleworth, John Savell.]

221.—Daniell Bridges of Drury Lane. 26 February 1724/5.

IN THE SHOPE—One large cask of tobaccoe about 130 *li.* waite, £6 10*s*.; two small casks of tobaccoe 54 pound waite, £2 9*s*. 6*d*.; one small cask of tobaccoe 17 pound waite, 11*s*. 4*d*.; a quantety of bees wax, 16*s*. 4*d*.; a small quantety of cheese and butter, 2*s*. 1*d*.; 2 pound of loafe sugar, and 12 pound of rice, 5*s*.; 12 pound of the hock end of baccon, 4*s*. 6*d*.; the nest of drawers containing small quantety of severall sort of things amounts to 11*s*. 7*d*.; sugar and plumbs in the drawers under the counter, 10*s*. 9*d*.; 1 quire and ½ of writeing paper, 9*d*.; 1 pound ¼ of green tea, 10*s*.; 4 parsells of Bohe tea, 6 *li.* 10 *oz.*, £3 5*s*.; peppers and seeds in severall paper bags, and ginger likewise, 4*s*. 8*d*.; small quantety of snuff and pots itt is in, 3*s*. 10*d*.; shott and gun powder, 18*s*. 6*d*.; tin cannaster and scalls, £1 5*s*. 6*d*.; the nest of drawers, shelves, and the old boxs, £2 7*s*.; brandy cags and glass bottles, 12*s*. 6*d*.; some whiteing and matches, 8*d*.; a coffee mill and tin lamps, 7*s*.; allome and some balls of packthread, 4*s*.; the old tubs, and iron pestell and morter, 13*s*.; old [?]siferies tobaccoe block and wast paper, 4*s*. 6*d*.; the window grates, 12*s*.; puter measures, 5*s*.; the 2 black boys, 3*s*.; the sine, the brase and leaden waites, 19*s*.; 4 pound of sope and brase cockes, 3*s*. 10*d*.; the liquers containe in severall wooden cask, 10*s*.; a chease taster and a nife, 9*d*.; the liquers contain'd in severall glass bottles, 12*s*. 6*d*.; a gallepott and a few capers, 6*d*.; 13 pound of anchoveys, 14*s*.; French barly, starch, and some whole brimstone, 4*s*. 1*d*.; tobaccoe pipes, red herrins, and links, 2*s*. 2*d*.; about 6 gallons of lamp oyle, 10*s*. 1*d*.; stone bottels and earthen panes, 3*s*.

IN THE SELLER—About one chaldron of coales, £1 10*s*.; two small washing tubs, 2*s*. 4*d*.

IN THE KITCHIN—A paire of grates, fire shoveles, tongs, poker, and a broune table, 13*s*.

IN THE SHOP—A small quantety of salt, and an old wooden measure, 3*s*.
Mony for the income—£3 3*s*.
Total Due—£33 9*s*. 3*d*. [No appraisers' names.]
On a separate sheet in a different hand—'Memorandum that Mr Daniell Bridges left ready cash in gold nine pounds nine shillings in silver one pound sixteen and six pence in halfpence and farthings fourteen shillings.'

Mrs. [Rebecca] Bredges. 20 May 1725.
Won fetheor bed and all belongin theor two, £4; another fethor bed and all belongin theor two, £4 5*s*.; won tronck, two chests, and a desk, 10*s*.; three pare of sheets, and a pare of pillow bears, two touells, two table cloaths, six napckings, and weaoring lining and close, £5; won tub, and a killdeoking, and a pres cobard, and a small cobard, and small impleyments, £1 10*s*.

In redey money left four pound thurteng shilling.
[Total—£19 18*s*. Appraiser—Richard Gregson.]
[This inventory is not numbered in the file; it is in a different hand from the previous document, but appears to be allied to it.]

222.—Mary Branwood, widow. 2 August 1725.

IN THE HALL—Two ovall tables, 7 chairs, one jack, 2 pair of cobirons, a fender, a warming pan, 2 pair of tongs, one fire shovell, one cleaver, one gridiron, one chopping knife, iron scure, & stool with a leaf, and other small implements, five candlesticks, box iron & heaters, one trammel, a curtain & rod, a still, & pot iron, and a salt box, one pair of bellows, an old candle box, and a stove for to heat lock iron heaters, two Bibles & other books, one cushion, 1*li.* 15*s.* 8*d.*

IN THE PARLOUR—One feather bed, bedstead and furniture thereto belonging, two chairs, one table, one stool, an old cubbard, an old deal box, a coverlett, a looking glass, 2*li.* 18*s.* 6*d.*

IN THE LITTLE BUTTERY—Three beere vessells, 21 quart bottles & seaven pints, one sieve, and other implements, six mugs and other earthen ware, three beerstalls, 1*li.* 1*s.* 9*d.*

IN THE CHAMBER OVER THE PARLOUR—One feather bed, bedsted, one pair of sheets, with the furniture to the bed, an old huctch, four chairs, 3 blankets, 2 pillows, a cushion, 2*li.* 16*s.* 6*d.*

IN THE CHAMBER OVER THE BUTTRYS—One bed with the furniture, a large trunk, a chair, & stool, a chest of drawers, one hutch, and two boxes, 7 pair of sheets, one silver cup and 7 silver spoons, 2 pair of window curtains, 12 napkins, 7 table cloths, 7 pillowbeers, 6 towels, 7*li.* 5*s.* 6*d.*

IN THE SMALL BEER BUTTRY & PASSAGE—One hogsheads, half hogsheads, rundlett, 9 pewter dishes, one cheese plate, 16 plates, and the earthen ware, 2 brass kettles, 2 boylers, a frying pan, 2 skillets, a brass ladle, a cullender, a skimmer, a wooden tunnel, a pestle & mortar, 1 powdring tub, & form, seven trenchers, a tinn tunnell, a milk stand, a wooden bottle, a fish plate, a tinn covering, 3 pewter porringers, a drugin box, a pasty pan bottom, a table, an old cupboard, a hand chopper, 5 towels, 4 earthen plates, leaden weights, 4 knives, 2 forks, 4*li.* 14*s.* 4*d.*

IN THE KITCHIN—A copper, and a kettle hung, a meshing tub and 8 other tubs, a kneeding trough, 2 pailes, and a hand bowl, a flasket, a spit, with other implements, & a little table, 2*li.* 16*s.*

IN THE CHAMBER OVER THE END OF THE MALTHOUSE—A feather bed, with bedstead, valents, curtains, coverlet & bases &c., one table, one hutch, 3 chairs, 2*li.* 7*s.* 6*d.*

IN THE MALT CHAMBER—Twelve sacks, 1 old chest, with other lumber, 13*s.*; & a pillion, 2*s.* 6*d.*

IN THE YARD—A wheel barrow, a pair of wheels, 1*li.* 5*s.*; a pair of harrows, horses harness, and the horse and mare, and a parcell of stack-wood, and other wood, 7*li.* 10*s.*

The wheat growing, 8*li.*
Toto—43*li.* 6*s.* 3*d.* [Appraisers—William Cook, William Green.]

223.—John Lugar. 22 February 1725/6.

IN THE HALL—One small table, one dresser, one spit, and other ode empliments of houshold stufe, 7*s.*

IN THE PARLOR—One bed & bedsted, 2 bolsters, one blancket & coverlid, one cubard, one table, 2 stools, 4 peweter dishes, one hutch, 6 chairs, £2 1*s.* 6*d.*

IN THE HALL CHAMBER—One bed and bedsted, one bolster, one blancket, one coverlid, a kneading trough, & warming pan, £1 2*s.*

IN THE CHAMBER OVER THE PARLOR—Two huches, 2 old boxes, one trunck, 6*s.*

IN THE BUTTRY—Two kettels, 2 skillits, one frying pan, & some other old lumber, £1.

IN THE BREWHOUS—One lead, seven tubs, one vessel, and tub stall, £1 5*s.*

His wearing cloths and mony in the testators purse, 10*s.*
[Total]—£6 4*s.* 6*d.* [should be £6 11*s.* 6*d.*].
[Appraisers—Edward Day, John Eare.]

224.—John Day the elder, of Highwood in Writtle, carpenter. 16 March 1725/6.

IN THE HALL—One long table, 6 joynt stooles, two other small tables, 4 old chairs, one cuberd, fire shovel and tongs, 3 small spits, 6 peuter dishes, 6 pleats, one bras candle stick, som other small implements, one clock, one worming pan, £2 10*s.*

IN THE PARLER—One indeferant bed, & bedsted with all belonging too it, one chest of drauers, one pres cubard, one small table, 2 sorry old chairers, £1 4*s.*

IN THE BUTTRE—Two half hogsheds, one iron porridg pots, 7*s.*

IN THE DARY—One chespres, one stand, 3 woden trays, and a few earthen pans, and other small implements, 7*s.*

IN THE BREWHOUSE—One small copper, four tubs, one bras cettle, other small things, £1 5*s.*

IN THE CHAMBER OVER THE PARLER—One sorry bed with a linciwolcy teeke [linsey-woolsey tick], and bedsted, one small table, three hutchis, 2 truncks, £1 10*s.*

IN THE HALL CHAMBER—Two beds with what belongs to them very mean, one cubbard, 2 huthis, £1 10*s.*

Two cows that are kept upon the Commans, £4.
Waring clothis and mony in his purs, £1 10*s.*
Linlin—4 pair of sheets, 6 napkins, 3 board cloths, £1 3*s.*
[Total]—£15 6*s.* [Appraisers—Samuel Shettleworth, William Middleton.]

225.—John Battle of Writtle. 24 September 1726.

In the hall—One press cupboard, a long table, a little table, three joined stools, six chairs, one form, a jack, a gridiron, two trammels, a warming pan, two spits, two brass candlesticks, three iron candlesticks, a small nesst of drawers, and other implements as two cup cobirons, &c., £2 10*s*.

In the parlour—The bedstead, bed & furniture, two old tables, eight chairs, window curtains & valents, a pair of tongs, a pair of cobirons, and other small things, £10.

In the further buttery—Three half hoggsheads, two kilderkings, and other small things, £1.

In the little pantry—Eight pewter dishes, a dozen pewter plates, a keep cupboard covered with haircloth, with other small things, £2.

In the small beer buttery—One half hogshead, & beer stall, two kettles, three skillets, four pewter dishes, with other small things, £1.

In the dairy—One chees press, one chirm, a chees stand, two chirm staves, two tubs, two forms, with other small things, £1 10*s*.

In the chamber over the hall—Two bedsteads, one bed and furniture, one chest, four pillows, sheets, pillowbeers, and table linnen, £6.

In the chamber over the parlour—A chest of drawers, one oval table, a stool, a little box, four chairs, two cobirons with brass heads, £1 10*s*.

In the chamber over the buttrey—One feather bed, beadsted, coverlet, curtains and vallens with the furniture belonging to it, window curtains & valants, a table, and four chairs, £5.

In the garret—The cheese there, £3.

In the chamber over the dairy—A bedstead, & bed, &c., £1 10*s*.

In the kitchin—Two brass brewing boylers, seaven tubs, one tub stall, one form, & other smal things, £3.

Corn in the barn where the wheat lyes—The wheat, £50.

In the barley barn—The barley, £30.

In the lower barn—Pease & oats, £8.

In the hay house & cow house—The hay, £10.

Waggons, carts, plows, & harrows, £12; corn skreen, fanns, bushell, sacks & shovels, £2.
Four horses, £20; horse harness, pannells, bridle, & saddle, £3.
Four cows, £10; thirty sheep, £7 10*s*.; one hog, one sow, & eleaven piggs, £4 10*s*.; sixteen geese, £1 10*s*.
Ready money and wearing apparrel, £5.
[Total]—£210 10*s*. [Appraisers—Laurence Hillyard, John Hillyard.]

226.—Joseph Downham of Hadleigh. 27 September 1726.

Four old chaires, 1*s*.; 3 old hutches, & joint stool, 5*s*. 6*d*.; 2 brass skillets, pott, frying pann, old brass copper, 12*s*. 6*d*.; 3 old cobirons, old sword, shoeing iron, pott hanger, & spitt, lead weight, 6*s*.; 23 pound of pewter at 6*d*. per pound, 11*s*. 6*d*.; old morter, 12 old trencher, 1*s*.

IN THE KITCHIN—Long table, 3 old chaires, covert, 5*s*. 6*d*.

IN BREWHOUSE—Things, &c., £6 17*s*.; [illegible], trough, kettle, few [more] odd things, 4*s*.

IN THE BEDCHAMBER—[?Tuinge sheet],3*s*., tub, hutch, 2*s*. 6*d*.; 2 old bedsteds, feather bed, & severall od things, £1.
[Total—£10 9*s*. 6*d*. Appraisers—John Mann, James Reason.]
[Note at foot of inventory in a different hand—'by household goods sold by Testator before his death & not delivered seven pounds when paid to Executor.']

227.—John Hillyard of Writtle, bricklayer. 21 January 1726/7.

IN THE HALL—One press cupboard, one deal dresser board with doors & drawers, one table, three chairs, one spinning wheel, an hour glass, a smal looking glass, two window curtains and valent, two cup cobirons, one other cobiron, a trammell, two small spits, a dripping pan, a coal dish, pistle & mortar, a pair of bellows, a fire shovell, a pair of tongs, and other small implements, £1 3*s*. 6*d*.

IN THE PARLOUR—One bedstead, curtains and valents & rods, one feather bed, bolster, one blanket, an old coverlet, four chairs, one table, three chests, window curtains and valents, £2 10*s*.

IN THE DAIRY—A cheespress, a stand, a chirm &c., a milk pan, and other earthen ware, a wooden tray, three small cheese motes, 7*s*. 6*d*.

IN THE BUTTERY—One hogshead, one old half hogs head, one kilderkin all old ones, two old kettles, thre small skillets, one pottage pot, four small old pewter dishes, one plate, a frying pan, one drinkstall, a pail, one tap tub, & other implements, £1 7*s*.

BREWING CONVENIENCYS—One small old brass boyler for wort, two tubs, one cowl, and a kneading trough, 14*s*. 6*d*.

IN THE CHAMBER OVER THE PARLOUR—One old fashioned bedsted, rods, curtains and valents, one feather bed, one bolster, one blanket, an old coverlet, a table, a stool, £1 10*s*.

IN THE CORN CHAMBER—Six quarters of oats, £3; six bushells of wheat some of it black, £1 2*s*.; six sacks, 13*s*.

IN THE STABLE—Three horses and a mare, £6 10*s*.; three collars, two pair of chain harness, four pair of plow harness, one pair of thilbals, three pair of bit halters, one cart saddle, £1 2*s*. 6*d*.

ABROAD—One waggon, and an old cart buck, £5 10*s*.; one plow and irons thereto belonging, harrow teeth, 8*s*. 4*d*.; three cows and a sow, £8 5*s*.; twenty nine sheep, £7 5*s*.
Twenty three acres of wheat growing, £38 10*s*.
Half a load of hay, and some oat straw in the barn, £1 5*s*.
Linnen—Three pair of coarse sheets, two pillowbeers, 7*s*. 6*d*.
Wearing apparrel and money in pocket, £5.
Toto—£86 10*s*. 10*d*. [Appraisers—Lawrence Hillyard, James Osborne.]

228.—John Plomer of Writtle. 1726.

The deceased's wearing apparell, & shaire, £3 17*s*. 6*d*.
Debt due from Benjamine Jefferson, £12 2*s* 6*d*.
Arrears of rent of the deceased's freehold estates at Writtle due at his death, £46.
[Total—£62. Appraisers—James Crush, Joseph Woodgate.]
[John Jefferyes noted as one of the executors.]

229.—John Godfrey of Writtle, miller. 14 February 1727/8.

IN THE HALL—One dresser and shelves, 8*s*.; three pewter dishes and twelve pewter plates, 11*s*.; one ovall table, one old deal leaved table, and five chairs, 9*s*. 6*d*.; one coal rack, fire shovel, tongs & bellows, 6*s*.; one spit, two slices, and one beef fork, 2*s*.

IN THE BREW-HOUSE—One copper, one kettle, & tubs, £1 16*s*.

IN THE BUTTERY—Seven drink vessells, and drink stall, £1.

IN THE CHAMBER—One bed and bedsted, two pair of sheets, and one table cloth, two tables, and an old bed in the garret, £2.

One old horse, 12*s*. 6*d*.
A rope and a pair of pully blocks the propper right of Benjamin Glanfield which were sold at the Water Mill as appears by the Inventory thereof for the sume of 5*s*.
Due to him at Rumford, £1 15*s*.
Wearing apparrell and ready money, £39 1*s*.
In all—£48 6*s*. [Appraisers—William Green, (blank) Bampton.]

230.—Abraham Stoakes. 14 September 1728.

Corn and hay, £10 2*s*. 6*d*.; mare and two colts, £7 10*s*.; cou and a calfe, £1 15*s*.; 9 sheep and 3 piges, £3 15*s*.; a cart, £1; implements of husbandre, 7*s*. 6*d*.

IN THE HORLL—2 tables, 1 form, 6 cheaeas, 6*s*.; other small trifels, 3*s*. 6*d*.

IN THE PALER—One bead and all thing belonging, £1 15*s*. 6*d*.; fouer cheaeas and a table, 5*s*. 6*d*.; puter and bars, £1 1*s*.

Small trifels in the dary, 9*s*.; vesels and tubs, 7*s*. 6*d*.
A trundle beed in the chamber, 19*s*.
Linin and a huch, 9*s*.
In money, £1.
In all—£31 6*s*. [Appraisers' names not given.]

231.—William Abrey of Writtle. 20 May 1729.

The deceased's wearing apparel and pocket mony, £5.
Twenty quarters of malt, £28; more malt, £35 17*s*. 6*d*.
A clock, £2.
[Total]—£70 17*s*. 6*d*. [Appraisers—Theophilus Lingard, Robert Kirkman.]

232.—Margaret Haward of Writtle, widow. 7 July 1729.

IN THE HALL—One pair of grates, fender, poker, hanger, fire-shovel, tongs, jack, pullies and weights, chaffing dish and brush, £1 14*s*. 8*d*.; four spitts, one iron dripping pan, 10*s*.; one pestle and mortar, one pepper and one drudging box, two brass cobiron heads and skimmers, 6*s*.; two warming panns, 4*s*. 6*d*.; a lock iron and two heaters, and four iron candlesticks, 3*s*. 6*d*.; a clock and clock case, £4 5*s*.; three oval tables, 13*s*.; seven rush chairs, 5*s*. 6*d*.; window curtains and six pictures, 8*s*.

IN THE PARLOR—The bedstedle, vallance & curtains, and curtain rods, three blankets, and one quilt, £3; one bed, one bolster, two pillows, £3 6*s*.; pair wainscot drawers, £1 1*s*.; two punch bowls, six slap basons and sugar pot, glasses, tea potts, & cups, 5*s*. 6*d*.; seeing glass, £1; table with the drawer, 5*s*.; six black rush bottom [chairs], 5*s*.; one pair of cobirons brass heads, 3*s*. 6*d*.; window curtains and pictures, 4*s*.

IN THE CHAMBER OVER THE PARLOR—Bedsted, curtains, vallance & curtain rods, one quilt, and three blankets, £2 5*s*.; one bed, one bolster, and two pillows—seventy four pound at eight pence per pound, £2 9*s*. 4*d*.; one table, four chairs, two punch bowls, one pair of window curtains, 9*s*.; one chest of drawers, 12*s*.

IN THE ROOM OVER THE HALL—Bedstedles, curtains, vallance, and curtain rod, one rug, one blanket, £1; one bed, two bolsters—seventy nine pound at seven pence per pound, £2 6*s*. 1*d*.; one livery cupboard, an old hutch, one stoole, 2*s*. 6*d*.

IN THE CHAMBER OVER THE PASSAGE—Bedsteds, curtains, vallance, and curtain rods, one rug, two blankets, £1; one bed, one bolster—seventy one pound at seven pence per pound, £2 1*s*. 5*d*.; one hutch, one table, three chairs, seven pair of sheets, five table cloths, and window curtains, £1 13*s*.

IN THE ROOM OVER THE SHOP—Bedstedles, curtains and vallance, one bed, one bolster—ninety two pound at six pence per pound, £2 10*s*. 6*d*.

IN THE ROOM OVER THE KITCHEN—One trundle bedstedle, flock bed, and bolster, 4*s*. 6*d*.; one bedstedle, 4*s*.; one close stool, 4*s*.; a powdering tub, 4*s*.; a fan, and chaffing seive, 1*s*.; five bushel wheat, £1 7*s*. 6*d*.; six sacks, 9*s*.

IN THE ROOM OVER THE SHOP—Seventy four pound iron at three half pence per pound, 9*s*. 3*d*.; a curtain and curtain rod, 6*s*.; a hutch, and side bed, 1*s*. 6*d*.

IN THE BUTTERY—Three half hogsheads, one kilderkin, one large stone bottle, one cupboard, two drink stalls, three shelves, one half peck, one seive, one basket, one hutch, £1 2*s*. 6*d*.

IN THE DAIRY—Two half hogsheads, two drink stalls, one stand, four shelves, and one dresser, £1 3*s*.; one frying pan, and one sauce pan, 5*s*.; twenty three pots and pans, 5*s*.; thirty knives and forks, 4*s*.; a pye board, cutting knife, milk seive, and rolling pin, 9*d*.

IN THE SLAUGHTER HOUSE—Three bushell of meal, 18*s*.; a kneading trough and a seive, 1*s*.

IN THE BREWHOUSE—Eight tubs, one coul, 13*s.*; two swill tubs, 3*s.*; copper & bars, £1 15*s.*; four brass kettles, one boyler, five brass skillets—sixty three pound at one shilling per pound, £3 3*s.*; one dozen and half of plates, 12*s.*; eleven pewter dishes—thirty five pound at eight pence per pound, £1 3*s.* 4*d.*; one bell metal pot, 10*s.*; one cheese press, rack, two pair iron cobirons, two pair trammels, one gridiron, one fender, one pair of bellows, one tin dripping pan, one tin coffee pot, one brass ladle, one fork, and two joynt stools, one table, two old chairs, one shovel, one spade, one mattock, a flaskett, two pails, one cullinder, one brass tea kettle, fifteen trenchers, & one scuer, £1 9*s.* 5*d.*

CART HOUSE—Two carts, copses, & ladders, and wheelbarrow, £5 2*s.*
Woodstacks & woods in the yards, £1 5*s.*; a grindstone, and winch, 5*s.*; hogs coat in the yard, 5*s.*

STABLE & HAY OVER & ADJACENT TO THE STABLE WITH THE ORCHARD—Hay over the stable, £4 10*s.*; one hay cock in the orchard, £9; apples, walnuts, and plumbs, £7 10*s.*; the mare and ronney horse, £6 10*s.*; the bayhorse and jack, £5; three pair of plow harness, two pair cart harness, two cart sadles, four collars, one pannell, three bit halters, three cruppers, one pair of false harness, £1 8*s.*
Harrows, 18*s.*; plough, &c., 10*s.*; a scith, 1*s.* 6*d.*; two rakes, three forks, 2*s.*
One cow, £2 15*s.*; coal, 4*s.*; riddle, & oat sive, 2*s.*; four hogs, £5.
Dung, 15*s.*; three acres wheat, £18; five acres oats, £12; two acres barley, £4 8*s.*
Grand Totall—£137 5*s.* 11*d.* [should be £136 18*s.* 3*d.*].
[Appraisers not named. Exhibited 11 June 1730.]

233.—William Grudgfield of Writtle. 18 July 1729.

IN THE HALL—Two tables, six chairs, one jack, two spits, three skillets, one bell metal pot, one iron pot, one brass pot, two spits more, two brass candlesticks, two iron ones, one brass mortar, one drudging box, one pepper box, one pair of cobirons, two brass kettles, twelve pewter dishes, eight pewter plates, three pewter porringers, four earthen quart mugs, four earthen pint mugs, and three half pint earthen mugs, a brass chaffing dish, a brass slice, a brass ladle, a dripping pan, a gridiron, & a pot iron, with many other small implements, £4 10*s.*

IN THE PARLOR—Three tables, eleven rush bottom chairs, two pair of cobirons, one fire shovel and tongs, and one pair of bellows, and a warming pan, £1.

IN THE BREWHOUSE—One copper, one mashing tub, one back, one under back, one working tub, and one starting tub, one hogshead, two kilderkins, one hop seive, and one funnel, one mash tub stall, and one drink stall, three keelers, three forms, one fire fork, and one peeler, a tap hose, & rudder, £5 10*s.*

IN THE CELLAR—Fourteen hogsheads of strong beer, and two empty kilderkins, six drinking stalls, a pipe ring, a powdering tub, two brass cocks, a pair of nippers, £53.

IN THE HALL CHAMBER—One feather bed, bedstedle, bolster, curtains, three pillows, one blanket & coverlid, an old chest of drawers, six cane chairs, one table, one trunk, £4 5*s*.

IN THE PARLOR CHAMBER—One feather bed, one bolster, one pillow, two blankets, a bedstedle, curtains and vallance, two chairs, one cupboard, a hutch, and one dozen & eight bottles, £3.

IN THE CELLAR CHAMBER—Two hutches, one kneading trough, one flower tub, one flasket, seven sheets, one table cloth, two chairs, £2.

IN THE YARD—Two hundred tiles, a parcell of round wood, and a horse, £3 5*s*.

Wearing apparel and ready money, £1 10*s*.
[Total]—£78. [Appraiser—G. Griffith. Exhibited 11 June 1730.]

234.—Thomas Harris of Writtle. 8 January 1729/30.

IN THE HALL—Three tables, three joyned stools, eight chairs, £1 2*s*.; eight pewter dishes, one warming pan, one spit, one mortar, one gridiron, two cobirons, one pair of tongs, one pair of bellows, one fire shovel, six candlesticks, five wedges, and other small implements, £2 4*s*.

IN THE PARLOR—One bedsted, curtains, bed blanket and coverlid, bolster and pillows, £3; four pair of sheets, 12*s*.; a press cupboard, a little table, one chair, a trunk, 6*s*.; one tub, one hutch, three drink vessels, 12*s*.

IN THE FIRST CHAMBER—One bedsted, bed, bolster, blankets, coverlid, curtains, vallance, a small parcel of wool, half a bushell of wheat, and a pillion, £2 12*s*.

IN THE FURTHER CHAMBER—One bedstead, curtains, vallance, bed, bolster, blankets, coverlid and all as they stand, and two hutches, £4.

IN THE CHEESE CHAMBER—The cheese, corn sacks, & other goods therein, £10.

IN THE DAIRY—Two kettles, one pottage pot, three skillets, two dishes, £2 1*s*.; four drink vessels, three tubs, one cheese press, one churn, one stand, and other implements, £1 15*s*.

IN THE BREWHOUSE—One copper, three tubs, one paile, a mattock, one spade, & other implements, £1 16*s*.

IN THE BARN—The wheat, £16; oates, £3; hay, £9.

IN THE STABLE—Two horses and furniture belonging to them, £4 10*s*.

WITHOUT DOORS—One cart, one plow, one pair of harrows, £4; six cows, and three calves, & three heifers, £25 5*s*.; three hogs, £5; twenty seven sheep, £6 10*s*.

Crop on the ground—Three acres of wheat, £6.
Wearing apparel and money in pocket, £5.
In all—£114 5*s*.
[Appraisers—John Green,[1] John Hilyard. Exhibited 11 June 1730.]

[1] Signs as William Green on the paper copy.

235.—Joseph Goodman of Writtle, miller. 19 May 1730.

IN THE HALL—Three pewter dishes, six plates, seven porringers, six chairs, one grate, two spits, one pair of tongs, one pair of bellows, and a fire shovell, two tables, one boyler, two skillets, a warming pan, and other small things besides, £2 10*s*.

IN THE BUTTERY—Three vessels, one kettle, one kneading trough, one frying pan, and other small things, £1 15*s*.

IN THE BEST CHAMBER—A bed, bolster, bedstedles, blanket & quilt, five chairs, one table, dishes, cups, &c., and other small things, £5.

THE LITTLE CHAMBER—Linnen, hutch, and bed, &c., £4.

Wearing apparel, £1.
Ready money, bills, &c., £30.
[Total]—£44 5*s*.
[Appraisers—William Green, Samuel Choate. Exhibited 19 May 1730.]

236.—Jonathan Sapsford of Sturgeons, Writtle. 20 January 1731/2.

IN THE WHEAT BARN—Wheat in the barn, £40; wheat straw, £3 10*s*.; wheat upon the ground, rent of land, and fallows, £96 11*s*.

IN THE BARLEY BARN—Barley in the barn, £40; barley straw & other straw, £11.

IN THE STABLE, &C.—Seven horses, £110; furniture for 6 horses, £6 6*s*.; hay, £12; fourteen cow cattle & 2 calves, £51 15*s*.; forty six sheep, £23; waggons, carts, plows, harrows, ladders, dew rakes, &c., necessaries, £30; dung and manure, £12; hogs and pigs, £6.

IN THE BREWHOUSE, DAIRY, AND CHEESE CHAMBER—Two coppers, a mashing tub, coolers, tubs, cheese presses, stands, cheesfats, dressers, milk coolers, cheeses, skillets, pots, pans, pork in the powdering tubs, &c., £33.

IN THE KITCHEN—One clock, a cupboard, tables, dressers, spits, chairs, cobirons, dripping pans, gridirons, &c., small things, £6 10*s*.

TWO SMALL BEER BUTTERIES—4 vessells, bottles, shelves, &c., £3.

THE SERVANTS CHAMBER—2 beds, bedsteadles, & coverings, £3.

IN THE HALL—One clock, 2 tables, 7 chairs, cobirons, &c., together with the closet, £7.

IN THE PARLOUR—One bed, bolster, bedsteadles & furniture, hang press, 3 small tables, 3 chairs, &c., small things, £5.

STRONG BEER CELLAR—7 vessells, drinkstalls, and a small table, £6.

ROOM OVER THE STRONG BEER CELLAR—A trunk, a box, & a few apples, £1.

ROOM OVER THE PARLOUR—One bed, bolster, bedsteadles with curtains and furniture, 1 chest of drawers, 1 hutch, 1 trunk, 1 pair of cobirons, 1 glass, 3 chairs, 1 joynt stool, 2 other stools, &c., small things, £7.

CLOSET OVER THE KITCHEN—One course bed, bedsteadles, &c., £1 10*s*.

CHAMBER OVER THE KITCHEN—One bed, bolster, pillows, bedsteadles, curtains & other furniture, with chest of drawers, trunk, chairs, one small hutch, and a joynt stool, &c., £8; 30 hundred of hops at 3 pound per cwt., £90; rye and turnips, £10; sacks, screw, shovels, & other materials for workmen, £5.

CHAMBER OVER THE HALL AND CLOSET—A bed, bolster, bedsteadles and furniture, 1 table, 2 looking glasses, cobirons, &c., a trunk, a box, 6 cane chairs, one stool, & earthen ware in the closet, £17.

Brass and pewter, £9.
Plate, £4.
Linnen, £30.
Wearing apparel & pocket money, £10.
Summa totalis—£697 2*s*. [should be £698 2*s*.].
[Appraisers—William Green, Samuel Choate. Exhibited 30 May 1732.]

237.—Philip Bright of Writtle. 28 July 1743.

IN THE HALL—One spit, one stool, two cobirons, one tramel, two pair of tongs, two firepans, a pair of bellows, a pott iron, one gridiron, one salt box, one cleever, two brass candlesticks, one skimer, one brass chafing dish, one pestle and morter, a pair of snuffers, one slice, one box iron and heaters, one flower box, one pepper box, one cupboard, four silver spoons, one form, two tables, two pailes, two skillets, one saucepan, six pewter dishes, six plates, one cullender, three coffee potts, two tunnells, one dresser, one lanthorne, one warming pan, six chairs, one clock and furniture, one settle, a parcel of earthen ware, one gun, £8 3*s*.

IN THE PARLOUR—Two hutches, two boxes, one desk, three chairs, two stools, one bedstead, one feather bed, one bolster, two blanketts, one rugg, curtains and furniture, five pillows, thirteen napkins, two table cloths, one apron, one cupboard, a parcell of old linnen, £3 10*s*.

IN THE BUTTERIES—Six vessels, two beer stalls, one boyler, one kettle, £2 10*s*.

IN THE GARRETTS—One iron beam, an old bed, and a parcel of lumber, £1 7*s*. 6*d*.

BEST CHAMBER—A cabinett, a suit of bed curtains, a bedstead, one feather bed, one bolster, one pillow, one couch, nine pair of sheets, twenty four napkins, £20.

DAIRY—One bason, one pan, two frying pans, one ladle, one skimer, a pair stilliards, £1 10*s*.

BREWHOUSE—One copper, one mash tubb, one press, two tubbs, a parcell of lumber, £3 10*s*.

YARD AND CART LODGE—Two waggons, one cart, a parcell of tools for husbandry, £10.

IN THE BARN—One bushel, one shovel, two fanns, sixty sacks, a parcel of wheat, a parcel of oats, a parcel of pease, £9 14*s*.; about thirty loads of hay, £37 10*s*.

COW HOUSE—Five cows, three calves, six piggs, £25 18*s*.

In the stable—One sadle, two bridles, five horses and their furniture, £14.

In the meadows & fields—One bull stagg, three heifers, £14; five sheep, four harrows, one plow with furniture, £3; 9 acres of fallow, three tilts, £9; four half acres of barley, £13 12*s.*; twelve acres of bullermung, £27 12*s.*; ten acres of clover seed, £20; three acres of wheat, £3; one acre horse beans, £3 12*s.*; a parcell of tares, £3; a parcell of earth & dung, £5.
[Total]—£239 8*s.* 6*d.*
[Appraisers—Tobias Green, Richard Barnes.]
[Exhibited 1 September 1743]

238—Theophilus Lingard of Writtle. 18 January 1743/4.

In the best room—A sacking bottom bedstead with blue mohair curtains lined with India Persian, a feather bed, bolster, and two pillows, three blankets, one quilt, a chest of draws, a dressing table and glass, six cane chairs, one elbow ditto, a stove grate, shovel, tongs, poker and holders, a hearth brush, a pair of window curtains and rod, a looking glass, the paper hangings of the room, £8 15*s.*

In the little room—A sacking bottom bedstead with stuff curtains, three old blankets, one blue rugg, a large chest, a small table, one chair, one stool, a pair of window curtains and rod, £1 18*s.* 6*d.*

In the striped bed room—A sacking bottom bedstead with camblett curtains, a feather bed, bolster, and four pillows, three blanketts, one coverlid, one counterpain, a chest of draws, five old chairs, one table a set of window curtains and rod, £4 15*s.*

In the garrett—A corded bedstead, a flock bed and bolster, two old blanketts, a tapstry covering, a corded bedstead, a feather bed and bolster, three blanketts, one coverlid, one pillow, a table, an old chair, a hutch, a box, and an old trunk, ten cucumber glasses, £3 15*s.* 6*d.*

In the maid's room—A corded bedstead with old curtains, a set of yellow ditto not put up, a feather bed, bolster, one pillow, two blankets, one rug, two old hutches, four old chairs, an old trunk, a brass kettle, one small ditto, two old water potts, a pair of garden sheers, a pair of cobirons, £3 0*s.* 2*d.*

In the best parlour—An ovall table, a looking glass, a corner cupboard, a round table, a cane couch and squab, six cane chairs, one elbow ditto, a stove grate, shovel, tongs, poker and fender, two pictures, a pair of window curtains and rod, the hangings of the room; on the stair case—twenty prints in frames, £5 9*s.* 10*d.*

In the pantry—Sixteen pewter plates, two small dishes, a dresser, a cubbard, a punch ladle, a flower tubb, seven tin patty pans, a roleing pin, two flower seives, fifty five pieces of Delph and earthen ware, a kneeding trough, and a meal tubb, a corn tubb, an old table, a bran tubb, a pyeboard, two pair of brass scales, three brass weights, two leaden ditto, a pair of stillyards and weight, £1 17*s.* 2*d.*

IN THE HALL—The coal racks, a pair of iron cheeks, fender, shovel, tongs, poker, and two hangers, one trevit, a gridiron, three scquers [skewers], a bird spit, a pair of large brass candlesticks, snuffers and stand, two pair of lesser ditto, snuffers and stand, a pestle and mortar, an old drudging box, five iron candlesticks, one tinder box, a box iron, three heaters, a brass candle-box, a warming pan, the jack as fixt, a pair of spit irons, one spit, a corner cupboard, a large table, three small ditto, an ironing board, eight rush bottom chairs, a small cupboard, a fire curtain and rod, two window curtains and rods, a pair of bellows, two maps, two tyn coffee potts, a quart decanter, three cruits, one pair glass salts, nine wine glasses, two tumblers, £4 18*s.*

IN THE CELLAR—Two hogsheads, five half hogsheads, two kilderkins, a woodden tunnell, two butter firkins, seven small runletts, three beer stalls, three brass cocks, £2 13*s.* 6*d.*

IN THE BUTTERY AND OUT CELLAR—Nine hogsheads, eight half hogsheads, three sauce pans, two skillets, two boilers, two kettles, ten puter dishes, fourteen plates, a pewter measure, a tin funnell, two lanthorns, two brass slices, nine pieces of wooden ware, six pieces of earthen ware, a frying pan, three pailes, a powdering tub, six drink stalls, thirteen dozen quart bottles, two dozen pints, a half hogshead, a copper, two cowles, two swill tubs, one marsh tub, seven wash and wort tubs, a cleaver, a dozen of knives and forks, £11 19*s.* 5*d.*

Plate and Linnen—Silver spoons, a pint cup, a porringer, a pair of fine sheets, a od ditto, four pair of middle ditto, five pair ordinary ditto, one damask table cloth, three diaper, two ditto, twelve pillow biers, six diaper napkins, ten od napkins, four od pieces, £10 4*s.* 8*d.*
For home made liquors, £10.

Out door stock—Two cows, two heiffers, forty eight sheep, and fifteen hogs and pigs, £38 18*s.*; five horses, and two colts, & all geers, £27 11*s.*; one waggon, five old carts, two plows, and three harrows, £15 5*s.*; thirty sacks, one bushell, one fan, thirty mauns, twenty bushell basketts, £3 16*s.* 2*d.*; five ladders, a parcell of working tools, one wheelbarrow, £1 6*s.* 6*d.*; a parcell of forks and rakes, one waggon tilt, one stack of hay, a parcell of straw, and a parcell chaffe, £12 8*s.* 6*d.*; a parcell of wood, a parcel old hurdles, and a parcell of coals, twenty bell glasses, two cucumber frames, and parcell greens, £5 4*s.*; a parcell of young trees, and a parcell of crab stocks, £1 12*s.*; seven roods of turnips, a parcell of parsnips, and a parcell of beans, £4 12*s.* 6*d.*; seven acres and half of wheat plowing and sowing, one acre of peas, £8 13*s.*; for plowing and sowing, and parcell [?]dung, £1 10*s.*; six acres plowing and diging parcell of ground, £2 12*s.*; for a parcell of plowing, diging and sowing, £2 2*s.* 3*d.*; two seives, one riddle, and a parcell of small measures, 10*s.*; for a parcell of apples and small seeds, £13 12*s.*; for wheat, oats, and tares, £19.
Ready money in the house, £20.
[Total]—£267 19*s.* 8*d.* [should be £247 19*s.* 8*d.*].
[Appraisers—Lancaster Noone, Tobias Green. Exhibited 24 May 1744.]

239.—Richard Reddings of Writtle, 1744.

IN THE HALL—Two tables, one form, six chairs, one joint stool, one warming pan, two cobiron, fire shovel and tongs, five pewter dishes, six plates, pestle and mortar, three candle sticks, and other small things, one spit, one gunn, £1 8*s*.

IN THE PARLOUR—One bed and bedstead, curtains, vallence, two blanketts, one rug, one cupboard, one hutch, four chairs, three half hogsheads, two kilderkins, £3.

IN THE BUTTERY—One half hogshead, two little washtubs, two porridge potts, one form, a few small earthen ware, 5*s*.

IN THE KITCHIN—One copper, two kettles brass, three tubs, and a cowl, a kneeding trough, two shovels, one spade, one hoppick, beetle, eleven wedges, mattock, & pickax, £3 6*s*. 6*d*.

IN THE CHAMBER OVER THE PARLOUR—One flock bed and what belongs to it, three hutches, one hanging press, three chairs, 13*s*.

IN THE CHAMBER OVER THE HALL—Twenty sacks, scales and weights, six bushells tares, eight bushells oats, one hen coop, one screen, one wire seive, a parcel of clover seed in the chaffe, one old chest, and other utensils, £3 16*s*.

IN THE STABLE—One horse, one mare, £6.

IN THE BARN—All the utensills in the stable, 15*s*.; a parcell of wheat to thrash, £4 10*s*.; two seam of peas to thrash, two seam of oats, £2 10*s*.; three seam of barley to thresh, £2 2*s*.

One dung cart, with ladders, ropes, and winch pins, £2; one long ladder, 5*s*.; one plough with all its utensils, 3*s*.
One cow, £2 10*s*.; two Welch calves, £3; twenty four sheep and lambs, £8 5*s*.; four harrows, 10*s*.; two fatt hogs, £3 10*s*.
One acre and half of wheat sown upon the ground, £3 3*s*.; three acres and half of clover land plowed once, 15*s*.; three load old and new hay, £3.
Four pair of sheets with some coarse table linnen, £1 12*s*.
Ready money and wearing apparell, £2.
[Total]—£62 13*s*. 6*d*. [should be £58 18*s*. 6*d*.].
[Appraisers—Samuel Shetwith, John Hardey.]

240.—John Portway of Writtle. 8 July 1749.

Twenty four acres wheat, and seven quarters and half wheat, £44; eleven ditto and half oats, four barley, three and half pease, £43 4*s*.; six loads of hay, four cows, twenty eight sheep, twenty two piggs, £47 15*s*.; three horses and furniture, one waggon, two carts, £26; five harrows, two rowls, three plows, and other husbandry goods, £7 18*s*.; one hundred and ninety loads of earth and dung, £8 11*s*. 8*d*.

One copper, one mashing tub, one working ditto, five ditto, £13.

One bed, one quilt, three blankets, two pillows, one chest drawers, one table, one glass, £11 9*s*. 6*d*.; two [beds], quilt, blankets, four chairs, one table, two iron doggs, £6 1*s.*; one [bed], quilt, two blankets, one table, two chairs, one chest, £2 9*s.*; one [bed], quilt, two [blankets], two pillows, six chairs, one table, £5 8*s.*; one [bed], one rugg, two blankets, £2 10*s.*

Fifteen dishes, four dozen plates, one crane, fender, tongs, fire shovel, poker, bellows, three tubs, nine chairs, and dresser, £7 16*s.*; three pots, three saucepans, brasses, glasses, and mugs, £4 2*s.* 6*d.*

Nineteen chairs, six ditto, five tables, jacks, fire shovel, tongs, £2 14*s.*

One copper, two skillets, seven tubs, pails, quarn, syder press, trough, £3 17*s.*

Wearing apparel, £5 4*s.*

An account of the liquors gauged and appraised by Robert Spurling—18⅔ hogsheads of old beer, £46 12*s.*; 13½ barrels of ale, £15 10*s.* 6*d.*; 1 hogshead of small beer, 10*s.*; 35 hogsheads, £17; 4 small casks, 16*s.*

Summe Total of this Inventory—£322 8*s.* 2*d.*

[Appraisers of first section of inventory—Tobias Green, Nathaniel Springham. Exhibited 6 October 1749.]

241.—William Goodde of Roxwell. [Undated.]

Forte qurteres of malt, 36*li.*; a leven quarteres of barle, 9*li.*

Thre hors, and tooue coues, 17*li.*; thirtene shepe, 6*li.*

A quarter of whet, 1*li.* 15*s.*; whet one the ground, barle falloue, 20*li.*

Other lumber, 2*li.*

Pese, 2*li.*

Owing by bond, 10*li.*

Summe is—103*li.* 15*s.*

[Appraisers—Thomas Warner, Thomas Sach.]

242.—Widdow Watts [for James Watts]. [Undated, *c.* 1660.]

IN THE HALLE—One long table, 8 joyned stowles, one long forme, one bench bord and back, 1*li.* 10*s.*; one coberd, 15*s.*; one little table, 2 lettle stoles, 4*s.*; 6 cheyers, one glascuberd, 12*s.*; 5 cussins, one bayer [*sic*] of bellows, with other implements, 8*s.* 6*d.*

IN THE CHAMBER OVER THE HALLE—One joyned bedstedle, 2 fether beds, one fether bolster, 2 fether pellows, one ruge, one payer of blankets, curtans, and vallance, 7*li.* 5*s.*; one pres cuberd, 10*s.*; one livere cuberd, 11*s.* 6*d.*; 2 joyned chest, one pox [box], 2 joyned stolles, 1*li.*; 2 chayers, 2 payer of cobierns, 2 payer of tongs, 2 fier shovels, and other implements, 1*li.* 1*s.* 6*d.*

IN THE CLOSET—One cuberd, table, and other implements, 5*s.* 6*d.*

All the pauter, 3*li.* 10*s.* 10*d.*

IN THE CHAMBER OVER THE KITCHIN—One joyned bedstedle, 2 chest, 2 trunks, one payer of cobbiarns, and other implements, 1*li.* 3*s.* 4*d.*

IN THE CHAMBER OVER THE BUTTRE—One bedstedle, one fether bed, one flock bed, 2 fether bolsster, 2 fether pellows, one coverlet, on payer of blankets, and curtins, 3*li.* 0*s.* 10*d.*; one halfe heded bedstedle, 2 flock beds, one coverlet, 2 blankets, 2 pellows, one bolster, 1*li.* 10*s.*; 2 chayers, one chest, one lettle forme, and others implements, 5*s.* 4*d.*

IN THE GARAT—One borded bedstedle, 2 trundle beds, 3 flock bed, 2 fether bolsters, one flock bolstors, 4 blankets, 1*li.* 10*s.* 6*d.*

IN THE CHESLE [?CHEESE] CHAMBER—2 owld tables upon darmons, with other implements, 5*s.* 4*d.*

IN THE CHICHIN—One table upon darmans, one long forme, one joyned stolle, one little table, 6 chayers, one settle, one short forme, one salt box, 1*li.*; 2 muskets, one fowlling pesse, one pike, 18*s.*; one jack, 4 spets, 3 driping pans, one clever, one shreding knife, one tin collender, one payer of cobbirns, fier shovell and tongs, 2 payer of tramels, and other implements, 1*li.* 10*s.*

IN THE DAYRE—One plonk, 2 charnes, 6 kellers, 5 bowls, 5 [?]mowts, 2 breds, one powdring tub, 3 small drink vessels, 4 shelfes, and others implements, 2*li.* 0*s.* 6*d.*

IN THE BUTTRE—One chespres, one charne, one hanging cuberd, and other implements, 7*s.* 10*d.*; all the brass in the buttre, and the lead in the kichin, 5*li.* 10*s.* 6*d.*

IN THE BRUHOWS—One copper, 6 tubes, one pelle, one forme, with other implements, 2*li.* 12*s.* 6*d.*

IN THE BOWLTING HOWSE—One kneding troff, one mele tube, one bowle, with other implements, 7*s.* 6*d.*

5 horsses and 2 colts, 18*li.*; cart harnes and plow harnes, and collers, and halters, and 2 panels, 3 roopes, 2*li.* 1*s.*; one wagon, 2 dungcarts, one owld cart boddey, 8*li.* 2*s.*; 8 cowes, one bull, 30*li.*; 3 yerling bollox, 3*li.* 15*s.*; 12 shepe, and 22 lambes yeare owld, 12*li.* 2*s.*; one sow, hogg, and 5 shetes, 2*li.* 18*s.*
Haye, 10*li.*; whet upon the grownd at 1*li.* 14*s.*, 34*li.*; barleland, 8 acors, 6*li.* 4*s.*; one plow and chaynes, 1 payer of harows, and other irons belonging to it, 1*li.*
One skrue, one quarne, one boshell, one fann, 1*li.* 6*s.* 8*d.*; 2 dawrakes, spades, shovels, mattox, with other implements, 12*s.*
His wareing aparell and money in his purs, 5*li.*
[Total—174*li.* 16*s.* 8*d.*]
[Appraisers—Henry Finch, John Woolmer.]
Money oweing by my husband James Watts in bond, 155*li.*
Left in my Cozen Bretts hands which my husband rec' p'd unto Richard Casse since my husbands death, 50*li.*
Debts without bond payed since, 50*li.*
Pd of the bonds, 85*li.*
All the debts which I have payed since my husbands death amounteth to 185*li.*

243.—Cristair Belsted. [Undated.]

IN THE HALL—On tabell, and a forme, with 2 chairs, and other impellments, 13*s.* 4*d.*

IN THE PALER—On old fether bed and bed stedl, on pres, and 2 chests, and a tabell, and other trifelling things, 3*li.*

IN A UPER CHAMBER—3 chests, on covrlet, and other impellments, 14*s.*; on chest, 2 pair of shets, a tabell cloth, on payr of pelober, and a dusen of napkens, 1*li.* 10*s.*

IN ON OTHER ROM—2 old flocke beds, and 2 old bed stedls, and other things, 14*s.*

IN THE BUTREY—2 bras ketls, 2 bras pots, and other impellments, 2*li.*

IN THE MILKE HOWS—On qarn, on ches, lar, and 7 pautr dishes, and other impellments, 1*li.* 10*s.*

His whet in the barn, and his haye in the haye howse, 10*li.*
On hors, and a mar and colt, 4*li.* 10*s.*; 2 cous por old ons, 3*li.*
On old dunkart, and a payr of whels, 2*li.*
His warin clothes, and his purs and mony, 2*li.*
In desperate debts, 79*li.* 8*s.* 6*d.*
The sum is—110*li.* 19*s.* 10*d.*
[Appraisers—Thomas Robinson, James Wattes. See fair copy, No. 18.]

244.—Edward Hawkins. [Undated.]
In bonds, 25*li.*
Corne & chafe, 2*li.* 10*s.*
Goods within doores, 1*li.* 10*s.*
Total—29*li.* [Appraiser—Thomas Browne.]

245.—[No name or date, *c.* 1720.]
AN INVETEARY OF LINEN AND WEAREING APARRELL.
One suite of red striped silk.
One suite of blew silk.
One scarfe.
Two peices of dammask containing 20 yd. moor or less.
Eight paire of sheets.
Two sifer rings, and two plaine rings, and one paire of silver buttons, one silver poringer, one silver snuff box.
Two large silver spoons, and two silver tea spoons.
Four pillobears, & two diaper table cloathes.
Three holland shirts, and one coarse shirt.
Five linen shifts, and 5 turnovers, and 2 muslin hoods.
Three coats, one wastcoate, and one paire of briches.
One fustin frock, two paire of stockines, and three wollen capes.
Two wiggs, and one wigg of Mr. Zach[r]. Bridgs, and one foloi Bible.
Two old wastcoats, [one paire of chest of drawers, one corner cubbard—deleted].

BRASS AND PUTER
Two dousson and 5 plaits, six puter dishes, and two boylers, three sauce pans, and three stew pans; two brace candle sticks, and one paire of snuffers; one peper box and drudger, one box iron and two heaters; one brase skimmer, and one copper coffee pot; one warming pan, and one gridiron.

IN THE FRONT CHAMBER
One paire of chest of drawers, and one corner cubbard; six cane chairs, one table, and one looking glass; foure larg pictures with gilt frames, and a parsell of small picturs; two beds and one bed stid, with its furneturs, and two larg cheests.

IN THE LITTLE CHAMBER
One bed and bed stid, and 1 paire of blankitts, and a rug, & 1 cane chaire.

IN THE LODGERS ROOME UP 3 PAIRE OF STAIRES
One bed and bed stid, one paire of sheets, and one paire of blanketts; one old Dutch table; one iron pott, a little pair of grates, and 4 old black chairs.

APPENDIX A

The three following inventories were found with the bonds listed in Appendix B, and are not regarded as part of the main series. They are not included in any of the tables or mentioned in the introductory notes.

246.—Joseph Lingard. 14 October 1712.

In ye Hall—3 Tables, 2 formes, 2 tramells, one goint stoole, 4 Chires, on Press Cupboard, 2 Cobyrins, 2 skilletts, on spitt, on Gridyron, on worme-ing pand, on Chefing Deesh, on pair of Tongs, 3 puter Dishes with other Implements, 1*li.* 6*s.*

In ye butrey—7 Tubbs, 2 Porridges Pott, on Kettle, on vessells, A Beethel and a wedges with other Implments, 1*li.* 2*s.*

In ye parler—On Bed and stedle, 3 Hutches, on vesell, 4 pewter Dishes, on pewter porringer, on Chaire, on box with other Implements, 1*li.* 2*s.*

In ye Milk House—A Neding Trofe, 2 vessell, 2 Hutches, 2 formes, Mele Tubbs with other Impls, 6*s.*

One Coper, 9*s.*

In ye Chamber over ye hall—On bed and stedle, 2 Hutches, 4 pond of wooll, 3 seme of wheat with other Implements, 7*li.*

In ye Chamber over ye parler—On bed and stedle, on Hutch with other Implementes, 12*s.*

On ho[r]se with Harness, 2*li.* 10*s.*
On pair of harrows, on plow, 2 dung cart, on Load Cart, 6*li.*
5 sheeps and wheats on ye grond, 3*li.* 10*s.*
Wheats in ye wheatt Barne, 6*li.*

In ye Barley Barne—Barley, on scren, on Bushel, on fan with other Implementes, 7*li.*
His wareing Apprarell and mony 2*li.*
[Total]—38*li.* 17*s.*
[Appraisers—Robt. Thornton, Rayden Cook.]

247.—Edward Boggas of Roxwell, gent. 29 Sept. 1702.

The wheate in the barne, 36*li.*; the Barley in the barne, 30*li.*; the Pease in the barne, 13*li.*; the Oates in the barne, 5*li.*; the Hay, 5*li.* 5*s.* 6*d.*
One Horse and the furniture belonging, 7*li.* 10*s.*; foure Cows, 10*li.* 2*s.* 6*d.*; one and thirty sheep, 12*li.*; the Hoggs, 5*li.* 6*s.*; 9 piggs, 2*li.* 16*s.*
One waggon, 2 dung Carts, a plow and a payer of Harrows, 8*li.* 7*s.* 6*d.*
One Screw and sacks and other Implements, 1*li.* 15*s.*
The hoppole, 5*li.*
The fallow, 3*li.*
The furniture in the Hall Chamber, 18*li.* 1*s.*
The furniture in the Parlor Chamber, 9*li.* 15*s.*
The furniture in the Chamber over the Seller, 5*li.* 1*s.* 6*d.*
The furniture in the Chamber over the Kitchin, 4*li.* 10*s.*
The furniture in the Chamber over the Dary, 1*li.*

In the Closet—bookes, a desk and a Cubord, *2li. 2s. 6d.*
The plate, *2li.* 10*s.*
The furniture in the Parlor, *6li.*
The furniture in the Hall, *2li.* 5*s.*
The furniture in the Kitchin, 5*li.* 5*s.* 1*d.*
Other Goods in the Kitchin, 3*li.* 5*s.*
The Goods in the Brewhouse, 5*li.* 1*s.* 6*d.*
The Goods in the Dary, 1*li.* 0*s.* 6*d.*
The Goods in the Seller, 2*li.* 18*s.* 6*d.*
The Linning, 5*li.* 10*s.*
His wearing apparell and money in his purse, 5*li.*
Sume totall is—223*li.* 0*s.* 1*d.* [should be 224*li.* 8*s.* 1*d.*].
[Appraisers—Tho. Wolfe, Robert Crush.]

248.—George Taverner of Writtle. 22 June 1704.

IN YE HALL—Two tables, one press cubord, one joynd form, 3 joynd-stooles, 4 chaires, 2 spitts, a gridiron, 3 cobbirons, fireshovell & tongs, with other odd things, 1*li.* 10*s.*

IN YE PARLER—One bedsted with one feather-bed, two feather bolsters, one Coverlid, 2 blanketts with curtains, one press-cubbord, 4 chaires, one joynd-stool, one worming-pan, 3*li.* 5*s.*

IN YE DAIRIE—Six tubbs, one keeler, one stan, one churn, one cheese press, scales & weights with other odd things, 1*li.* 6*s.* 8*d.*

IN YE BUTTERIE—4 halfe-hogsheads, 2 drink-stalls, one saddle & pillion with other odd things, 1*li.* 7*s.* 6*d.*

IN YE BREWHOUSE & BUTTERIE—8 tubbs, 2 coppers, 3 kettles, one iron pott, one brass pott, 4 skilletts, one halfe hogshead, 6 barrills, one kneading trough, 2 drink-stalls with odd things, 5*li.* 17*s.* 6*d.*

THE PARLOR CHAMBER—Two joynd bedsteds, 2 feather beds, 3 feather bolsters with curtains, 2 blanketts, 2 coverlids, one table, 2 joynd forms, 3 chaires, 5 chests, one hanging-press, a payre of andirons, 4*li.* 7*s.* 6*d.*

IN YE SERVANTS CHAMBER—Two bedsteds, one feather bed, one flock bed, 3 blanketts, with odd things, 1*li.* 10*s.*

Pewter, 1*li.* Linen 3*li.*
Wheat in ye Barn 5*li.* One skreen, one bushell, 10 sacks, 17*s.* 6*d.*
Hey in ye house 1*li.* 10*s.*

IN YE CART HOUSE—One wagon, one tumbrell, a payre of harrows, one plow with irons, 5*li.* 5*s.*

3 kows, 7*li.* 10*s.*; one hogg, a sow & 10 piggs, 2*li.* 12*s.*; 13 sheep & one lamb, 3*li.* 10*s.*; 2 horses with collers & harness, 7*li.* 15*s.*
4 acers of wheat growing, 12*li.*; 6 acers of barley growing, 12*li.*; one acre & halfe of oats & tears, 1*li.* 5*s.*; 13 acres fallow once plowd, 2*li.* 12*s.*
His wearing apparell & money in his pockett, 4*li.*
[Total]—89*li.* 0*s.* 8*d.*
[Appraisers—Wesson Stylman, Will Boosey. Exhibited 22 June 1704.]

APPENDIX B

THE obligation to produce an inventory was in the form of a bond, half in Latin and half in English. The Latin portion of a typical example[1] may be translated as follows:—

Know all men by these presents that We, Mary George of Writtle in the County of Essex, widow, and John Price of Terling in the said County, yeoman, are held and firmly bound unto the Reverend John South, Bachelor of Laws, in [and throughout the whole] peculiar and exempt jurisdiction of Writtle in the County of Essex, Official or Commissary lawfully constituted, in Six hundred pounds of good and lawful money of England, to be paid to him the said Reverend or his certain Attorney, executors, successors or assigns. For the good and faithful payment of which sum we bind ourselves and each of us for the whole and our heirs, executors and administrators, firmly by these presents sealed with our seals. Dated the sixth day of the month of November in the year of the reign of our Lord Charles by the grace of God King of England, Scotland, France and Ireland, defender of the faith, and so forth the fourteenth and in the year of our Lord 1638.

Then follows the English half of the document:—

The Condicion of this Obligacion is such that if the abovebounden Marye George the Relict and Administratrix of all and singuler the goods Chattles and Creditts of John George late of Writtle deceased doe make or cause to be made a true and perfect Inventory of all and singuler the goods rights creditts and Chattles of the said deceased which shall or may come to the hands possession or knowledge of the sayd Marye George And the same soe made doe exhibite into the Regestry of the sayd Mister John South the next to be holden in the parishe of Writtle aforesayd, and the same goods well and truly doe administer (that is to say) doe pay the debts of the sayd deceased so farr as the sayd goods and Chattles will thereunto extend and as the law doth chardge And also doe make a true and perfect Accompte of and uppon hir sayd administration when shee shall thereunto be Lawfully called. And such parte and portion of the sayd goods as shalbe found remayning uppon the sayd accompte shall distribute and dispose according to the discretion of the above named Mister John South or some other competent Judge in that behalfe for the tyme being And lastly that the abovebounden Mary George and John Price theire heires executors and administrators doe at all tymes heereafter clearely acquitt defend and same harmelesse the above named Mister John South and all other the officers and ministers by reason of graunting the said letters of administration Then this obligacion to be voyd or els to stand in force

Sealed signed and delivered

in the presence of

the marke of

Anthony A Toppin

the marke of

Marye S George (L.S.)

[Signed] John Price (L.S.)

[Signed] William Howson Notarie Publique

[1] D/APw P3 is the E.R.O. catalogue mark of the list of Bonds on pp. 279-82. See also Inventory No. 19.

Name of Deceased	*Parish*	*Persons Bound*	*Relationship to Deceased*	*Date of Bond*	*Inventory No.*
John Barnes	Writtle	Susanna Barnes of Writtle	widow	30 Aug. 1637	
		John Barnes [of Blank]			
John Taverner	Writtle	Michael Taverner of Writtle, husbandman		15 Jan. 1638	17
Francis Banks	Roxwell	Francis Banks of Roxwell, husbandman		15 Jan. 1638	13
		Anthony Toppin of Writtle, cordwainer			
Thomas Rainberd	Roxwell	John Raineberd of Roxwell, weaver		13 Feb. 1638	16
		Reynold Sumner of Roxwell, gent.			
John George	Writtle	Mary George of Writtle	widow	6 Nov. 1638	19
		John Price of Terling, yeoman			
John Burrowes	Writtle	Helen Burrowes of Writtle	widow	6 Nov. 1638	10
		Thomas Borne of Writtle, sawyer			
Christopher Bellsted	Writtle	Thomas Hills of Writtle, yeoman		18 Oct. 1639	18, 243
John Turnedge	Writtle	Ann Turnedge of Writtle	widow	18 Oct. 1639	
William Bearman		Elizabeth Bearman of Writtle	widow	7 May 1640	22
		John Lavender of Ingatestone, yeoman			
Thomas Coleman	Roxwell	John Coleman of Roxwell, husbandman		12 Jan. 1641	
		William Branwood of Writtle, glover			
Charles Clarke	Writtle	Henry Emson of Writtle, yeoman[1]	son-in-law	9 May 1661	26
Thomas Sharpe	Writtle	Catherine Sharpe of Writtle	widow	20 April 1663	32
John Collins		Elinor Collins of Roxwell	widow	1 Aug. 1670	
John Stookes		Parnell Stookes of Roxwell	widow	17 June 1672	
Richard Nutting		Sarah Nutting of Writtle	widow[2]	1 June 1687	142
John Flacke yeoman	Roxwell	William Flacke of Roxwell, husbandman	son	9 Oct. 1700	187
		Matthew Flacke of Roxwell, husbandman			
		Edmund Bogg of Roxwell, yeoman			
Robert Butler clerk	Roxwell	Elizabeth Butler of Roxwell	widow	30 Sept. 1703	
		James Reeve of Chignal St. James, clerk			
		John Searle of Willingale Doe, clerk			
Edward Boggas gent.	Roxwell	Elizabeth Boggas of Roxwell	widow	8 June 1704	247
		Charles Ley of Roxwell, clerk			
		Matthew Ryley of Roxwell, fellmonger			
George Taverner yeoman	Writtle	John Taverner of Writtle, yeoman	son	22 July 1704	248
		Joseph Lea of Writtle, gent.			
		John Hubbard of Writtle, blacksmith			
Matthew Manning	Writtle	Rebecca Manning of Writtle	widow	16 May 1706	
		Joseph Lea of Writtle, gent.			

[1] Acting for Mary Emson his wife, daughter of deceased who appointed Mary Clarke (buried at Writtle, 18 Dec. 1659) executrix of his will. A bill of Emson's disbursements amounting to £26 *2s. 5d.* is preserved [D/APw P2].

[2] Sarah Nutting was a spinster by occupation; this bond is not executed.

Name of Deceased	*Parish*	*Persons Bound*	*Relationship to Deceased*	*Date of Bond*	*Inventory No.*
Thomas Bickner	Writtle	Mary Bickner of Writtle	widow	16 May 1706	
		Thomas Bickner of Writtle, tallow-chandler	son		
		John Hubbard of Writtle, blacksmith			
		Daniel Barnard of Writtle, butcher			
Jane Marriage widow	Roxwell	John Cooper of Roxwell, yeoman	brother	16 May 1706	
		Thomas Cooper of Roxwell, yeoman			
John Saffold	Writtle	Mary Saffold[1]	widow	22 Nov. 1706	
John Saffold	Writtle	John Saffold of St. Peter-le-Poer, London, domestic servant	son	9 Dec. 1706	
		John Willimot of All Saints-by-the-Tower, London, citizen and founder			
		Walter Betts of St. Mary, Whitechapel			
William Moody	Writtle	Hannah Green *alias* Moody	mother	1706[2]	
Henry Car	Writtle	John Hilliard[3] of Writtle		1706[2]	
Henry Bright widower	Roxwell	John Bricknock of Roxwell, yeoman	son-in-law	5 June 1707	192
		Richard Wolfe of Writtle, yeoman[4]			
		Henry Cooke of Great Bardfield, clerk			
Robert Hilliard	Writtle	Elizabeth Hilliard of Writtle	widow	27 May 1708	193
		Laurence Hilliard of Writtle, yeoman			
		Christopher Lingard of Writtle, gardener			
Henry Mansfield	Roxwell	Sarah Mansfield of Roxwell	widow	16 June 1709	194
		Henry Mansfield of Roxwell, yeoman			
		Christopher Lingard of Writtle, gardener			
William Paveley bachelor	Writtle	Elizabeth Paveley of Writtle, widow	mother	21 Jan. 1708	
		Robert Paveley of Writtle, singleman			
Thomas Robjant	Writtle	Elizabeth Robjant of Writtle	widow	16 June 1709	195
		Laurence Robjant of Blackmore, yeoman			
John Sapsford widower	Writtle	John Warner of Wickford, yeoman[5]		3 June 1710	
		John Stradling of Writtle, webster			
Thomas Lucas	Writtle	Elizabeth Lucas of Writtle	widow	3 June 1710	
		Christopher Lingard of Writtle, gardener			
John Nash	Roxwell	Mary Nash of Roxwell	widow	3 Jan. 1712	197
		Richard Allin of Roxwell, maltster			
		Robert Branard of Roxwell, cordwainer			
Henry Isaacson widower	Roxwell	George Isaacson of Roxwell, husbandman	son	1 April 1714	201
		Henry and Thomas Isaacson of Roxwell, husbandmen			

[1] Renounces probate in favour of John Saffold, son of deceased, to whom letters of administration are granted. See also next entry.

[2] Bond not executed.

[3] For Mary his wife, widow of deceased.

[4] For Dorothy, wife of John Bricknock and daughter of deceased.

[5] Principal creditor, and administrator.

Name of Deceased	Parish	Persons Bound	Relationship to Deceased	Date of Bond	Inventory No.
Isaac Day	Roxwell	Sarah Day of Roxwell	widow	5 April 1716	202
		Edward Day of Norton Mandeville, carpenter			
		William Pool of Roxwell, yeoman			
Thomas Crush widower	Roxwell	Thomas Crush of Baddow, yeoman	grandson	25 Aug. 1711	
		Thomas Heyton of St. Sepulchre's, London, victualler			
		Hamlet Toone of St. Faith's, London, butcher			
John Taverner bachelor	Writtle	John Adams of Chelmsford, tallow-chandler		23 Aug. 1712	
		Thomas Bickner of Writtle, tallow-chandler[1]			
		John Haward of Writtle, butcher			
Joseph Lingard	Roxwell	Mary Lingard of Roxwell	widow	9 July 1713	246
		John Asser of Roxwell, yeoman			
Thomas Crush[2]		James Crush of Chelmsford, mercer		23 July 1714	
		John Crush of Berners Roothing, yeoman			
		Abraham Classon of Good Easter, grocer			
		Henry Sandford of Chelmsford, innholder			
Thomas Wolfe widower	Roxwell	Thomas Wolfe of Roxwell, yeoman	son	5 April 1716	
		Nathaniel Osborne of Writtle, yeoman			
		William Green of Writtle, yeoman			
Stephen Chalke	Roxwell	Anne Chalke of Roxwell	widow	29 June 1717	204
		William Fuller of Morrell Roothing, yeoman			
		William Chalke of Good Easter, yeoman			
Thomas Saffold	Writtle	William Saffold of Twickenham, yeoman	nephew	7 June 1718[3]	
		John Fox and William Gibbs, both of St. Bridget's *alias* St. Bride's, London, yeomen			
John Saffold	Writtle	William Saffold of Twickenham, yeoman	son	25 June 1718	
		John Fox of St. Bridget's, London, yeoman			
Henry Turnedge	Roxwell	Hester Turnedge of Roxwell	widow	6 June 1720	207
		Thomas Wolfe of Roxwell, yeoman			
		George Francis of Roxwell, butcher			
Sarah Hilliard widow	Writtle	John Hilliard of Writtle, yeoman	son	20 April 1720	
		John Wood of Writtle, blacksmith			
Matthew Flack	Writtle	Martha Flack of Writtle	widow	21 April 1720	
		John Wood of Writtle, blacksmith			
		Thomas Jones of Writtle, yeoman			
Robert Butler bachelor	Writtle	Reginald Branwood of Writtle, carpenter		19 April 1721	
		James Fuller of Writtle, gent.[4]			
		Thomas George of Writtle, gardener			

[1] For Mary, wife of John Adams, sister and administratrix of John Taverner. Certificate enclosed with bond states that Mary Taverner of Reads relinquishes her right of administration of her son's [John Taverner] estate to her daughter Mary Adams.

[2] Sole executor of Mary Crush, late of Roxwell, widow.

[3] In respect of the goods left unadministered by Lydia Saffold, widow and administratrix of Thomas Saffold.

[4] For Elizabeth, wife of Reginald Branwood and mother of deceased.

Name of Deceased	*Parish*	*Persons Bound*	*Relationship to Deceased*	*Date of Bond*	*Inventory No.*
John Freeman bachelor	Writtle	John Glascock of Bobbingworth, yeoman John Homer of St. Clements Danes, Middlesex, ironmonger[1] Robert Rookby of St. Gregory, London, gent.		13 Nov. 1721	213
Thomas Ramsey	Writtle	Hannah Ramsey of Writtle John King of Writtle, gent.	widow	24 May 1723	
Rebecca Bridges	Writtle	Zachariah Bridges of Writtle, yeoman Thomas Sorrell of Writtle, collar-maker Nathaniel Osborne of Writtle, yeoman	son	20 May 1725	221
John Isaacson	Roxwell	Henry Isaacson of Roxwell, husbandman Thomas and George Isaacson of Roxwell, husbandmen	brother	29 Nov. 1726	
John Godfrey	Writtle	Charity Godfrey of Writtle Emma King of St. Giles, Cripplegate, London, widow William King of St. Giles, Cripplegate, London, watch-maker	widow	21 March 1727	229
Thomas Cheveley[2] widower	Roxwell	George Cheveley of Roxwell, yeoman Thomas Wolfe of Roxwell, yeoman John Brecknock of Roxwell, yeoman	son	11 June 1728	
Jeremiah Argull bachelor	Writtle	Richard Argull of Little Waltham, wheelwright Thomas George of Writtle, husbandman	brother	20 May 1729	
Abraham Stokes	Writtle	Susannah Stokes of Writtle Thomas George of Writtle, husbandman	widow	20 May 1729	230
William Aubury bachelor	Writtle	Simon Aubury of Writtle, wheelwright William Osborne of Writtle, yeoman Reginald Branwood of Writtle, carpenter	brother	20 May 1729	231
Reginald Branwood, senior	Writtle	Elizabeth White of Writtle, widow Nathaniel Springham of Writtle, gent. John Phillips of St. Andrew, Holborn, gent.	daughter	5 June 1759	

[1] For Anne, wife of John Glascock and sister of deceased.

[2] It may be mentioned here that members of the Cheveley family were coroners of Writtle from 1664 to 1837 (see D/DP M 608/1-17).

INDEX OF SUBJECTS

The references in heavy type are to the Introduction (pp. 1-70): those in roman type are to the Inventories, NOT to pages.

The references in heavy type are to the Introduction (pp. 1-70); those in roman type are to the Inventories, NOT to pages.

The references in heavy type are to the Introduction (pp. 1-70); those in roman type are to the Inventories, NOT to pages.

The references in heavy type are to the Introduction (pp. 1-70); those in roman type are to the Inventories, NOT to pages.

The references in heavy type are to the Introduction (pp. 1-70); those in roman type are to the Inventories, NOT to pages.

The references in heavy type are to the Introduction (pp. 1-70); those in roman type are to the Inventories, NOT to pages.

The references in heavy type are to the Introduction (pp. 1-70); those in roman type are to the Inventories, NOT to pages.

The references in heavy type are to the Introduction (pp. 1-70); those in roman type are to the Inventories, NOT to pages.

The references in heavy type are to the Introduction (pp. 1-70); those in roman type are to the Inventories, NOT to pages.

The references in heavy type are to the Introduction (pp. 1-70); those in roman type are to the Inventories, NOT to pages.

The references in heavy type are to the Introduction (pp. 1-70); those in roman type are to the Inventories, NOT to pages.

The references in heavy type are to the Introduction (pp. 1-70); those in roman type are to the Inventories, NOT to pages.

The references in heavy type are to the Introduction (pp. 1-70); those in roman type are to the Inventories, NOT to pages.

The references in heavy type are to the Introduction (pp. 1-70); those in roman type are to the Inventories, NOT to pages.

The references in heavy type are to the Introduction (pp. 1-70): those in roman type are to the Inventories, NOT to pages.

The references in heavy type are to the Introduction (pp. 1-70); those in roman type are to the Inventories, NOT to pages.

The references in heavy type are to the Introduction (pp. 1-70); those in roman type are to the Inventories, NOT to pages.

INDEX OF PERSONS AND PLACES

Names in the lists of bonds on pp. 278-282 are not included.

Refs. in heavy type are to INVENTORIES of persons mentioned, NOT to pages; in roman type to persons mentioned in Inventories, NOT to pages; in italic to the Introduction (pp. 1-70).

Refs. in heavy type are to INVENTORIES of persons mentioned, NOT to pages; in roman type to persons mentioned in Inventories, NOT to pages; in italic to the Introduction (pp. 1-70).

Refs. in heavy type are to INVENTORIES of persons mentioned, NOT to pages; in roman type to persons mentioned in Inventories, NOT to pages; in italic to the Introduction (pp. 1-70).

Refs. in heavy type are to INVENTORIES of persons mentioned, NOT to pages; in roman type to persons mentioned in Inventories, NOT to pages; in italic to the Introduction (pp. 1-70).

Refs. in heavy type are to INVENTORIES of persons mentioned, NOT to pages; in roman type to persons mentioned in Inventories, NOT to pages; in italic to the Introduction (pp. 1-70).

Refs. in heavy type are to INVENTORIES of persons mentioned, NOT to pages; in roman type to persons mentioned in Inventories, NOT to pages; in italic to the Introduction (pp. 1-70).